A **Typographic Workbook**

a primer to history, techniques, and artistry

Second Edition

Kate Clair
Cynthia Busic-Snyder

WILEY

John Wiley & Sons, Inc.

Published by John Wiley & Sons, Inc., Hoboken, New Jersey
Published simultaneously in Canada

For general information on our other products and services or for
technical support, please contact our Customer Care Department within
the United States at (800) 762-2974, outside the United States at
(317) 572-3993 or fax (317) 572-4002.

Wiley also publishes its books in a variety of electronic formats. Some
content that appears in print may not be available in electronic books.

Library of Congress Cataloging-in-Publication Data:

ISBN-13: 978-0-471-69690-2
ISBN-10: 0-471-69690-0

Printed in the United States of America

10 9 8 7 6 5 4 3 2

Table of Contents

Preface

The study and practice of type and typography is both art and science combined with a rich social and technological evolution over the last five and a half centuries, poised for an interesting and innovative future. Although the rules of typesetting are old and the technologies for the creation and distribution of printed materials continue to change, the primary intent remains: quality typography that supports the meaning and understanding of the words it represents. Great typography often results from a strong foundation in the historical development of writing and printing, the clear ability to identify subtle characteristics of typeform design according to a defined context, and the successful mastery of the almost infinite number of minute details involved in specifying and setting text.

Typography has become a subject area of specialized study—a subset of the general practice of graphic design. Digital technologies have shifted the responsibility of quality typesetting from the professional service bureau typesetter to the designer who is also responsible for the overall design aesthetic, print production management, and often the client communication and coordination. Whereas less than two decades ago the designer was able to focus on the composition and leave the minutiae to someone else, this is no longer the case in the digital age of personal computers and publication design. The graphic design student must now take responsibility for expanding their experiences and expertise in a number of supporting subjects related to design.

A Typographic Workbook integrates historical and technical typographic information into a single publication with the intent to provide a learning guide for students and a reference for practicing professionals. Various faces are used from one chapter to the next, intended to illustrate a small portion of the wide range of typeface choices and the visual results, and help with the development of an aesthetic understanding and appreciation for foundation-level typography. Extensive examples illustrate both the preferred methods and techniques, contrasted with numerous examples of undesirable settings with explanations of the differences.

This edition of the text includes short exercises intended to support the information presented by encouraging the learner to refer to contemporary internet resources; skill-building exercises encouraging the exploration of the concepts, rules, and theories discussed; review questions that emphasize the important facts and test understanding of the content; a detailed historical perspective of typography as a communication medium; and comprehensive set of three appendices.

Included in the historical perspective is a revised approach to copy fitting with a character-per-pica chart and expanded exercises. The approach to learning typographic layout has been expanded to include information on standard paper and envelope size charts as well as industry standard folds for publications. Appendix A illustrates numerous fonts indicating the designer(s) and design context. Appendix B lists and defines the key concepts presented in the text. Appendix C lists the key players in the abridged typographic history presented, with a concise bibliographic description when possible. It is my hope that the information provided, a mesh of the old and the new, sparks a special interest towards creating functional and beautiful typographic compositions while laying the foundation for intermediate and advanced studies in graphic design.

Cynthia Busic-Snyder

Acknowledgments

Special thanks to my family and close friends for their patience as I pursued this tangent endeavor. Your encouragement made this project possible.

Thanks go to my good friend and mentor, Charles Wallschlaeger who knows when to pat me on the head and send me on my way. I am especially appreciative to Kimberly Elam who continues to provide professional inspiration and quiet encouragement.

Special thanks to my good friend and mentor Stan Harris who continues to enlighten me on the ways of life and letterpress printing.

Thanks to my parents, who taught me that "good enough" isn't, I think.

The students I see daily give this project meaning and substance as they continue to teach me new things with their creative questions and innovative solutions. Thank you for challenging me to do my best as I attempt to keep up with each of you.

The professionalism exhibited by John Wiley & Sons, Inc. Senior Editor Margaret Cummins, Senior Editorial Assistant Rosanne Koneval and Senior Production Editor Leslie Anglin have been exemplary. I appreciate their consistent patience, support and encouragement.

MPB *This one is for you.*
ICNLYLOM.

Ancient Writing Systems

Ancient is generally defined by Western culture as "before the fall of the Western Roman Empire, 476 CE." Few remember to consider the highly developed societies of the ancient Egyptians, Greeks, and Romans with their magnificent architecture, legal systems, epic plays, elaborate religious rituals and myths, comfortable homes with indoor plumbing, and carefully developed writing systems. Many believe that these societies' technological developments would not have been possible without written communication.

The study of written communication is somewhat synonymous with the study of the history of civilization. In prehistoric times, before writing systems were developed, there was no recorded history; knowledge of past events was orally communicated from generation to generation. It is possible that if there had never been written records, the history of the world would be condensed to the point that one human could commit it to memory.

1.1 Cartouche of Egyptian queen Cleopatra II, who ruled approximately 69–30 BCE. A *cartouche* (called *shenu* in ancient Egyptian) is a series of hieroglyphics enclosed by an oval or rectangular band representing the name of a royal or divine persona.

Key Concepts

ancient
boustrephedon
cartouche
cuneiform
demotic script
hieratic script
hieroglyphics
iconography
ideograph
logogram
mnemonics
papyrus
parchment
phaistos disk
phonemes
phonetic
phonogram
pictograph
rebus
Rosetta Stone
Semitic languages
syllable
typography

Already subjective in nature, the experience and recollection of events are further affected by personal interpretation and editing; if there were no written record, it would be impossible to know any of the details of the earliest cultures and the the lives of ordinary people who lived in them.

Because lettering and *typography* (the style, arrangement, and appearance of type) are tied closely to available manufacturing technology, writing substrates (clay, stone, or parchment) reflect the raw materials and mechanical abilities of a particular society. Much knowledge of ancient cultures comes to us via secondhand parchment copies of papyrus scrolls, made by monks during the Middle Ages. Most original papyrus texts no longer exist, as they deteriorated in the moist Mediterranean climate, while many of the copies on *parchment* (which is made from animal skins) survived. Contemporary translations, therefore, are based on copies that are assumed to be fairly accurate reproductions of the original texts.

Prehistoric Societies

Trying to imagine human existence prior to oral and written communication is difficult. Scientists debate when the ability to enunciate a spoken language evolved. Archeological evidence of fire use, tool making, and cooperative activities predates the evolution of a biological capacity for speech, indicating the probable use of extensive nonverbal communication.

As verbal communication developed, it became easier for humans to interact with and assist one another in organized activities, as well as structure their lives communally to achieve more comfortable, more predictable, and safer lives.

Development of Oral Communication

Oral communication allowed humans to communicate feelings, thoughts, concepts, techniques, and procedures. It brings forth the question of whether thought as we conceive of it today was even possible before humans developed the capacity to express it in words, or whether the expression of thoughts, hopes, and fantasies become possible because humans developed the means of expression through refined speech.

The earliest evidence of agriculture occurs in the Nile River valley in Egypt, the Tigris and Euphrates River valleys in Mesopotamia, and the Yangtze River valley in China. Since the first civilizations developed in these

P   A   L   E   O   L   I

Aboriginal rock engravings | Venus of Willendorf | Hand axe | Sharpened stone tools | Namibian cave paintings

30,000 BCE | 29,000 BCE | 28,000 BCE | 27,000 BCE | 26,000 BCE | 25,000 BCE | 24,000 BCE | 23,000 BCE | 22,000 BCE | 21,000 BCE

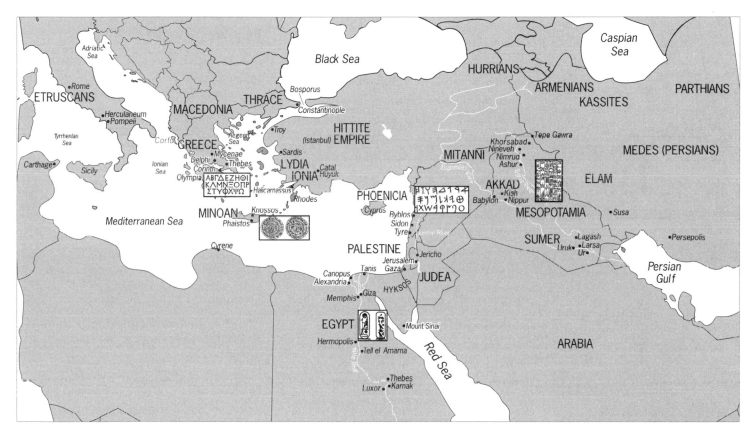

areas, it may be safe to assume that a hospitable climate and agricultural knowledge were two of the most significant contributing factors to the development of human civilization. Because humans no longer spent the majority of their time battling the elements and gathering food, they could devote more time refining their living conditions.

Anthropologists believe that the domestication of animals was a strong factor in the development of human societies. Nomadic tribes used domesticated animals to help

1.2 Early language centers and writing are believed to have evolved in areas surrounding the Mediterranean Sea, from Greece to Mesopotamia.

1.3 Timeline illustrating the development period of prehistoric tool making, cave painting, and agriculture from 30,000 BCE to 9000 BCE.

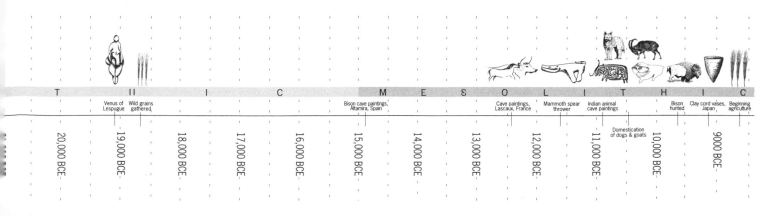

1.4 Simple pictographs are somewhat representative in appearance. At top is a pictograph for an ox, and below is the pictograph for mountains.

1.5 Cylinder seals were rolled into wet clay to show ownership, to indicate the contents of containers, and/or to commemorate events or for ceremonial purpose. The wet clay could be wrapped over the top of a vessel to prevent tampering. These seals were used in Mesopotamia as early as 1500 BCE.

them more easily transport food and shelter resources. In both nomadic and agrarian societies, domesticated animals could be slaughtered as necessary for sustenance.

With the basic necessities of life attended to, humans turned their attention to refining tools, maintaining the political organization of the tribe, perfecting healing arts, defending against predators and pondering the stars, skies, nature, and spiritual ideals. When information was communicated by word of mouth, certain people were entrusted with the "memory" of the tribe. They were chosen by the tribe's elders to memorize the myths, legends, and genealogies of the community. Sacred knowledge and techniques of healing were passed down orally as well. *Mnemonics*, the use of reminder devices used to help recall large amounts of information, were developed by these ritual specialists and historians. Often relieved of the menial tasks of fulfilling the basic day-to-day needs of the tribe, such individuals were invested with social power and political status in the community.

The tribal historians and other specialists often had the exclusive power to choose their successors, deciding to whom they would pass the knowledge of the tribe for the next generation. This prestigious position required great accuracy in the recall and telling of important information, so many years were devoted to training and memorization. Most of these specialists were respected elders by the time they assumed the position.

Respect for elders in the community was unquestioned. Some indigenous peoples associate the various stages of aging (commonly based on hair color) with status within the tribe. In fact, in some Native American

Puzzling Evidence

Archeologists have long held that written language was first developed in Mesopotamia, where cuneiform tablets date from 3200 BCE. New evidence emerging from China, however, raises a new question of who may have been first to pen their thoughts.

Tortoise shells etched with symbols have been excavated from the Jiahu site in Henan province in central China. The shells found appear to be part of a funerary ritual in Neolithic graves that have been dated to 7000–5800 BCE. If the incised symbols can be taken as a written language, they will predate what was previously the earliest known written language in China by more than three thousand years, and the written language of Mesopotamia by more than two thousand years.

The tortoise shells, some stone tools, and several bone musical instruments have been incised with up to sixteen different symbols and geometric shapes either identical or very similar to the jiaguwen pictographs used in the second millennium BCE and found at the Yinxu archeological site, generally accepted as evidence of the first written language of China.

Some archeologists point to the great similarity of the symbols and their artifactual context between the Jiahu and Yinxu sites and argue that the Jiahu symbols were part of early attempts at an organized information system.

Others hold that the symbols are isolated geometric decorations, and although they may have had religious significance, they do not represent an early written language.

What are your thoughts? At what point would religious or decorative *iconography* (the pictorial illustration or set of illustrations representing a subject) begin to be recognized as a pictographic written language?

languages the word for "gray-haired" means "knowledgeable" and the term for "white-haired" means "close to the knowledge of the gods." This linkage between thought and word is one example of how language and our perceptions of reality are connected.

Since all communication was verbal, it was contemporaneous. Before the invention of writing, no one could speak directly to anyone not living at the same time. For ideas, concepts, and practices to have lasting influence, they had to be restated by each succeeding generation and could not help but be influenced and altered by personal interpretation, inaccuracies, embellishments, and memory lapses. As a result, there is a limitation to the accuracy of nonwritten transmission of information over time.

Still, today many spoken languages exist that have no written form. It may seem logical to use an existing alphabet (Roman, Cyrillic, Arabic, etc.) to transcribe them. But because of broad historical associations among certain societies, political and economic and cultural features of those societies, the languages used in those societies, the languages used in those societies and the alphabets used to write those languages, the choice of an existing alphabet to transcribe a previously nonwritten language may be fraught with political consequences. Ultimately, the written form of a language must develop out of the culture of the people who practice it for it to make total sense.

Early Writing Societies

Developed writing systems have been discovered in Sumeria, Egypt, China, and India. Cuneiform is dated to approximately 3200 BCE; hieroglyphics are dated to approximately 3000 BCE; precursors to the Chinese system of writing date to around 1800 BCE; and Sanskrit is dated to approximately 1500 BCE. The introduction of writing allowed these cultures to more rapidly develop complex sociopolitical organizations, as it enabled them to record codes of law, history, literature, philosophy, medicine, mathematics, scientific discoveries, and religious practices.

The single expression of an idea in a visual form cannot be considered an alphabet. For instance, the cave paintings in Lascaux, France, dating back to somewhere between 30,000 and 12,000 years ago, communicate the form of animals but do not qualify as pictographic communication. Because they do not add up to a codified system of standardized symbols, and they are not used repeatedly in a consistent, standardized manner to represent the same concept over a period of time, they are considered images and not a system of writing.

Repetition of agreed-upon shapes is the essence of a writing system. In order to communicate, the simplified drawings must be recognizable and easily interpreted by larger numbers of a population.

Pictograph-Based Writing Systems

Early picture writing employed simplified drawings to represent objects. This is assumed to be the first step in developing most written languages. Called *pictographs* (the simplified drawings of objects), these drawings may have been introduced into use for a variety of reasons. Some historians assume that writing began with small tags of clay inscribed with pictographs that were attached to jugs by string intended to

Fact Find! What other languages can you find that use other alphabets? What about Greek? Cyrillic? Log on to to your favorite search engine and find an Internet reference to help you create your comparison. Print out the results for discussion. List some of your ideas in the space provided below. Be sure to cite your sources correctly!

_____

_____

_____

_____

_____

_____

_____

_____

_____

_____

_____

_____

URL: http://

URL: http://

Date visited:

1.6 The combination of the top two pictographs, an ox and mountain range, results in the final ideagraph on the bottom, meaning "wild ox."

represent the contents of the vessels during shipping. Others have speculated that writing was used to record gifts to the temples, as people were required to give offerings each year. Another theory posits that writing evolved as a means to indicate ownership; a small distinctive mark or series of marks on an object designated to whom it belonged or by whom it was crafted. Still others theorize that pictographs developed out of drawing as a shorthand means to record memorable events. Exactly how and why writing systems were developed is unclear. What is clear, however, is that distinct but possibly related

alphabets developed in different ancient cultures in different geographic locations within a relatively short period of time.

Pictographs are appropriate for the representation of people, places, and things but are not efficient for communicating complex and abstract ideas, emotions, concepts, and actions. Modern examples of pictographs indicate gender-separate restroom facilities, overnight lodging, eating areas, acceptable smoking and nonsmoking environments, and eating establishments. Pictographs are vital in communicating simple meaning in the absence of a common language or script. As the

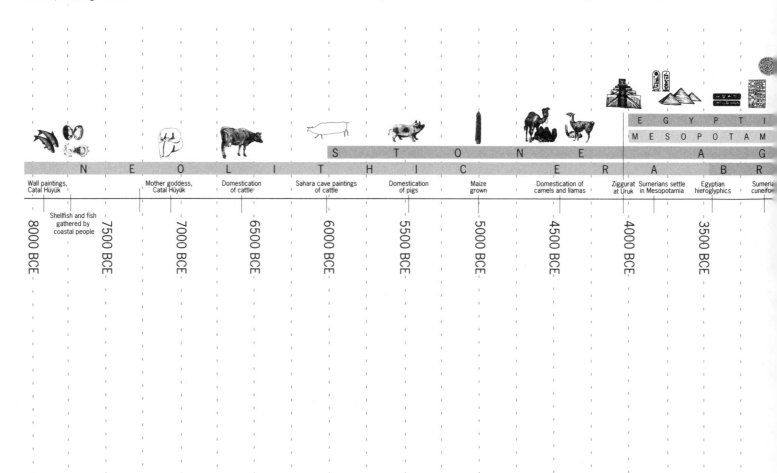

uses for written communication expanded, it was necessary for the written language to express a greater variety of concepts.

From Pictographs to Ideographs

Pictograph-based languages evolved into written systems that allowed the representation of abstract thought rather than simply representing objects. As pictographs were assigned meaning that went beyond a simple visual representation of a tangible thing, they were transformed into a slightly more complicated form of writing known as an ideograph. An *ideograph* (or

1.7 Modern pictographs and ideographs communicate simple messages across multiple languages and cultures.

1.8 The timeline below shows the expansion of literacy, the dissemination of knowledge, and the growth of typographic forms over the centuries.

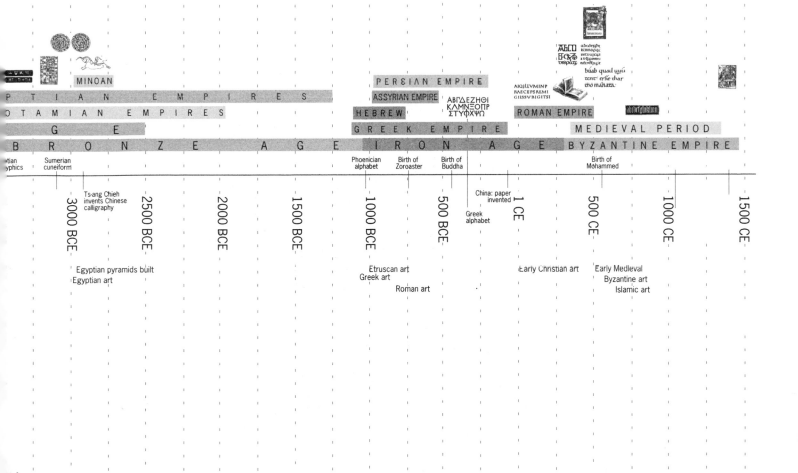

1.9 Ideographs combine pictographs to communicate more complex concepts and messages.

ideogram) is the combination of two or more pictographs intended to represent a concept— for example, the pictographs of a woman and a child may combine to represent the idea of "pregnant" even though it does not show a literal interpretation of a pregnant woman.

Ideographs, in other words, are pictographs that come to mean something other than their original intent. For example, the pictograph of "hand" changed to an ideograph when it is combined with other symbols to convey the concepts of "to give," "to greet," "to offer," or "to take"—actions or concepts associated with the hand in some way. Ideographs mark the true beginning of a written language.

There is an element of abstraction to ideographs, so they may not be instantly understood when seen. They often require interpretation and translation. Each culture developed a specific set of ideographs that reflected it spiritual beliefs and its political, economic, and social structure.

The Semitic Languages

The *Semitic languages* comprise the languages in the Middle East, an area today that includes the countries of Syria, Lebanon, Israel, Palestine, Jordan, Cyprus, Turkey, Iraq, Egypt, Iran, Kuwait, Saudi Arabia, Bahrain, Qatar, United Arab Emirates, Oman, and Yemen.

Semitic languages fall into four groups. North Peripheral includes Akkadian, which was spoken in Assyria and Babylonia and which is the oldest Semitic language. It stopped being used as a literary language in the first century CE. North Central includes Hebrew (the language of Israel today); Aramaic; and Ugaritic and Phoenician, both

of which no longer exist. South Central includes the Arabic language in nearly all of its dialects, as well as Maltese, which is an offshoot of Arabic. South Peripheral includes South Arabic dialects and Amharic, as well as other Ethiopian languages.

Sumerian Cuneiform

The Sumerian culture arose in Mesopotamia in the region between the Tigris and Euphrates Rivers, known as the "fertile crescent" (present-day Iraq). The soil in this area is rich and productive, but much of the surrounding land is limited in its ability to sustain agriculture. The land has low-lying hills surrounding it to the north that act as a natural barrier preventing attack from that direction. The regular supply of freshwater from the two rivers enabled the culture to grow its own food and become a sedentary, agricultural society.

Eventually the Sumerians developed written forms of communication. At first every character represented one word, but many words lacked unique symbols. For these, symbols of related objects were used (a foot could mean both "to go" and "to stand," in addition to meaning "foot").

Abundant clay from local riverbeds served many purposes, among them making writing tablets. The clay tablets could be inscribed with a stylus while still moist, then laid in the sun to dry. As both the stylus and the tablet-making processes developed, the style and form of the written messages changed in appearance. By 3100 BCE a codified system of pictographic symbols called *cuneiform*, existed.

By approximately 2500 BCE scribes had shifted from using a pointed stylus to draw

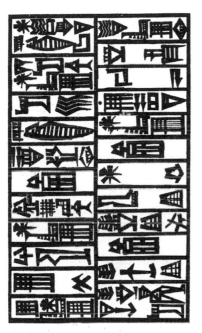

1.10 Old Akkadian pictographs of ancient Babylonia, from the time of King Sargon, predate the wedge-shaped cuneiform writing.

1.11 The wedge-shaped characters of cuneiform are stacked in vertical rows.

in the clay tablet to using a triangular stylus pressed into the clay, the hallmark of cuneiform writing. Characters had evolved into combinations of wedge-shaped strokes, further abstracting the symbols composing the written language. In its early stages cuneiform was written from top to bottom. During the third millennium BCE this changed into writing from left to right, and also the signs changed: they were turned on their sides.

Cuneiform writing developed into a mixture of logograms and syllables. A *logogram* is a sign that represents an entire word and *syllables* represent certain sounds. Cuneiform writing mixed these two symbol types.

Eventually the Sumerians were conquered by the Assyrians from northern Mesopotamia. The Assyrians were quick to adopt cuneiform as a practical writing system. Cuneiform writing has been used in several languages, and was in use for about 3000 years. When Aramaic spread as the predominant language in the seventh and sixth centuries BCE, its alphabet (derived from Phoenician script) gradually replacing cuneiform writing. The last example of cuneiform writing dates to 75 CE. Western scholars deciphered the cuneiform systems in the 1840s.

Early cuneiform employed ideograms, though later these symbols came to be used as phonograms. *Phonograms* are signs that represent sounds—either whole words, syllables, or *phonemes* (a language's distinctive sounds).

A logogram or logograph is a single written symbol that represents an entire word or phrase. For example, the symbol 8 is a logogram that is pronounced "eight" in English. Compared to alphabetical systems, logograms have the disadvantage that a large

Fact Find! What are examples of logograms, other than numerals, used today? Can you find a modern definition or interpretation? Log on to to your favorite search engine and find an Internet reference to help you answer the question. Be sure to cite your source(s) correctly!

_____

_____

_____

_____

_____

_____

_____

_____

_____

_____

_____

URL: http://

URL: http://

URL: http://

Date visited:

Meaning	Pictograph	Sideways	Cuneiform	Assyrian
orchard				
to walk				
star				
goose				
sun/day				
plowing				
fish				
ox				
boomerang				

1.12 Pictographs were transformed into hieroglyphs, script hand, hieratic script, and demotic script, shown right.

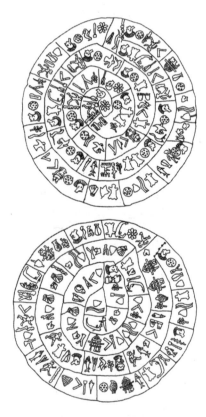

1.13 Drawings of the Phaistos Disk exemplify the use of early pictographs. The Phaistos Disk has not yet been deciphered and translated into a modern language.

number of them are needed to be able to write down a large number of words. An advantage is that one does not need to know the language of the writer to understand them—everyone understands what 1 means, whether they call it one, eins, uno, or ichi.

Cuneiform required deciphering for understanding to come about; they could not be intuitively identified and so immediately impart understanding to the reader.

Minoan Writing

A significant piece of evidence alluding to early writing outside of Mesopotamia is found on the island of Crete and is attributed to the Minoans (a culture named after their ruler, King Minos). The remains

of this writing are limited as the Minoan culture is believed to have been decimated by a tidal wave caused by a volcanic eruption on a neighboring island. Among artifacts found in archeological excavations of the ancient city of Phaistos that include the Minoan alphabet is a clay disk with symbols spiraling to or from the center.

Found in 1908 at the ruins of the Minoan palace, the *Phaistos Disk* is dated to approximately 1700 BCE. The text is made up of sixty-one words, with forty-five different symbols occurring a total of 241 times. The symbols portray recognizable objects such as human figures and body parts, animals, weapons, and plants.

1.14 Ancient clay tablet inscribed with cuneiform.

Some scholars think the text is a prayer and the language is Greek. Another theory also suggests that the language of the disk is Greek, but claims that it contains proof of a geometric theorem. Others feel that the disk contains a magical text, possibly a curse, and that the language of the disk in Indo-European. Finally, some believe that this alphabet may provide a link between ancient hieroglyphics and ancient Phoenician. The debate continues.

Written Languages Remain Undeciphered

Like the script on the Phaistos Disk, a number of writing systems have been discovered but remain partially or completely undeciphered today. Among them is Vinca or Old European, found on many artifacts excavated from archeological sites in southeast Europe, especially near Belgrade. These samples date between 6000 and 4500 BCE.

The Indus script, named for the valley in India where it was found, dates to approximately 3500 BCE. Sometimes referred to as Harappa script, little is known about the language or the people who utilized it. Some think it may be a form of a Dravidian Language.

A script that first appeared around 2900 BCE in the kingdom of Elam in southwest Persia (modern Iran) is named Proto-Elamite and has yet to be deciphered. So does a script used between 2250 and 2220 BCE called Old Elamite.

Linear A is a script used between 1800 and 1450 BCE on the island of Crete. Although it has not been proven, historians believe that Linear A may be related to Linear B writing, which has been deciphered.

The Etruscan alphabet has been deciphered, but the Etruscan language remains poorly understood. It is assumed to have developed from the Greek alphabet when the Greeks colonized southern Italy, starting in the middle of the sixth century BCE.

Meroitic is an extinct language that was spoken in the Nile Valley and northern Sudan until the fourth century, CE. Although the Meroitic script has been deciphered, little is known about the language it represented.

Rongo Rong is a script representing the Polynesian language Rapa Nui, spoken on Easter Island. Knowledge of the script was lost during the 1860s and has yet to be rediscovered.

What Is a Rebus?

A *rebus* is a series of pictographs of short words combined to have the reader verbally sound out longer words or phrases; it is a mode of expressing words and phrases by pictures of objects whose name resembles those words, or the syllables from which they are composed. An example might include the combination of

moon + light = moonlight, *or* eye + ball = eyeball.

The invention of the rebus allowed the creation of complex words.

A combination of the pictographs of the sea and the sun results in a rebus meaning "season." The phoenetic sound of each word combine to sound out a new word (season) with new meaning (the natural division of temperate zones, sometimes marked astrologically).

The Voynich Manuscript, named for Wilfred M. Voynich, the antique-book dealer who acquired it in 1912, is a lavishly illustrated, 234-page codex written in an unknown script. Numerous attempts have been made to decipher the text to no avail. One theory that survives is that the manuscript was written by the Franciscan friar Roger Bacon sometime during the thirteenth century.

Egyptian Hieroglyphics

Egyptian pictographic *hieroglyphics* (a writing system that used pictographs to represent words and sounds) are believed to have originated around 3000 BCE. Magnificent examples of hieroglyphs found in Pharaoh's tombs date to approximately 2900 BCE. The highly detailed carved stone tablets required much patience to produce and this level of effort is not seen in everyday written records from ancient Egypt. The hieroglyphs popularly used for historical, legal, and business records consisted of simplified symbol systems to speed the writing process.

Hieroglyphics commonly run in vertical columns, read from top to bottom but not always starting with the far right column. All the people and animals face the same direction in any given passage. To read hieroglyphics, read into or toward the front of the human or animal symbols. The vertical columns are separated by thin rules and delineated by one or two colored horizontal rules across the top and bottom of the adjoining columns.

In hieroglyphics the same *phonetic* (spelling that corresponds to pronunciation)

1.15 The fluid appearance of these hieroglyphs was produced with a reed brush on papyrus.

Object	Pictograph	Hieroglyph	Script hand	Hieratic script	Demotic script
animal skins tied together					
vessel					
harpoon					
papyrus bundle					
whip					

1.16 Pictographs were transformed into hieroplyphs, script hand, hieratic script, and demotic script.

sound could be represented by a variety of symbols depending upon the scribe's geographic location or education. Over three hundred symbols had to be known in order to "read" the story or message. The Egyptians never simplified the system to the twenty-four consonant sounds needed to represent the utterances of their spoken language.

Hieroglyphics evolved into a system of communication that was constructed in a rebus-like fashion. This transition to the use of the rebus device marks the beginning of a phonetic relationship between the spoken word for an object and the objects they represent; there is a detachment from the physical object of the pictograph. A rebus must be deciphered, unlike pictographs, which need only to be identified.

Further embellishments to the manner in which a pictograph was written could add significant meaning to a word or name. For instance, Egyptian pharaohs were believed to be direct descendents of the gods. Their

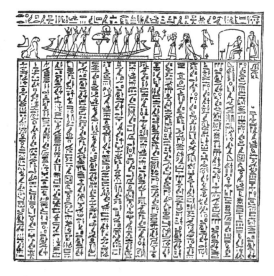

1.17 In this example the Egyptian hieroglyphics are organized into vertical columns divided by column rules. Each column was read in the direction faced by the symbols.

names were written in hieroglyphs enclosed with the ankh to signify immortality.

Hieratic Script

Pictorial hieroglyphics became more simplified with the invention of papyrus and reed brushes. By 1500 BCE a calligraphic style known as *hieratic script* (meaning "priestly writing") began to appear. Hieratic script was used for religious literature exclusively for a time, until its gradual adaptation for commerce and business uses. It is characterized and influenced by the development of the reed pen as a writing tool, so the characters are more abstract and simplified than previous forms of lettering.

Demotic Script

Around 500 BCE the hieratic script eventually evolved into *demotic script*, (demotic means "of the people"). This writing style is visually simplified even more compared to hieratic script.

Throughout history, the dissemination of knowledge and the ability to read and write have often been reserved for the chosen few: the elite, the scholars, the ruler, and the priests who controlled the religious rituals and early forms of taxation. Those who could read were pursued for advice in all types of disputes and emergencies; their knowledge and judgment were highly respected. In many cultures the scribes—those who could write—were believed to hold power over human life; if an Egyptian scribe wrote your name in the Book of the Dead, it meant that your time in this world had expired.

Although ordinary people could use demotic script, the average working person did not have access to the education required to interpret or write the information using the system. Doubtless the scribes did little to remedy this situation, as it helped to perpetuate the class system and ensure their necessity in society.

The transition away from hieroglyphics was gradual, eventually giving way to demotic script, and ultimately there was no one left who was able to read the ancient Egyptian writing.

Ancient Writing Systems Evolve

A majority of scholars agree that by 1500 BCE ancient Phoenicia had established a phonetically based alphabet consisting of twenty-two characters. This ancient Phoenician alphabet is believed to be the basis of the Greek and Roman alphabets, and hence of the alphabet used in much of the Western world today.

Phoenicia was considered the gateway to the Middle Eastern lands and all the goods and foods its people produced. The Phoenicians were a seafaring and merchant people located at the crossroads

Papyrus

Papyrus is a paper-like material made from the papyrus bulrush that grew wild along the banks of the Nile River. Papyrus is made by soaking the bamboo-like plant in water, then stripping the inner fibers. These fibers are beaten flat and then aligned in a parallel fashion. A second layer of flat fiber strips is placed crosswise to the first. Layered with cloth, the fibers are placed under great pressure to dry. Individual pieces of papyrus, measuring approximately 9 x 15 inches are joined to create scrolls up to 30 feet in length.

When papyrus became a common writing substrate in about 2400 BCE, a reed brush was found to be the perfect writing tool. The pictographs took on a fluid, sinuous, graceful appearance when drawn using a brush. Corners became rounded as the speed of the scribe increased; often several hieroglyphics were constructed from one continuous, flowing stroke.

Exercise Objectives

Upon completion of this exercise, readers will be able to:

- Understand the challenges associated with assigning meaning to images and constructing a system of visual communication

- Identify and discuss some characteristics of pictographic writing

- Outline design decisions in the combining of images intended to communicate to someone other than themselves

- Explore the possibility of multiple interpretations of pictographs within different communication contexts

life	house	water
woman	plant	man
to see/vision	knife	distant lands
lake/body of water	hand	water snake
fronds	basket	cloth
mouth	tied	ground snake
vessel	courtyard	foot
horizon	hill	to support
seat	tree	fire
servant	vulture	reed/writing
beetle/change	to cry	to seek or find
swallow	arm/to give	owl/watchful
sun	sun's rays or energy	animal halter
bread	lamp/torch	to walk or to go

Hieroglyph Writing Exercise

Traditionally, hieroglyphs are stacked vertically, with all characters facing the same direction (either left or right). Combine a number of symbols to create a short story or message. Write your English interpretation along with the hieroglyphic story for later reference in the space allotted.

Copy only your hieroglyphic message onto a blank sheet of paper and exchange messages with another student. Determine if each of you can decipher the story as written. Make a note of the difficulties you encounter during your process of interpreting the unfamiliar message.

What topic(s) would you like to have written about had you known a greater quantity of symbols?

....

....

....

Was the resulting story interesting and creative or relatively limited and straightforward? Why?

....

....

....

Compare your experience with this exercise and what you imagine to be that of a young person learning to write for the first time. What about learning to pronounce and write a foreign language? What are the similarities between these situations?

....

....

....

....

....

of international trade. The Phoenician language was in use along the coast of Syria, Lebanon, and Israel, as well as in Phoenician colonies all around the Mediterranean Sea, as far west as northern Morocco. The Phoenician language was very close to Hebrew and Moabite. The oldest archeological traces of Phoenician date back to eleventh century BCE.

Because of their diverse trade and travel, the culture of the Phoenicians was influenced by many other peoples who lived around the Mediterranean Sea, including the Greeks, Minoans, Etruscans, and Sumerians. The Lebanese, Maltese, Libyans, and even some Somalis, along with certain other island folk in the Mediterranean, still consider themselves descendants of Phoenicians.

The Phoenician alphabet was developed around 1200 BCE from an earlier Semitic prototype. The alphabet was a unique approach to writing. Oral speech was broken down into a series of sounds and a written symbol was assigned to each sound, freeing written communications from the literal visual translations originally used in other written languages. This simplified the number of symbols required to write and read the message. With fewer symbols to memorize, learning to read and write became a less arduous task. Literacy spread among the general population. The Phoenician alphabet also was used to transcribe other oral languages into written versions, making early translation and cross-cultural communication possible. The Phoenician alphabet and language spread quickly in the region as a result.

From this alphabet the Greek alphabet, which forms the basis of all European alphabets, was derived. The alphabets of

1.18 Ancient Phoenician characters inscribed on a piece of the interior of a bowl.

Writing Compared to Plowing

For a while, Greek writing read from right to left on the first line, then reversed and read from left to right on the following line, and so forth, across the page in a snake-like fashion, flipping asymmetrical letters. This structure was named "*boustrephedon*" and comes from the Greek words meaning "as the ox plows the field." Although you may think that eventually it is just as easy to read backwards, with some practice, it is still difficult to read text when you have to constantly flip the letters to discern them.

1.19 Comparing the form of Phoenician characters, on the left, with early Greek characters, on the right, reveals the resemblance between the two.

1.20 Hieroglyphs used in ancient Egypt to depict the seasons, from top to bottom: akhet—winter, a time of sowing; pert—spring, a time of growing; shemu—summer, a time of inundation.

the Middle East and India are also thought to derive indirectly from the Phoenician alphabet. Ironically, the Phoenicians themselves are largely silent on their own history—Phoenician writing has largely perished, since their characteristic writing material was papyrus and has disintegrated. What we know of them comes from their neighbors, the Greeks and the Hebrews.

By approximately 800 BCE the use of the Phoenician alphabet had spread to ancient Greece. To write the alphabet the Greeks used an ivory or metal stylus to inscribe wax tablets. The Greeks simply borrowed the original twenty-two characters and adapted them for their own needs. Five consonants were changed to vowels to account for the sounds in the Greek language that had no Phoenician equivalent. The first vowels were alpha, epsilon, iota, omicron, and upsilon. The Greeks introduced three new consonants which were appended to the end of the alphabet in the order in which they were developed. There were several variants of the Greek alphabet, most important were western (Chalcidian) and eastern (Ionic) Greek; the former gave rise to the Etruscan alphabet and the latter to the Roman alphabet.

The Rise of Ancient Greece

The year 500 BCE is considered the peak of arts and learning during the Golden Age of Greece, approximately three hundred years after the adoption of the Phoenician alphabet. With the expansion of the Greek Empire under the rule of Alexander the Great (from 356 to 323 BCE) Greek culture spread. The growth of the Hellenistic culture caused the spread of the Greek alphabet (precursor to our

1.21 The Rosetta Stone is believed to have been carved around 200 BCE. The same inscription is written in three different alphabets.

own) as far as Egypt, Mesopotamia, and India. When Alexander died, his generals parceled out the lands of his empire, creating smaller kingdoms. Despite the resulting lack of unification, the effects of the common language and writing system prevailed.

Recovering Ancient Egyptian Hieroglyphics

As demotic became more widespread, understanding of hieroglyphics faded away, and ultimately there was no one left who was able to read the ancient Egyptian writing. A large portion of the hieroglyphic texts were difficult to decipher because of their religious nature, since the names of the gods were no longer recognized. Until the discovery of the *Rosetta Stone*, hieroglyphics had not been completely or correctly deciphered. The Rosetta Stone held the key to translating and understanding

Chapter One Review

ancient hieroglyphics. The stone was unearthed by Napoleon's men in 1799 when they invaded Egypt. This elaborately inscribed stone displays one message in three different forms: ancient Greek, Egyptian hieroglyphics, and demotic script. Using the ancient Greek inscription as a map, archeologist Jean-François Champollion decoded the order and sounds of the hieroglyphs in 1822. Champollion also posed theories, later proved correct, about the structure of the demotic script on the Rosetta Stone. The discovery and transcription of the writing led to the deciphering of other hieroglyphic inscriptions.

Circle one answer for each definition to indicate the correct key concept term for each. When necessary, determine whether the phrase provided is true or false.

1. The year 5100 BCE is considered the peak of arts and learning during the Golden Age of Greece, aproximately three hundred years after the adoption of the Phoenician alphabet.
    a. True
    b. False

2. Pictures and/or pictographs assembled in an order so as to represent the syllables in a word or words, from which meaning can be deciphered.
    a. Hieroglyphic
    b. Demotic script
    c. Cuneiform
    d. Rebus

3. Anthropologists believe that the domestication of animals was a strong factor in the development of human societies.
    a. True
    b. False

4. To sound or utter any of the abstract units of the phonetic system of a language that correspond to a set of similar speech sounds.
    a. Phoneme
    b. Semitic languages
    c. Ideograph
    d. Syllable

5. Tortoise shells etched with symbols have been excavated from the Jiahu site in Henan province in central China. The shells found appear to be part of a funerary ritual in Neolithic graves that have been dated to approximately 12,000–7800 BCE.
    a. True
    b. False

6.   Pictorial material relating to or illustrating a subject or the traditional or conventional images or symbols associated with a subject and especially a religious or legendary subject; the imagery or symbolism of a work of art, an artist, or a body of art.

    a.   Iconography
    b.   Pictograph
    c.   Mnemonics
    d.   Hieroglyphic

7.   The Assyrians were quick to adopt cuneiform as a practical writing system. Cuneiform writing has been used in several languages, and was in use for about 3000 years.

    a.   True
    b.   False

8.   The pith of a plant cut in strips and pressed into a paper-like substrate or material to write on.

    a.   Parchment
    b.   Rosetta Stone
    c.   Papyrus
    d.   Cartouche

9.   Repetition of agreed-upon shapes is the essence of a writing system.

    a.   True
    b.   False

10.   A character or symbol used to represent a word, syllable, or phoneme.

    a.   Phonogram
    b.   Ideograph
    c.   Rebus
    d.   Parchment

11.   Today many spoken languages exist that have no written form.

    a.   True
    b.   False

12.   An Egyptian script that lasted for about 1000 years following hieratic script, and belongs to the last period of ancient Egyptian history. This script was used for business and literary purposes. It has a cursive form, signs are more flowing and joined, and the signs themselves are more similar to one another, making it slightly more difficult to read.

    a.   Hieratic script
    b.   Semitic languages
    c.   Demotic script
    d.   Cuneiform

13.   Most original parchment texts no longer exist, as they deteriorated in the moist Mediterranean climate, while many of the copies on papyrus survived.

    a.   True
    b.   False

14.   A symbol that is used to wholly communicate a simple message without words, such as in traffic signs and restroom door signage. This may be used as a signature, otherwise known as a distinctive mark indicating identity, such as a corporate logo.

    a.   Hieroglyphic
    b.   Pictograph
    c.   Mnemonic
    d.   Rebus

15.   Some historians assume that writing began with small tags of parchment inscribed with pictographs that were attached to jugs by string intended to represent the contents of the vessels during shipping.

    a.   True
    b.   False

16. The oval band symbolizing continuity encloses hieroglyphs of a god's or pharaoh's name into one visual entity.
    a. Phonogram.
    b. Cartouche
    c. Rebus
    d. Ideograph

17. With the expansion of the Greek Empire under the rule of Frederick the Great (from 356 to 323 BCE), Greek culture spread.
    a. True
    b. False

18. A sign or character that represents and idea or concept, often comprised of two or more pictographs.
    a. Pictograph
    b. Cartouche
    c. Ideograph
    d. Syllable

19. The Semitic languages comprise the languages in the Far East, an area today that includes the countries of Syria, Lebanon, Israel, China, Palestine, Jordan, Cyprus, Turkey, Iraq, Egypt, Iran, Kuwait, Saudi Arabia, Bahrain, Qatar, United Arab Emirates, Oman, and Yemen.
    a. True
    b. False

20. A name used to designate a group of Asiatic and African languages, namely: Hebrew and Phoenician, Aramaic, Assyrian, Arabic, Ethiopic (Geez and Ampharic).
    a. Hieratic script
    b. Semitic languages
    c. Demotic script
    d. Hieroglyphic

21. Around 500 BCE the hieratic script eventually evolved into demotic script (demotic means "of the people"). This writing style is visually complicated compared to hieratic script.
    a. True
    b. False

22. Representing speech sounds by means of symbols that have one value only; of or relating to spoken language or speech sounds.
    a. Phonogram
    b. Pictograph
    c. Phonetic
    d. Ideograph

23. Found in 1908 at the ruins of the Minoan palace, the Phaistos Disk is dated to approximately 3700 BCE. The text is made up of fifty-one words, with eighty-five different symbols occurring a total of twenty-four times.
    a. True
    b. False

24. A black basalt stone found in 1799 that bears an inscription in hieroglyphics, demotic characters, and Greek and is celebrated for having given the first clue to the decipherment of Egyptian hieroglyphics.
    a. Hieratic script
    b. Semitic languages
    c. Demotic script
    d. Rosetta Stone

25. Hieroglyphics commonly run in horizontal rows, read from right to left. All the people and animals face the left in any given passage.
    a. True
    b. False

26. Of or relating to a time early in history, or to those living in such a period or time; especially of or relating to the historical period beginning with the earliest known civilizations and extending to the fall of the western Roman Empire in 476 CE.
    a. Phonetic
    b. Boustrephedon
    c. Rosetta Stone
    d. Ancient

27. A written language of characters formed by the arrangement of small wedge-shaped elements and used in ancient Sumerian, Akkadian, Assyrian, Babylonian, and Persian writing.
    a. Cuneiform
    b. Hieratic script
    c. Demotic script
    d. Hieroglyphic

28. Because of their diverse trade and travel, the culture of the Phoenicians was influenced by many other peoples who lived around the Mediterranean Sea, including the Greeks, Minoans, Etruscans, and Sumerians.
    a. True
    b. False

29. Writing with alternating lines in opposite directions; one line is written from left to write, then the next line is reversed (mirrored) and written from right to left. The Greeks called this Phoenician method of writing in alternating directions a word which means "like the ox plows a field."
    a. Hieratic script
    b. Boustrephedon
    c. Demotic script
    d. Typography

30. Before the discovery of the Rosetta Stone, hieroglyphics had been completely and correctly deciphered.
    a. True
    b. False

31. A writing system developed in ancient Egypt that used pictographs to represent words and sounds.
    a. Hieroglyphic
    b. Pictograph
    c. Mnemonic
    d. Parchment

32. The style, arrangement, and appearance of typeset matter; typography is sometimes seen as encompassing many separate fields from the type designer who creates letterforms to the graphic designer who selects typefaces and arranges them on the page.
    a. Hieratic script
    b. Logogram
    c. Demotic script
    d. Typography

33. A device, such as a formula, verse, or rhyme, used as an aid in remembering; a technique of improving the memory.
    a. Mnemonic
    b. Cartouche
    c. Rebus
    d. Ideograph

34. The smallest conceivable expression or unit of speech; a unit of spoken language that is next bigger than a speech sound and consists of one or more vowel sounds alone or of a syllabic consonant alone or of either with one or more consonant sounds preceding or following.
    a. Ideograph
    b. Pictograph
    c. Syllable
    d. Logogram

35. Greek culture spread. The growth of the Hellenistic culture caused the spread of the Greek alphabet (precursor to our own) as far as Egypt, Mesopotamia, and India.
    a. True
    b. False

Lettering during the Roman Empire and Middle Ages

The lettering of the precursors of our English language developed throughout the Roman Empire and its decline into the Middle Ages, up to the Renaissance. The Celtic, Carolingian, Romanesque, and Gothic lettering styles formed a bridge to the letterforms known today.

Because each predominated in a particular area at a particular time, differences in lettering and illumination style provide today's scholars with the clues necessary to identify the geographical location and time period where a given medieval manuscript originated.

During the Middle Ages, lettering developed in two general directions. The first included a number of similar styles showing Celtic influence, followed by the introduction of a consistent hand under the rule of Charlemagne. This period ended with the Romanesque variations. The second is characterized by a Gothic flavor, branching into Rotunda, Textura, Bartarde, and various Humanistic styles simultaneously.

2.1 Medieval illustrations depict the hardships suffered by those enduring the plagues in Europe during the Middle Ages.

The Impact of the Roman Empire

For approximately forty years beginning in 185 BCE the Roman Empire waged war intermittently against the Greeks. Their intent was to extend their empire by conquering neighboring lands. In 146 BCE the Romans finally were successful in their effort to overrun Greece.

The Roman alphabet, considered to be the earliest known version of our own modern alphabet, was derived from the Greek alphabet via the Etruscans, who settled north of Rome. During Roman military encroachment and empire expansion, the twenty-one-letter alphabet was spread throughout England, Spain, Egypt, and the Persian Gulf.

Roman Triumphal Arches

Romans conquered foreign lands and forced the people into slavery. Huge triumphal arches built across main thoroughfares of the conquered

2.2 Below: Timeline illustrating the development of typefaces during the Middle Ages.

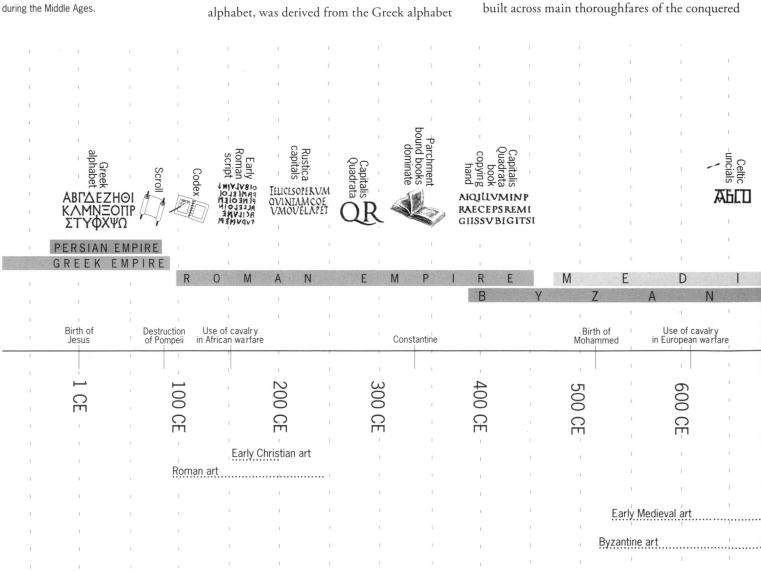

cities were the constant reminders of Roman pride and conquest. The conquered populations saw on a daily basis commemorative inscriptions emblazoned on the large arches. The Romans also engineered and built (with slave labor) many of the first roads and bridges connecting the cities of their empire in order to more easily move troops and supplies to new locations.

One lovely example of the structure and weight of Roman capitals is the inscription at the base of Trajan's column in Rome, carved around 114 CE. This inscription is regarded as the finest extant example of chisel-cut lettering. It shows the introduction of *serifs* (the horizontal extensions at the end of a stroke on a letterform), which were not seen in earlier examples.

In approximately 100 CE the Roman Empire was at its strongest, dominating the areas we currently refer to as Europe, Egypt, and parts of Mesopotamia and northern Africa. Part of the success in unifying this extensive

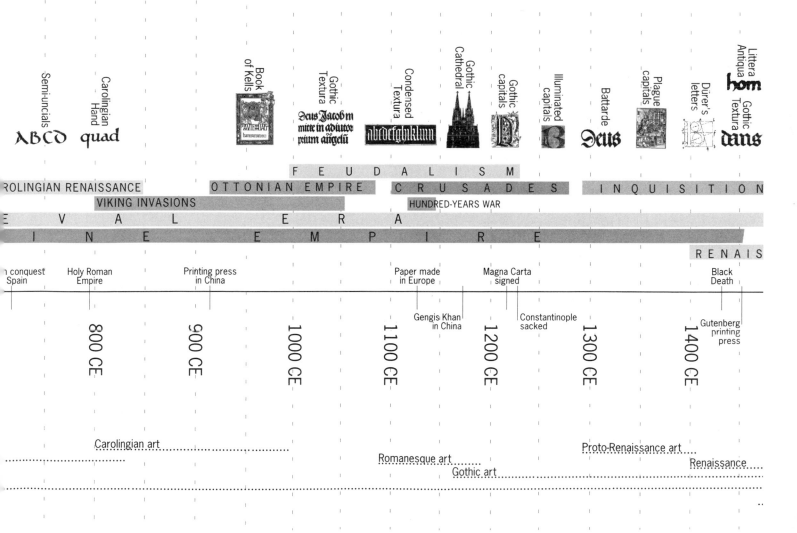

2.3 The Roman Empire at approximately 100 CE is indicated by the lined area of the map.

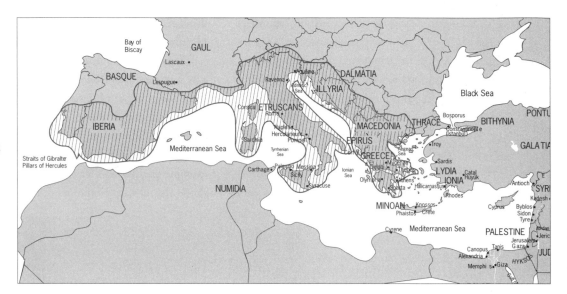

2.4 Etruscan script from approximately 600 BCE.

2.5 Engraved Capitalis Quadrata from Trajan's column illustrates the precisely balanced and well-proportioned letterforms of the Roman alphabet in approximately 114 CE.

area is attributed to the use of a single language (Latin), a primary writing style, and a consistent government structure.

Roman Lettering

Just as the Greeks borrowed the alphabet from the Phoenicians, the Romans borrowed from the Greeks. The Romans adapted much of Greek civilization, including pieces of their culture, art, philosophy, legal system, and the written alphabet.

Roman lettering was a fine art. For years later scholars believed that the serifs were necessitated by the stonecutting technique, in order to create clean, precise "stops" for the strokes of the letters using a chisel. Recent studies suggest, however, that the serifs may have been created by the reed letterer, who laid out the text in paint or ink on the stone, to be used as a guide by the stonemason. The stonemason followed the reed brush strokes, creating thick and thin strokes and serifs just as in the hand written version. After being cut into the stone, the letters were filled with red paint to look like writing on papyrus, but most

of the inscriptions that remain today have lost their coloring.

Capitalis Quadrata to Rustica

Capitalis Quadrata is the written counterpart to the classic carved Roman capitals. Written with a reed pen, the thick and thin strokes incorporate an organic unity of curves and straight lines that form square-shaped capitals. A condensed version of Capital Quadrata, named *Rustica* came into popular use between 100 BCE and 100 CE. Less rigidly constructed, the Rustica capitals saved space, reducing use of expensive parchment and papyrus. The Rustica lettering style allowed scribes to compress the quantity of information that would fit into a given space, often accommodating 50 percent more content. Eventually the letters were linked to increase the speed with which they were written.

Constantine Ends Christian Persecution

By 325 CE, Christianity was a widely recognized religion. The Roman Empire adopted Christianity and the formerly pagan people

ABCDEFGHI JKLMNOPQ RSTUVWXYZ

2.6 The Roman letterforms, top, were drawn on stone before being chiseled. Once the letters were engraved in stone, they were usually painted with red ochre paint for greater readability.

no longer persecuted Christians. Around 330 the emperor *Constantine* united the Eastern and Western portions of the Roman Empire and expanded into the area known today as Russia. He set up garrisons, or small bands of military personnel, in the conquered lands to ensure that he would receive tribute and taxes from the conquered people. The capital of the Roman Empire was moved from Rome to Constantinople, named after him.

The Roman Empire Divided

In about 395 the Roman Empire divided into eastern and western factions, ending the religious cohesiveness of the empire. That same year, the empire was overrun by northern outsiders called the *Visigoths* (the western group of Goths

who sacked Rome and created a kingdom in present-day Spain and southern France). At first the Romans lost control of distant, outlying areas, but gradually the invaders overthrew Rome. Shortly thereafter, around 476 CE, the eastern division of the empire was overrun by Germanic barbarians who ransacked and looted the cities, leading to the Romans' final downfall.

The Scroll versus the Codex

Most Roman documentation was written on scrolls. *Scrolls* (rolled documents) were constructed of papyrus. Papyrus was too fragile to fold into pages because it would crack, so long documents were rolled for storage and transportation. The vertical strands on the back side of papyrus make it a poor writing surface, so scrolls only accommodated writing on one side.

An early form of the book was known as a *codex*. This consisted of two wax-coated boards tied together along one edge. The pointed end of a stylus was used for writing in the soft wax, and the flat end of the stylus was used for erasing. The wax booklet was intended for temporary communication, notes, and correspondence and was used by students and scribes in training.

Later versions of the codex incorporated *parchment* (writing substrate made from animal skin) which could also be used on both

ABCDEFGHIJK LMNOPQRST UVWXYZ

ABCDEFGHI JKLMNOPQ RSTVWXYZ

2.7 By approximately 300 CE the square Roman capitals appeared shorter, wider, and with thicker strokes than Capitalis Quadrata, top. Rustica from approximately 500 CE, bottom, is a condensed face written with an angled pen.

2.8 An example of ancient Roman script commonly found in daily application of written documents such as business notations, loan documents, and other accounting records.

Tools and Letters

Ancient Roman writing, formed with flat-tipped reed pens, still affects the look of many of our contemporary typefaces, as reflected in the weight variations. The angle of the pen, in addition to the direction of pen movement, produced lines of different widths. The thickening of the lines, especially on curved letters, is called *stress*. The appearance of our own writing styles and typefaces are reflections of the tools employed in their creation.

sides. Parchment could be folded and stitched. Gradually codices became recognized as a choice among Christian scholars, as they were easier to use. In contrast to a lengthy scroll, the parchment codex used less material, took up less room in storage, and was less cumbersome when searching for a specific area of text.

The form of early books evolved from the codex, with a left-hand page (*verso*) and a right-hand page (*recto*). Although both scrolls and codices survived side by side from about 1 CE to about 400 CE, the practicality of the codex format eventually dominated.

Roman Script

Business transactions, bookkeeping, and correspondence from approximately 400 CE were written in script. This popular handwriting style was faster to use than capitals and required less space and fewer materials to communicate ideas. It was thought to be easier to read and is often identified as the beginning of lowercase letters as we know them today.

These letterforms were dramatically different from the original Roman capitals, and were characterized by long sweeping flourishes. Local chanceries and government scribes developed individual variations on the everyday cursive style, introducing *ligatures*, *ascenders*, and *descenders*.

2.9 Adobe Garamond Pro includes special glyphs called ligatures. A ligature is a combination of two or more connected letterforms. Ascenders are portions of a letterform that extend above the x-height of the form, and descenders are portions of the letterform that extend below the x-height of the form.

2.10 Examples of the uncial lettering illustrate regional and personal style differences in character form most commonly associated with the Celts.

Christianizing of Ireland and the Celtic Lettering

Shortly before the fall of Rome, around 430 CE, the missionary Saint Patrick set out with Bible manuscripts, intent on converting Ireland. Perhaps because Ireland was geographically removed from the mainland of Europe, it was not frequently subjected to invasions by nomadic tribes or warriors. This allowed *Celtic* (pertaining or relating to the Welsh, Cornish, or Scots Gaelic peoples) manuscripts and lettering design to flourish without much outside influence.

Celtic lettering and decoration innovations marked new directions in letterform shape and illustration styles, with extraordinary variation and geometric ornamentation. Introductory pages to each of the gospels use the whole page to illustrate one word or phrase magnificently. The complex interlacing of precise Celtic scrollwork is dotted with animals and supernatural creatures carefully executed with attention paid to minute details. Bright, intense colors are set adjacent to one another to intensify the thick texture of twisted ornamentation, highlighted with gold leaf. The rounded letterforms, with both upper- and lowercase clearly defined, are carefully *letter spaced* and *word spaced* to improve legibility.

The Crumbling Empire Leads to Feudalism

Rome was sacked by a succession of invaders, beginning around 410 CE—first the Visigoths, followed by the *Burgundians, Vandals, Franks, Ostrogoths,* and *Lombards.* Following their participation in the conquest of the Western Roman Empire, these Germanic tribes settled throughout Europe and Iberia, founding kingdoms. Except for the Franks, all have disappeared. Rome was ravaged once again around 533 CE when the Byzantine (eastern roman) emperor Justinian's armies attempted to regain control of the city. As the city became less safe, people moved to the estates of landed nobles in the countryside, trading their liberty for protection by the lord. These vassals, or people who held land from a feudal lord and received protection in return for homage and allegiance, were required to guarantee defensive military service in case of attack.

Following the fall of the Roman Empire in 476 CE, the centers of civilization were looted and Western society fell into the Dark Ages. *Feudalism,* an economic system where serfs or indentured slaves worked for the wealthy lord in exchange for protection, took hold.

Each feudal lord set up a small, self-sufficient community, so the need to interact with other communities and travel was limited. Usually medieval communities were surrounded by a

2.11 Monastic orders were reponsible for the preservation of ancient texts through copying texts to preserve and disseminate knowledge; often men born to a low societal status joined a religious order to earn the opportunity for education and social respect.

protective wall or set up on a high land mass for protection. Since most people were settled within these enclosed communities, they no longer looked to conquer new lands or build new empires. On the other hand, cultural life was hampered because there was no forum for the interaction of ideas, philosophies, or influences.

The Roman Christian church emerged as the unifying force in Europe, with the power of the clergy unquestioned. The Christian notion of an all-powerful, father-like God was prominent in all facets of daily life. At the same time, there was a great belief in evil spirits among the average population carried over from the days of pagan belief and worship.

Secluded monasteries were established for religious orders, so learning and copying of biblical

Parchment

Parchment is a writing substrate that is made from the skin of goats and calves. *Vellum* is the highest quality of parchment, made from newborn calf skin. The fur was removed from the skin surface, which was smoothed by techniques utilizing stones and liquid washes before being stretched over a frame and left to be dried and bleached by the sun.

Unlike papyrus, both sides of parchment could be written on without the ink seeping through. A number of scholars believe that parchment allowed for the evolution from scrolls to books since it was usable on both sides, and could be folded without cracking. The terms *recto* and *verso,* which identified the right and left pages in a book spread, came from the description of the sides of the sheet of parchment. *Recto* referred to the good side or the smooth inside of the skin, while *verso* referred to the back, or less smooth side of the skin.

There were disadvantages to parchment. Even though both surfaces could be written upon, it was more expensive to manufacture than papyrus, hence, the production of books using parchment was very expensive. Because they were costly, books were collected by rulers, as symbols of their great wealth and power.

2.12 Variations in Celtic knotwork B's illustrate the creativity and imagination that went into the interpretation of letterforms, often used to illustrate and illuminate texts copied by religious orders.

αbcdeꝼᵹhıȷ klmnopqr stᴜʋwxyʒ

2.13 Uncials were named for the grid used to construct the letterforms. This wide style of calligraphy eventually developed a second variation of small uncials, or *minuscules* called half-uncials. The half-uncials are believed to have evolved into the lowercase letterforms known today.

ABCDEF GHIJKLM

2.14 These very linear, strongly vertical *majuscule* (uppercase) letterforms are of Celtic origin, but vary greatly from the Uncial style. This style is often referred to as *Runic* since it appears to follow many of the characteristics seen in Nordic Runes.

texts was limited to geographically isolated areas. Monks raised their own animals and crops for food; they lived a peaceful life of quiet religious practice and study.

In the monasteries, many of the ancient texts were copied. Some of the manuscripts produced by the monks were sold to provide money for necessities they could not produce themselves, while others were produced for the monks' own libraries. It is these copies on parchment, rather than the papyrus originals, that survive today in small numbers. These parchment manuscripts reveal the different regional styles of lettering that developed during the medieval era.

Celtic Round Uncials

From the Celtic lands emerged a more rounded form of the Roman alphabet called Uncials. *Uncials* (from Latin *uncia*, meaning a twelfth part, referring to the measurement of an inch) are believed to be the precursor of our upper- and lowercase letters. Many scholars feel that uncials grew out of a desire to have small letters in biblical manuscripts for the pragmatic purpose of saving parchment. The new letterforms were quicker to write, compared to earlier lettering styles, and provided the opportunity for monks and scribes to develop beautiful letterforms for sacred texts.

Celtic uncials were distinguished by their roundness, their diminished serifs, and their subtle ascenders and descenders. In the interest of saving time, corners were rounded off. Uncials appear to be lowercase letters, but often sentences were begun with the same uncial characters used in the rest of the sentence.

From the development of the Phoenician alphabet through the introduction of uncials, all prior Roman letters had been uppercase. The introduction of *half-uncials* provided the

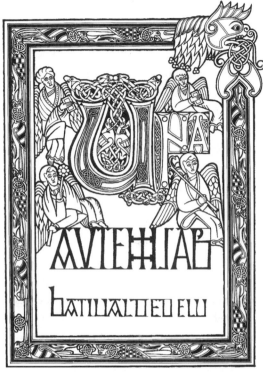

2.15 Page 285 recto from the Book of Kells (Luke 23:56 through 24:1) infers the resurrection of Christ, as Joseph of Arimathea and others gather to anoint the body and find the rock rolled away from the entrance of the tomb, and the body of Jesus missing.

foundation for lowercase or *minuscule* letters. These half-uncials began to appear in documents around the year 600. Eventually ascenders and descenders were extended, evolving into the letterforms known today. The letterforms developed regional stylistic variations. The practice of reading to oneself influenced the increasing use of small letters because scaled-down books could be more easily transported to different locations for meditation and reflection. Also, the distinctions between upper- and lowercase letters meant that words were more legible.

Lettering as a Declaration of Faith

The ornamentation of early papyrus scrolls was limited to the carving of the sticks to which the scroll was attached. As the demand for Bibles in the codex format increased, greater importance was placed on creating beautiful copies of the sacred word. Monks copying the sacred text became imaginative and competitive, and were committed to penning a beautiful Bible to exalt their God. The reference to God as the "light" led to the use of gold leaf in the *illumination* of the words. Initial caps, identifying the beginning of a new section, became highly stylized, including images of the characters featured in the story (called *histrionic capitals*) while the covers of the Bibles were embedded with jewels.

The concept of illuminating was a double entendre, as it was meant to make clear the stories of the Bible as well as to brighten the page with bright colors and reflective gold and silver accents. The average person of the time period could not read, since this skill was reserved for wealthy nobles and those within the church community. Most commoners relied on the pictorial carvings and paintings in churches to recall the scenes from the Bible, as well as the stories and lessons that accompanied them.

A Unifying Force in Lettering

During the early Middle Ages (500 to 750) the lands of the Roman Empire had disintegrated into independent feudal communities, causing the Latin language to evolve into regional dialects. Strong military leaders' attempts to conquer and consolidate large territories into kingdoms continued. By 768 CE, the Gauls' leader, *Charlemagne*, was known for being a strong military leader, as well as a ruler who favored learning and the arts.

A standardized lettering style was decreed throughout the empire, which extended through much of the area that comprises modern-day Europe. Charlemagne appointed an English monk scholar, *Alcuin of York*, to oversee the copying of many ancient manuscripts. Many assume that Alcuin was a Celtic-trained monk as he assembled a large number of letterers at Charlemagne's court at Aachen in 789 CE. He chose a hand that was similar to Celtic uncials

2.16 Monks copying and binding books.

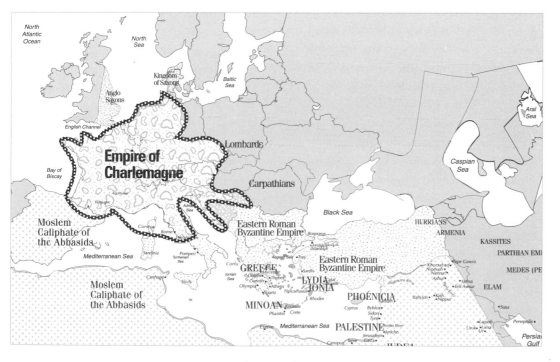

2.17 The Carolingian manuscript hand was codified during Charlemagne's reign. This example is believed to have been written around 800.

2.18 Empire of Charlemagne around the time of his death, approximately 814.

2.19 An illustration of the variations in Romanesque characters and the practice of enclosing or insetting characters inside another to conserve space.

2.20 An engraving of Romanesque lettering includes a variety of letterforms.

2.21 Gothic lettering was practiced and perfected using a grid that helped the calligrapher determine correct proportions for each letterform while maintaining consistent vertical strokes.

as the imperial lettering style. Alcuin is credited with the introduction of the *Carolingian* (meaning during the reign of Charlemagne) style of lettering that was dictated as the standard copying text.

Like Celtic uncials, the *Carolingian hand* is a style of writing in which the characters are round and full. There is a twisting of the pen throughout the downward stroke of the ascenders, giving a slightly tapered appearance to the letters. This standardized hand brought about a uniform lowercase Roman alphabet. By this time (800 CE) the use of larger uncials to introduce a sentence was common practice; however, standardized punctuation and word spacing were not adopted until the 1400s, following the invention of printing.

During Charlemagne's reign a class of scribes was employed to copy secular texts. These commercial letterers were employed by book merchants who pressured them to write with greater speed. It is believed that this practice of encouraging greater speed affected the style of Carolingian hand that spread throughout Europe. These scribes were hired to draw up contracts, loan documents, legal agreements, and deeds, in addition to the copying of texts for the educated elite of the day.

On Christmas day, 800, Pope Leo III crowned Charlemagne the emperor of the Holy Roman Empire, a move calculated to gain military support against invaders intent on the overthrow of Rome. However, it was not long before Vikings began to raid by land and sea, intermittently attacking Europe from about 830. The Lindisfarne Monastery was ransacked in 793, Ireland was invaded in 835, and France in 843, followed by England in 851. These raiders had no appreciation of the culture they were destroying; they stole items made of precious metals and melted

2.22 The practice of Gothic hand lettering illustrates letterform variations.

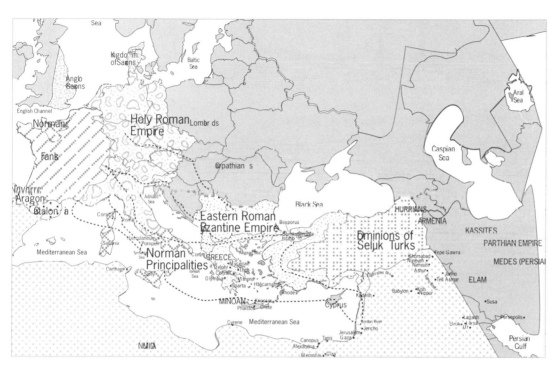

2.23 Gothic Textura is characterized by a condensed, vertical structure and a boxlike aesthetic conveyed by the diagonal counterforms and serifs.

2.24 Map illustrating the various routes of movement during the Crusades.

them down. Since the monasteries were known to have elaborate gifts donated by wealthy patrons, they were a prime target for attack.

By 1000, the Carolingian hand had evolved into many variations and was widely used by monks copying ancient texts. This set the stage for the Italian Renaissance printing fonts as they were mistaken by printers as an ancient hand from Roman times. The development of typography slowed with the decline of Charlemagne's empire during the barbarian raids. Eventually Charlemagne's empire was divided among his three sons, and the visual standards of the empire deteriorated into regional variations once again.

The Romanesque Hand Invites Innovation

The *Romanesque* lettering style formulated between 800 and 1000 is characterized by the extensive manipulation of the forms, which feature innovative additions to the strokes.

Inspired by earlier Celtic and Rustica lettering, the Romanesque integrates insets, overlaps, and fused letters in manuscripts and engravings. Inventive geometric experimentation and the truncation of crossbars freed the lettering from the prior austere standardization, with creative results. Multiple forms of the same letter were used in a single manuscript to showcase the scribes' talent and creativity. Romanesque-era lettering differs according to location and is so varied that the influences are difficult to trace.

The Development of the Gothic Textura Hand

There was little consistency in the reigning powers during the seventh and eighth centuries, although the Pope played an important role from time to time. Isolationism in small feudal communities continued, and the era was marked by great devotion to religion. Natural phenomena were explained as curses or blessings from an almighty power. Pilgrimages to faraway lands

2.25 The ornamentation of initial caps during the Gothic period (above) remained intricate but was more structurally restrained along the vertical and diagonal axis of the composition than the Celtic hand styles (below).

1. Select a letterform and begin exploring possibilities for adding decorative swashes. You may trace, photocopy, or scan the letters provided (facing page).

2. Reflect the design along a horizontal axis.

3. Reflect the design once again, along a vertical axis.

4. Overlap the outline of the letterform and the decorative area of the design.

5. Determine which areas will be in front and which areas will be in back..

6. Continue refining the details and separating front and back elements in the composition.

7. Explore options for addition of shade and shadow with various sizes of lines within the decorative area of the design. Experiment by drawing on the base art of the letter _M_ provided, left, before working on your own solution.

Illustrated Initial Exercise

Papermaking and Printing in Ancient China

The Greeks were still writing on papyrus scrolls while the Chinese were mass-producing printed works in 300 CE, a full 1,200 years before the Europeans!

Ts'ai Lun was credited with the development of paper in China in about 100 CE. He used an assortment of vegetable fibers such as mulberry tree bark, bamboo, silk, cotton rags, linen, and hemp. These natural fibers were soaked in water and beaten until they broke down into a pulp. Using a wooden frame with a screen attached to one side, he lowered it into the watery pulp mixture. Gently shaking the screen as he brought it up out of the water, he was able to create an even coating of fibers against the screen. The thin mat of plant fiber was flattened, weighted, and pressed until it was dry.

By 270 CE the Chinese were printing from woodblocks. Areas of a solid wood block were carved away, leaving a raised surface. A water-based ink was rolled onto the raised surface and allowed to soak into the wood grain. A piece of paper was applied to the surface and rubbed to transfer the image from the woodblocks to the paper. Often multiple blocks were arranged to print on a single sheet of paper, and could be inked in different colors.

were a commonplace homage of faith, a means of purifying oneself from past sins, proof of one's devotion, or a means to gain heavenly grace. During this era, marked by the importance placed on honor, purity, and chivalry, commoners did not question clergy.

The evolving *Gothic* character was angular and condensed; heavy vertical strokes were dominant, causing the curves to all but disappear. These *black letters* were made with great precision and were evenly spaced to such an extent that the texture on the page resembled woven fabric; for this reason it was referred to as *Textura*.

There were not larger spaces between words, and the copy extended from the left margin to the right in two vertical columns, without exception. This complete use of the page is difficult for the contemporary reader to decipher, as there was little indication of the beginning and ending of words or sentences. A few variations on lowercase letterforms evolved to assist readers in distinguishing between letterforms, such as the dot over the lowercase *i* (the tittle), to help readers distinguish it from a stroke of an *n*, *m*, or *u*. The length of ascenders and descenders was shortened and the vertical space between lines of text was reduced to economize on parchment, resulting in text that is difficult to read.

Because religious texts were the most commonly reproduced at this time, and because this Gothic lettering style was used at the same period of time, unavoidable associations between the two have resulted. The Gothic black letter hand still resonates with religious overtones hundreds of years later. Many historians compare the strong, vertical, angular style to the spires of Gothic architecture from the same period of time.

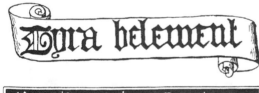

2.26 Round majuscule letters (top), known as Lombardic, were plump and curvilinear, in contrast to the Gothic Textura.

2.27 The banner example (top) illustrates how the Lombardic and Gothic Textura styles were mixed to create visual contrast and interest, as compared to the example (bottom) which is composed exclusively of the strong vertical Textura hand.

Mediterranean Expansion of Muslims

The Muslim Arabs expanded across Persia, Arabia, and the north coast of the Mediterranean at an unprecedented rate between 620 and 730, bringing political stability and their religion, Islam, to the lands they conquered. The Muslims ruled Arabia, Palestine, parts of ancient Persia, and Egypt by 650.

Their next expansion included North Africa, and by 711 they crossed from Morocco to Spain at the Straits of Gibraltar. They continued, overtaking Spain, and were not stopped until 732, when they reached the Pyrenees, which provided France with a natural barrier. Sicily was invaded in 827, with Rome attacked about twenty years later, in 846. Because St. Peter's Cathedral was not enclosed within Rome's protective walls, it was looted. With this great conquest by the Arabs came the opportunity to control all the shipping throughout the Mediterranean.

Beginning in 1096 and continuing until about 1291, the *Crusades*, or Holy Wars, were fought by Christians from Central Europe against the Middle East. Turkey, Syria, and Arabia were attacked, as well as the Holy Land. (Since the area surrounding and including Jerusalem is considered sacred by three different religions, it remains an area of dispute today.)

Development of Rag Paper in Europe

Books became cheaper during the Middle Ages once it was discovered that paper could be made from rags and plant fibers, creating an alternative to expensive parchment. The lower cost of paper allowed faster, less expensive book production. The growing middle class of guild members was becoming more literate, and it became possible for them to afford books. Soon rag paper became plentiful throughout Europe.

Around 1100 papermaking was introduced in Sicily, and by the end of the 1200s a small paper mill was well established in Fabriano, Italy. Paper mills grew rapidly along rivers because the power of the running water was used to turn great water wheels for production, and also because the papermaking process required large quantities of water. France followed and within fifty years built paper mills as well. These different mills began using watermarks to identify and distinguish themselves. A *watermark* is a design embossed into a piece of paper during its production used for identification of the paper and papermaker. The watermark is visible when the paper is backlit.

The Late Gothic Period

The feudal societies of the Middle Ages transitioned into settled cities as the powers of local lords brought about the establishment of reasonable laws, which curtailed much local crime, allowing the development of trade. Increased agriculture supported international trade, and money began to replace land as a measure of wealth.

Universities were founded in cities and a broader spectrum of society received a formal education. Universities necessitated the use of books in greater quantities, so the demand for craftsmen involved in the production of books grew as well. Guilds of craftsmen organized and began training apprentices for the workforce in many areas, but those specializing in lettering, ornamentation, and binding were particularly popular. Since a number of the universities were secular, there was a transition away from the religious monopoly on education and book production; besides the traditional clerical Latin translations, classical Greek and Roman texts moved into popularity by the end of the era. The study of the ancient Roman and Greek texts developed into a philosophical movement known as humanism. This school of thought placed humans at the center of the universe, without divine intervention.

From approximately 1200 through 1400 the Gothic aesthetic in art and architecture was at its height throughout Europe. Supported by flying buttresses, the spires of cathedrals soared ever higher in their attempt to reach up to heaven. Vast areas of stained glass depicted Biblical stories, making it easier for the clerics who taught and preached to illustrate the concepts. Monasticism was at its peak, with many different orders. Churches were built in small towns along pilgrimage routes.

2.28 Rotunda lettering is believed to have been adapted from earlier Gothic lettering, although it is wider and less ornate—perhaps it is a hybrid produced by a combination of Gothic and Carolingian.

2.29 Carefully executed Gothic lettering results in a gracefully elegant aesthetic solution, but it is difficult for contemporary readers to decipher.

2.30 Northern Gothic lettering shows the difference between the full majuscule letters and the minuscule letters; the difference in the wider letterform of the uppercase provides a visual break and a point of emphasis among the strong vertical lowercase forms.

2.31 Illustrative capital letters often reflect contemporary philosophies or social concerns, such as these, drawn during the time of the "Black Death."

Fact Find! What other examples can you find of the calligraphic lettering styles to compare? Uncials, Gothic Textura or Lombardic? Can you find examples of technique to replicate these styles of lettering on your own? Log onto to your favorite search engine and find an Internet reference to help you create your comparison. Print out the results for discussion. List some of your ideas in the space provided below.

_____

_____

_____

_____

_____

_____

_____

_____

_____

URL: http://

URL: http://

URL: http://

Date visited:

During the thirty years between 1347 and 1377, more than forty percent of the population —that is, more than twenty-five million people— died when the bubonic plague hit Europe. It is frequently referred to as the *Black Death*, because the victims turned black from the plague. The plague was brought by fleas that lived on rats, which came on cargo ships bringing goods from the East. The disease spread rapidly with the existing unsanitary living conditions of the time, and for most victims death came within four days of the onset of symptoms.

Historians believe that a number of religious monuments were built during this time as a symbol of celebration and thanks by survivors. A number of illustrations, bookplates, and initial capital letters represent the plague as a skeleton coming to whisk the living away unexpectedly.

Rotunda Compared to Gothic Lettering

By the early 15th century, Gothic black letter, known as Textura, and Rotunda lettering had emerged. *Rotunda* (also referred to as *Humanistic Hand*, or *Littera Antiqua*) was a more open and round style that was preferred in France and Italy. The condensed Gothic black letter remained popular in Germanic areas into the 1900s. Both of these styles became models with the onset of experimentation with movable type and printing.

Littera Antiqua was inspired by the six-hundred-year-old Carolingian writing forms, combining square Roman capitals with curving, round, lowercase letters. Scholars who read ancient Roman manuscripts that had been copied during the Carolingian period thought that they were reading original texts copied in a writing style developed during the time of ancient Rome, hence the name Littera Antiqua, meaning "ancient letters." Littera Antiqua was the formal style of lettering used for secular manuscripts, so it served to differentiate lay texts from religious texts in many areas of Europe.

Chapter Two Review

Setting the Stage for the Renaissance

Cities began to grow in size and importance, around 1450, just before the Renaissance (which refers to the "rebirth" of learning) bringing about occasional political strife and turmoil. Art was created primarily under the patronage of wealthy lords, politicians, and religious leaders. The de' Medici family in Florence, Italy, was known for sponsoring great works of art and architecture during the Renaissance, as were a number of the Popes, who comissioned religious sculpture, architecture, and frescoes.

When the Turks closed the overland routes to India and the Far East, nations seeking spices and silks began to sponsor explorers to find alternate routes. This led to Christopher Columbus' journey to America in 1492, and Vasco da Gama's successful journey to India in 1497 by sailing around the southern tip of Africa. Humans began to understand enough about world geography and the earth's forces to explain them in natural terms instead of supernatural terms. Humanism flourished during the Renaissance.

Circle one answer for each definition to indicate the correct key concept term for each. When necessary, determine whether the phrase provided is true or false.

1. Black letters that were made with great precision and were evenly spaced to such an extent that the texture on the page resembled woven fabric were referred to as _____.
   a. Textura
   b. Frescoes
   c. Rotunda
   d. Bartarde

2. Part of the success of the Roman Empire in unifying Europe, Egypt and parts of Mesopotamia and northern Africa is attributed to the use of a single language (Latin), a primary writing style, and a consistent government structure.
   a. True
   b. False

3. The study of the ancient Roman and Greek texts developed into a philosophical, secular movement known as _____. This school of thought placed humans at the center of the universe, without divine intervention.
   a. Humanism
   b. Black Death
   c. Feudalism
   d. Monasticism

4. By 270 CE the Chinese were printing from woodblocks.
   a. True
   b. False

5. The western group of Goths who sacked Rome and created a kingdom in present-day Spain and southern France
   a. Muslims
   b. Ostrogoths
   c. Visigoths
   d. Burgundians

6. Around 330 CE the emperor Constantine united the Eastern and Western portions of the Roman Empire and expanded into the area known today as Russia.
    a. True
    b. False

7. Around 1100, papermaking was introduced in Sicily, and by the end of the 1200s a small paper mill was well established in Fabriano, Italy.
    a. True
    b. False

8. A design embossed into a piece of paper during its production used for identification of the paper and papermaker. It is visible when the paper is backlit.
    a. Inital capital
    b. Codex
    c. Watermark
    d. Religious monument

9. Ts'ai Lun was credited with the development of paper in China in about 100 CE.
    a. True
    b. False

10. The written counterpart to the classic carved Roman capitals. Written with a reed pen, the thick and thin strokes incorporate an organic unity of curves and straight lines that form square-shaped capitals.
    a. Rustica
    b. Rotunda
    c. Carolingian
    d. Capitalis Quadrata

11. From approximately 1200 through 1400 the Gothic aesthetic in art and architecture was at its height throughout Europe.
    a. True
    b. False

12. An early form of the book.
    a. Uncial
    b. Codex
    c. Rotunda
    d. Scroll

13. Alcuin of York is credited with the introduction of the _____ (meaning during the reign of Charlemagne) style of lettering that was dictated as the standard copying text.
    a. Textura
    b. Rotunda
    c. Rustica
    d. Carolingian

14. The Muslim Arabs expanded across Persia, Arabia, and the north coast of the Mediterranean at an unprecedented rate between 620 and 730, bringing political stability to the region.
    a. True
    b. False

15. Believed to have been a combination of bubonic and pneumonic plagues that entered Europe along Eastern trade routes, it swept across Europe between 1347-1350.
    a. Humanism
    b. Black Death
    c. Feudalism
    d. Black Letter

16. A condensed version of Capitalis Quadrata that came into popular use between 100 BCE and 100 CE.
    a. Textura
    b. Rotunda
    c. Rustica
    d. Bartarde

17. Books became cheaper during the Middle Ages once it was discovered that paper could be made from rags and plant fibers, creating an alternative to expensive parchment.
    a. True
    b. False

18. Just as the Greeks borrowed the alphabet from the Phoenicians, the Romans borrowed from the _____.
    a. Mesopotamians
    b. Greeks
    c. Muslims
    d. Italians

19. One lovely example of the structure and weight of Roman capitals is the inscription at the base of Charlemagne's column in Rome, carved around 114 CE. This inscription is regarded as the finest extant example of chisel-cut lettering.
    a. True
    b. False

20. It was spread by rats carrying infected fleas, and eliminated between one-fourth and one-third of the population in its first wave.
    a. Feudalism
    b. Black Death
    c. Crusades
    d. Pneumonia

21. Inspired by earlier Textura and Rotunda lettering, the Romanesque integrates decorative insets, overlaps, and fused letters in manuscripts and engravings.
    a. True
    b. False

22. _____ lettering is believed to have been adapted from earlier Gothic lettering, although it is wider and less ornate—perhaps it is a hybrid produced by a combination of Gothic and Carolingian.
    a. Bartarde
    b. Romanesque
    c. Rotunda
    d. Carolingian

23. During the Gothic era, multiple forms of the same letter were used in a single manuscript to showcase the scribes' talent and creativity.
    a. True
    b. False

24. Beginning in 1096 and continuing until about 1291, the Holy Wars were fought by Christians from Central Europe against the Middle East. The correct term for this campaign is called
    a. Islam
    b. Crusades
    c. Black Death
    d. Feudalism

25. Because religious texts were most commonly reproduced using a Gothic lettering style, unavoidable associations between the two have resulted. The Gothic black letter hand still resonates with religious overtones hundreds of years later.
    a. True
    b. False

26. A standardized lettering style was decreed throughout the empire of this leader, which extended through much of the area that comprises modern-day Europe.
    a. Constantine
    b. Ts'ai Lun
    c. Charlemagne
    d. Alcuin of York

27. Uncials (from Latin uncia, meaning a twelfth part, referring to the measurement of an inch) are believed to be the precursor of our upper- and lowercase letters.
    a. True
    b. False

28. Rome was sacked by a succession of invaders, beginning around 410 CE—first the Visigoths, followed by the
    a. Vandals, Ostrogoths, Burgundians, Lombards, and Franks.
    b. Burgundians, Vandals, Franks, Ostrogoths, and Lombards.
    c. Ostrogoths, Burgundians, Vandals, Lombards, and Franks.
    d. Franks, Burgundians, Ostrogoths, Vandals, and Lombards.

Circle one answer to correctly
identify each example.

29. **abcdefghi
jklmnopqr
stuvwxyz**

   a. Textura

   b. Rotunda

   c. Carolingian hand

   d. Half-uncials

30. SMBADO

   a. Lombardic

   b. Rotunda

   c. Gothic

   d. Celtic lettering

31. abcdefghi
jklmnopq
rstuvwxyz

   a. Etruscan script

   b. Rotunda

   c. Carolingian hand

   d. Celtic lettering

32. ABCDEFGhi
JKLMNOPQ
RSTWXYZ

   a. Textura

   b. Rotunda

   c. Carolingian hand

   d. Uncials

33.

   a. Roman script

   b. Rotunda

   c. Carolingian hand

   d. Celtic lettering

34. ABCDEFGHI
JKLMNOPQ
RSTVWXYZ

   a. Roman script

   b. Rustica

   c. Etruscan script

   d. Celtic lettering

35.

   a. Lombardic

   b. Rotunda

   c. Gothic

   d. Etruscan script

Renaissance Typography and Printing

The changing economies and emerging political stability of the late Middle Ages fostered the growth of cities. The increasing complexity of social organization encouraged the development of craftsmen's guilds and trade networks. Universities were founded in the burgeoning cities, and students were attracted to these centers of learning, art, and culture. Thus, the stage was set for the Renaissance, during which a resurgence of interest in ancient Roman and Greek thought led to the philosophical movement known as humanism.

In Europe, printing with movable, reusable type developed during the Renaissance and is considered an epochal event in the course of human development. A modern comparison is the development and widespread distribution of the personal computer, which has brought about similar changes in the speed and dissemination of information.

3.1 With a simple platen press, up to two hundred pounds of pressure per square inch may be applied to the page to make a clean impression. A great deal of physical labor was involved in printing using this method. Today, these platen presses are used for assembling covers on handmade books.

Key Concepts

Bartarde
Book of Hours
bracketing
chase
Civilité
Cloister Old Style
colophon
copperplate engraving
42-Line Bible
furniture
italic
kerning
libraire juré
movable type
Old Style
Papal Chancery
precision mold
press bed
quoins
Reformation
registration
Renaissance
Roman typeface
set width

The Renaissance

Often described as the "rebirth of learning," the *Renaissance* lasted approximately two centuries, from the mid-1400s to the late 1600s. The rebirth included a fascination with the artifacts, architecture, and language of ancient Greece and Rome. The writing, music, theater, philosophy, medicine, and law of the ancient cultures were held up as ideals, in sharp contrast to the predominantly Christian-based learning of the Middle Ages. Many ancient works found their way into print as book printing became more common and less expensive.

The Beginning of Printing

The refinement of the printing press, the innovation of *movable typ*e (reusable, individual letters cast in metal or carved in wood), and the manufacture of greater

Fact Find! Although the dates for the Renaissance are generalized here, there are different Renaissance periods in different areas of Europe, with emphasis in different areas of the arts and the humanities. List two examples of more specific dates and locations for the Renaissance period. Be sure to cite your source(s) correctly!

URL: http://

URL: http://

Date visited:

Capitalis Quadrata book copying hand
AIQILLVMINP RAECEPSREMI GIISSVBIGITSI

Celtic uncials
ABCD

Half-uncials
ABCD

Carolingian hand
quad

of Kells

CAROLINGIAN RENAISSANCE   OTTO
VIKING INVASIONS
R E   M E D I E V A L
B Y Z A N T I N E

Birth of Mohammed | Use of cavalry in European warfare | Muslim conquest of Spain | Holy Roman Empire | Printing press in China

400 CE   500 CE   600 CE   700 CE   800 CE   900 CE

Carolingian art
Early medieval art
Byzantine art

quantities of cheaper paper allowed the increase of book production. From the time when oral tradition dominated human interaction through the development of formal writing systems, never had there been such an enormous leap in communication as following the development of Gutenberg's printing technology. This process was much less expensive than the previous hand-copied editions, allowing more widespread dissemination of the written word. The broad availability of books encouraged greater literacy among commoners, since the mass reproduction of texts enabled a greater number of landowners and merchants, as well as many members of the guilds, access to and ownership of books; no longer were books exclusive to nobility.

Johann Gutenberg is credited with the development of movable, reusable type.

3.2 Timeline highlighting the transition from the Roman Empire to the Middle Ages, with examples of popular lettering styles of the period.

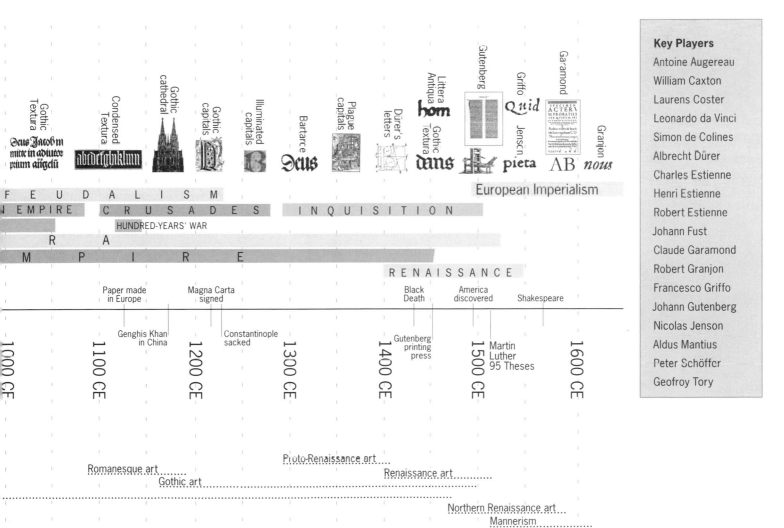

Key Players

Antoine Augereau
William Caxton
Laurens Coster
Leonardo da Vinci
Simon de Colines
Albrecht Dürer
Charles Estienne
Henri Estienne
Robert Estienne
Johann Fust
Claude Garamond
Robert Granjon
Francesco Griffo
Johann Gutenberg
Nicolas Jenson
Aldus Mantius
Peter Schöffer
Geofroy Tory

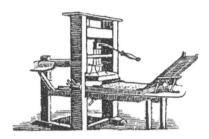

3.3 This press is similar to the one modified and perfected by Gutenberg.

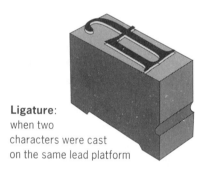

Ligature: when two characters were cast on the same lead platform

3.4 Gutenberg used 270 different pairs of ligature letters in the printing of his 42-Line Bible so that the end result would more closely resemble the versions hand-copied by scribes.

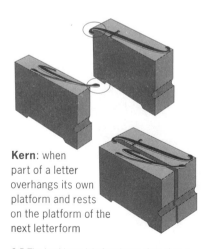

Kern: when part of a letter overhangs its own platform and rests on the platform of the next letterform

3.5 The lead base (platform) was shaved on a number of characters to create kerned pairs, for easier reading and to mimic handwritten texts.

Certainly Gutenberg's commitment to refinement of the printing process and to solving a series of problems and challenges is legendary. Some historians argue that *Laurens Coster* of Holland developed the art of printing slightly before or around the same time as Gutenberg; others argue that Coster merely stole some of Gutenberg's trial forays into printing. Still others propose that we know too little of the actual details of Gutenberg's life to credit him with the invention of printing. This controversy remains an unresolved, contentious issue among historians.

Gutenberg: The Metal Craftsman

The generally accepted version of the printing story is that Gutenberg, an accomplished metalworker and caster, was working toward developing a technique of printing text for books as early as 1438. He joined with goldsmith *Johann Fust*, who agreed to underwrite the cost of Gutenberg's printing experiments, provided Gutenberg repay him.

Gutenberg adapted a press that was originally used to press grapes for winemaking. He developed a method of casting metal type in single pieces that varied in width but maintained a precise and consistent height. He developed a *chase* (a rectangular iron frame in which pages or columns of type are composed) to hold the type in position on the printing press bed. Finally, he formulated inks to the correct consistency for use with lead cast type, and perfected techniques for *registration* (accurate alignment of type and images), for clean and precise impressions, and for keeping the edges of the printed page ink-free. In short, Gutenberg worked out the details that made printing a viable reproduction process.

Movable, Reusable Type

Gutenberg's brilliant innovation was the production of individual, reusable characters, rather than casting an entire page as one solid piece. The printing process required that Gutenberg cast each piece of type to the exact same depth for inking and the exact same height so that they would align along the baseline, but also find a means to cast different widths to accommodate different letter widths—from a lowercase *i* to an uppercase *M*. Gutenberg perfected the process with an ingeniously simple precision mold. First a punch was cut of the letter from hardened iron. Next, the punch was driven into the brass matrix to a precise depth to create the negative mold, from which the final lead alloy character was cast.

The *precision mold* was composed of two L-shaped pieces of metal that could be opened and closed to accommodate letters of varying widths while constraining the height and depth to consistent measurements. The negative brass impression of the letter, known as the brass matrix, was placed into the top of the mold. A mixture of molten lead, antimony, and tin was poured into the precision mold. The mold was quickly clamped shut and swung around by a rope to force the molten metal into all the small pieces of the letter and to prevent air bubbles from being trapped in the molten metal. Air bubbles would result in an imperfect raised letter or one that would deform under the pressure of the press, rendering it worthless.

Once the precision mold cooled, it was opened to remove the cast letter. Each cast letter was smoothed, and all burrs were removed. This was a labor-intensive process, but the letters could be used over and over. Ultimately it was faster to cast the individual letters than to copy a single page by hand. Gutenberg and his workers (hired metal-smiths accustomed to working in fine detail) cast over 15,000 lead characters for his first Bible (known as the *42-Line Bible* for the number of lines of text set on each page).

Imitation of a Hand-Copled Book

Gutenberg's ultimate goal was to create a manuscript that looked as though it had been hand-lettered by a scribe. Since there was no other form of writing or lettering available to Gutenberg at the time, it was logical that he would copy the existing standard. To approximate the handwriting of the scribes, Gutenberg cast almost 270 pairs of kerned or ligature pairs of characters as one punch. Since the *set width* (the space around a letter and the letter itself) is an inherent part of each cast lead piece, those characters that appeared too far apart underwent *kerning*, which referred to the practice of filing away a portion of the base of one character, allowing part of the letter to rest on the base of the adjacent character. (Today, the term *kerning* refers to the adjustment of the space between letters within a single word, with a goal of increasing legibility.)

The First Printing Ink

Oriental ink, which was thin and soaked into the wood type, then into the paper, produced a blurred edge to the characters and images and would not work for Gutenberg's printing process. It is likely that he borrowed his ideas about ink formulation from oil paint introduced in the early 1430s. Gutenberg's ink had enough

1. Steel punch with raised letter carved by a punchcutter

2. Punch is stamped into brass matrix

Brass matrix

3. Matrix is inverted and secured onto top of mold

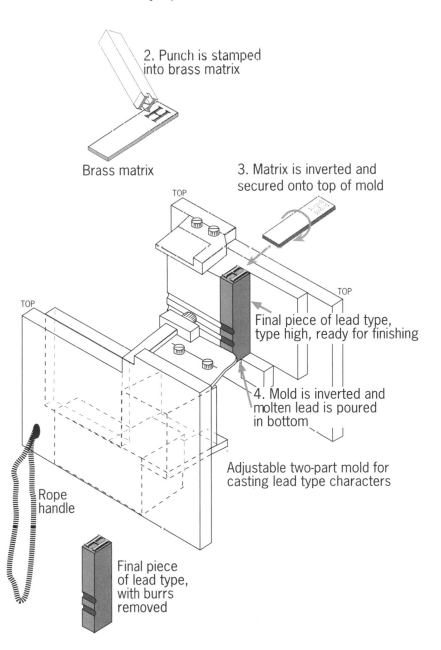

TOP

TOP

TOP

Final piece of lead type, type high, ready for finishing

4. Mold is inverted and molten lead is poured in bottom

Adjustable two-part mold for casting lead type characters

Rope handle

Final piece of lead type, with burrs removed

3.6 This drawing roughly depicts Gutenberg's precision mold, and illustrates the process for casting a single piece of lead type, beginning with the cutting of the punch.

Wood furniture

Chase

Quoins are used
to lock type and
furniture in place

3.7 Photograph of a chase with wood type, handset using wood furniture, and quoins to lock it into place.

tackiness to stick to the nonporous surface of the metal letters, yet transferred to paper under pressure. If the ink was too runny, it would stick to the background areas of the type as well as the raised surfaces of the letters, creating a mess. The final mixture consisted of boiled linseed oil with lead and copper added to create a rich blackness.

Composing a Page

It was necessary to hold the type in position on the press as pressure was applied to the platen to transfer ink to the sheet of paper, parchment, or vellum. The individual letters were set into lines, and then the lines were organized appropriately and locked into a *chase* (the metal or cast iron frame set on a platen press that stabilizes handset lead type in letterpress printing), using *quoins* (expandable furniture) and *furniture* (wood and metal spacers to maintain the position of type) for proofing. Gutenberg relied on a paper mask placed over the perimeter of the bed to prevent any excess ink from spoiling the clean page margin.

Printing the 42-Line Bible

The Gutenberg Bible was a two-volume work, measuring roughly twelve inches wide by sixteen inches tall, with a total of 1,282 pages in both. Most copies were printed on rag paper, with approximately one-quarter of them printed on vellum. Only 48 of the estimated 180 original copies are known to exist today.

Scholars believe that Gutenberg printed his 42-Line Bible between 1450 and 1456 in Mainz, Germany. One page of the Bible contained four thousand to five thousand pieces of type. A stock of fifteen thousand to

The Use of Colophons

The word *colophon* comes from Latin, and means "finishing stroke." A colophon is an inscription, monogram, or cipher containing the place and date of publication and the printer's name. It was originally placed on the last page of a book. Johann Fust and Peter Schöffer used the printer's mark above in the colophon of each Gutenberg Bible.

Colophons were first used when someone who had hand-copied a book completed the task by signing and dating the last page. Sometimes the scribe would add a short phrase about himself, including his location or the reason why he had undertaken the writing of the particular text. This tradition carried over into early printed editions of books, when the printer included a printer's mark in the colophon as a means of identifying and authenticating the work.

Today, colophons are used only in limited-edition books. Modern colophons include information about the press, the paper, the printer, the designer, the illustrator, the paper, the ink, and the length of the run or edition. Most limited-edition books are numbered, just as an edition of an original etching, serigraph, or lithograph would be numbered.

twenty thousand pieces of type had been cast to allow the printing of a page while another was being composed. A proof was pulled, and errors were corrected for all copies of the book, allowing for a consistent product, unlike the hand-copied versions, which included numerous different errors in each edition.

This process of producing a book cost a fair amount of money. Johann Fust, who had helped finance Gutenberg, foreclosed on the loan in November 1455 and locked him out of the print shop once the process was refined. This act prevented Gutenberg from selling the books, which had consumed five years of his life's work and which were only a few months from completion.

Peter Schöffer, Gutenberg's assistant, was brought in as a partner by Fust to manage the press. Together they finished printing approximately 180 Bibles and made a fortune once the Bibles were signed and sold the following August.

Assembly-Line Book Production

Numerous historians consider Gutenberg's workshop to be one of the earliest examples of assembly-line production. Unlike earlier craftsmen, who handled a project from start to finish, each person in Gutenberg's shop worked on a single phase of the process: composing, printing, or binding.

Both the news and the technology spread quickly. In the area of Germany where Gutenberg practiced, other shops quickly established themselves. Many believe that Gutenberg set up a separate press following Fust's foreclosure on his first shop, although records indicate that, destitute, he was taken on as a craftsman for the

3.8 Gutenberg's Bible, printed between 1450 and 1455, is believed to be the earliest example of a full-length book printed in the Western world.

3.9 Gutenberg's printing shop is believed to be one of the earliest examples of assembly-line production. These woodcuts illustrate the composers, press operation, and inking of the type.

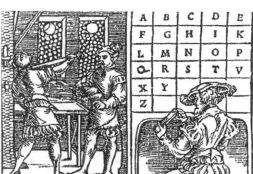

3.10 Nicolas Jenson's Roman typeface was so popular in France that it completely replaced black letter styles preferred by Germanic peoples.

3.11 Example of the Humanistic hand, popular for everyday writing and correspondence during the Renaissance.

archbishop of Mainz in 1465. Gutenberg died in relative poverty three years later.

A number of early printed books were sold at the same price a scribe would have been paid to hand-copy them, even though the books cost less to produce, since most could not distinguish between the two. When people became more discerning, the printed books were considered inferior to the hand-lettered counterparts. Some of the lettering guilds had printed books outlawed in their precincts because they were afraid that their members would be put out of work. On the contrary, many scribes began laying out books for the press composers by producing hand-lettered prototypes, and their workload increased.

Early Typefaces

The earliest typeset faces were modifications of scribes' hand-lettered alphabets. Gradually, books departed from the manuscript model, and typefaces were cut that used Littera Antiqua as a model hand. Some typefaces were designed specifically for printed books—with smaller but more legible letterforms. The resulting books were more compact and required less material, making books more affordable.

Many of the typefaces cut were variations of a historical lettering form, such as uncials or Carolingian. This marked the beginning of typographic design, establishing typography as an art to be studied and pursued separate from the art of lettering.

The Spread of Printing: Jenson in Italy

As the printing trade spread to Italy book buyers came to prefer the typefaces produced there, rather than Gothic Textura. They favored a Roman style, such as Littera Antiqua, and liked the more open texture and rounded shape of Rotunda. By 1458, French engraver *Nicolas Jenson* was dispatched from the mint at Tours, where he made coins, to Mainz by King Charles VII. He was to bring back information on the new art of printing. Due to the unstable monarchy in France, Jenson settled in Italy and never returned to France.

Jenson developed the first pure *Roman typeface*, characterized by contrast between the thick stem and thin hairline strokes; serifs were blunt and heavily bracketed with an oblique stress. The baselines of the individual letters aligned more accurately in Jenson's type than in any other printed font of the era. The capital letters were shorter in height than the ascenders, so they did not stand out significantly. The lowercase *e* has a distinctive slanted cross stroke. This typographic style became known as *Old Style*; however, after leaving Germany, versions of Jenson's type remain today as *Cloister Old Style*. Old Style exhibits a soft, organic feel, as the serifs appear to grow out of the stem. The often gently rounded serifs are cup-shaped, with generous *bracketing* (the straight or curved transitional area between the letterform stroke and the serif).

Printing in England

The first printed book in England was created by *William Caxton*, a wealthy silk merchant turned printer. After studying printing and working for a number of years in Bruges, Flanders, Caxton set up shop in England around 1478. The first book printed in the English language was set in a flourishing, angular Gothic face called *Bartarde*. Popular in France at the time, it is considered a fusion of Rotunda and Gothic Textura.

Gothic faces were more widely accepted in England than they were in France and Italy, and their popularity lasted much longer there.

Eventually royalty limited the printing industry to the cities of London, Oxford, and Cambridge by requiring all manuscripts to be submitted to a censor and a license obtained.

The Religious Reformation

In 1517 Martin Luther nailed his ninety-five theses to the door of the church in Wittenberg, Germany, calling for reform in Catholicism. Upon his refusal to recant his ideas, Luther was excommunicated and his works became the basis of the Protestant *Reformation*. Other reformists broke from the church in France and Switzerland as well. When Henry VIII wanted to divorce his wife,

he was unable to do so through the Catholic Church and broke away, forming the Church of England in 1534. The Reformation sparked great upheaval in Europe, and a number of wars resulted. No longer did a unifying spiritual force link the different countries.

At the Council of Trent in 1545, the Counter-Reformation movement called for changes within the Church. Brought about as a reaction to growing Protestantism, these changes included centralizing the Catholic church, issuing a catechism to the faithful, reinforcing the authority of the Pope and the Bishops, and generally heightening the persecution of heretics and publishers who printed materials for the Protestant Reformation. In the face of continued religious persecution, many religious groups moved to more hospitable areas or set off, like the Puritans, to settle a new land where they would be free to worship as they wished.

The Pinnacle of the Renaissance

The 1500s mark the height of the Renaissance in Europe. In addition to the renewed interest in ancient Greek and Roman culture, aesthetics, and philosophy, the spread of books increased literacy, even among the lower classes. Writing was no longer limited to a few scribes, but was learned and practiced more widely.

One of the most popular and widely available texts of the time was the *Book of Hours*. This medieval book evolved out of the monastic cycle of prayer which divided the day into eight segments of "hours": Matins, Lauds, Prime, Terce, Sext, Nones, Compline, and Vespers. By the early fifteenthth century the book had developed into a variety of portable sizes to be used in private devotions, as

3.12 William Caxton's font for English printed texts was influenced by the Germanic black letter style.

3.13 William Caxton's printing mark used to identify his work.

3.14 Sample of Bartarde, which incorporates some of the flourishes and curves of Rotunda along with the strong vertical emphasis and condensed form of Textura.

opposed to communal worship. As popularity increased, an efficient system of book production and trade developed to supply the demand. A thriving economy developed around the production of these Books of Hours. Books of Hours remaining today include some of the finest examples of medieval art.

Printers of the 1500s began to face the problem of state and religious censorship of their work. Ideas expressed in classic Greek and Roman texts were often contrary to those held by local clergy or royalty. Eventually the humanist philosophy (which placed man, rather than God, at the center of the universe) gained acceptance throughout Europe despite attempts to prevent its spread.

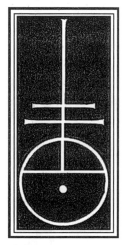

3.15 Nicolas Jenson's printer's mark.

Intertwining Printeries: The Estienne Family and Simon de Colines

Henri Estienne was the founder of a family of Parisian and Genevan printers of the sixteenth and seventeenth centuries. By 1502, at the time of his death, he was a well-established printer in Paris with more than a hundred beautiful texts to his credit. His foreman, *Simon de Colines*, succeeded him in the business and eventually married his widow.

Like Estienne, Colines became a *libraire juré*, a select printer to the university in Paris. He printed texts used in the study of the liberal arts, theology, and medicine, the Bible, Books of Hours, and editions of classical and contemporary literature. He produced more than 750 editions over twenty-six years.

Years later Henri's son *Robert Estienne* took over his father's print shop, while Simon de Colines moved a few doors away and began his own business. Robert, who was considered a great scholar, shifted the

3.16 Robert Estienne's printer's mark is believed to have been drawn by Geofroy Tory.

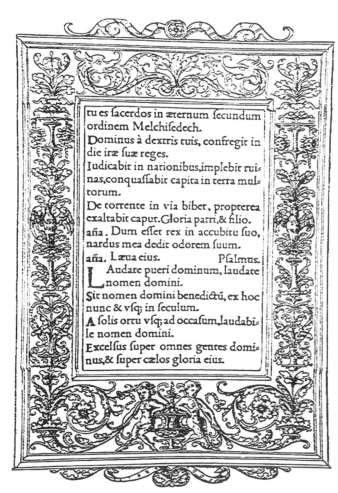

3.17 A decorated page from the Book of Hours, printed by Simon de Colines circa 1540.

emphasis of the business to the printing of editions of works by classical authors, dictionaries and lexicons, and critical editions of the Bible. The olive tree printer's mark used by Robert's press was designed by *Geofroy Tory* who is believed to have been a proofreader for Robert's father, Henri. Some of the popular Estienne fonts of the time were designed by *Claude Garamond*, who would later lend his name to a well-known font. Although scholars assumed that Simon de Colines and Robert Estienne took up separate careers, there is evidence to the contrary. A substantially large number of the authors and texts found in the more than five hundred editions produced by Robert Estienne are identical with Colines'.

As a humanist who upheld the cause of the Reformation, Robert sustained continual attacks by noted faculty from the University of Paris following the printing of a series

3.18 Simon de Colines' printer's mark.

3.19 Decorative woodcut initial *I* by Charles Estienne around 1545 (Paris, France).

3.20 Decorative metal-cut initial *I* by Robert Estienne around 1536 (Paris, France).

of the New Testament of the Bible. He lost favor with the king and moved to Geneva in 1550. He continued to produce significant historical works there until his death.

Charles Estienne, one of Robert's brothers, succeeded him in the management of the family print shop in Paris in 1551. Charles was educated in medicine, so the emphasis of the shop's printed works became medicine and agriculture. His most famous editions include one of the earliest encyclopedias appearing in France.

Eventually the second Henri Estienne, Robert's son, inherited the press set up by Robert, on the express condition that it would not move from Geneva. Considered the greatest scholar of the family, the younger Henri issued editions of Greek and Latin works, and wrote valuable treatises on the French language. The editions he printed are not considered to equal the works of his father in beauty and typographic art.

Despite a number of social and personal difficulties, the Estienne family continued to hold a prominent place in the printing industry throughout the seventeeth century.

Aldus Mantius as Publisher

During the early 1490s, about the time of Christopher Columbus' voyages to America, the Italian scholar and tutor *Aldus Mantius* envisioned low-priced printed books as a means of making ancient manuscripts available to students, as well as a means for making money. At the age of forty, Aldus signed on with a financial backer and a printer, and began printing reference books. This business venture changed the concept of books; no longer was the unwieldy, large book limited to the lectern, from which scholars

3.21 Example of the font Francesco Griffo cut for Aldus Mantius' books.

read aloud to students. He printed smaller, easily transportable books for individuals to read to themselves.

The design of Mantius' books took on a more modern aesthetic. In 1495 a calligraphic Roman typeface developed by *Francesco Griffo* was commissioned. This typeface incorporated varying weights of hairline and stem strokes with delicate serifs. Griffo's typeface appeared more uniform in the shape, size, weight, and scale of the characters than Jenson's and was legible at a much smaller size.

First and foremost, Mantius was a businessman, and he continually experimented with ideas to produce books at a lower cost, allowing for a higher profit margin. His modern book layout was established using a more open and airy design, minus the heavy borders previously incorporated. This was a cost-saving measure—without borders, the press setup time was shortened, resulting in faster production and less cost. The smaller type allowed Mantius the opportunity to compress more information into a smaller space, using fewer materials and further reducing the cost of producing the individual product.

Influenced by the *Papal Chancery* cursive handwriting, Aldus Mantius worked with Francesco Griffo to develop the first *italic* type in 1506. Originally italic type was intended as a lowercase book typeface only, and relied on the Roman capital letters (nearly a quarter century passed before italic capital letters appeared). Mantius discovered that the italic characters were much narrower than the Roman characters and proceeded to set entire books in the italic version to conserve space, again helping him keep the cost of book production as low as possible.

One of Mantius' most famous works, *Hypnerotomachia Poliphili*, was a distinctive typographic masterpiece using clear-cut Roman letters, richly ornamented with decorative woodcuts. *Albrecht Dürer* was commissioned to illustrate the text, bridging the gap between the Gothic and Humanist typographic traditions.

Mantius was a fastidious editor and proofreader, and his books set the standard for accuracy in spelling and syntax. His successful and accurate translations were made available to scholars and students alike. He created a high-quality book with consistent content at affordable production rates, and his work became well known throughout the region. Mantius' forward thinking and effort helped Venice become a printing center that exported many small, affordable books.

The Letter as Art

In the 1500s, during the Renaissance in Europe, book design and type design evolved as a formal area of study. Painters and sculptors were dependent on the patronage of the wealthy, and they broadened their practice to include different skills so as to produce what their patrons desired. As a result, many artists became fine letterers and calligraphers. Lettering was considered an art, as important as drawing and writing poetry.

This expansion of individual skills followed the philosophy of the Renaissance period and allowed an artist with many talents to explore a variety of employment opportunities. Artists often worked in different media, creating woodcuts for printing in addition to paintings, drawings, and sculptures. Type was seen as an additional form of artistic expression, and the artists did

3.22 Giovanni Battista Palatino's uppercase *B* with some of the construction lines indicating the thought behind the letterform design. Palatino was a letterer who published writing guides to teach correct lettering technique.

3.23 One of Mantius' pocket-sized books using Griffo's italic for the lowercase. The uppercase letters are in roman at the beginning of each line. Because the italic font was thinner, it was used for the entire text to conserve space.

not view themselves as separate from the graphic arts and graphic design practices, as is common today.

Renowned artists of the Renaissance felt that the proportions of the perfect letter were as predictable as those of the human body. In his *De Divina Proportione* of 1509, *Leonardo da Vinci* analyzed the construction of letterforms using geometric elements. He also compared the proportions of letters to the human body.

In 1525 Albrecht Dürer wrote an essay entitled "On the Just Shaping of Letters" as part of a treatise on applied geometry. Dürer constructed letters by inscribing them in

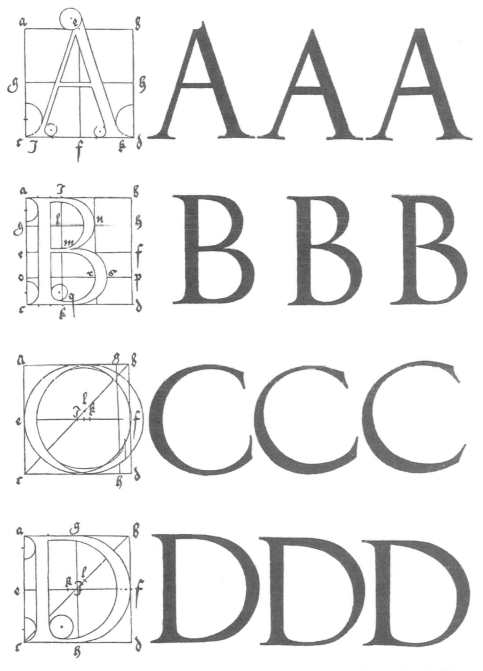

3.24 Albrecht Dürer's construction of capital letters. Artists such as Dürer saw letters and lettering as a legitimate avenue for their expertise in scale and proportion.

Fact Find! Albrecht Dürer was a famous Northern Renaissance painter and engraver. What are some of his significant contributions during the Renaissance? What characteristics define his work? Can you find out any information on his education and training? List a few sentences describing your find below, and cite your Internet source(s) correctly.

_____

_____

_____

_____

_____

_____

_____

_____

_____

_____

_____

_____

URL: http://

URL: http://

Date visited:

3.25 This *Book of Hours*, printed by Geofroy Tory, first appeared around 1525. The delicate woodcut illustration was made using fine-grained boxwood. The composition embodies a sense of proportion and classic elegance; the dark bird near the top in a center position creates a dominant focal point.

a square of a specific size, then building the character from the elements of the square and the arcs of circles. Complete instructions and alternative designs for each letter are provided in his text. Although commonly known for his impressive woodcut illustrations, he made a significant contribution to the field of typography with this essay.

Geofroy Tory Establishes Bookmaking as an Art

Parisian printer, typographer, and author Geofroy Tory studied in Italy and was a well-known professor before going to work as an editor for the elder Henri Estienne. After Henri Estienne's death, Tory returned to Italy to study drawing and engraving and worked as a bookbinder. He was famous for his intricate and beautiful initials, borders, illustrations, and design of printer's marks.

Tory's *Book of Hours* appeared around 1525 and was significant in that the type he used was not modeled after handwriting styles. This work helped to establish the practice of designing books as an art form in France, and his distinctive high-quality work earned him an appointment to King Francis I.

One of Tory's most significant writings was *Champfleury*, dated around 1529, in which he outlines and elaborates on the theory behind the design of his Roman capitals. With the exception of Albrecht Dürer's works, most earlier treatises on letterform design over the previous decades had been in Italian.

Tory believed that one of the tendencies of this era was the desire of the elite to conceal knowledge from the rest of the population. In recognizing and understanding knowledge as power, his concerns revealed a new social understanding.

Geofroy Tory is known for introducing accents, the apostrophe, and the cedilla into printed French texts.

France Offers a New Look in Type: Garamond

Claude Garamond's most noted accomplishment was the development of a Roman typeface that moved away from the calligraphic forms of the day. Just as earlier forms of writing were affected by and evolved from the tools and the substrate used, Garamond was sensitive to the fact that the printed word relied upon a metal substrate. His letters moved away from mimicking the traditional hand-lettered forms and toward refined, accurate, consistent forms made possible by this medium. His Roman typefaces were introduced around Paris in 1530.

Garamond was not a printer, but having grown up in the family printing business, he was well versed in the processes. He established a business exclusively to cast letters and sold them to printing shops. Garamond was the first full-time punch cutter and type founder, separating the foundry from the printing workshop. He studied under *Antoine Augereau*, a contemporary of Simon de Colines.

3.26 Example of a cover using Civilité from 1557 illustrates the French style of Renaissance Roman type.

Garamond cut a face, based on the Aldus Roman face, that bears his name and is considered one of the finest in typographic history. The Old Style face was readily and widely accepted, and was used almost exclusively in Europe for two hundred years. With simplicity and careful blending of letters into legible, classic forms, the type allowed tighter word spacing which resulted in a more even visual tone when printed. Garamond understood that there are more lowercase letters than uppercase letters on a page, and therefore paid special attention to their design. The lowercase letters in Garamond are as beautiful as the uppercase letters, and he started the trend to using lowercase letters in book titles where previously only capital letters had been used.

The wide acceptance of Garamond's work is credited with France's move away from the black letter style, and his style monopolized the printing industries in France

and Italy well into the 1700s. Variations on Garamond's faces, based on the same basic forms, are still popular today.

Prevalence of Italic and Script Faces

Robert Granjon, an apprentice of Claude Garamond's, cut ten outstanding italic faces. One of these was a companion to the Roman Garamond face, incorporating graceful descenders and small hooks at the end of the final strokes instead of serifs. The lowercase *k* had a loop, replacing the upper diagonal stroke. The new italic faces hinted at their handwriting origins but clearly were designed for the printed page, with careful attention given to the advantages and constraints of the medium.

In 1577 Granjon cut a typeface intended to simulate everyday handwriting rather than formal hand-lettering. His most famous, based on the popular handwriting style of the day, *Civilité*, is considered the first cursive face. This face linked lowercase letters and led to the development of a class of specialized script faces.

Handwriting as a Status Symbol

During the Renaissance, fancy script faces and elaborate handwritten documents that were cut into a copperplate were an instant success. Complicated handwriting with flourishes and curlicues, thick and thin contrast in the strokes, and the linking of letters was considered a sign of status. Many people were employed as handwriting masters during this period, but oddly enough, Granjon's Civilité was one of the few script faces cast in lead. As the writing trends changed fairly quickly during this time, with the explosion of experimentation and rapid

3.27 Granjon italic features delicate strokes, and the majuscule letterforms are slanted just as the lowercase letterforms are, unlike earlier italic styles which slanted only the lowercase and maintained Roman uppercase forms.

3.28 An early example of a page printed in the English language about the "English Usurer." The letter *U* pronunciation and letterform did not become separate from the *V* until much later. Early works incorporate the letter *V* where modern works would use the letter *U* today.

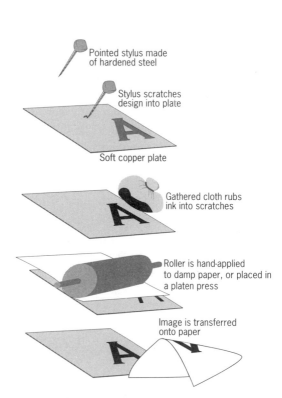

Pointed stylus made
of hardened steel

Stylus scratches
design into plate

Soft copper plate

Gathered cloth rubs
ink into scratches

Roller is hand-applied
to damp paper, or placed in
a platen press

Image is transferred
onto paper

3.29 The process of creating a copperplate for printing involves
the use of a hardened steel engraving stylus and a soft, polished
copperplate. The stylus is used to scratch an image into the plate
surface. Ink was applied to the plate, with any excess carefully
removed. Ink remained in the surface scratches so that when a
damp sheet of rag paper was laid on the surface and put under
pressure, the image transferred to the paper. Because copper
is soft enough to draw on with the stylus, it would not maintain
clarity and detail for a large number of impressions.

development of faces, Civilité was considered somewhat illegible and so it faded in popularity.

By the 1600s, *copperplate engraving* was used to re-create the popular scrollwork of the writing masters because it could reproduce the fine lines of the trendy scripts. Copperplate illustrations were more refined than those created on woodblocks, since the medium could hold fine hairlines for details and for cross-hatching shaded areas, creating the illusion of depth.

Whereas lead type was relatively durable and could be re-used, the soft copperplates were inscribed with a single message, and once two hundred or so impressions were printed, the plate had to be repaired or ground down to be inscribed once again. Both media had found their niche in the printing industry.

Printing Innovations

Printed materials during the Renaissance reflected the artistic sensibility of the era. The dark borders filling every inch of available space popular in hand-lettered texts of the Middle Ages were gone. Presswork was refined, and a high degree of accuracy, consistency, and cleanliness was common among the finest printers of the time.

The majority of books published during this period were of a religious nature, though toward the end of the seventeenth century many were secular. Contributions included the design of the Old Style families of type, small capitals, italic faces, printer's marks, type registration on the printed page, two-color printing, colophons, and movable type. Noted contributors to the innovations of the period include Gutenberg, Coster, Jenson, Mantius, Garamond, and Granjon.

Estimates suggest that the number of books expanded 180-fold, with approximately fifty thousand housed in Europe's monasteries and libraries in the 1450s but nine million in 1500. Over thirty-five thousand different editions were printed in the first fifty years following the invention of printing. This boom grew to include not just books, but also short-lived broadsides, posters, and leaflets.

By 1500, printing establishments existed in 140 cities on the continent. A number of historians argue that without printing technology, the political revolutions (American and French) that ensued over the next centuries would not have been possible. Printing enabled the dissemination of ideas over great distances without requiring large assemblies of people. Ideas about human rights became widespread, and language was standardized throughout Europe. Printing led to the democratization of information as less expensive books were produced, allowing the lower classes equal access to information previously reserved for the wealthy.

Chapter Three Review

Circle one answer for each definition to indicate the correct key concept term or key player for each. When necessary, determine whether the phrase provided is true or false.

1. The first printed book in England was created by William Caxton, a wealthy silk merchant turned printer.
   a. True
   b. False

2. The practice of filing away a portion of the base of one character, allowing part of the letter to rest on the base of the adjacent character.
   a. Registration
   b. Copper plate engraving
   c. Kerning
   d. Bracketing

3. Often described as the "rebirth of learning," the _____ lasted approximately two centuries, from the mid-1400s to the late 1600s
   a. Ottonian Empire
   b. Reformation
   c. Renaissance
   d. Papal Chancery

4. To approximate the handwriting of the scribes, Claude Garamond cast almost 270 pairs of kerned or ligature pairs of characters as one punch.
   a. True
   b. False

5. A Parisian printer, typographer, and author who studied in Italy and was a well-known professor before going to work as an editor for the elder Henri Estienne.
   a. Robert Estienne
   b. Albrecht Dürer
   c. Nicolas Jenson
   d. Geofroy Tory

6. Goldsmith who agreed to underwrite the cost of Gutenberg's printing experiments, provided Gutenberg repay him.
   a. Johann Fust
   b. Albrecht Dürer
   c. Nicolas Jenson
   d. Peter Schöffer

7. The precision mold was composed of two N-shaped pieces of metal that could be opened and closed to accommodate letters of constant width while varying the height and depth measurements.
   a. True
   b. False

8. Whereas lead type was relatively durable and could be reused, the soft copper plates were inscribed with a single message, and once two hundred or so impressions were printed, the plate had to be repaired or ground down to be inscribed once again.
   a. True
   b. False

9. One of his most significant writings was *Champfleury*, dated around 1529, in which he outlines and elaborates on the theory behind the design of his Roman capitals.
   a. Aldus Mantius
   b. Geofroy Tory
   c. Francesco Griffo
   d. Albrecht Dürer

10. An apprentice of Claude Garamond's, who cut a famous typeface, based on the popular handwriting style of the day, named Civilité, which is considered the first cursive face.
   a. Aldus Mantius
   b. Nicolas Jenson
   c. Robert Granjon
   d. Albrecht Dürer

11. The first book printed in the English language was set in a flourishing, angular Gothic face called _____.
    a. Civilité
    b. Gothic Textura
    c. Bartarde
    d. Rotunda

12. One of Aldus Mantius' most famous works *Hypnerotomachia Poliphili* was a distinctive typographic masterpiece using clear-cut Roman letters, richly ornamented with decorative woodcuts and illustrated by:
    a. Henri Estienne
    b. Albrecht Dürer
    c. Leonardo da Vinci
    d. Peter Schöffer

13. He believed that one of the tendencies of this era was the desire of the elite to conceal knowledge from the rest of the population. In recognizing and understanding knowledge as power, his concerns revealed a new social understanding.
    a. Henri Estienne
    b. Albrecht Dürer
    c. Geofroy Tory
    d. Peter Schöffer

14. In the 1300s, during the Renaissance in Europe, book design and type design evolved as a formal area of study. Painters and sculptors were dependent on the patronage of the wealthy, and they broadened their practice to include different skills so as to produce what their patrons desired.
    a. True
    b. False

15. He is known for introducing accents, the apostrophe, and the cedilla into printed French texts.
    a. Johann Fust
    b. Robert Granjon
    c. Nicolas Jenson
    d. Geofroy Tory

16. One of the most popular and widely available texts of the Renaissance in Europe was the Book of Hours.
    a. True
    b. False

17. The Old Style face was readily and widely accepted, and was used almost exclusively in Europe for three hundred years.
    a. True
    b. False

18. His foreman, Simon de Colines succeeded him in the business and eventually married his widow.
    a. Johann Fust
    b. Henri Estienne
    c. William Caxton
    d. Geofroy Tory

19. Robert Granjon understood that there are more lowercase letters than uppercase letters on a page, and therefore paid special attention to their design.
    a. True
    b. False

20. Jenson's first pure Roman typeface characterized by contrast between the thick stem and thin hairline strokes; serifs were blunt and heavily bracketed with an oblique stress.
    a. Civilité
    b. Cloister Old Style
    c. Bartarde
    d. Papal C hancery

21. Printing enabled the dissemination of ideas over great distances without requiring large assemblies of people.
    a. True
    b. False

22. He was taken on as a craftsman for the archbishop of Mainz in 1465 and died in relative poverty three years later.
    a. Henri Estienne
    b. Johann Gutenberg
    c. Charles Estienne
    d. William Caxton

23. In his *De Divina Proportione* of 1509, Leonardo da Vinci analyzed the construction of letterforms using geometric elements.
    a. True
    b. False

Typography During Colonization and Industrialization

Beginning in the seventeenth century, mechanization made type production increasingly faster. In that same era, printers are often credited with producing the literature that spread concepts of freedom and liberty, encouraging the American and French revolutions and the other political movements they inspired. During this period, typography transitioned from clean, practical, readable text faces to the highly ornate faces seen in early advertisements dating from the Victorian era.

4.1 This capital letter *A* captures the essence of the excessive decoration indicative of the Rococo era.

Colonial Era Typography

Colonization of America began in the sixteenth century by individuals looking for economic opportunity and freedom from religious oppression. The first permanent colony was the 1607 settlement at Jamestown, Virginia. The Pilgrims landed in Plymouth, Massachusetts, and the Dutch settled in New Amsterdam (New York) in 1623, escaping the absolutist monarchs of Europe.

In Europe, playwright William Shakespeare died in 1616, seven years before his entire collection of works was published in 1623. Bach and Vivaldi lived at the end of this century, and operas began to appear onstage. Baroque music and art were in style. Printed works for recreational purposes became more common, and the printing industry flourished in the 1600s and 1700s despite the lack of technological innovation in the equipment.

Some historians see the Baroque style as connected to the Counter-Reformation of the Roman Catholic Church, which emphasized spirituality and the emotional aspects of the Catholic religion. *Baroque*

art is seen as based on the expression of emotion in vibrant colors. Some Baroque artists turned to classical themes while others placed Christian heroes in ancient settings.

Novels, journals, and political pamphlets became widely available to the

4.2 Timeline emphasizing the context of colonial and industrialized innovations in typography.

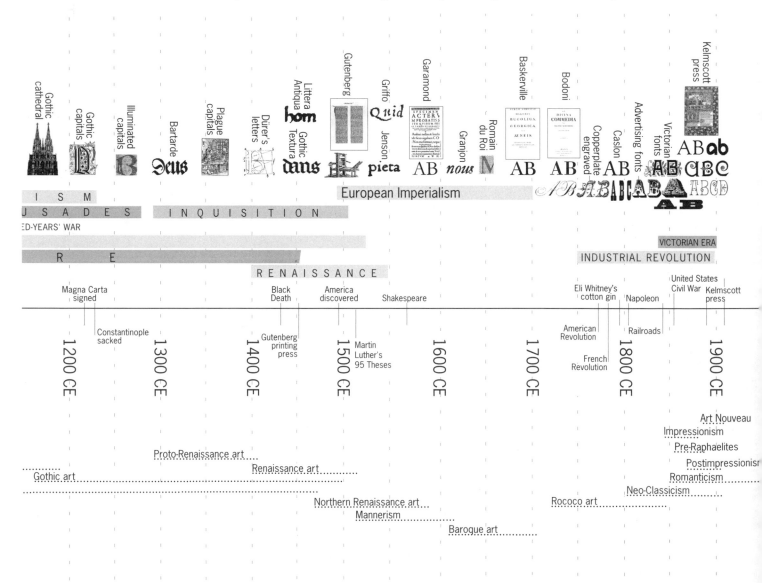

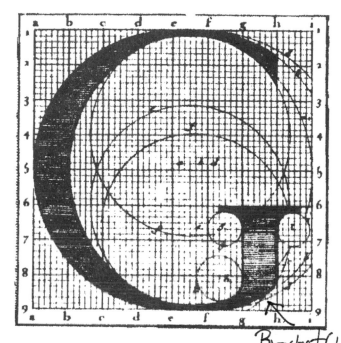

4.3 Left: An example of the letter G of the Romain du Roi font designed by the French Academy of Sciences to be a mathematically and geometrically perfect font.

rts. Les Hérétiques domptez, la Maiſo
ite Royale reſtablie, rendoient le Roy
. Mais il manquoit au Roy un fils qu
ıis ans de mariage ſans enfans luy avoı
n avoir iamais. Enfin. Dieu touché des

Bracket (transition)

emerging European middle class, and there was an unquenchable thirst for the printed word. Novels had tremendous impact on morals and cultural norms. Posters and broadsides, as well as newspapers (the first was printed in Strasbourg in 1609), were found in most cities throughout Europe. In Amsterdam, books were printed in condensed type to fit into vest pockets. The first Bible was printed in English by *Robert Baker* in 1612.

Reportedly the first printing press was established in the American colonies in 1640. By 1775 there were fifty printers in the thirteen colonies, despite the tax on paper and advertising. These presses spread the word of the revolution throughout the New World faster and more consistently than word of mouth could, encouraging a unified front for a strong rebellion.

A Mathematically Perfect Font

In 1692 King Louis XIV of France ordered the French Academy of Sciences to develop its own geometric formula for the correct construction of letterforms. A committee of scholars and mathematicians developed a detailed theory of design based on a grid of 2,304 squares. In 1702 *Philippe Grandjean*, royal punch cutter, cut a face called the *Romain du Roi* (Roman of the king) in keeping with the geometric proportions established by the academy. This is the first recorded face based on precise mathematical analysis and consistency, as compared to the artistic approaches used by calligraphers previously. The face exaggerated the difference in weight between the stem and hairline stroke, reduced bracketing, and created thin, horizontal, squared-off serifs. This face was reserved for exclusive use by the royal printing office of France and any other use was considered a crime.

Rococo-Era Typography

In the 1720s, a flowery, ornamental style of design and fashion known as *Rococo*, appeared in Paris. This style of design reflected a monarch who lived lavishly— a

4.4 This example of the Romain du Roi font shows that many of the details of the original design were lost as the punch cutters worked by hand from much smaller reproductions of the detailed drawings.

Key Players

Robert Baker

John Baskerville

Stephenson Blake

Giambattista Bodoni

William Austin Burt

William Caslon

William Caslon IV

Firmin Didot

Henry Fourdrinier

Philippe Grandjean

John Handy

Friedrich Koenig

Aloys Senefelder

Darius Wells

4.5 The decorative initial *E* illustrates the French preference for ornate, three-dimensional leaves accented by contrasting curvilinear texture.

4.6 Letterpress compositor assembling letters for a page from the shallow drawers, called *California job cases*.

Setting Letterpress Type

Letterpress type is set by hand, one character at a time. Typographic characters are sorted into different small compartments of a large, shallow drawer, called a *California job case*. The capital or majuscule letters were sorted into the top drawer, or upper case, while the small or minuscule letterforms were sorted into the lower case, resulting in the names we use today.

lifestyle that was soon overthrown in favor of a government fueled by the people in the French Revolution. The royals continued to enjoy a life of extravagance and frivolity, unaware of the anger that was brewing in the hearts of those condemned to lives of misery and poverty.

The flamboyance of the style of the Rococo-era art and typography was expressed as fine lines and curvilinear flourishes. Copperplate engraving was best suited to reproducing this style, rather than the rigidity of letterpress printing. The handwriting craze of earlier years experienced a renaissance, with calligraphic masters creating elaborate cards exhibiting their talents to lure students. These elaborate flourishes and scrollworks were sought after as a sign of refinement by the upper classes, which remained completely out of touch with the harsh reality of the living conditions of the poorer classes throughout Europe.

Letterpress Printing

The earliest printing presses were constructed by modifying the design of a fruit press. The original platen press included a large horizontal press bed with a frame around it. All type or images intended for printing were precisely .918 inch tall, called *type high*. Accuracy in the bed dimensions as well as the composite type was required; any blocks or lead taller than type high could tear the paper or printing substrate, while any imagery less than .918 inch would not be inked correctly, resulting in a poor if nonexistent impression. Precise depth was essential for even distribution of ink and a uniform impression.

The frame around the press bed was shorter than .918 inch so that it would not be inked or print. The wood or lead type was arranged on the press bed, and then furniture (blocks of wood and metal) was placed between the sides of the type and the sides of the chase. The combination of the furniture shapes locked the type in place to prevent it from shifting under the high pressure of the platen during printing. Preliminary test prints, called *proofs*, allowed the pressman to check for a clean, crisp impression.

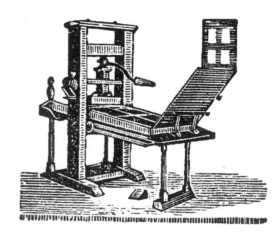

4.7 The earliest pressure presses were used by placing a sheet of paper between the type and a platen.

Letterpress printing is a variation of the original platen press. In the beginning, letterpress printing was limited to a horizontal and vertical compositional structure or layout. It was not until Dada artists experimented with more free-form compositions, composed directly on the printing press bed, did printed works move away from the highly structured compositions. It is a complicated process that involves practice and patience; packing behind the

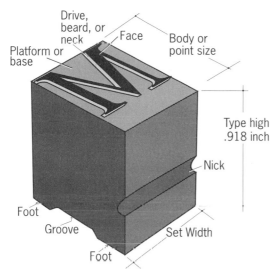

4.8 A piece of lead type. The dimension of the height of the piece of lead measures .918 inch, while the letterform is a raised surface above that dimension. That way, only the raised letter is inked and the recessed background remains clean.

type is sometimes required to accurately meet type high dimensions in all areas to be printed. Ink has to be mixed with oil to an exact viscosity for a clear, clean impression. Temperature and humidity affect both the ink and the paper, so trial-and-error methods of proofing are required until the perfect impression results.

Typography During Colonial Expansion

Colonial expansion became a necessity for obtaining the raw materials needed for expansion in European countries, as well as a source of tax revenue for the kingdom. The colonies provided a ready market for the goods manufactured in Europe. While the French aristocracy contributed money to support the American colonies in their move toward independence, their own lower classes became more and more dissatisfied. Ironically, a number of historians are convinced that the success of the American Revolution in the colonies inspired the French peasants to incite a fight for freedom a decade later in 1789.

The end of the eighteenth century saw the steam engine become a mainstay in a number of manufacturing industries. The first one was placed in a cotton-spinning factory in Nottinghamshire in 1785. Eli Whitney is credited with the invention of the cotton gin in 1793, the same year Louis XVI and Marie Antoinette were executed by guillotine in France. Following the Reign of Terror (in which any noble person could

4.9 William Caslon's Old Face, below, was known for the clarity of the lowercase letters and the accurate alignment of the baselines. Many believed these characteristics allowed for easier reading.

ENGLISH ROMAN.

Quousque tandem abutêre, Catilina, patientia noſtra? quamdiu nos etiam furor iſte tuus eludet? quem ad finem ſeſe effrenata jactabit audacia ? nihilne te nocturnum præſidium palatii, nihil urbis vigiliæ, nihil timor populi, nihil conſenſus bonorum omnium, nihil hic munitiſſimus
ABCDEFGHIJKLMNOPQRSTVUW

be sentenced to guillotine death by verdict of the lower classes as a crowd, a young general named Napoleon Bonaparte seized dictatorial power in France in 1799.

Type Fashion in England

Around 1730, goldsmith *William Caslon* designed a type that included Roman and italic, called Old Face. This typestyle was an instant success in England. It maintained balanced proportions, and the thick strokes of the letters had a slightly heavier weight than was seen in other contemporary type, increasing its legibility. In contrast to the light-type Romain du Roi, there were no flourishes to distract the reader. Although the font relies on an organic style, it has

4.10 The 1664 Bill of Mortality is an example of English printing incorporating italic and Roman fonts within an illustrative frame.

ll preferve my former authority

wifh me joy in the other of my l

to the firft, if to mean well to

ld to approve that meaning to e

may be confidered as maintaini

nt you have heard is certainly tri

ing thofe fentiments effectual to t

: in daring freely to fupport

4.11 John Baskerville's font is crisp and light in texture as compared to its predecessors.

A 26-Letter Alphabet

Throughout the 1700s there were mix-ups over the use of the letters *I, J, U, V,* and *W.* As a result, *J, U,* and *W* were assigned separate sounds and full recognition, resulting in the 26-letter alphabet we know today.

more refinement in the weights of the strokes than Garamond. Caslon's Old Face quickly became the standard for books printed in English. The first editions of both the Declaration of Independence and the Constitution were printed in Caslon, so to this day the Caslon Old Face italic and swash capitals still convey an antique American feeling.

Writing Master Turns Type Designer

John Baskerville, an accomplished stone-cutter, began his professional career as a writing master in the 1700s. After making money as a manufacturer of japanned ware (objects layered with lacquer and then decoratively carved), he returned to letters and printing at the age of forty one. Like Gutenberg, Baskerville perfected many elements of the printing process. He was interested in all phases of the production process: he designed type, carefully casted it, refined the technique of "packing" the press, introduced new papers with a smoother surface, improved press designs, and refined ink formulas to achieve a rich purple-black.

Considered a *Transitional Style* type (orginally called "improved type" during the late 1700s), the *Baskerville* font marks the beginning of the influence of printing mechanization on the field of type design. The new typeface (in Roman and italic) was introduced in England by Baskerville with his publication of an edition of Virgil's works in 1757. The precise, extremely thin strokes and straight serifs in a relatively heavy face were a departure from the cruder, craftsmanlike faces seen in examples of Old Style. The new Baskerville

PUBLII VIRGILII

MARONIS

BUCOLICA,

GEORGICA,

ET

AENEIS.

BIRMINGHAMIAE:
Typis JOHANNIS BASKERVILLE.
MDCCLVII.

4.12 A layout by John Baskerville, above, illustrates an open and spacious style devoid of extraneous decorative elements.

font was straight, with a vertical stress and flatter serifs. This face reflected a number of qualities seen in Romain du Roi, the mathematically engineered face.

Baskerville has been recognized as the first pure type designer, distinguishing him from those who were also punch cutters (*John Handy* was Baskerville's punch cutter). He is considered one of the earliest type designers to create and refine his letter-forms on paper rather than directly cutting the punches in metal. Baskerville considered the goals, possibilities, and constraints of the whole printing process during the drawing of a typeface.

Knowing at the outset of the design that he did not want a heavy impression of the letters pushed into the paper, he made his own extremely black printing ink by boiling linseed oil, aging it with black resin, and burning the lampblack himself. A committed perfectionist, he searched for a smoother printing surface and eventually developed the first woven paper. Rejecting the traditional laid texture, he hot-pressed the surface of damp paper to ensure added smoothness. During the printing process, he packed the blanket behind the sheet of paper with harder material than was usually used, achieving a crisper result.

Baskerville's work is identified by the generous use of white space incorporated into the layout, and the lack of extraneous ornamentation; it relied exclusively on the typography to convey meaning and feeling

4.13 A layout by Giambattista Bodoni illustrates a typical layout known for its clean, crisp composition and contrast in size.

ousque tandem abutêre,
ilina, patientiâ nostrâ?
dacia? nihilne te noctur

4.14 Bodoni's Modern Font.

in the composition. Initially his efforts were met with criticism, as many complained that the paper was too smooth and the ink too black. Some thought that the reflection caused by clean, smooth paper with large areas of blank space would hurt their eyes. Unfortunately, John Baskerville died before knowing that his printing innovations and commitment to excellence were widely accepted by the general public.

Typography in Italy

In 1788 in Parma, Italy, *Giambattista Bodoni* introduced the first *Modern Style* typeface, with extreme weight variations between the thick and thin strokes. The round letters were narrow with thin serifs that were not attached to the stem (no bracketing). The geometric precision of this face imparts a classical feel with its vertical stress and small x-height in proportion to the capital letter height, as well as in the details seen in the sharp right angles of the serifs and the ascenders that are the same height as the capital letters. There is a mechanical consistency to the design, as Bodoni used repetition of shape to create similar letters throughout the alphabet.

It is possible that Bodoni was familiar with, and found inspiration in, the work of French designer *Firmin Didot*, who in turn was likely influenced by the Romain du Roi. The Modern Style faces of *Bodoni* and *Didot*

Fact Find! After multiple reproductions and deterioration over time, the examples of early classic faces are difficult to discern. Search the Internet for modern versions of Baskerville, Bodoni, and Didot, then print them out for class discussion. In the space below, identify the type designer and foundry who developed the contemporary variations you found. Analyze a few of the letterforms and list the similarities and differences to begin to better understand the subtleties of typographic design.

_____
_____
_____
_____
_____
_____
_____
_____
_____
_____
_____

URL: http://

URL: http://

URL: http://

Date visited:

AVIS

AUX SOUSCRIPTEURS

DE

LA GERUSALEMME

LIBERATA

IMPRIMÉE PAR DIDOT L'AÎNÉ

SOUS LA PROTECTION ET PAR LES ORDRES

DE MONSIEUR.

LES ARTISTES choisis par MONSIEUR pour exécuter son édition de LA GERUSALEMME LIBERATA demandent avec confiance aux souscripteurs de cet ouvrage un délai de quelques mois pour en mettre au jour la première livraison. Il est rarement arrivé qu'un ouvrage où sont entrés les ornements de la gravure ait pu être donné au temps préfix pour lequel il avoit été promis : cet art entraîne beaucoup de difficultés qui causent des retards forcés ; et certainement on peut regarder comme un empêchement insurmontable les jours courts et obscurs d'un hiver long et rigoureux. D'ailleurs la quantité d'ouvrages de gravure proposés actuellement par

4.15 Firmin Didot's layout, right, was typically a classically understated arrangement with center-aligned headings and justifed text, resulting in a balanced composition.

Plus beau, plus fortuné, toujo
Ton règne ami des lois doit br
Tous nos droits affermis signal
Le ciel t'a confié les destins de
Qu'il exauce nos vœux, qu'il
De ta carrière auguste exempt
Que sa bonté pour nous prolc

4.16 Firmin Didot's Modern font.

economies was under way. Some made the transition overnight, selling their farms and moving to cities to find viable employment for survival. The path to the Industrial Age was littered with many unemployed and many overworked among a few who prospered, emphasizing the contrast in social status. Great changes in the society and the economy were reflected in the art and literature of the time.

As the *Industrial Age* gained momentum, the 1800s saw even faster production of goods and services as steam power was deployed in all areas of the manufacturing process. English slums grew at a staggering rate, as many who were barely getting by on meager farms moved to the cities in search of work. Squalid living conditions were exacerbated by overcrowding.

Eventually a middle class emerged from these political and economic revolutions. As the standard of living of the working classes improved, they were better able to afford the goods and services made available through industrialization. Wealth was no longer measured by land ownership, but by capital investment. The growing urban population demanded inexpensive goods. Advertising of such products resulted in an explosion of printed materials. Through the creation of the middle-class consumer, Industrialization had given birth to a market economy, as well as an entirely new and immense opportunity for the printed word.

Many European countries had colonized distant lands during exploration for inexpensive raw materials. Under the pretense of "Christianizing" the natives, the church expanded its hold as well. As Napoleon's rise to power continued in

may have been influenced by changes in the engraver's tool, a thin, pointed stylus used to mark on metal plates. As this tool was refined over time, the creation of more precise letterforms became possible.

The Dawn of Industrialization

As the 1700s closed, political revolutions had occurred in both America and France, and a transition from an agrarian, handcraft society to mechanized, mass-produced

CASLON

France, he attempted to militarily take over larger areas of Europe. Napoleon's defeat by Wellington at Waterloo in 1815 led to greater definition of independent national identities throughout the century. In 1860 Italy was united as one nation, and in 1870 Germany was unified under Bismarck, more clearly defining borders and territories.

Printing Gains Momentum

In 1803, Englishman *Henry Fourdrinier* engineered a continuous-roll papermaking machine, revolutionizing paper manufacturing. By 1840 it was possible to make paper out of wood in one continuous sheet. This resulted in a paper product that was consistent, plentiful, and inexpensive compared to the old process of making one sheet at a time by hand. The consistency in the paper weight and surface texture allowed innovations in printing presses to increase speed and accuracy.

In 1814 *Friedrich Koenig* built two steam-powered presses for the *Times* of London. Prior to Koenig's mechanized presses, 250 sheets per hour was considered fast on the handpresses. These new Koenig presses were capable of printing up to 1,100 sheets per hour—a 440 percent increase in production.

Eventually the addition of curved printing plates and inking rollers added to the speed of the production process. By 1851 printing presses commonly ran 20,000 sheets per hour. The mechanical advancements made information affordable, accessible, and timely for more people. Literacy increased as a result.

Introduction of Sans Serif Fonts

All printed type through the early 1800s had been serif. The introduction of *sans serif* (without serifs) type in 1816, by *William Caslon IV*, was referred to as *Grotesque* in Europe and *Gothic* in America as many felt it was barbaric-looking and strange. By 1832 the novelty of the sans serif aesthetic had worn off, and Stephenson Blake and Co. (a Sheffield typefoundry started by William Garnett and John Stephenson, and financially supported by James Blake) produced a broad range of sans serif faces that soon became popular in the United States.

A New Era in Typography: Advertising

In 1820 the application of typography moved from the use of predominantly book faces to the increased use of decorative display faces. The Industrial Revolution was in full swing, with economic expansion never before seen. Dramatic changes in society continued, and large groups of immigrants

4.17 William Caslon IV's sans serif font was unpopular when it was introduced, and therefore the name coined for it was *Grotesque*.

4.18 Heather Lightface features swirls and decorative finials.

4.19 Above: Arboret, a fanciful Victorian era font, is indicative of the popular, highly ornate style that emerged during the Industrial Revolution.

4.20 Far right: Large posters, called bills, evolved as the mass-marketing medium of the Industrial Revolution era.

4.21 Right: Tall vertical fonts were cut from wood. The exaggerated serifs and unusual condensed proportions created a dark headline intended to catch the viewer's attention.

4.22 Karmac is another example of a Victorian font that employs the use of decorative curlicues to evoke viewer interest.

were rapidly absorbed into the American workforce, often exploited as inexpensive labor.

To serve the needs of the growing manufacturing sector, advertising became more prevalent. Unusual display faces emerged for use on posters, stationery, catalogs, timetables, trade cards, and other necessities of a manufacturing and marketing economy. Manufacturers felt the need to draw greater attention to their own products and services within the crowded visual environment by developing ornate, shadowed, and three-dimensional-looking fonts. Large 2-inch and 3-inch fancy variations of fonts became the norm, suitable for shouting out the messages about new wares.

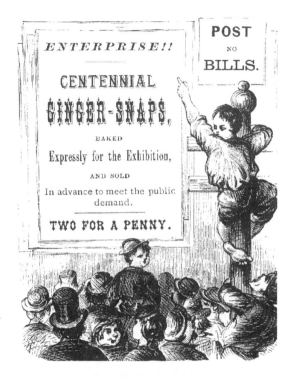

These large headlines were cut from wood since it was lighter and less expensive than cast lead. Larger-sized type became more popular, and by 1827 the American *Darius Wells* (New York inventor and printer) was known for producing large hand-cut wood type. There was no limit to the size of type that could be printed, and variations in the type width became popular. Condensed and extended versions of the large wood type found popularity as well. Wells eventually developed a mechanical router (called the vertical revolving cutter) so that he could produce wood type more

ABCDEFGHIJ KLMNOPQR STUVWXYZ

4.23 Coffee Can is a font that was widely used on signs and posters for circuses during the Victorian era, and it is still associated with the circus today.

4.24 The availability of prepackaged foods brought about the need to create unique product identites with the intent of developing consumer brand loyalty.

quickly and accurately. In 1828 he released the first catalogue of typefaces known in the United States.

Sans serif typefaces were mixed into the compositions to add to the bold, black look of the page intended to draw greater viewer attention. New type forms evolved, exhibiting thick, black strokes and heavy slab serifs. These fonts acquired the name *Egyptian* due to England's preoccupation with the archeological discoveries and expeditions taking place simultaneously along the Nile River. With stems and *slab serifs* of nearly equal weight, they were considered highly visible in crowded advertising broadsides. One example of type from the period, P. T. Barnum, with swelled, stretched, three-dimensional incised, shaded letters was designed to catch the attention of the buying public.

The emphasis on selling goods drove the type design of the period. Formerly, changes in typography had been driven by the available tools, materials, and technology available to printers and by their sense of

aesthetics. The output was reading material in the form of books and pamphlets. But now the shift was driven by the manufacturing industry, and the needs of advertisers influenced the aesthetic issues of type design.

The Practical Writing Machine

A primitive *typewriter* was patented in 1714, but it was not until 1829 that *William Austin Burt* patented a practical writing machine in the United States. The earliest models produced only capital letters and primarily embossed the letters, so they were usually only considered as a tool to prepare materials for the blind. Eventually the modern typewriter became the writing machine of choice for the male secretaries, replacing their neatly written business correspondence and records.

The typefaces for the refined machines resembled Bodoni, but the thin serifs did not allow the operator to make multiple copies in any significant quality. The mechanics of the typewriter were such that

4.25 The typewriter allowed the preparation of professionally finished documents. Almost every business office had a male secretary to type formal contracts and correspondence.

AaBbCcDdEeFfGgHhIi

4.26 Monospaced fonts allow the same amount of horizontal space or set width, no matter what the character is; modern fonts are optically spaced, so the set width varies according to the width of individual characters.

4.27 The practice of fitting typography together like a jigsaw puzzle extended beyond poster design into package and label designs during the Victorian era.

the letters were monospaced on the resulting printed page. *Monospacing* refers to the equal spacing of letters within a word, so that all the wide letters such as *W* take up the same amount of space as the letter *i*.

The monospaced letters made it difficult for readers to read fluidly, causing an uneven staccato rhythm. To compensate for this technical difficulty, serifs of the thinner letters were extended to fill a larger horizontal space. The new typewriter lettering became known as *pica*, and typewriters proliferated.

The typewriter allowed individuals the opportunity to create finished, printed-looking documents in the privacy of their own homes and offices. Typing caught on very quickly in the business sector, and within a couple of decades typewriters were standard equipment in business offices, bringing about the decline of the use of scribes for writing out formal legal documents and for transcribing court documents. With the invention of the electric typewriter in 1935 came variable spacing options, causing more designers to become interested in the design of type styles for the typewriter.

Stone Chromolithography Printing

The *lithographic printing* process is based on the principle that oil and water do not mix. Images are drawn on a stone with a grease marker. The stone is coated with a mixture of water and gum arabic, which does not adhere to the image area. When

an oil-based ink is applied to the stone surface, it adheres only to the image area and can be printed.

Invented around 1796 by *Aloys Senefelder*, the lithographic printing process did not gain commercial popularity until the beginning of the 1900s. Because the artist or designer drew directly on the stone, this method allowed a great deal of freedom and spontaneity in type design and imagery, as well as the opportunity to use multiple colors. The theater industry took advantage of this media, creating lavish and colorful posters. Type gracefully and often whimsically swept across labels and posters with an ease not seen in the traditional letterpress productions.

The Victorian Era Influences Typography

The last half of the 1800s is commonly referred to as the *Victorian era*, after Queen Victoria, who ascended the British throne in 1837 at the age of eighteen. She ruled the kingdom until 1901. The era was marked by social optimism, strong moral and religious beliefs, and emphasis on correct manners and social conventions. A naive sweetness and romance marked this era, attributed to the ruling sentiment of a youthful queen. This time brought about a gentler social attitude toward children, partially exhibited by the wide publication of children's books.

A love of minute detail and intricate decoration marks the architecture, furniture, clothing, and artistic styles of the period.

ABCDEFGHIJKLMN
OPQRSTUVWXYZ&!!

ABCDEFG
HIJKLMN
OPQRSTU
VWXYZ

4.28 Extremely tall fonts such as Tombola (top) and wide, highly extended fonts such as Lambada (bottom) enabled poster printers to fit the intended message into the allowed space; one word could be made to fit an entire line of justified type if necessary.

When Victorian aesthetics were applied to type design, however, often the result was not promising. It frequently led to filigreed and embellished typefaces that were nearly impossible to read. Many Victorian faces feature curlicues intertwined with natural, leafy themes not seen since the Middle Ages. Today, few faces from this period find application in modern compositions, as their poor legibility prohibits their use.

Documenting the American Civil War

A portion of the Victorian era coincides with the American Civil War (1861–1865), followed by Reconstruction in the Southern states. Ostensibly the reason for the war was philosophical opposition to race-based slavery; however, the largely industrial-based economy of the North was in direct conflict with the plantation economy of the South, and this schism fueled the war as well. The American Civil War was the first to be documented photographically, and firsthand accounts were carried in newspapers. Over a million American men lost their lives during the bloody war, and with the advent of photojournalism the craving for timely news of the individual battles propagated the wide distribution of daily newspapers.

Chapter Four Review

Circle one answer for each definition to indicate the correct key concept term or key player for each. When necessary, determine whether the phrase provided is true or false.

1.   The introduction of sans serif type in 1816 by this person was referred to as Grotesque in Europe and Gothic in America as many felt it was barbaric-looking and strange.
   a.   Giambattista Bodoni
   b.   William Caslon IV
   c.   John Baskerville
   d.   Robert Baker

2.   Art from this period is seen as based on the expression of emotion in vibrant colors. Artists of the time turned to classical themes while others placed Christian heroes in ancient settings.
   a.   Victorian era
   b.   Rococo era
   c.   Colonial expansion
   d.   Baroque era

3.   A primitive typewriter was patented in 1714, but it was not until 1829 that William Austin Burt patented a practical writing machine in the United States.
   a.   True
   b.   False

4.   Many faces from this period of time feature curlicues intertwined with natural, leafy themes not seen since the Middle Ages.
   a.   Industrial Age
   b.   Rococo era
   c.   Victorian era
   d.   Baroque era

5.   The lithographic printing process is based on the principle that oil and water mix.
   a.   True
   b.   False

6.   Developed by the French Academy of Sciences, this is the first recorded face based on precise mathematical analysis and consistency, as compared to the artistic approaches used by calligraphers previously.
   a.   Bodoni
   b.   Romain du Roi
   c.   Grotesque
   d.   Old Style

7.   The lithographic printing process was invented around 1796 by _____; however, the process did not gain commercial popularity until the beginning of the 1900s.
   a.   Aloys Senefelder
   b.   Friedrich Koenig
   c.   William Austin Burt
   d.   Darius Wells

8.   Reportedly the first printing press was established in the American colonies in 1640. By 1775 there were fifty printers in the thirteen colonies, despite the tax on paper and advertising.
   a.   True
   b.   False

9.   Preliminary test prints that allowed the pressman to check for a clean, crisp impression.
   a.   Platen
   b.   Furniture
   c.   Chase
   d.   Proofs

10.   Around 1730, this goldsmith designed a type that included Roman and italic, called Old Face. This typestyle was an instant success in England.
   a.   William Caslon
   b.   Firmin Didot
   c.   John Baker
   d.   Philippe Grandjean

11. In 1702 Philippe Grandjean, royal punch cutter, cut a face called the Romain du Roi (Roman of the King).
   a. True
   b. False

12. In 1788 in Parma, Italy, he introduced the first Modern Style typeface.
   a. Giambattista Bodoni
   b. Firmin Didot
   c. John Baskerville
   d. Philippe Grandjean

13. The flamboyance of the style of this era of art and typography was expressed as fine lines and curvilinear flourishes.
   a. Victorian era
   b. Rococo era
   c. Industrial Age
   d. Baroque era

14. In 1803, this Englishman engineered a continuous-roll papermaking machine, revolutionizing paper manufacturing.
   a. Stephenson Blake
   b. John Handy
   c. Friedrich Koenig
   d. Henry Fourdrinier

15. The geometric precision of this Modern Style face imparts a classical feel with its vertical stress and small x-height in proportion to the capital letter height, as well as in the details seen in the sharp right angles of the serifs and the ascenders that are the same height as the capital letters.
   a. Caslon
   b. Baskerville
   c. Bodoni
   d. Didot

16. He printed the first Bible in English in 1612.
   a. William Austin Burt
   b. Darius Wells
   c. Robert Baker
   d. William Caslon IV

17. Like Gutenberg, he perfected many elements of the printing process. He was interested in all phases of the production process: he designed type, carefully casted it, refined the technique of "packing" the press, introduced new papers with a smoother surface, improved press designs, and refined ink formulas to achieve a rich purple-black.
   a. Giambattista Bodoni
   b. Firmin Didot
   c. John Baskerville
   d. Henry Fourdrinier

18. Blocks of wood and metal placed between the sides of the type and the sides of the press bed.
   a. Press bed
   b. Furniture
   c. Type high
   d. Chase

19. Some historians see the Rococo style as connected to the Counter-Reformation of the Roman Catholic Church, which emphasized spirituality and emotional aspects of the Catholic religion.
   a. True
   b. False

20. These fonts acquired the name Egyptian due to England's preoccupation with the archeological discoveries and expeditions taking place simultaneously along the Nile River.
   a. Sans serif
   b. Serif
   c. Slab serif
   d. Hairline serif

21. All type or images intended for letterpress printing were precisely .918 mm tall, called type high.
    a. True
    b. False

22. John Baskerville's punch cutter:
    a. Aloys Senefelder
    b. John Handy
    c. Robert Baker
    d. Darius Wells

23. To compensate for the technical difficulty of reading mono-spaced letters, serifs of the thinner letters were extended to fill a larger horizontal space. The new typewriter lettering became known as pica, and typewriters proliferated.
    a. True
    b. False

24. In 1814 he built two steam-powered presses for the *Times* of London. Prior to Koenig's mechanized presses, 250 sheets per hour was considered fast on the hand-presses. These new presses were capable of printing up to 1,100 sheets per hour.
    a. William Austin Burt
    b. Aloys Senefelder
    c. Friedrich Koenig
    d. Henry Fourdrinier

25. Monospacing refers to the equal spacing of letters within a word, so that all the wide letters such as *W* take up the same amount of space as the letter *i*.
    a. True
    b. False

26. A New York inventor and printer was known for producing large hand-cut wood type and the first type catalog.
    a. William Austin Burt
    b Darius Wells
    c. Robert Baker
    d. Aloys Senefelder

Early Twentieth-Century Typography

The world continued to change rapidly as Charles Darwin published his 1859 *Origin of Species*, shocking Victorian society. Commercialism and industrialization managed to creep into almost every aspect of American and European life. Great innovation and excitement ushered in the new century, with Sigmund Freud's psychological theories, long-distance communication via telegraph, the visual interpretations of the French Impressionists, and the connection of the American continent from east to west by rail.

5.1 The Wright brothers completed the first engine-powered flight in Kitty Hawk, North Carolina in 1903.

During the first two decades of the 1900s, significant innovations in science and technology were introduced. Electric light became a brighter alternative to gas light. In 1901 the first radio transmission from Britain to America was completed by Guglielmo Marconi; in 1903 the Wright brothers completed their first engine-powered flight; in 1905 rotary offset lithography was introduced by Ira Rubel; in 1908 Henry Ford produced the first fifteen Model T motor cars.

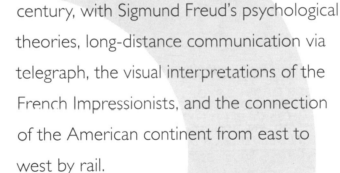

evolving from new printing technology and industrialized mass production. In opposition was a nostalgic look back that brought about a revival of lost vehicles for expression by small presses of Great Britain and America.

The Arts and Crafts Movement

In contrast to the mass production of banal products, the *Art Workers Guild* was formed in 1884. The primary intent was to create functional products that also involved great aesthetic deliberation and intent. The movement praised the work of individual craftsmen, since the artists were convinced that the faster production of manufactured goods compromised design quality and resulted in ugly products of poor quality. *William Morris* and his followers yearned for a return to the values of individual craftsmanship not seen in industrial production.

The *Arts and Crafts movement* intended to produce high-quality, well-designed home goods such as furniture, fabric, books, wallpaper, and architecture. Because the goods produced as a result of the crafts resurgence were handmade, however, they were affordable only to the wealthy. What began as an attack on mass production evolved into a kind of elitism. Historians argue whether this movement had a positive effect in the end, raising the aesthetic standards and construction quality of manufactured products.

Kelmscott Press

William Morris established *Kelmscott Press* in 1889, looking to books printed in the 1500s for inspiration. After studying printing, paper-making, bookbinding, and type design for three years, he began producing books. His books were oversized tomes that included Morris' own Roman typeface after the style of Nicolas

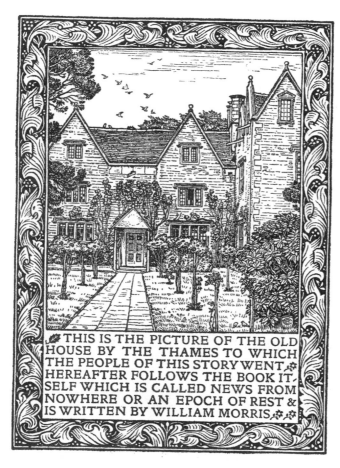

5.2 A page printed by the Kelmscott Press, right, illustrates William Morris' elaborate home and printing facilities.

5.3 A sample of William Morris' Golden typeface, above, was made popular by its use in many Kelmscott Press publications.

In 1909 Russian ballet was introduced to European audiences, and artists experimented in the Surrealist and Cubist styles of painting.

The tension between the old and the new forms of technology manifested itself in a number of ways. One force was the new practices

5.4 A page from *Canterbury Tales* printed by Kelmscott Press, circa 1896. These oversized books were reminiscent of the Middle Ages when books were handcrafted on substrates with irregular surfaces. The imperfect handmade paper used by Kelmscott Press was part of the political statement against industrialization.

5.5 The nameplate used to identify books produced by Kelmscott Press symbolized the beautiful but imperfect handcraft by the Arts and Crafts movement.

Key Players

Josef Albers
Herbert Bayer
Peter Behrens
Morris Fuller Benton
A. M. Cassandre
Georges Claude
Theo van Doesburg
Otto Eckmann
Lyonel Feininger
Eric Gill
Bertram Goodhue
Frederic Goudy
Walter Gropius
Edward Johnston
Wassily Kandinsky
Paul Klee
Rudolf Koch
El Lissitzky
Filippo Marinetti
Otto Mergenthaler
Laszlo Moholy-Nagy
Piet Mondrian
William Morris
Stanley Morrison
Paul Renner
Ira Rubel
Kurt Schwitters
Jan Tschichold
Henry Van de Velde

Jenson. The type was a heavier, blacker face surrounded by ornate woodcut borders and ornamental initials inspired by the medieval manuscripts. Morris' fastidious craftsmanship extended from the composition to the rag linen paper exclusively produced for all his printing. Through his efforts, printing was reaffirmed as an art form, as opposed to a mechanical process devoid of human input. The use of beautiful and lavish decoration was considered to enhance the emotional experience of the book. Morris cut three faces: the first named

Golden, another named Chaucer, and the last Troy. Although these faces did not become popular during this time, Morris championed the notion that well-designed pages affect the reader's perception and comprehension. His work supported the proliferation of private presses and limited-edition books throughout Europe and American.

Morris applied the same care and perfection to his furniture design, wall hangings, fabric, and wallpaper. His everyday works for the home were works of art and he is sometimes

Neon Lights up Type

Neon sign technology was first successfully demonstrated in France in 1910 by French chemist and inventor *Georges Claude*. His first patent was granted in 1915. In 1923, Claude and his company, Claude Neon, introduced neon gas signs to the United States by selling two to a Packard car dealership in Los Angeles, California. Earle Anthony purchased the two signs reading "Packard" for $24,000. Neon lighting quickly became a popular fixture in outdoor advertising, and by 1930 there was a booming neon sign industry.

Neon signs are created by bending hollow glass tubes into shapes, limited only by the scale and expertise of the artisian. The tubes are filled with gas (usually neon or argon) and an electrode is attached to each end of the tube. When the sign transformer is turned on, the gas molecules become excited and emit light.

This scientific discovery dramatically changed the general public's perception of typography and signage as glowing script and sans serif fonts appeared against the dark night sky.

referred to as one of the earliest industrial designers.

Page Type Composition Speeds Up

Although printing technology had advanced greatly since Gutenberg's time, the setting of type had made only one technological leap in several hundred years. Originally known as hot type because it was cast in molten lead, each letter was laid in a galley or composing guide one character at a time. This meant a great amount of handwork went into composing the daily newspapers. In the late 1800s the New York newspapers offered a half-million-dollar reward to anyone who could improve the type composing process, cutting the required time by 25 percent. Three thousand patents were issued to inventors who worked on mechanized typesetting machines, competing for the award.

In 1886 *Otto Mergenthaler* designed the first *Linotype* machine. The linotype machine's *matrices* or molds of letters are linked to a corresponding key on a typewriter keyboard. As the operator types, the matrices are aligned through a tube, adjacent to one another. All characters, including minuscule and majuscule letters, numerals and punctuation marks, have a corresponding key on the keyboard and a corresponding matrix. Once the operator has typed to the correct column width and word ending, a button is pressed and the molten lead is poured into the matrices creating a line of cast type in one piece—hence the name Linotype.

The molten lead cools quickly, is shaken out of the matrix, and lands next to the previous typeset line. The edge of each line of type is notched along the top and bottom edges so that they align accurately and lock together. The original matrices return to their original

5.6 Model 5 Linotype standard keyboard typesetting machine.

positions via a mechanical combination of chains and pulleys, ready for the process to create the next line of type.

If the Linotype operator types a word incorrectly, the line may be discontinued or it may be cast then removed from the column of type. After realizing they had made a mistake, composers often ran their finger across the keyboard creating a nonsense phrase to bring a proofreader's attention to the incorrect line.

Spacing on the Linotype machine was its greatest limitation. Kerning can be accomplished and justification is possible, but both require keystroking on the part of the operator during the input process.

Mergenthaler's hot-type method could compose ten times faster than the hand composition method. The increase in productivity allowed newspapers to produce more copies at a lower price. Because less time was required in the composing room, the newspapers reached press sooner and timely editions were more quickly available to the general public.

Technological change continued to proceed, and by 1911 the Linotype machine was able to carry three magazines of matrices at one time and change fonts at the press of a lever. Reacting to competition by *Monotype*, a new linecasting machine was developed by *Intertype* in 1912 following the expiration of the Mergenthaler patent. In 1918 the *New York Times* purchased a number of Intertype casters which helped to firmly establish the new competition in the industry.

Mergenthaler's Linotype machine also meant that entire composing rooms of twenty people who worked to assemble a newspaper in a day were replaced by only three operators. The same efficiency that brought about positive economic changes for the printing industry caused hardship for those who became unemployed. Former type composers found themselves looking for new training and other employment.

Setting headline type was still done by hand with wood type, since this task was beyond the capabilities of both the Monotype and Linotype machines. Although Monotype was able to strengthen its market position by 1914, when it became capable of casting larger type (up to 24 points in size), it was not until the Ludlow machine was developed that wood-letter industry moved into decline.

Art Nouveau

The aesthetic influence of the Victorian era and the Arts and Crafts movement flowed together to create the *Art Nouveau* movement (called *Jugendstil* in Germany). Based on graceful, sinuous, curving lines and images of svelte young women, the style frequently appeared

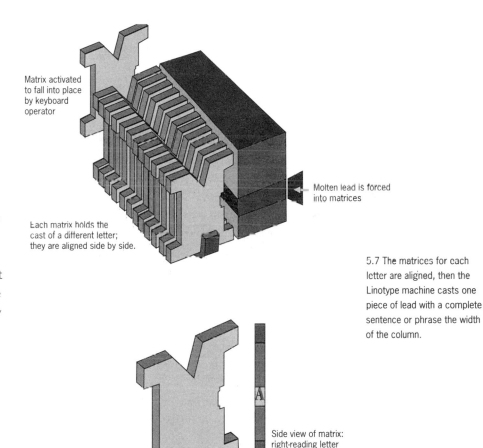

Matrix activated to fall into place by keyboard operator

Each matrix holds the cast of a different letter; they are aligned side by side.

Molten lead is forced into matrices

5.7 The matrices for each letter are aligned, then the Linotype machine casts one piece of lead with a complete sentence or phrase the width of the column.

Side view of matrix: right-reading letter is recessed

Matrix: letterform cast in brass

in posters. There was a renewed interest in hand lettering as it could be incorporated easily into works printed using stone lithography. Alphonse Mucha's posters display an elegant integration of type and illustration possible when the illustrator/artist is also the typographer.

The most distinctive Art Nouveau typeface was designed by *Otto Eckmann* for the Klingspor foundry around 1900; its aesthetic was a blend of organic themes from Jugendstil and a form of black letter traditional to Germany incorporating the medieval pen and open bowls on letterforms. This distinctive display face was not

5.8 An illustration of a single line of cast lead type from a Linotype machine.

5.9 A book cover in the Art Nouveau style incorporates stylized flowers with writhing stems and caps to create a sense of movement.

highly legible due to the complex decorative style.

German designer *Peter Behrens* was influential through out his career, beginning with illustrative work in the Jugendstil. Around 1900 he designed faces for Klingspor foundry, the most popular of which was Behrens Roman. It was similar to Otto Eckmann's type, but slightly less florid and more visually related to the German black letter forms.

Behrens is noted for his wide-ranging variety of design styles and for the progression in his aesthetic ideals during his career. At approximately the same time as he designed Behrens Roman, he designed a book set in sans serif entitled *Feste des Lebens,* which was an abrupt shift from the Textura style. Historians often cite this as a precursor to the changes from Germanic black letter to bold sans serif faces in Europe.

One of Behrens' most noted accomplishment is the development of the visual identity for AEG, which involved the design of several company tradmarks between 1907 and 1914. AEG (Allemeine Electricität-Gesellschaft), originated in 1887 as the German Edison society for applied Electricitaet which was the German equivalent of General Electric in the United States.

Type for Mass Production

Morris Fuller Benton was asked to develop a new sans serif aesthetic for the *American Type Founders* (ATF). Franklin Gothic was among the new sans serif designs he produced just after the turn of the century; subtle details in the thinning of strokes where round strokes join stems distinguished these from other heavier sans serif fonts. During a similar period of time, *Frederic Goudy* designed Copperplate Gothic

5.10 Book cover graphic illustrating a symmetrical Art Nouveau composition.

(not a true Gothic), with tiny serifs used to hold character definition, and *Bertram Goodhue* created Cheltenham, a popular display type for advertising, that was noted for its robust flexibility, as it was cut in a wide range of weights and sizes.

Offset Lithography

In 1905 *Ira Rubel* introduced *offset lithography.* Refined in the 1930s, the main concepts behind offset lithography remain similar today. In offset printing, the images and type that constitute a final layout or composition are pasted onto board. Continuous-tone images, such as photographs, are converted to halftones, and areas of photoset type are accurately arranged. A negative film is made using a photographic process; this film is placed on an aluminium alloy printing plate and exposed. Once prepared, the aluminum plate is attached to a cylinder on the printing press. The image from this plate is offset onto the surface of a rubber roller, then printed onto the sheet of paper. The paper never touches the printing plate.

Offset lithography helped to revolutionize the industry: press preparation time was reduced, and the presses could run faster with the plates on cylinders than with flat platens containing lead type. Although offset lithography is the most popular form of commercial printing today, it took fifty years for it to dominate the industry.

An Aesthetic Revolution

By the end of the first decade of the 1900s, profound changes across Europe sparked new interpretations of visual language. The fracturing of realism sprang into prominence with *Cubism* and Futurism, while Suprematism and Constructivism extended the visual revolution into pure abstraction of content. The works of Georges Braque and Pablo Picasso expressed the ideals of Cubism by abstracting

three dimensional space into two dimensions. The artists compressed and contrasted the reality of planes in three-dimensional space while adding a consideration of the fourth dimension of time. The deviation from reality inherent in this abstraction from the third and fourth dimensions provides a foundation for many of the artistic visual explorations in abstract compositions. Experimentation with these ideas incorporating typography is seen around 1911 and 1912 in papiers collés (collage) constructions.

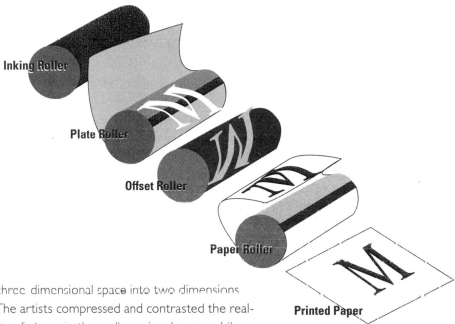

5.11 The process of offset lithography includes a plate that picks up ink from a roller. The inked plate transfers the image onto a rubber offset roller, which, in turn, transfers the image to the sheet of paper.

Franklin Gothic

5.12 ITC Franklin Gothic Book, Copperplate Gothic 29a, and ITC Cheltenham Bold are contemporary versions of fonts developed for printing and mass production in the early 1900s.

COPPERPLATE GOTHIC

Cheltenham

Fact Find! Search the Internet for examples of Art Nouveau and Art Deco fonts. See if you can find both original examples and contemporary reproductions for your analysis. Print out and clearly label your discoveries for class discussion. In the space below, list the primary visual characteristics of each period, as seen in the font samples collected. What are the differences and what are the similarities? Be sure to cite your source(s) correctly!

_____

_____

_____

_____

_____

_____

_____

_____

_____

URL: http://

URL: http://

URL: http://

URL: http://

Date visited:

Baskerville
Bodoni
Romain du Roi
Copperplate engraved
Caslon
Advertising fonts
Victorian fonts
Kelmscott press
Constructivism
Dada

VICTORIAN ERA

INDUSTRIAL REVOLUTION

DIGITAL REVOLUTION

Eli Whitney's cotton gin
Napoleon
U.S. Civil War
Kelmscott Press
World War I
World War II
International Typeface Corporation
Apple Macintosh computer

American Revolution
Railroads
AIGA founded
Phototypesetting

French Revolution

1700 CE   1800 CE   1900 CE   2000 CE   2100 CE

Art Nouveau   Abstract expressionism
Impressionism   Color field painting
Pre-Raphaelites   Pop art
                               Op art
Postimpressionism
Romanticism   Minimalism
Neo-Classicism   Conceptualism
Rococo art   Performance art
                  Cubism
                  De Stijl   Earth-site art
                  Fauvism   Photorealism
                  Expressionism   Postmodernism
                  Constructivism
                  Dada
                  Futurism
                  Surrealism
                  Bauhaus
Arts and Crafts movement

5.13 Facing page: Timeline illustrating the context of typographic styles and trends during the twentieth century.

Futurism began with the distribution of a manifesto by *Filippo Marinetti*, out of rebellion against the corrupt and confused Italian government. The Futurist movement was at its height from 1909 until 1918. Futuristic painters Giacomo Balla, Carlo Carra, and Gino Severini also drew on the use of typographic materials by incorporating newspapers and other print in their work.

The Italian Futurists Ardengo Soffici and Filippo Marinetti created typographical experiments using found and constructed type, reinventing literary communication. Marinetti explored the interconnectedness of the meaning of the written word and the aesthetic associated with it; his free-form layouts are typographic puns and wordplays that challenge the linear nature of reading.

Post-War Typographer: Rudolf Koch

Rudolf Koch, a teacher of calligraphy at the Arts and Crafts School in Offenbach, was inspired by William Morris' books. Koch was a deeply reverent Christian with distinctly medieval preferences in type. He developed personal variations of some of the traditional medieval faces.

After he returned from serving during World War I, he continued designing typefaces for the Klingspor type foundry. In 1923 he designed the heavy face Neuland, chiseling the all-caps font from the metal punches without preliminary drawings. This experimental face has been copied and revived many times by a number of different foundries.

Eva Antiqua, Kabel, Koch Antiqua, Locarno, Neuland Star, Stempel Kabel, and Wilhelm Klingspor Gotisch are other fonts designed by Koch. The sans serif face Kabel, is frequently used today. It is a beautiful, legible face that conveys a carefree playfulness. The angled terminals make the characters appear to dance and skip along the baseline.

Frederic Goudy's Inspired Private Press in the United States

Frederic Goudy was inspired by the books produced by William Morris, as were many other American printers. The emphasis on excellent-quality paper and impeccable presswork exemplified by the Kelmscott Press raised the overall standards in the printing industry. Goudy is credited as being

5.14 Rudolph Koch's Neuland font has been revived countless times by numerous foundries over the last six decades.

The War to End All Wars

With the outbreak of World War I, on August 14, 1914, the atmosphere of innovation and improvement suddenly changed. The war produced more casualties than the total sum of every war since. Worldwide, ten million lives were lost by the time Germany surrendered on November 18, 1918. Estimates on record show that approximately one-quarter of the male population of this generation was lost in warfare. The devastation and loss from the war were so significant that it was believed society had learned its lesson, hence the notion that there would never be another global conflict of this magnitude.

Also in 1917, the Bolsheviks overthrew Czar Nicholas II and started a Communist society under Lenin. The Bolshevik Revolution caused the loss of approximately five million lives in Russia. Stalin later annihilated millions of farmers and property owners in the process of instituting state ownership and control.

The horrible devastation and repercussions that resulted sparked a number of changes in philosophy that fueled new art movements and aesthetic styles.

abcdefghijklmnopqrstuvwxyz 1234567890
ABCDEFGHIJKLMNOPQRSTUVWXYZ

5.15 Kabel Light

abcdefghijklmnopqrstuvwxyz 1234567890
ABCDEFGHIJKLMNOPQRSTUVWXYZ

5.16 Kabel Book

abcdefghijklmnopqrstuvwxyz 1234567890
ABCDEFGHIJKLMNOPQRSTUVWXYZ

5.17 Kabel Heavy

abcdefghijklmnopqrstuvwxyz 1234567890
ABCDEFGHIJKLMNOPQRSTUVWXYZ

5.18 Kabel Black

ABCDEFGHIJKLMNOPQRSTUVWXYZ 1234567890
ABCDEFGHIJKLMNOPQRSTUVWXYZ

5.19 Goudy Old Style Small Caps and Old Style Figures

abcdefghijklmnopqrstuvwxyz 1234567890
ABCDEFGHIJKLMNOPQRSTUVWXYZ

5.20 Goudy Sans Regular

abcdefghijklmnopqrstuvwxyz 1234567890
ABCDEFGHIJKLMNOPQRSTUVWXYZ

5.21 Goudy Old Style Regular

abcdefghijklmnopqrstuvwxyz 1234567890
ABCDEFGHIJKLMNOPQRSTUVWXYZ

5.22 Goudy Old Style Italic

the first full-time American type designer, running his own Village Press until it was destroyed in a fire.

During his career Goudy cut 122 beautiful, functional faces, often based on inspiration from the Renaissance and from the humanist movement in typography. He cut the face Goudy Old Style, which reveals a visual relationship to the calligraphic pen. He wrote a number of books on lettering and edited journals that dealt specifically with book design and layout.

Edward Johnston and Eric Gill: Classic Letters

The whimsical embellishments characteristic of Victorian-era type in previous decades precipitated a desire for simpler, streamlined typefaces. While some looked to the Roman classics for inspiration, others referred to the original sans serif face introduced in 1816. *Edward Johnston*, a central figure in the English revival of fine calligraphy and the study of letters, devoted most of his life to teaching the art of lettering. In some historical accounts, Johnston is considered the primary mover in England's resurgence in handcrafted lettering. In his classes he trained a generation of fine calligraphers in many different lettering, calligraphic, and script faces while encouraging high-quality craft through disciplined dedication and inspired teaching.

In 1915 Frank Pick, then the director of London Transport, commissioned Johnston to design a typeface for the London Underground corporate identity. This font, now known as Johnston Sans, is a creative departure from earlier sans serif faces, and illustrates a tremendous amount of innovative exploration of individually character forms. Some of the lowercase

5.23 Above: General Bullseyes, 1916–19, drawn by Johnston, or more likely one of the London Transport printers, was bolder than the normal Johnston Sans.

letterforms take on characteristics of traditional uppercase letterforms, as seen in the decorative tail of the letter q. Although classified as a sans serif font, there are slight variations in the angular nature of the terminals that add character and visual interest. Alternate forms of the letters *a* and *g* are offered in the original drawings of the font, possibly to bring variety to the signage and allow a range of possible combinations.

Johnston wrote a number of books on lettering to further interest in the field, and is considered one of the definitive sources on typography from this period. Publications

5.24 The final design for Johnston Sans lowercase, dated July 1916.

5.25 The final design for Johnston Sans uppercase, dated June 1916.

abcdefghijklmnopqrstuvwxyz 1234567890
ABCDEFGHIJKLMNOPQRSTUVWXYZ
5.26 Perpetua Regular

abcdefghijklmnopqrstuvwxyz 1234567890
ABCDEFGHIJKLMNOPQRSTUVWXYZ
5.27 Perpetua Italic

abcdefghijklmnopqrstuvwxyz 1234567890
ABCDEFGHIJKLMNOPQRSTUVWXYZ
5.28 Perpetua Bold

abcdefghijklmnopqrstuvwxyz 1234567890
ABCDEFGHIJKLMNOPQRSTUVWXYZ
5.29 Gill Sans Light

abcdefghijklmnopqrstuvwxyz 1234567890
ABCDEFGHIJKLMNOPQRSTUVWXYZ
5.30 Gill Sans Light Italic

abcdefghijklmnopqrstuvwxyz 1234567890
ABCDEFGHIJKLMNOPQRSTUVWXYZ
5.31 Gill Sans

abcdefghijklmnopqrstuvwxyz 1234567890
ABCDEFGHIJKLMNOPQRSTUVWXYZ
5.32 Gill Sans Italic

abcdefghijklmnopqrstuvwxyz 1234567890
ABCDEFGHIJKLMNOPQRSTUVWXYZ
5.33 Gill Sans Bold

abcdefghijklmnopqrstuvwxyz 1234567890
ABCDEFGHIJKLMNOPQRSTUVWXYZ
5.34 Gill Sans Bold Italic

5.35 A visual comparison between Kabel Light by Rudolph Koch (gray) and Gill Sans Light by Eric Gill (outline), one of Edward Johnston's protégés. At first glance the text sizes of these fonts appear similar, but in reality they have significant differences in structure and shape.

include *Writing and Illuminating and Lettering*, London 1906, and *Manuscript and Inscription Letters for Schools and Classes and for Use of Craftsmen*, London, 1909.

Eric Gill, one of Edward Johnston's students, began a career as a letterer and a stonecutter. The first typeface he designed, Perpetua, was a traditional serif face inspired by classical models. He made a break with classic faces in 1928 with his design Gill Sans. Although this is a sans serif face, many of the letters have beautiful calligraphic details. Once introduced in England, it received rave reviews. It has stylistic characteristics in common with Johnston's Railway type. Other well-known faces by Eric Gill include Joanna and Bunyan.

The Roaring Twenties

The 1920s, known as the Roaring Twenties, were a time of celebration and freedom, a societal rebound from the shock and devastation of World War I. Although the world was at peace, Europe was struggling to recover from the war, with Germany suffering the most. The German mark was so devalued that baskets of money were required to purchase a single loaf of bread. Many resorted to using the worthless currency as fuel, burning it in their furnaces when winter set in.

Design in the decade between the World Wars is varied, and many different influences in the art world have resulted in typographic counterparts. Art Deco, Futurist, Constructivist, Art Nouveau, Suprematist, Impressionist, Expressionist, Cubist, De Stijl, Surrealist, Jugendstil, Dadaist, Social Realist, and Bauhaus ideas coexisted in art and design circles throughout Europe. It is difficult to establish a linear timeline, as so many of them were simultaneously in vogue.

Dada Rejects Typographic Messages

Dada rejected the organization of type on the page and instead encouraged its use as an expressive medium. The Dadaists created layouts by intuitive placement of type and abstract elements that appeared random. They rejected the rigid horizontal and vertical format that had straitjacketed printing of the past, and introduced a new typographic sense. They composed on the press bed using an assortment of letters in various sizes. Boxes, bars, and rules were incorporated in ways that represented letterforms. They felt that the chaos they created in their compositions justifiably represented the sense of the era. The

philosophical nihilism and angst among survivors of war was compounded by the physical and psychological scars left by the conflict. The confusing, sometimes offensive, sometimes poetic Dada compositions were widely rejected, although their work liberated printing practices and expressed incredible energy and innovative exploration.

Art Deco

Art Deco is characterized by its technically elaborate, geometrically linear designs, which usually incorporated the use of bilateral symmetry. Decorative frames are often included as part of the composition, along with dark areas of tone or color, geometric shapes, and multiple, thin parallel lines.

5.36 Left: Typographic composition in the Dadaist style.

5.37 Art Deco–style frame, illustrating the strong contrast in line work, the symmetrical composition and the decorative borders, indicative of this style.

abcdefghi jklmnopq rstuvwxyz 1234567890 ABCDEFGHI JKLMNOPQR STUVWXYZ

5.38 Broadway, designed by Morris Fuller-Benton in 1925 is characteristic of the Art Deco style. Considered somewhat whimsical today, it is commonly found on theater advertisements and marquees.

abcdefghijklmnopqrstuvwxyz 1234567890
ABCDEFGHIJKLMNOPQRSTUVWXYZ

5.39 Peignot Light

abcdefghijklmnopqrstuvwxyz 1234567890
ABCDEFGHIJKLMNOPQRSTUVWXYZ

5.40 Peignot Demi

abcdefghijklmnopqrstuvwxyz 1234567890
ABCDEFGHIJKLMNOPQRSTUVWXYZ

5.41 Peignot Bold

abcdefghijklmnopqrstuvwxyz 1234567890
ABCDEFGHIJKLMNOPQRSTUVWXYZ

5.42 Bauhaus 93

5.43 Constructivist typographic layout.

A. M. *Cassandre* (Adolphe Jean-Marie Mouron) was a type and graphic designer of the Art Deco period, known for his design of the typeface Peignot. In addition to the Art Deco influence, Cassandre was influenced by the Cubist style, in which the artists attempted to represent multiple views of the subject in one composition. He struggled for simplicity; his typefaces explore contrast in weight while introducing innovative interpretations of letterforms. Fonts by Cassandre include Bifur, Acier, Acier Noir, Peignot, Touraine (with Charles Peignot), and Cassandre, created over four decades.

The Bauhaus Aesthetic: Kandinsky and Bayer

The *Bauhaus*, a German school of design was founded after World War I. Das Staatliches

Bauhaus emerged from a prewar school run by the Belgian architect and designer *Henry Van de Velde*, who had made a mark with his work in the Art Nouveau style. The emergence of a new typographic sense is seen in the work of the faculty and students which is based on new ideas in composition from the aesthetic and technological influences of the time.

The postwar "form follows function" and "less is more" design ideologies originated from their philosophy. Architect *Walter Gropius* (formerly an assistant to Peter Behrens) founded the school in 1919, soon recruiting *Laszlo Moholy-Nagy, Wassily Kandinsky, Paul Klee, Lyonel Feininger,* and *Josef Albers.* Their form of modern art was seen as contrary to traditional German ideals, and first the Nazis forced the school to move and then to close completely in 1933. Although the original Bauhaus existed for only

5.44 A Kandinsky poster designed by Herbert Bayer follows the Constructivist ideas of composition, with angled bars supporting and clarifying the typographic hierarchy.

abcdefghi
jklmnopqr
stuvwxyz

5.45 Herbert Bayer's Universal font in which he attempted to eliminate the need for different uppercase and lowercase letterforms.

fourteen years, the philosophical foundation set here continues to have strong repercussions in visual style and visual education today.

In his 1925 essay "Contemporary Typography — Aims, Practice, Criticism," Moholy-Nagy predicted that a great deal of typographic communication would be replaced by sound recordings and film images. He asserted that the practice of typography needed to be raised to a more expressive and powerful visual aesthetic that would embrace the machine-print production technology. He taught that the idea of tension and contrasting visual elements could be achieved through the disposition of type. Typographic signs were moved from their primary use as borders and decorative elements into positions of emphasis and meaning. He encouraged students to attempt the design of a functional typeface of "correct proportions" without individual, extraneous decoration.

A student of the Bauhaus, *Herbert Bayer*, devoted a great deal of his studies to typography. In 1925, when the school moved to Dessau, Bayer became the first head of a new typography workshop, where he remained until 1928. He explored the idea of taking a sans serif font to a logical extreme as his "universal type,"

wherein he attempted to serve all typographic needs by reducing the letters to their most basic forms; he discarded capitals, claiming them unnecessary. This typographic innovation was considered successful at the time, but it was not widely reproduced. Bayer continued his creative work throughout his lengthy career.

The Bauhaus taught that "clean" design and the use of good-quality materials resulted in "good design." The goal was to achieve a well-designed object or space that could be manufactured using industrial technology of the time, which was in direct opposition to the philosophy of the Arts and Crafts movement. Once the school was closed, many of the instructors immigrated to the United States and continued to teach, where they influenced several generations of artists, designers, and architects.

De Stijl Movement in the Netherlands

The *De Stijl* movement appeared in the Netherlands around 1917. *Piet Mondrian*'s paintings commonly are touted as the typical example of this style, characterized by the abstract geometric forms arranged according to universal principles of compositional balance. Generally, heavy black bars, placed at right

5.46 De Stijl layout incorporates geometric forms with compositional balance.

angles, separated typographic information from the rest of the composition. Like other movements, De Stijl attempted to reject the values of the former economic and philosophical basis for composition as it moved away from representational imagery.

Theo van Doesburg (born Christian Emil Marie Küpper) applied De Stijl ideology to many of his creative endeavors and in 1919 developed a typeface called An Alphabet, based exclusively on a square. Curves and diagonals are completely omitted in favor of a modern, geometric aesthetic. Although never a commercial success, the face still resonates with a contemporary feeling.

Russian Constructivism: El Lissitzky and Kurt Schwitters

Following the spread of the Bauhaus philosophy and the rise of Bolshevism in the 1920s, an increasing number of fine artists transitioned from the canvas to the study of design in other media. In Russia, the ideas of De Stijl, Cubism and Futurism gave way to *Constructivism* and *Suprematism.* Soviet art, much like the art of the rest of the Western world at the time, was an attempt to express meaning through the simplest possible means with basic color and shape. The distinguishing feature of the Soviet Constructivism and Suprematism movements arose from the Communist and utilitarian ideology of Soviet culture at the time. "Art for art's sake" was renounced, as those practicing turned their attention to book, magazine, exhibit, and type design, in which Soviet artists of the early twentieth century sought to create the utilitarian art for the new Soviet state.

The Constructivist style is characterized by the use of simple, bold, angled planes, linear angled elements, and a strong use of the

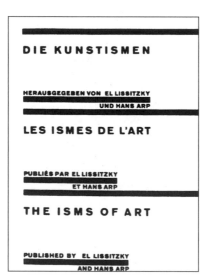

5.47 Cover of The *Isms of Art* by El Lissitzky from 1924 uses dark horizontal rules to create the compositional repetition while organizing the information within the format.

5.48 *Beat the White with the Red Wedge*, 1919, by El Lissitzky, is exemplary of the Constructivist style, which combines angular shapes and asymmetrical balance.

diagonal. Constructivist designer *El Lissitzky* created innovative typographic layouts, breaking from the restraints of vertical and horizontal stress in his compositions. He incorporated techniques of photomontage, letterforms constructed of geometric shapes, and rules in red, white, and black. Lissitzky lectured widely on Constructivism, spreading the philosophy and practice in the creative communities. His ideas evolved and were propagated through progressive art schools in the newly established Soviet Union such as Vkhutemas (Higher State Artistic-Technical Workshops) and Vitebsk (A Public Higher School of Art), where Kandinsky and Chagall practiced and taught.

Another innovative designer, *Kurt Schwitters* was close to El Lissitzky in the 1920s, although his work is a different synthesis of Dadaism, Constructivism, and De Stijl. He often worked in conjunction with Lissitzky and Theo van Doesburg to create innovative typographic solutions. Schwitters' methods of laying type over bold rules establishes a visual grid while interrupting blocks of type; rules and images contrast to create asymmetrical layouts. Schwitters experimented with the development of an alphabet that linked the sounds of the letterforms to the visual characteristics,

5.49 Jan Tschichold's cover for an insert on typographic design from 1925 that revolutionized German typesetting.

Influenced by the Bauhaus and Constructivist ideals of minimalism, Tschichold explored the use of asymmetrical layouts, diagonals and sans serif geometric typefaces, clearly organized within a grid structure. While teaching in Munich under the direction of Paul Renner, in 1928 he codified his typographic principles in *The New Typography*, for a wider audience of designers, printers, and letterers. Decoration was deemed unnecessary, and the idea that clear communication should dictate all layout decisions was set forth. Color within the composition was achieved by balancing light, bold, condensed, and extended sans serif typefaces. White space was viewed as an integral and essential element of any layout. Just prior to World War II, he began to revise these views and reassess the value of classical type and layout.

5.50 Examples of Paul Renner's Futura in a variety of weights and sizes.

altering the weight so that heavier forms represented vowels.

Minimal Typographic Design: Jan Tschichold

Jan Tschichold's early typographic compositions revolved around this need for clear communication of the message. Although not formally trained in art or design, Tschichold is considered one of the most important practitioners of *die neue typographie* which developed in Europe between the World Wars. As well as redesigning Penguin Books typefaces and layouts around these principles of simplicity, he also produced a small number of critically important typefaces.

A Geometric Typeface: Paul Renner's Futura

Artist, teacher, painter, typographer, and author *Paul Renner* was a central figure in the German artistic movements of the 1920s and 1930s, becoming an early and prominent member of the Deutscher Werkbund while creating his first book designs for various Munich-based publishers. Renner taught with Jan Tschichold at the Bauhaus in the 1930s and was a key participant in the heated ideological and artistic debates of that time. Like others from the Bauhaus, Renner was arrested and dismissed from his post by the Nazis.

Renner designed Futura in 1927. This font is based on simplified, geometrically shaped letterforms. Early exploratory versions of this face show the designer's innovative approach, as many alternate characters were unusual interpretations of traditional letterforms that added

abcdefghijklmnopqrstuvwxyz 1234567890
ABCDEFGHIJKLMNOPQRSTUVWXYZ

5.51 Futura Light

abcdefghijklmnopqrstuvwxyz 1234567890
ABCDEFGHIJKLMNOPQRSTUVWXYZ

5.52 Futura Book

**abcdefghijklmnopqrstuvwxyz 1234567890
ABCDEFGHIJKLMNOPQRSTUVWXYZ**

5.53 Futura Bold

abcdefghijklmnopqrstuvwxyz 1234567890
ABCDEFGHIJKLMNOPQRSTUVWXYZ

5.54 Futura Condensed Regular

abcdefghijklmnopqrstuvwxyz 1234567890
ABCDEFGHIJKLMNOPQRSTUVWXYZ

5.55 Futura Condensed Demi

**abcdefghijklmnopqrstuvwxyz 1234567890
ABCDEFGHIJKLMNOPQRSTUVWXYZ**

5.56 Futura Condensed Extra Bold

an irregular syncopation to the page. Even though the bowls varied in height, the stark geometry of the sans serif face was a departure from the classical approach to type design.

In the final type design, the round characters were based on a perfectly geometric circle, and the angled characters on triangles. Eventually the collection was broadened to include a whole family of faces, including thirteen variations in weight. Futura is still frequently used, as it has a beautiful economy of form and a strong sense of balance and functionality.

The Great Depression

The decade of economic depression in the United States began with the Wall Street crash of 1929. International trade had screeched to a halt with the passage of the Hawley-Smoot Tariff Act, which placed high taxes on imported goods. Now, with the onset of the depression, banks closed and businesses failed. Soup lines in cities became a common sight as unemployment sky rocketed. Food was scarce in metropolitan areas because the cost of shipping crops and livestock to market was more than what Midwestern farmers could charge for their products.

By 1934, fascist dictator Adolf Hitler had come to power in Germany, Benito Mussolini ruled in Italy, Francisco Franco headed Spain, and Joseph Stalin ran the Soviet Union. The demoralized public looked to these extremist leaders to vanquish the difficult conditions of their daily lives through idealistic ideologies. Unfortunately, they had traded their freedom for a promise of stability and a comfortable future that turned out to be fiction.

Franklin D. Roosevelt was elected to the White House in 1932 by a clear majority, and

presidential manipulation of the U.S. Supreme Court allowed the policies of the New Deal to be implemented. Roosevelt instituted the most extensive public-spending policies the country had ever known, and today many economic historians believe this action deepened and extended the Depression, though it provided a safety net for many.

Type for Daily Newspapers

During the Depression, daily newspapers were a consistent source of information both on the economic state of the country and on possible employment. Eventually typefaces were developed specifically for Linotype technology and the demands of the newspaper industry, which had to withstand wear on high-speed printing presses, avoid the possibility of the ink filling in the eye of the lowercase e, and allow the greatest number of letters to the inch while maintaining clear legibility. Not since the days of Baskerville had printing technology had such an impact on the design of typefaces. These very practical considerations caused those in the newspaper industry to realize the interdependence of the different phases of production, and to better address the design of type to ensure a viable solution for their typographic dilemma.

A contemporary study conducted by the font design firm Ascender Corporation found that the ten most popular typeface families used by today's newspapers are Poynter, Franklin Gothic, Helvetica, Utopia, Times, Nimrod, Century Old Style, Interstate, Bureau Grotesque, and Miller. Many of these typefaces were designed to accommodate the special constraints newspaper production poses.

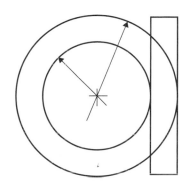

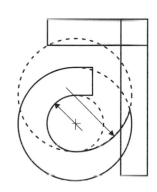

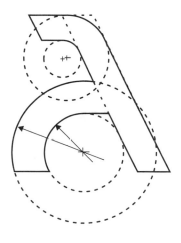

5.57 An analysis of Paul Renner's alternate designs for his Futura font.

abcedfghijklmnopqrstuvwxyz 1234567890
ABCEDFGHIJKLMNOPQRSTUVWXYZ

5.58 Times New Roman

abcedfghijklmnopqrstuvwxyz 1234567890
ABCEDFGHIJKLMNOPQRSTUVWXYZ

5.59 Times New Roman Bold

Times New Roman was designed by Stanley Morrison, with Victor Lardent in 1932. The constraints of the printing presses were considered in the design of this type family in order to achieve an optimal number of characters per line with maximum readability.

The United States at War

With Japan's attack on Pearl Harbor, Hawaii, in 1941, the United States entered World War II. Despite efforts to abstain, Americans were flung into the middle of a global conflict as they were finally starting to experience a recovery from a decade of economic depression. The war ended with the decision by President Harry S. Truman to drop the first atomic bombs on Hiroshima and Nagasaki, Japan, on August 6, 1945. Japan surrendered, and fighting in Europe eventually ended as Adolf Hitler and other Communist and Fascist rulers were deposed. Resources and markets for new typefaces disappeared in the all-consuming war effort; the environment shifted away from the one of typographic experimentation experienced in the late 1930s. The war resulted in a demand for propaganda posters prepared by the government to support the unified effort, marking the beginning of decline for the poster medium.

The 1950s represented the beginning of the Cold War and the buildup of military weapon arsenals by the Soviet Union and other Eastern bloc industrial powers. In this decade, a technological revolution set space travel as a guidepost for a country's military power. Women had entered the workforce during World War II out of necessity, and their participation continued following the war. As a result of the World War II GI Bill, which guaranteed free college tuition to veterans, Americans became better-educated and more mobile. From 1950 to 1953 America was involved in the Korean War conflict, which ended during the presidency of Dwight D. Eisenhower.

New York City was established as the center for graphic design activity during this period of time, as seen in the work of American designers Lester Beall, Paul Rand, and Bradbury Thompson. The conscription of young men into the armed forces coupled with the rationing of paper dampened the innovation of design work in Europe following the war periods. Television became common in American homes, and Abstract Expressionism was a major topic among New York City art critics. Polyester fabric came into vogue, frozen foods were introduced in the groceries, reel-to-reel tape recorders were invented, plastics became popular, and in 1957 the Soviets launched Sputnik, kicking off the international race to the moon.

Chapter Five Review

Circle one answer for each definition to indicate the correct key concept term or key player for each. When necessary, determine whether the phrase provided is true or false.

1. In his 1925 essay "Contemporary Typography — Aims, Practice, Criticism," he predicted that a great deal of typographic communication would be replaced by sound recordings and film images.
    a. El Lissitzky
    b. Henry Van de Velde
    c. A. M. Cassandre
    d. Laszlo Moholy-Nagy

2. Franklin Gothic was among the new sans serif designs he produced just after the turn of the century for the American Type Founders; subtle details in the thinning of strokes where round strokes join stems distinguished these from other heavier sans serif fonts.
    a. Rudolph Koch
    b. Morris Fuller Benton
    c. Eric Gill
    d. Wassily Kandinsky

3. Neon sign technology was first successfully demonstrated in France in 1910 by this French chemist and inventor.
    a. Lyonel Feininger
    b. Piet Mondrian
    c. Georges Claude
    d. A. M. Cassandre

4. In contrast to the mass production of banal products, this was formed in 1884. The primary intent was to create functional products that also involved great aesthetic deliberation and intent.
    a. Kelmscott Press
    b. Art Workers' Guild
    c. Art and Crafts movement
    d. Monotype

5. The works of Georges Braque and Pablo Picasso expressed the ideals of this movement by abstracting three-dimensional space into two dimensions.
    a. Cubism
    b. Suprematism
    c. Art and Crafts movement
    d. Futurism

6. Times New Roman was designed by Stanley Morrison, with Victor Lardent in 1932. The constraints of the printing presses were considered in the design of this type family in order to achieve an optimal number of characters per line with maximum readability.
    a. True
    b. False

7. In 1915 the director of London Transport commissioned him to design a typeface for the London Underground corporate identity.
    a. Eric Gill
    b. Edward Johnston
    c. Peter Behrens
    d. Frederic Goudy

8. The Bauhaus, a German school of design, was founded after World War I. Das Staatliches Bauhaus emerged from a prewar school run by this Belgian architect and designer who had made a mark with his work in the Art Nouveau style.
    a. Paul Klee
    b. Piet Mondrian
    c. Henry Van de Velde
    d. Walter Gropius

9. He was a type and graphic designer of the Art Deco period, known for his design of the typeface Peignot.
    a. Paul Renner
    b. Henry Van de Velde
    c. A. M. Cassandre
    d. Kurt Schwitters

10. In 1886, he designed the first Linotype machine.
    a. Otto Eckmann
    b. Ira Rubel
    c. Henry Van de Velde
    d. Otto Mergenthaler

11. This style, which first appeared in the Netherlands, is characterized by the abstract geometric forms arranged according to universal principles of compositional balance.
    a. Art Deco
    b. De Stijl
    c. Futurism
    d   Jugendstil

12. The distinguishing feature of the Soviet Constructivism and Suprematism movements arose from the Communist and utilitarian ideology of Soviet culture.
   a. True
   b. False

13. The aesthetic influence of the Victorian era and the Arts and Crafts movement flowed together to create this movement. Based on graceful, sinuous, curving lines and images of svelte young women, the style frequently appeared in posters. Based on graceful, sinuous, curving lines and images of svelte young women, the style frequently appeared in posters.
   a. Art Deco
   b. Surrealism
   c. Futurism
   d. Art Nouveau

14. This leader of the Arts and Crafts movement produced high-quality well-designed home goods such as furniture, fabric, books, wallpaper, and architecture.
   a. Walter Gropius
   b. Ira Rubel
   c. Morris Fuller Benton
   d. William Morris

15. Futurism began with the distribution of a manifesto by this person, out of rebellion against the corrupt and confused Italian government. The movement was at its height from 1909 until 1918.
   a. Filippo Marinetti
   b. Wassily Kandinsky
   c. El Lissitzky
   d. Lazlo Moholy-Nagy

16. Because the goods produced as a result of this movement, were handmade, however, they were only affordable to the wealthy. What began as an attack on mass production evolved into a kind of elitism.
   a. Art Nouveau
   b. Art Workers Guild
   c. Art and Crafts movement
   d. American Type Founders

17. He designed Futura in 1927, a font based on simplified, geometrically shaped letterforms.
   a. Paul Renner
   b. Edward Johnston
   c. Peter Behrens
   d. Lyonel Feininger

18. These artists created layouts by intuitive placement of type and abstract elements that appeared random. They rejected the rigid horizontal and vertical format that had straitjacketed printing of the past, and introduced a new typographic sense.
   a. Cubists
   b. Dadaists
   c. Suprematists
   d. Futurists

19. One of his most noted accomplishment is the development of the visual identity for AEG, which involved the design of several company tradmarks between 1907 and 1914.
   a. Edward Johnston
   b. Paul Klee
   c. Peter Behrens
   d. Herbert Bayer

20. Reacting to competition by this company, a new linecasting machine was developed by Intertype in 1912 following the expiration of the Mergenthaler patent.
   a. Linotype
   b. Art Workers Guild
   c. Monotype
   d. American Type Founders

21. He lectured widely on Constructivism, spreading the philosophy and practice in the creative communities. His ideas evolved and were propagated through progressive art schools in the newly established Soviet Union such as Vitebsk (A Public Higher School of Art), where he and Chagall practiced and taught.
   a. Laszlo Moholy-Nagy
   b. El Lissiztky
   c. Peter Behrens
   d. Paul Klee

Technology Changes the Designer's Role

The second half of the twentieth century ushered in dramatic changes in the type industry. Changes in technology have brought the classic art out of the hands of specialists and into the realm of the graphic designer, with both positive and negative consequences. Although technological innovations were slow to catch on following World War II, the availability of the personal computer in the 1980s brought about philosophical changes and an explosion of creative design both in the creation of typefaces and in the typesetting of traditional fonts.

6.1 Classic tools such as the California job case became obsolete with the move to photocomposition in the typesetting industry.

Key Concepts

casting off
character counting
characters per pica
cold type
copy fit
cpp
elite
galley
International Typeface
    Corporation
masters
photographic negative
Photon
photosensitive
phototypesetting
pica
proofreader's marks
U&lc
WYSIWYG

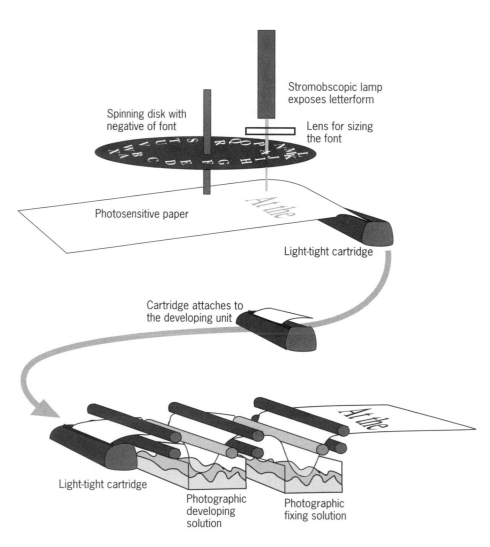

Spinning disk with
negative of font

Stromobscopic lamp
exposes letterform

Lens for sizing
the font

Photosensitive paper

Light-tight cartridge

Cartridge attaches to
the developing unit

Light-tight cartridge

Photographic
developing
solution

Photographic
fixing solution

6.2 A diagram of the phototypesetting process. The letter
is exposed onto photosensitive paper by a beam of light
projected through a negative. The paper is processed through
a number of photographic chemicals to develop the typeset
copy.

Transitioning from Hot Type to Cold Type

The transition from Linotype or hot type to *phototypesetting* or *cold type* was gradual. Some designers who favored lead type argued that photoset type was not as clear or crisp. Despite some experimentation with the conversion of a linotype machine in the 1920s, it took three decades for phototypesetting to become widely available. In 1949, *René Higonnet* and *Louis Marius Moyroud* piloted a phototypesetting machine at the American Newspapers Publisher Association Conference. This prototype set type from photographic negatives, called *masters*. Eventually named *Photon*, this phototypesetting machine was produced for sale by 1954.

In contrast to the older process of using molten lead to cast type matrices and slugs, with phototypesetting nuances in typographic detail could be more closely controlled. Removing the burden and constraints of casting type in metal allowed for the development of new faces not previously possible in cast lead. Type was crisp and blacker and could be enlarged up to 500 percent without effect on its integrity. Photocomposition was an economical leap as well, since it eliminated some steps in the production process.

Phototypesetting machines work by creating a negative of each character. The *photographic negative* is placed between an enlarging lens and *photosensitive* paper. A computer interface allows the typesetter to identify the desired point size, and then a light exposes the photosensitive paper and develops a character. With one negative of a font, typesetters can set type between 4 points and 36 points in size. The font negatives are designed as precise discs or ribbons that rotate at high speed to expose the characters after the correct size, alignment, and column specifications are set by the operator. Following exposure, the photosensitive paper is loaded into a light-safe cassette and developed

OVAL
OVERLAPPING
TWISTED

6.3 Photocomposition opened up new possibilities for setting type with special effects that were previously impossible using lead type.

photographically in a series of rollers and chemical baths.

The advent of photocomposition meant that designers were no longer constrained by type size, letter spacing, or leading dimensions, and so they began to explore new compositional possibilities. Type could be set along a curve; it could be photographically extended or condensed, or set at an oblique angle even if the original face was not. Type could be used to create textures and easily overlapped because the lead did not have to be cut away by hand for these special effects. Phototypesetting allowed the return of typography as an art, since spacing for legibility could be tightly controlled. There was a great proliferation of new typefaces, since the labor-intensive step of cutting new punches for each size of a new face was eliminated. By the early 1960s phototypesetting machines had eliminated vertical and horizontal spacing limitations, allowing operators to work at dizzying speed.

Technology Changes the Designer's Role in the Production Process

In addition to bringing on an explosion in the availability of typefaces and revolutionizing the compositional possibilities, the technological requirements of phototypesetting altered the responsibilities of the designer in the pre-press production process.

Whereas the roles of printer and graphic designer were commonly practiced by the same individual during the early days of hot type, the invention of cold type continued to increase the division of responsibilities in the workplace that had evolved with the invention of the Linotype machine. The widespread introduction of phototypesetting demanded the emergence of specialists well versed in the technological aspects of typesetting. These specialists learned the fine art of typesetting, paying special attention to spacing, punctuation, font identification, computerized encoding for specific point sizes, and the like, making for a full-time profession in itself—the same person who designed the typographic composition seldom did the typesetting for the job.

Formalized education in the graphic arts industry evolved into the complementary areas of printing and typesetting technologies or compositional theory and practice. For almost forty years, the graphic designer concentrated on solving compositional problems for clients, and communicated that aesthetic to the typesetter and printer, in the process shifting to more of a management and coordination role. The designer would meet with the client and propose a number of compositions. Once one was approved, the designer would specify the copy for the typesetter, prepare the mechanical art for the printer, and oversee the printing production by coordinating with the printer.

Fitting Copy

In this age of widespread computer technology, seldom is a designer required to *copy fit*. A time-consuming practice of a bygone era when graphic communicators and artists were responsible for preparation of the composition and of the final mechanical artwork, it is seldom understood or practiced in whole today.

Key Players
Edward Benguiat
Aaron Burns
Alessandro Butti
Seymour Chwast
Freeman Craw
Dan Friedman
Adrian Frutiger
April Greiman
René Higonnet
Armin Hoffman
Herb Lubalin
Max Meidinger
Louis Marius Moyroud
Aldo Novarese
Ed Rondthaler
Emil Ruder
Wolfgang Weingart
Hermann Zapf

Try This! First, estimate the number of characters in the following passage, and record this number in the space below. Next, count the characters in the following paragraph of text and record this number as well. What is the difference? How did you arrive at your answer? Write a short explanation of your process.

```
   "Come, my head's free at
last!" said Alice in a tone
of delight, which changed
into alarm in another
moment, when she found that
her shoulders were nowhere
to be found:  all she could
see, when she looked down,
was an immense length of
neck, which seemed to rise
like a stalk out of a sea
of green leaves that lay
far below her.

   "What CAN all that
green stuff be?" said
Alice.  "And where HAVE my
shoulders got to?  And oh,
my poor hands, how is it
I can't see you?"  She was
moving them about as she
spoke, but no result seemed
to follow, except a little
shaking among the distant
green leaves.
```

Copy fitting is a procedure approached in either one of two ways. In the first it is used to determine the correct typeface, size, line measure, and spacing required to fit text into the available space. In the second method, the type size, line measure, and spacing are established and then the amount of space required is determined. In short, copy fitting measures the amount of space that the manuscript will fit into when it is set in the designated font. Three variables are required for copy fitting: the total number of characters in the typewritten manuscript, the number of *characters per pica* (cpp) in the typeface and typeface size specified for the resulting set type, and the size of the area in the composition to be filled with type.

In the past, the final manuscript for a design was typed on a typewriter. Typewriters were available with one of two fonts, either *pica* (10 characters per horizontal inch) or *elite* (12 characters per horizontal inch). Regardless of the type size, typewriters printed monospaced letters, meaning that each uppercase and lowercase letter occupied the same horizontal space (that is, it used the same set width). On a page of a typed manuscript, the letters in each line would nearly align with the letters in subsequent lines, so the designer or graphic artist would count the characters in a few lines of type and work with average numbers. Since most manuscripts today are created on word processors, the digital type is optically spaced. Optically spaced manuscripts from modern computers are more difficult to correctly estimate, as there is greater variation in the number of characters that fit on a single line of text, so it is necessary to output the text in a monospaced font such as courier, to achieve accurate copy fitting results.

The first step in copy fitting is to determine the number of characters in the traditionally typed manuscript. This phase is called *character counting*, and the result is used to determine if the information will fit, or how it will fit into the allotted space in the final composition. This phase of advance planning is essential to avoid unforeseen problems with typeface design selections; the calculations minimize the additional costs incurred to have type set and reset by the service bureau when it does not fit in the composition as planned. (Modern word processing software applications are able to provide character and word counts, which eliminates the need for this step in the process.)

Count the number of characters in several lines of typed copy; include one or two of the longest lines of text, and four to six lines of average length. Be sure to include any punctuation marks and a single space after the end of each sentence. If you are working from a modern manuscript from a computerized word processing software application with the text set in Courier, count a larger number of lines before averaging—seven to nine instead of four to six.

Add the total number of characters together. Divide the total number of characters counted by the number of lines that were counted. This results in the average number of characters per line of typed text. Now, multiply the average number of characters per line (from the previous step) times the total number of lines in the typed manuscript to find out the total number of characters that need to fit in the designed composition.

Having determined an estimate of the total number of characters, the process of selecting a font begins. Service bureaus supply sample books of the fonts they own to local design and printing firms who use their typesetting services. The designer selects a font and refers to the *cpp* (characters per pica) chart that coincides with the selection.

Type specimen books of old provided a cpp chart for each size of each font offered. If no cpp chart is readily available, the lowercase conversion method helps estimate the number

It was so long since she had been   38
anything near the right size, that   35
it felt quite strange at first; but   36
she got used to it in a few minutes,   37
and began talking to herself, as   33
usual. "Come, there's half my plan   35
done now! How puzzling all these   34
changes are! I'm never sure what   33
I'm going to be, from one minute to   37
another! However, I've got back to   35
my right size: the next thing is, to
get into that beautiful garden—how
IS that to be done, I wonder?" As she
said this, she came suddenly upon
an open place, with a little house
in it about four feet high. "Whoever
lives there," thought Alice, "it'll
never do to come upon them THIS size:
why, I should frighten them out of
their wits!" So she began nibbling
at the righthand bit again, and did
not venture to go near the house till
she had brought herself down to nine
inches high.

6.4 The alternating gray and white areas each indicate approximately ten characters in a monospaced font.

The average number of characters per line of copy is calculated by adding the ten lines of counted characters together and dividing by the number of lines—in this case, ten.

The resulting number is multiplied by the total number of lines in the passage to provde an estimate of the total number of characters to be fitted into the designated space.

353 ÷ 10=**35**.3

This method is only an estimate. According to a popular word processing software application, the total number of characters in this paragraph including spaces is 832.

24 lines x **35** characters per line=**840**

6.5 A copy fitting table helps to estimate the amount of space required for the text once the character count is complete.

Set the lowercase alphabet in the appropriate size with the desired spacing for the final composition. Measure the line length in points, and match that dimension to the closest number in the leftmost column of the chart. The column indicated by 1 lists a close approximation of the number of characters per pica. Subsequent columns provide the number of characters per line according to a given column width or line length.

For example, if the lowercase alphabet measures 98 points, then there are 3.55 characters per pica, and 57 characters will fit into one line of a column measuring 16 picas wide. If there are 771 characters in the article to be set, then 771 ÷ 57 = 14 lines of text (always round up to the next number if there is any remainder).

The vertical space required for the text is based on the amount of leading specified. If the text is set on 12 points, then 14 picas is the required column depth for that amount of text at the given size.

Length of lowercase alphabet, measured in points

Number of characters per pica

Length of line to be set, measured in picas

	1	7	8	9	10	11	12	13	14	15	16	17	18	19	20	22	24	26	28	30	32	34	36	38
60	5.80	41	46	52	58	64	70	75	81	87	93	99	104	110	116	128	139	151	162	174	186	197	209	220
62	5.61	39	45	51	56	62	67	73	79	84	90	95	101	107	112	123	135	146	157	168	180	191	202	213
64	5.44	38	44	49	54	60	65	71	76	82	87	92	98	103	109	120	131	141	152	163	174	185	196	207
66	5.27	37	42	47	53	58	63	69	74	79	84	90	95	100	105	116	126	137	148	158	169	179	190	200
68	5.12	36	41	46	51	56	61	67	72	77	82	87	92	97	102	113	123	133	143	154	164	174	184	195
70	4.97	35	40	45	50	55	60	65	70	75	80	84	89	94	99	109	119	129	139	149	159	169	179	189
72	4.83	34	39	43	48	53	58	63	68	72	77	82	87	92	96	106	116	126	135	145	155	164	174	184
74	4.70	33	38	42	47	52	56	61	66	70	75	80	85	89	94	103	113	122	132	141	150	160	169	179
76	4.58	32	37	41	46	50	55	60	64	69	73	78	82	87	92	101	110	119	128	137	147	156	165	174
78	4.46	31	36	40	45	49	54	58	62	67	71	76	80	85	89	98	107	116	125	134	143	152	161	170
80	4.35	30	35	39	44	48	52	57	61	65	70	74	78	83	87	96	104	112	121	131	139	148	157	165
82	4.24	30	34	38	42	47	51	55	59	64	68	72	76	81	85	93	102	110	119	127	136	144	153	161
84	4.14	29	33	37	41	46	50	54	58	62	66	70	75	79	83	91	99	108	116	124	133	141	149	157
86	4.05	28	32	36	40	45	49	53	57	61	65	69	73	77	81	89	97	105	113	121	129	138	146	154
88	3.95	28	32	36	40	43	47	51	55	59	63	67	71	75	79	87	95	103	111	119	127	134	142	150
90	3.87	27	31	35	39	43	46	50	54	58	62	66	70	73	77	85	93	101	108	116	124	131	139	147
92	3.78	26	30	34	38	42	45	49	53	57	61	64	68	72	76	83	91	98	106	113	121	129	136	144
94	3.70	26	30	33	37	41	44	48	52	56	59	63	67	70	74	81	89	96	104	111	118	126	133	141
96	3.63	25	29	33	36	40	44	47	51	54	58	62	65	69	73	80	87	94	102	109	116	123	131	138
98	3.55	25	28	32	36	39	43	46	50	53	57	60	64	67	71	78	85	92	99	107	114	121	128	135
100	3.48	24	28	31	35	38	42	45	49	52	56	59	63	66	70	77	84	90	97	104	111	118	125	132
102	3.41	24	27	31	34	38	41	44	48	51	55	58	61	65	68	75	82	89	96	102	109	116	123	130
104	3.35	23	27	30	33	37	40	43	47	50	54	57	60	64	67	74	80	87	94	100	107	114	120	127
106	3.28	23	26	30	33	36	39	43	46	49	53	56	59	62	66	72	79	85	92	98	105	112	118	125
108	3.22	23	26	29	32	35	39	42	45	48	52	55	58	61	64	71	77	84	90	97	103	110	116	122
110	3.16	22	25	28	32	35	38	41	44	47	51	54	57	60	63	70	76	82	89	95	101	108	114	120
112	3.11	22	25	28	31	34	37	40	43	47	50	53	56	59	62	68	75	81	87	93	99	106	112	118
114	3.05	21	24	27	31	34	37	40	43	46	49	52	55	58	61	67	73	79	85	92	98	104	110	116
116	3.00	21	24	27	30	33	36	39	42	45	48	51	54	57	60	66	72	78	84	90	96	102	108	114
118	2.95	21	24	27	29	32	35	38	41	44	47	50	53	56	59	65	71	77	83	88	94	100	106	112
120	2.90	20	23	26	29	32	35	38	41	44	46	49	52	55	58	64	70	75	81	87	93	99	104	110
122	2.85	20	23	26	29	31	34	37	40	43	46	48	51	54	57	63	68	74	80	86	91	97	103	108
124	2.81	20	22	25	28	31	34	36	39	42	45	48	51	53	56	62	67	73	79	84	90	95	101	107
126	2.76	19	22	25	28	30	33	36	39	41	44	47	50	52	55	61	66	72	77	83	88	94	99	105
128	2.72	19	22	24	27	30	33	35	38	41	44	46	49	52	54	60	65	71	76	82	87	92	98	103
130	2.68	19	21	24	27	29	32	35	37	40	43	46	48	51	54	59	64	70	75	80	86	91	96	102

of characters per pica (cpp). Estimating the number of characters and lines typed copy will occupy in its typeset form is called *casting off*. At best this process is an approximation that allows for a 5 to 10 percent margin of error.

To convert a typeset line consisting of the letters *a* through *z* into cpp, first measure the sample in points. Then divide the number 353 by the length of the typeset lowercase line (in points) to arrive at the number of characters per pica. This is not as accurate as using the cpp chart supplied by the type foundry, so some allowance for slightly longer or shorter paragraphs must be considered.

As a precaution, remember that the same font of the same name will vary slightly from one service bureau to another in terms of subtle design variations, different set widths, and varying character per pica values. This is due to the fact that the different service bureaus may have purchased their version of a font from a different foundry. In traditional typesetting, it is important to use the same service bureau for the complete job to ensure consistency.

Type Specification

Type specification is the process of communicating to the typesetter at the service bureau the information necessary to achieve the desired final type output. Correct and complete type specification consists of the following details:

Indication of the correct name of the font

Indication of the correct style, including Roman, italic, weight, and width variables

The correct size of the selected type in points, including the correct leading (this is written as the font size over the leading dimension, so 10 point type set with 2 additional points of vertical space would read as 10/12).

The desired paragraph alignment: flush left/ragged right, flush right/ragged left, justified, or centered

The width of the column, indicated in picas and points

The dimension of the paragraph indents (traditionally an em space) and/or any additional leading required at the end of one paragraph before the following paragraph begins

Whether the text is to be set in all caps, all lowercase, or traditional upper- and lowercase. Often the original manuscript is typed to indicate these preferences, but it is a good practice to reinforce the message in writing to the service bureau.

Any special treatment, such as an initial cap or drop cap at the beginning of a story or article; both horizontal alignment (perhaps the first line hangs instead of indents) and vertical alignment (perhaps the drop cap is 3 lines high but aligns with the baseline of the second line of type, so it extends above the height of the first line of type), and size and/or font for certain elements (such as an ornamental script or embellished Egyptian font).

Proofreading Tips

Proofreading your document is probably the most important task in the preparation of text for typesetting and printing. Grammar and spelling checkers in most software applications catch most mistakes, but *most* doesn't mean *all*! Typesetting errors reduce the credibility of the content in the article or text; after all, if the author cannot pay attention to correct spelling, grammar, and typesetting, then there is a chance that the content is not accurate either. Of course, that is only an impression or assumption on the part of the reader, but it may be a

---

Try This! Write the correct specifications for this paragraph of text so that the typesetter will understand what you want it to look like after it is set.

As there seemed to be no chance of getting her hands up to her head, she tried to get her head down to them, and was delighted to find that her neck would bend about easily in any direction, like a serpent. She had just succeeded in curving it down into a graceful zigzag, and was going to dive in among the leaves, which she found to be nothing but the tops of the trees under which she had been wandering, when a sharp hiss made her draw back in a hurry: a large pigeon had flown into her face, and was beating her violently with its wings.

Font:

Font size:

Leading:

Alignment:

Column width:

Special instructions:

Now, switch specs with a peer and have him/her set your type on your computer according to your specifications. Be sure to have him/her follow the specifications exactly! See if it looks as you intended.

well-founded concern. Here are a number of tips to help you become a thorough proofreader:

Read the entire document to establish a feeling for layout and content before searching for errors.

Read a second time to check for consistent punctuation and correct spelling.

The third time, read the entire document aloud, including headlines and subheads, to catch any duplicate words or missing words.

Check the proper names of people, places, and things against a credible source.

Verify numerals. Call phone numbers to be sure that they reach the desired personnel; check any addition, subtraction, multiplication, or other mathematical formula.

Check for consistent use of abbreviations, acronyms, italics, and bold face.

Is artwork positioned correctly and clearly captioned? Proof the photographer's credit against a credible source for title and spelling.

Is the use of fonts consistent throughout—that is, are there any unusual font changes? In justified text, mark up any awkward hyphenation (too many in a row, or improperly placed) or rivers of white space (multiple areas of large word spacing caused by justified alignment).

Be sure that the headlines, body copy, gutters, and margins are consistent throughout the document.

The Mark and Its Definition

Mark	Definition
ℓ	Delete the word, character, or punctuation mark it touches. Often the item to be deleted is circled if there is any possibility of confusion about which item(s) are to be left out.
¶	Start a new paragraph.
∧	Insert a letter, word, or punctuation mark. Some proofreaders circle the item to be inserted, while some do not. The insertion mark must be accurately and clearly placed.
⌐	Move into or connect with line of text above.
___	Set the underlined character, word, or phrase in italic.
～～	Set the underlined character, word, or phrase in bold.
≡	Set the underlined character, word, or phrase in uppercase, also called all caps.
/	When marked through an uppercase character, it indicates a change to lowercase.
⌐_	Indicates insertion of a line break, meaning to move the rest of the text past this point onto the next line of typeset copy.
STET	Ignore the changes indicated and leave the original wording or format.
#	Space is required. When written as "open up #" the typesetter will understand the intent to add room in the text.
◠	Lessen or close up a space.
∽	Transpose the enclosed characters, words, or phrases.
‖	Align vertically.
No¶	Remove paragraph indent.

The Mark as Written in Edited Text	The Resulting Appearance
delete extra chaaracter.	Delete extra character.
¶Start a new paragraph here since the topics are somewhat unrelated.¶This is a good place to change subjects.	Start a new paragraph here since the topics are somewhat unrelated. This is a good place to change subjects.
Include the missing leter.	Include the missing letter.
This sentence has a ⌐ line break in an unusual place. Move this line to eliminate the awkward space.	This sentence has a line break in an unusual place. Move this line to eliminate the awkward space.
An italic or oblique font may indicate vocabulary words or key phrases in the text.	An *italic* or *oblique font* may indicate vocabulary words or key phrases in the text.
A bold font provides emphasis and attracts the reader's attention to phrases in the text	A **bold font** provides emphasis and **attracts the reader's attention** to phrases in the text.
Uppercase or all caps may be used for headings or subheads to visually differentiate them from the body copy in a composition	UPPERCASE or ALL CAPS may be used for headings or subheads to visually differentiate them from the body copy in a composition.
When marked through an UpperCase character, it indicates a change to lowercase.	When marked through an uppercase character, it indicates a change to lowercase.
Once in a while, adding a break eliminates a hy-phenation or a resulting awkward widow or orphan in typesetting.	Once in a while adding a break eliminates a hyphenation or a resulting awkward widow or orphan in typesetting.
STET-ℓ Ignore the changes indicated.	Ignore the changes indicated.
Space is required; when written as "open up #" the typesetter will understand intent to add room inthe text.	Space is required, when written as "open up #" the typesetter will understand intent to add room in the text
Lessen or close up a space. This may be used when a word such as can not is set incorrectly, or when there are two spaces in place of one space.	Lessen or close up a space. This may be used when a word like cannot is set incorrectly, or when there are two spaces in place of one space.
Transpose teh enclosed characters, words, or phrases so that they sense make to the reader.	Transpose the enclosed characters, words, or phrases so that they make sense to the reader.
|Align vertically so that the lines in the text are all flush against the same margin.	Align vertically so that the lines in the text are all flush against the same margin.
no¶ The paragraph should be set so that there is no indent at the first line.	The paragraph should be set so that there is no indent at the first line.

chart is continued on next two pages

Proofreader's Marks

The first sheet of typeset copy provided by the service bureau or typesetter is called a *galley*, or galley proof. Someone other than the designer and the typesetter reviews the typeset copy, checking it against the original manuscript to be sure that it reads correctly and that there are no typesetting mistakes. In the event that there are changes or mistakes to be corrected, this is indicated in a color that is easy to discern against the galley. Special marks, called *proofreader's marks* or proof correction marks, are used to indicate changes. Even with the use of digital typesetting on personal computers, these marks are still employed today.

Type Design During the Second Half of the Twentieth Century

Type design during the second half of the twentieth century saw the revival of classic fonts as well as a number of movements toward a new aesthetic. In Europe, the early emphasis was on highly organized compositions with a direct and clear hierarchy of information, which later spurred a reaction in the form of a period of exploration and of experimentation with compositions that some found illegible, and grunge typography, or textured digital and handwritten fonts in free-form compositions inspired by personal experience and an individual sense of aesthetic.

Adrian Frutiger's Numbered Univers Family

Adrian Frutiger, a Swiss-born designer, developed an entire family of sans serif faces, named Univers, from 1954 through 1957. The family encompassed a variety of weights, italics, condensed, and extended fonts. Frutiger optically adjusted portions of the typeface to ensure an optically even visual texture. He devised a numeric system to identify the twenty-one visual variations within the family. Organized within a matrix, Univers 55 is considered the standard

The Mark and Its Definition

Mark	Definition
═	Set copy in small caps.
sp	Spell out word or term completely.
wf	Wrong font.
⌐	Move text right according to the distance indicated in picas, points, and/or em or en spaces.
⌐	Move text left according to the distance indicated in picas, points, and/or em or en spaces.
]·[	Center copy.
#	Close up and delete space.
∨"	Insert quotation marks.
∨'	Insert an apostrophe.
∧ 1/N	Insert an en dash or nut dash.
∧ 1/M	Insert an em dash.
⌊⌋	Lower item indicated.
⌈⌉	Raise item indicated.
²	Insert superior (superscript) figure or letter.
₂	Insert inferior (subscript) figure or letter.

The Mark as Written in Edited Text	**The Resulting Appearance**
A combination of caps and small caps is commonly used for headlines or for introducing a new section.	A COMBINATION OF CAPS AND SMALL CAPS is commonly used for headlines or for introducing a new section.
The first (10) exhibitors gained entrance to the show through the south door.	The first ten exhibitors gained entrance to the show through the south door.
Pay attention to the font used throughout.	Pay attention to the font used throughout.
• Move text right to align the subsequent lines of bulleted text, so that the bullet creates a hanging indent and all text aligns.	• Move text right to align the subsequent lines of bulleted text, so that the bullet creates a hanging indent and all text aligns.
Sometimes the type is not set correctly, so this is an indication to move text one or more lines over to the left, as in a block quote, or to remove a hanging indent.	Sometimes the type is not set correctly, so this is an indication to move text one or more lines over to the left, as in a block quote, or to remove a hanging indent.
Align the text in the middle of the column instead of flush left or flush right.	Align the text in the middle of the column instead of flush left or flush right.
This is helpful when more than one space is typed at the end of a sentence. There should be only one space after a period.	This is helpful when more than one space is typed at the end of a sentence. There should be only one space after a period.
The other day Sally asked, "Would you like to go shopping with Mother and me?"	The other day Sally asked, "Would you like to go shopping with Mother and me?"
That's not mine, it belongs to Harry.	That's not mine, it belongs to Harry.
The violin recital is scheduled for Thursday, March 5th, from 7:00 to 9:00 p.m.	The violin recital is scheduled for Thursday, March 5, from 7:00–9:00 p.m.
"I'd really like to take my Groovy Girl doll to class next week, you know, the one with yellow hair?"	"I'd really like to take my Groovy Girl doll to class next week—you know, the one with yellow hair?"
Be sure that all the text aligns along the baseline of the sentence.	Be sure that all the text aligns along the baseline of the sentence.
Be sure that all the text aligns along the baseline of the sentence.	Be sure that all the text aligns along the baseline of the sentence.
Superior figures are often used in mathematical formulae to indicate exponential relationships, such as $4^2 = 16$.	Superior figures are often used in mathematical formulae to indicate exponential relationships, such as $4^2 = 16$.
Inferior figures are often used in chemical formulae to indicate the number of atoms, such as H_2O.	Inferior figures are often used in chemical formulae to indicate the number of atoms, such as H_2O.

"Serpent!" scremed the Pigeon.

"I'm NOT a serpent!" said Alice indignantly. "Let me alone!'

"Serpent, I say again!" repeated the Pigeon, but in a more subdued tone, and added with a kind of sob, "I've tried every way, and nothing seems to suite them!'

"I haven't the leeast idea what you're talking about," said Alice.

"I've tried the rots of treees, and I've tried banks, and I've tried hedges," the Pigeon went on, without attending to her; "but those serpents! Theres no pleasing them!"

Alice was more and more puzzled, but she thought there was no use in saying anything more till the Pigeon had finished.

"As if it wasn't trouble enough hatching the eggs,' said the Pigeon; "but I must be on the look-out for serpents night and day! Why, I haven't had a wink of sleep these threee weeks!" "I'm very   sorry you've been annoyed," said Alice, who was begining to see its meaning. "And just as I'd taken the hihest tree in the wood," continued the Pigeon, raising its voice to a shriek, 'and just as I was thinking I should be free of them at last, they must needs come wriggling down from the sky! Ugh, SerpEnt!"

"But I'm NOT aserpent, I tell you!" said Alice. "I'm a—I'm a--"

"Well! WHT are you?" said the Pigean. "I can see you're trying to invent something!'

"I--I'm a litttle girl," said Alice, rather DoubtfUlly, as she remembered the number of changes she had gone through that day.

"A likely story indeed!" said the Pigeon in a tone of the deepest contempt. "I've seen a goOd many little girls in my time, but never ONE with such a neck as that! No, no! You're a serpent; and there's no use denying it. I suppose youll betelling me next that you never tasted an egg!"

"I HAVE tastd eggs, certainly," said Alice, who was a very trutful child; "but little girls eat eggs quite as much as serpents do, you know."

"I don't believe it," said the Pigeon; "but if they do, why then they're a kind of serpent, thatsall I can say."

This was such a new idea to Alice, that she was quite silent for a minute or two, which gave the Pigeon the opportunity of adding, "You're looking for eggs, I know THAT well enough; and what does it matter to me whether youre a little girl or a serpent?" "It matters a good deal to ME," said Alice hastily; "but I'm not looking for eggs, as it happens; and if I was, I shouldn't want YOURS: I don't like them raw."

Copy fitting Exercise

Use the text on the facing page for this exercise. Begin by marking the text using proofreader's marks to correct it.

Estimate the number of characters in the passage.

Determine the space required for the following situations. Show your calculations in the space allowed, so that you can get assistance in determining the strengths and weaknesses of your calculations.

How many lines of type will fit into a column 15 picas wide using:

Fenice Regular 10/13   abcdefghijklmnopqrstuvwxyz

_____

_____

_____

_____

Futura Book 9/13   abcdefghijklmnopqrstuvwxyz

_____

_____

_____

ITC Garamond Book 13/13   abcdefghijklmnopqrstuvwxyz

_____

_____

_____

_____

How many lines of type will fit into a column 20.5 picas wide using:

Goudy Old Style 11/13   abcdefghijklmnopqrstuvwxyz

_____

_____

_____

_____

Bodoni Bold 14/14   abcdefghijklmnopqrstuvwxyz

_____

_____

_____

_____

_____

Helpful hints:

Do not forget that each time a new character speaks, a new paragraph begins.

During the days of typewriters, the only way to indicate the em dash was to use two hyphens in a row. Replace these with an em dash.

Check all quotation marks to be sure that they are double quotation marks instead of single quotation marks.

Follow the tips for proofreading so that you will be sure to catch all spelling errors and typos.

Pencil in the character count per line in the margin to help you remember those you have counted. The greater the number of lines you count, the more accurate your estimate will be.

The copy fitting tables and directions are on page 104 for your reference.

You will need an accurate point/pica ruler for this exercise.

How much of the text from the facing page will fit into this space (indicated by the outline), using Janson Text 55 Roman, set 10/13?

abcdefghijklmnopqrstuvwxyz

Show your calculations below. Will all of the text fit? If not, how many lines will be left over?

_____

_____

_____

_____

_____

_____

_____

_____

_____

_____

_____

_____

_____

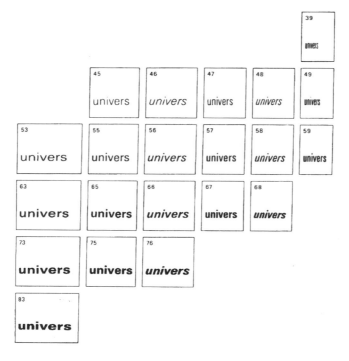

6.6 Relationship between the weights and styles of Adrian Frutiger's Univers (Deberny & Peignot promotional booklet, 1954) SPBL.

weight and proportion. As the face becomes bolder (Univers 75), the number of the font becomes larger, as the weight becomes lighter, the number is smaller (Univers 45). Weight is organized vertically from lightest to boldest, changing by ten digits on a scale reading 45, 55, 65, and 75. The face width changes on a horizontal scale of odd numbers: the standard-weight face, for example, includes the numbers 53 (extended), 55, 56, 57, 58, and 59 (condensed). Subsequent variations are located above and below the 50s. Even numbers in the scale are italic versions of its predecessor, an odd-numbered Roman version of the same weight and width.

The Swiss Design Style: Meidinger's Helvetica

In 1950s a new typographic design movement emerged in Switzerland and Germany. Based on an underlying grid structure, an asymmetrical arrangement of compositional elements, and the incorporation of different weights of sans serif type, this style offered multitudes of creative possibilities. One of the primary underlying philosophies of this movement was to override the individual personal style of the designer in favor of clear, concise communication of the intended message—an idea that originated in the teachings of the Bauhaus philosophy.

During the mid-1950s, *Max Meidinger* designed Helvetica for the Haas type foundry in Switzerland. Using a larger x-height, considered to be more legible than Univers, Helvetica was an immediate success. Numerous designers joined in the task of creating variations in weight and width of the Helvetica family, so there is less visual consistency than with Frutiger's Univers family. Helvetica embraces graceful curves and a slightly less geometric structure than Univers. Over the years, Helvetica's popularity brought about overuse, as it flooded the visual market on everything from

abcdefghijklmnopqrstuvwxyz 1234567890
ABCDEFGHIJKLMNOPQRSTUVWXYZ

6.7 47 Univers Light Condensed

abcdefghijklmnopqrstuvwxyz 1234567890
ABCDEFGHIJKLMNOPQRSTUVWXYZ

6.8 57 Univers Condensed

abcdefghijklmnopqrstuvwxyz 1234567890
ABCDEFGHIJKLMNOPQRSTUVWXYZ

6.9 67 Univers Bold Condensed

highway signage to food packaging and clothing label tags. As a result, it has lost its visual impact and slipped into the realm of generic application and impact.

A Classic Type Designer: Hermann Zapf

Hermann Zapf's work spanned four decades, beginning in the 1950s. Beginning as an accomplished calligrapher, he turned his hand to commercial type design. With Palatino in 1950, Melior in 1952, and Optima in 1958, he established himself as a talented and prolific designer.

Optima is a highly legible, humanistic sans serif typeface inspired by sans serif inscriptions from Florence, Italy, in the 1400s. Using slightly thicker, splayed ends of the strokes of letters to replace serifs, the result is simple and graceful, not cold and mechanical. Zapf worked with inspiration from the past but was able to imbue it with modern legibility and sensibility.

Fenice: Novarese's Elegant Font

Working in Italy, *Aldo Novarese* and *Alessandro Butti* designed the new sans serif typefaces Microgramma and Eurostile. Both typefaces share features of a highly engineered, square, spartan aesthetic. Intended to be tightly fitted characters that create a compact look in the composition, Microgramma is exclusively uppercase while Eurostile includes both upper- and lowercase letterforms.

Aldo Novarse went on to design other fonts, including ITC Novarese, ITC Fenice, and ITC Mixage. All of these fonts were designed with attention to the balance of weight and form.

Freeman Craw: A Designer of Stable Faces

American *Freeman Craw* designed three typefaces quite popular at the time: Craw Clarendon, Craw Modern, and Ad Lib. All are balanced, stable, and industrial-looking. They have a large x-height in proportion to the cap height (especially Craw Modern) and the characters are

abcdefghijklmnopqrstuvwxyz 1234567890
ABCDEFGHIJKLMNOPQRSTUVWXYZ

6.10 Linotype Palatino Regular

abcdefghijklmnopqrstuvwxyz 1234567890
ABCDEFGHIJKLMNOPQRSTUVWXYZ

6.11 Linotype Palatino Regular

abcdefghijklmnopqrstuvwxyz 1234567890
ABCDEFGHIJKLMNOPQRSTUVWXYZ

6.12 Linotype Palatino Regular

abcdefghijklmnopqrstuvwxyz 1234567890
ABCDEFGHIJKLMNOPQRSTUVWXYZ

6.13 Linotype Palatino Regular

abcdefghijklmnopqrstuvwxyz 1234567890
ABCDEFGHIJKLMNOPQRSTUVWXYZ

6.14 Optima Roman

abcdefghijklmnopqrstuvwxyz 1234567890
ABCDEFGHIJKLMNOPQRSTUVWXYZ

6.15 Optima Italic

abcdefghijklmnopqrstuvwxyz 1234567890
ABCDEFGHIJKLMNOPQRSTUVWXYZ

6.16 Optima Oblique

abcdefghijklmnopqrstuvwxyz 1234567890
ABCDEFGHIJKLMNOPQRSTUVWXYZ

6.17 Optima Bold

abcdefghijklmnopqrstuvwxyz 1234567890
ABCDEFGHIJKLMNOPQRSTUVWXYZ

6.18 Optima Bold Italic

abcdefghijklmnopqrstuvwxyz 1234567890
ABCDEFGHIJKLMNOPQRSTUVWXYZ

6.19 Optima Bold Oblique

abcdefghijklmnopqrstuvwxyz 1234567890
ABCDEFGHIJKLMNOPQRSTUVWXYZ
6.20 ITC Fenice Light

abcdefghijklmnopqrstuvwxyz 1234567890
ABCDEFGHIJKLMNOPQRSTUVWXYZ
6.21 ITC Fenice Regular

abcdefghijklmnopqrstuvwxyz 1234567890
ABCDEFGHIJKLMNOPQRSTUVWXYZ
6.22 ITC Fenice Bold

abcdefghijklmnopqrstuvwxyz 1234567890
ABCDEFGHIJKLMNOPQRSTUVWXYZ
6.23 ITC Fenice Ultra

abcdefghijklmnopqrstuvwxyz 1234567890
ABCDEFGHIJKLMNOPQRSTUVWXYZ
6.24 Novarese

abcdefghijklmnopqrstuvwxyz 1234567890
ABCDEFGHIJKLMNOPQRSTUVWXYZ
6.25 Novarese Italic

abcdefghijklmnopqrstuvwxyz 1234567890
ABCDEFGHIJKLMNOPQRSTUVWXYZ
6.26 Novarese Bold

abcdefghijklmnopqrstuvwxyz 1234567890
ABCDEFGHIJKLMNOPQRSTUVWXYZ
6.27 Novarese Bold Italic

abcdefghijklmnopqrstuvwxyz 1234567890
ABCDEFGHIJKLMNOPQRSTUVWXYZ
6.28 Eurostile

abcdefghijklmnopqrstuvwxyz 1234567890
ABCDEFGHIJKLMNOPQRSTUVWXYZ
6.29 Eurostile bold

slightly extended in width. The beauty of these faces is seen in the sensitivity he paid to the contrast of the thick and thin strokes.

International Typeface Corporation

Known as ITC, the *International Typeface Corporation* was based on the guiding principle of designing type for legibility. Founded in 1970 by *Aaron Burns*, *Herb Lubalin*, and *Ed Rondthaler*, ITC was a foundry known for the redesign of older classics, improving their legibility and visual balance and adapting them to phototypesetting technology. The most common updates included increasing the proportion of the x-height to the capital letters and opening the counterforms for more clarity.

ITC drew on the expertise and typographic archive already built by Lubalin and Burns while continuing to bring in new designers and designs licensed across manufacturers, which meant that the designer benefited directly from the royalties for usage based on the subsequent success of a font, face, or family.

However, as photocomposition companies and service bureaus multiplied, photographic technology made it possible for a supplier to duplicate the master matrix of characters in a face. Upon duplication of the desired face, the supplier was able to rename the face and therefore avoid paying any royalties to the original designer. The same photographic technology that had advanced the practice of typesetting and printing technology had become a double-edged sword, robbing many type designers of a livelihood from their chosen profession. The first issue of the ITC magazine *U&lc*, designed by Herb Lubalin, appeared in 1973. It included an attack on this kind of type piracy.

Today, ITC purchases the rights to newly developed faces, commissions designs from contemporary type designers, and reviews existing classic faces for possible improvement. ITC faces are licensed and may be purchased

abcde
ghijklm
nopqrstu
vwxyz
1234567890
ABCDEF
GHIJKLM
NOPQRSTU
VWXYZ

6.30 Examples of ITC Benguiat, originally designed by Ed Benguiat.

throughout Europe, Asia, and North America. ITC faces are consistent, so that no matter where the font is purchased, the output results are exactly the same

Edward Benguiat: A Prolific Type Designer

American corporate designer *Edward Benguiat* has designed over five hundred successful typefaces. The font named after him, Benguiat, incorporates interesting angles and curves, with heavily bracketed, sharp, and pointed serifs. His fonts are unique, showing a great deal of experimentation and original, fresh inspiration. He designed ITC Benguiat Gothic,

ITC Tiffany, ITC Souvenir, ITC Bookman, ITC Panache, and ITC Korinna.

Type Design in the 1960s

The post–World War II period of economic strength brought on a new wave of expansion in American industry. The United States dominated the manufacturing world as American factories supplied goods for recovering European countries, and the American gross national product reached a new high. John F. Kennedy succeeded Eisenhower in the White House. Baby boomers came of age, taking society by storm in their self-declared antiestablishment roles as beatniks, hippies, and flower children. The college-age population led politically active lives, helping to bring about a formal women's liberation movement and fueling the civil rights movement. America seemed to be defined by fairly prosperous, comfortable, middle-class consumers.

Type design in the 1960s borrowed inspiration from Op art and other psychedelic movements. The neon colors in vogue at the time rendered many typographic compositions illegible, and a resurgence of hand lettering echoed the swirling, dizzying effects often inspired by psychedelic drug use. Applications of organically formed letters were taken to the extreme, challenging viewers to figure out the intended message.

Seymour Chwast's Whimsical Typefaces

Primarily known as an illustrator, *Seymour Chwast* designed five popular typefaces that embodied the aesthetic of this era: Artone, Blimp, Filmsense, Myopic, and Buffalo. Artone implies the sense of platform shoes and bell-bottom pants by using an extremely high slab serif and obvious bracketing. Blimp is a round, pumped-up sans serif that incorporates a linear gradient. Filmsense is a sans serif face with rounded characters using black, white, and gray tones to define the forms. Myopic relies on the repetition

abcdef

6.31 Examples of Clarendon, originally designed by Freeman Craw.

Fact Find!   Search the Internet for typographic examples from Pushpin Studio. Who are the principal designers/illustrators? What well-known works were created by this group? What are the visual characteristics of much of their work? Print out examples for visual comparison, and list them below. Be sure to cite your sources correctly!

_____

_____

_____

_____

_____

_____

_____

_____

_____

_____

_____

URL: http://

URL: http://

URL: http://

URL: http://

Date visited:

of the form of the letter to communicate the illusion that it is stacked, and Buffalo is a modified bold sans serif. These display faces are clearly dated and cannot be separated from their affiliation with the 1960s.

Herb Lubalin's Flair for Innovative Typography

Herb Lubalin was a type designer who fully explored the advantages of phototypesetting. He used type to express emotions, concepts, and ideas typically portrayed in compositions by photography or illustrative imagery. In addition to being renowned for his intuitive sense of graphic design, he developed a number of type designs, including Avant Garde, Serif Gothic, and Lubalin Graph.

Avant Garde evolved from the lettering design for the masthead of the magazine of the same name, for which he served as art director. Unable to find characters that embodied the visual impact he desired, Lubalin simply created his own. This font is known for its extensive selection of alternate characters and unusual ligatures that Lubalin designed based on his preference for tight letter spacing.

Serif Gothic is an elegant, curvilinear face. It has small, delicate spur serifs. Lubalin Graph is a slab serif variation on Avant Garde. He retained the proportions of the Avant Garde letterforms, created custom ligatures, and added the square Egyptian slab serifs. Lubalin was a cofounder of the International Typeface Corporation, and his popular design style was seen in their typographic publication *U&lc* for years.

Type Design During the Radical 1970s

The 1970s in the United States were ushered in by the sexual revolution, the introduction of birth control pills, and free love. Recreational drug use was commonplace and included drugs funneled into the country from outside sources. The miniskirt, marijuana use, and long hair for

6.32 Fonts designed by Seymour Chwast reflect his illustrator's style and sense of humor.

both sexes joined the platform shoes, bell-bottoms, hip huggers, and fake eyelashes leftover from the 1960s. The smiley face and rock music were hip. America was embroiled in Vietnam abroad and antiwar demonstrations at home. The peace sign became the symbol for the war protest movement. Television brought the harsh reality of war to American living rooms, and the nation waffled in its support of the fighting troops.

John F. Kennedy and Martin Luther King, Jr. had been assassinated in the '60s. The radical black power group known as the Black Panthers had largely disbanded. Although the phrase "Black is beautiful" was popular in most urban areas, racial dissent and segregation were prevalent in rural areas and southern states. Although women had made progress toward social equality, with *Roe v. Wade* finally passing in 1973, avoiding additional deaths of many young women caused from complications of illicit abortions.

President Richard M. Nixon brought the troops home from Vietnam and signed the last balanced budget the United States has experienced. Secretary of State Henry Kissinger made strides toward peace in the Middle East, Nixon

abcdefghijklmnopqrstuvwxyz 1234567890
ABCDEFGHIJKLMNOPQRSTUVWXYZ

6.33 ITC Benguiat Book

abcdefghijklmnopqrstuvwxyz 1234567890
ABCDEFGHIJKLMNOPQRSTUVWXYZ

6.34 ITC Benguiat Bold

abcdefghijklmnopqrstuvwxyz 1234567890
ABCDEFGHIJKLMNOPQRSTUVWXYZ

6.35 ITC Bookman Light

abcdefghijklmnopqrstuvwxyz 1234567890
ABCDEFGHIJKLMNOPQRSTUVWXYZ

6.36 ITC Bookman Demi

abcdefghijklmnopqrstuvwxyz 1234567890
ABCDEFGHIJKLMNOPQRSTUVWXYZ

6.37 ITC Souvenir Light

abcdefghijklmnopqrstuvwxyz 1234567890
ABCDEFGHIJKLMNOPQRSTUVWXYZ

6.38 ITC Souvenir Demi

abcdefghijklmnopqrstuvwxyz 1234567890
ABCDEFGHIJKLMNOPQRSTUVWXYZ

6.39 ITC Avant Garde Gothic Book

abcdefghijklmnopqrstuvwxyz 1234567890
ABCDEFGHIJKLMNOPQRSTUVWXYZ

6.40 ITC Avant Garde Gothic Demi

abcdefghijklmnopqrstuvwxyz 1234567890
ABCDEFGHIJKLMNOPQRSTUVWXYZ

6.41 Lubalin Graph Regular

abcdefghijklmnopqrstuvwxyz 1234567890
ABCDEFGHIJKLMNOPQRSTUVWXYZ

6.42 Lubalin Graph Bold

6.43 One of the most famous typographic designs by Herb Luballn was for a magazine that never materialized. The *O* encloses the ampersand, creating the womblike reference.

6.44 Lubalin's design for the masthead of the first issue of *Avant Garde* magazine set the stage for the development of a complete font by the same name.

6.45 This poster is illegible, as the type becomes part of the fluid illustration. Letterforms are distorted and integrated into the image, enticing the viewer to decipher the message therein.

Fact Find! Search the Internet for compositional examples by Armin Hoffman. What did you discover about his life and his work? Prepare a list of significant milestones in this master's career. Be sure to cite your sources correctly!

_____

_____

_____

_____

_____

_____

_____

_____

_____

_____

_____

_____

_____

URL: http://

URL: http://

URL: http://

Date visited:

visited Communist China, and nuclear détente agreements were signed with the Soviet Union, marking the beginning of the end of the Cold War era. The scandalous Watergate hearings ended with Nixon's epochal resignation from the presidency.

During the late 1970s Japan launched a subtle economic war on the United States by flooding the market with inexpensive consumer goods. American companies were forced to reorganize to compete in a global economy. The Abstract Expressionists were pushed aside by Op art and Pop art artists in New York. Happenings and performance art gained notoriety, followed by the Conceptual, Environmental, and Minimal artists.

In the art world, the Minimalist aesthetic spilled over into the practice of graphic design, helping support a resurgent interest in the Swiss style applied to design layout.

Following almost a decade of disco music, polyester leisure suits, the oil embargo, the Iran hostage crisis, and a sweater-clad President Jimmy Carter reminding Americans to set their thermostats at 65°F, the country slipped into economic recession. Import cars traveled farther on a tank of gas and lessened the time American consumers spent in long lines at the pumps, resulting in foreign-built cars grabbing a large share of the automotive market.

The general public began to turn to jogging, yoga, transcendental meditation, encounter groups, and psychoanalysts for answers. Baby boomers settled down with families, and radical political protest faded.

Wolfgang Weingart

The International style of typographic design (also known as the Swiss style in which compositions are characterized by the use of grids, simplicity and clarity of communication, and sans serif type) had spent two decades gaining momentum, just in time for the ideals to be

6.46 1959 poster by Armin Hoffman for a Basel theater production of "Giselle."

questioned. The Swiss typography of *Emil Ruder* and *Armin Hoffman* established at the Basel Kunstgewerbeschule, or School of Design was considered dogmatic by former student *Wolfgang Weingart*. Recognition of his talent led Ruder and Hoffman to invite Weingart back to Basel to present an alternative perspective. In accepting a position there, Weingart placed himself in the middle of a new circle whose influence spread across Europe to the United States.

Teaching at Basel's School of Design, Weingart began to build complex, highly personal page compositions out of a vocabulary of grids, bars, open spaces, and simple letterforms. Compositional inspiration evolved from combinations of train ticket snippets, receipts, and other collected objects from his experiences. Recalling the "new typography" proposed by Jan Tschichold five decades earlier, Weingart's revival of avant-garde practices became known as the "new typography" in the 1970s and 1980s.

American designer *Dan Friedman* began his studies at the Kunstgewerbeschule in 1968, the same year Weingart began teaching there.

April Greiman returned from her studies in Switzerland to work in Los Angeles in 1976, helping to combine the new typography with American culture by interjecting energetic fragments from punk culture. West Coast designers Friedman and Greiman are among Weingart's most noted followers.

As American students returned to the United States to share their educational experiences, studies of the new typography flourished at the Cranbrook Academy of Art, and the Michigan-based school became known as a center for experimental design throughout the 1970s and 1980s. This search for a new aesthetic to revive expression in composition was known as American New Wave typography. Weingart initiated a compositional and theoretical reaction to Modernist typography that quickly spread and shaped graphic design in the United States.

The Dawning of the Digital Age

Corporate design was highly structured by the end of the 1970s. Strict program guides determined the grid layout and typeface choices of corporate communication in the 1980s. This decade included the savings-and-loan crisis, unbridled government spending, the rise of the environmental movement, and the election of President Ronald Reagan. Punks, skinheads, skateboards, and rap music were considered "awesome." Compact-disc players, home camcorders, silk ties, the Walkman, fiber optics, lasers, and genetic engineering were all new. The outbreak of HIV/AIDS changed the sexual scene, while aerobics and weight lifting replaced recreational drug use.

Rates of cigarette smoking fell and Americans began consuming slightly healthier foods. Personal computers made their way into many American homes by the end of the 1980s, just as television had done three decades prior. Silicon Valley emerged in California. Southern cities

6.47 This 1981 composition by Wolfgang Weingart was created by layering film. It is a worldformat poster for the Kunstgewerbemuseum Zürich "Schreibkunst."

experienced tremendous growth as many people moved to the Sunbelt.

The PC was launched by IBM in 1980 and was widely cloned, as competitors copied the system hardware and made it possible to run the same software applications. Business applications moved into the hands of office workers in addition to highly trained white-collar professionals, changing the workforce and increasing corporate productivity in the 1980s. Apple launched a personal computer in 1984 that set the standard for *WYSIWYG* (what you see is what you get) presentation and user-friendly graphic interface. Desktop publishing exploded as typesetting skills and other print production skills migrated from print shops to offices everywhere.

Designers began to handle their own typesetting with software applications such as Quark XPress and Adobe PageMaker (then owned by Aldus), resulting in a period of relative crudeness that reflected designers' lack of sensitivity to the nuances of character construction and spacing. The transfer of fonts from photocomposition technology to digital technology began in response to the demands of the industry. The practice of graphic design shifted to digital formats in about ten years— only a small amount of time compared to how long it took to make the transition from hand lettering to hot type, or the transition from hot type to cold type, as each of these changes spanned several decades.

Toward the end of the 1980s, the Postmodern and Memphis styles had infiltrated graphic and industrial design practices. Postmodernism was based on an eclectic approach to design, embracing diversity and contradiction. A postmodern approach rejects the distinction between low and high art forms. It favors the eclectic mixing of ideas and forms. Postmodern compositions promote parody, irony, and playfulness. Memphis design (originally a Milan-based design collective) was expressed through high contrast of geometric forms, colorful pattern and colors, especially with regard to furniture. In opposition to twentieth-century modernism's fixation on function over decoration and form over style, Memphis challenged accepted notions of "good taste" and provocatively embraced ornament and decoration.

Although there were some typefaces designed according to the aesthetic of these styles, typestyles developed by many prominent designers were influenced by the Retro movement. Rather than look for futuristic inspiration for new designs, they relied on the artifacts of the past. Contemporary messages were organized by reusing and reissuing past aesthetic ideas, including Dadaist type design, Constructivist design, woodblock-like illustrations, and photomontage techniques, making the old new once again.

Chapter Six Review

Circle one answer for each definition to indicate the correct key concept term or key player for each. When necessary, determine whether the phrase provided is true or false.

1. Type design in the _____ borrowed inspiration from Op art and other psychedelic movements. The neon colors in vogue at the time rendered many typographic compositions illegible, and a resurgence of hand lettering echoed the swirling, dizzying effects often inspired by psychedelic drug use.
   a. 1950s
   b. 1960s
   c. 1970s
   d. 1980s

2. His work spanned four decades, beginning in the 1950s. Beginning as an accomplished calligrapher, he turned his hand to commercial type design. With Palatino in 1950, Melior in 1952, and Optima in 1958, he established himself as a talented and prolific designer.
   a. Dan Friedman
   b. Adrian Frutiger
   c. Hermann Zapf
   d. Aaron Burns

3. This procedure is used to determine the correct typeface, size, line measure, and spacing required to fit text into the available space.
   a. Character counting
   b. Phototypesetting
   c. Copy fitting
   d. Type specification

4. A Swiss-born designer who developed an entire family of sans serif faces, from 1954 through 1957. The family, named Univers, encompassed a variety of weights, italics, condensed, and extended fonts.
   a. Max Meidinger
   b. Adrian Frutiger
   c. Ed Rondthaler
   d. Wolfgang Weingart

5. By the early 1960s these machines had eliminated vertical and horizontal spacing limitations, allowing operators to work at dizzying speed.
   a. Typewriter
   b. Intertype caster
   c. Phototypesetting
   d. Linotype

6. This American corporate designer has designed over five hundred successful typefaces. The font named after him incorporates interesting angles and curves, with heavily bracketed, sharp and pointed serifs.
   a. Hermann Zapf
   b. Seymour Chwast
   c. Edward Benguiat
   d. Dan Friedman

7. This is the process of communicating the to the typesetter at the service bureau information necessary to achieve the desired final type output.
   a. Character counting
   b. Copy writing
   c. Copy fitting
   d. Type specification

8. As a precaution, remember that the same font of the same name will vary slightly from one service bureau to another in terms of subtle design variations, different set widths and varying character per pica values. This is due to the fact that the different service bureaus may have purchased their version of a font from a different foundry.
   c. True
   d. False

9. In 1949, these two men piloted a phototypesetting machine at the American Newspapers Publisher Association Conference.
   a. Armin Hoffman and Wolfgang Weingart
   b. Alessandro Butti and René Higonnet
   c. Aldo Novarese and Freeman Craw
   d. René Higonnet and Louis Marius Moyroud

10. The first sheet of typeset copy provided by the service bureau or typesetter is called a _____.
   a. Photographic negative
   b. CPP chart
   c. Galley
   d. Proof

11. With one negative of a font, phototypesetters can set type between 4 points and 87 points in size
   a. True
   b. False

12. Founded in 1970, this company was a foundry known for the redesign of older classics, improving their legibility and visual balance and adapting them to phototypesetting technology.
   a. American Newspapers Publisher Association
   b. Pushpin Studio
   c. Photon
   d. International Typeface Corporation

13. A computer interface allows the typesetter to identify the desired point size, and then a light exposes the photosensitive paper and develops a character during this process.
   a. Phototypesetting
   b. Character counting
   c. Copy fitting
   d. Hand composing

14. Apple launched a personal computer in 1984 that set the standard for WYSIWYG presentation and user-friendly graphic interface.
   a. True
   b. False

15. He was a co-founder of the International Typeface Corporation, and his popular design style was seen in their typographic publication *U&lc* for years.
   a. Hermann Zapf
   b. Ed Rondthaler
   c. Edward Benguiat
   d. Herb Lubalin

16. Primarily known as an illustrator, he designed five popular typefaces that embodied the aesthetic of the 1960s: Artone, Blimp, Filmsense, Myopic, and Buffalo.
   a. Seymour Chwast
   b. René Higonnet
   c. Freeman Craw
   d. Herb Lubalin

17. During the mid-1950s, Max Meidinger designed Helvetica for the Haas type foundry in Switzerland.
   a. True
   b. False

18. Teaching at Kunstgewerbeschule, he began to build complex, highly personal page compositions out of a vocabulary of grids, bars, open spaces, and simple letterforms. He initiated a compositional and theoretical reaction to Modernist typography that quickly spread and shaped graphic design in the United States.
   a. Emil Ruder
   b. Wolfgang Weingart
   c. Louis Marius Moyroud
   d. Armin Hoffman

19. Proofreading your document is not important task in the preparation of text for typesetting and printing, since typesetting errors do not affect the credibility of the content in the article or text.
   a. True
   b. False

20. After working on the design of Microgramma and Eurostile, he went on to design other fonts, including ITC Novarese, ITC Fenice, and ITC Mixage. All of these fonts were designed with attention to the balance of weight and form.
   a. Max Meidinger
   b. Seymour Chwast
   c. Aldo Novarese
   d. Alessandro Butti

Contemporary Typography and Digital Technology

The spread of personal computers transformed type design in the late 1980s and early 1990s. The 1984 release of the Macintosh computer revolutionized the type and graphic design industries by providing the first user-friendly digital tool. Designers April Greiman, Rudy VanderLans, and Zuzana Licko eagerly latched onto the technology and immediately began to explore the new visual language made possible by the introduction of digital technology, setting the stage for a new era.

Since the time of Gutenberg, hundreds of years had been spent developing perfectly proportioned, legible font designs and printing technology to support the perfection of the printed word. But a change in the approach and philosophy of contemporary type designers evolved with the new digital technology, with less emphasis being laid on legibility and more on experimentation and communication of the message through the aesthetics of the typeface. Type designers began to explore type design as a means for personal expression and communication, positioning type as an aesthetic force in the new millennium. Typefaces could be designed more easily for specific applications, communicating a fresh approach and a more focused meaning through the compositional aesthetic.

7.1 Designers used to work with T-squares, triangles, and rubber cement or hot wax adhesive to paste-up typeset galleys in preparation for printing.

Key Concepts
Apple Macintosh
bit-map
bubble jet printers
daisy wheel printer
dot matrix printer
dpi
Émigré magazine
hinting
imagesetter
image operator
ink jet printers
laser printing
Multiple Master
OpenType
PostScript
ppi
rasterize
TrueType
PDL

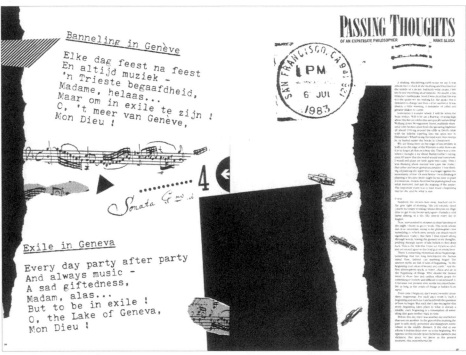

7.2 Page spread from *Émigré*, issue 1.

7.3 Page Spread from *Émigré*, issue 3.

ÉMIGRÉ Magazine

Working with the facilities available to him at the time, designer *Rudy VanderLans* developed the first issue of *Émigré magazine* in 1983–84. The Macintosh computer was not yet widely available, so the first few issues were created using typewritten text and photocopied reproductions of imagery. The layouts, done with traditional low-tech paste-up methods were free-form and expressive.

The magazine shook the traditional design world as its influence worked its way across the United States from its origin on the West Coast. In a letter to potential advertisers, Rudy VanderLans wrote, "The focus of *Émigré* is on the unique perspective of contemporary poets, writers, journalists, graphic designers, photographers, architects, and artists who live or have lived outside their native countries. Their influence on culture is diverse and significant: they import it and export it; they offer new interpretations, comparisons, ideas, and a certain universal wisdom acquired through juggling conflicting values and lifestyles."

The magazine set the stage for more exploration as young designers became inspired by the integration of typography and imagery in ways that broke the traditional grid and emphasized meaning and the search for meaning through composition. With the introduction of the *Apple Macintosh* personal computer, the look of the magazine and the techniques used to produce it evolved. The second issue of *Émigré* in 1985 was produced on the first version of the 128K Apple Macintosh computer. VanderLans was able to generate primitive imagery using the simple MacPaint software application, while his partner *Zuzana Licko* explored the possibilities

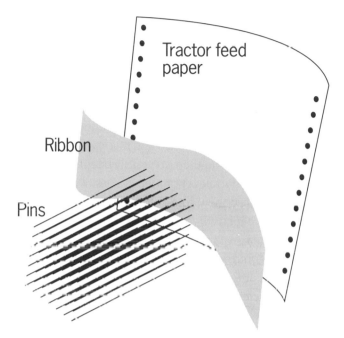

Tractor feed paper

Ribbon

Pins

7.4 A diagram of the dot matrix printing technology, where a series of pins arranged in rows strike against a ribbon onto paper to create images of letters on tractor-fed sheets of perforated paper.

Chicago
Chicago

7.5 Chicago, a font designed by Charles Bigelow specifically for output by dot matrix printer technology and for monitor display (top), was later redesigned for use with laser printer technology (bottom).

Dot matrix type

7.6 Letterforms are printed using a series of tiny dots pressed into a ribbon, much like the original typewriter technology. Based on 72 dpi, the output was somewhat difficult to read.

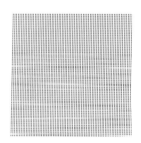

7.7 Example of the dot matrix grid.

Key Players
Charles Bigelow
Neville Brody
Matthew Carter
Barry Deck
Chuck Geschke
April Greiman
Jeffery Keedy
Max Kisman
Zuzana Licko
Robert Slimbach
Carol Twombly
Erik van Blokland
Rudy VanderLans
Just van Rossum
John Warnock

for type design in the new media. She began to produce fonts for the low-resolution technology, proving that individual designers could now design and produce typefaces with little constraint. Her first fonts—Emperor, Émigré, and Oakland—worked within the constraints of the available printer technology.

Since its inception, *Émigré* has expanded. In 1985 the company began to offer the Macintosh digital fonts created by Zuzana Licko and now distributes a number of faces of other *Émigré* designers and contributors. Not long after, the company began selling T-shirts, posters, and contemporary digital music CDs.

Dot Matrix, Daisy Wheel, and Ink Jet Printing Technology

Dot Matrix Output

Look closely at the output from a *dot matrix printer* to see the separate tiny dots that constitute each letter. Each dot on the paper is the result of a tiny pin hitting the inked ribbon against the sheet of paper.

The number of pin wires in a dot matrix printer head ranges from 35 pin wires (five horizontally and seven vertically) to 576 (twenty-four horizontally by twenty-four vertically). The larger the number of pins, the smaller the size of each pin and the closer they are to each other. This results in a more accurate and smoother image than those produced by a printer with fewer pin wires, or less resolution.

The first dot matrix fonts were monospaced, just as they were on typewriters. Considered a step backward by type purists, the result included awkward spaces and a primitive aesthetic of a bygone era; many preferred to continue with traditional typesetting or electric typewriter output.

Fonts designed by *Charles Bigelow* for the original Apple ImageWriter printer include Chicago, a font that was created specifically for use with the new digital technology and which provided a solution that worked well on a computer monitor with 72 *ppi* (pixels per inch) and 72 *dpi* (dots per inch) dot matrix printers. Working within the limitations of the

Heat plate heats ink, creates bubble

Ink forced through nozzle by expansion of bubble

Ink reflows into nozzle when contracts

7.8 The nozzle of a cartridge of a bubble jet printer, illustrating how the buble forces ink through in microscopic drops.

new technology provided a new challenge for type designers.

To improve the appearance of dot matrix output, Apple introduced a creative feature on their "Best" version of the printing mode on the ImageWriter. Each line was printed over twice, with the second impression slightly offset from the first to smooth out the appearance. This feature took twice as long to print, but the separate dots were no longer visible and the output was discernibly darker.

Daisy Wheel Printing

Printing technology evolved rapidly during the mid- to late 1980s as printer manufacturers experimented with alternatives to the dot matrix technology. One short-lived but popular solution was a printer that incorporated typewriter technology with computer technology, resulting in the *daisy wheel printer*. Raised characters were carried on a rotating daisy wheel. When a character was activated by the software application, the raised letter on the wheel was pressed against an inked ribbon onto the paper, leaving a typed impression. Although the final output was considered superior to that of the dot matrix printer, the impact and speed of the mechanism resulted in a great deal of noise. In addition, if bold or italic variations of the face were required, the rotating wheel had to be changed.

Ink Jet and Bubble Jet Technology

Similar to dot matrix printers, *ink jet printers* and *bubble jet printers* form characters from combinations of very small dots. The printer head slides back and forth across the page as the carriage in the printer moves the paper vertically. Tiny nozzles spray ink, so there

is little noise (unlike the dot matrix or daisy wheel printer) and the small areas of liquid ink run together, forming continuous tones that are more even and black areas that are more solid than previously possible. Ink jet and bubble jet printers can work in full color, unlike the single-color dot matrix or daisy wheel printers. They use four cartridges (cyan, magenta, yellow, and black) that mimic the commercial printing process.

Thermal bubble technology, commonly referred to as bubble jet, is used by manufacturers such as Canon and Hewlett-Packard. In a thermal inkjet printer, tiny resistors create heat, and this heat vaporizes ink to create a bubble. As the bubble expands, some of the ink is pushed out of a nozzle onto the paper. When the bubble pops, a vacuum is created. This pulls more ink into the print head from the cartridge. A typical bubble jet print head has 300 or 600 tiny nozzles, and all of them can fire a droplet simultaneously.

Often ink jet and bubble jet printing can be finicky about the type of paper or film used, and the final output often requires a short drying time so that the ink will not smear. The technology has greatly improved over the years and is still widely available for relatively affordable residential color output.

Zuzana Licko

Some of the first digital fonts designed by Zuzana Licko provided an alternative to costly professional typesetting and primitive typewriter fonts. The Emperor family is built on a series of pixel dimensions maintaining one-pixel stems to two-pixel counterforms; only the height of the letterforms changes, altering the proportions. The Universal family is based on the use of one-pixel stems to

Emperor

OAKLAND

Emigre

7.9 Emperor, Oakland, and Émigré, designed by Zuzana Licko,were designed for use with a 72 dpi computer screen and a dot matrix printer.

M o d u l a

Citizen

Triplex

7.10 Modula, Citizen, and Triplex were three of the first faces designed by Zuzana Licko using PostScript technology for output by a laser printer.

Variex

Variex

Variex

7.11 Variex, designed by Zuzana Licko and Rudy VanderLans in 1989, include three weight variations (light, regular, and bold). The font includes elements of both upper- and lowercase forms so there are not two separate cases in this font.

three-pixel counterforms, while the Oakland family uses a two-pixel stem and two-pixel counterform measurement.

The font designs generated by Licko embraced the dot matrix printing technology of the time. The typographic image on the computer screen was a fairly accurate representation of the image output from the printer. By 1985 *laser printing* technology was introduced, and the type designs Licko had produced for the dot matrix printer technology became obsolete, but the principles she had used to create the type were still completely valid. Her first high-resolution *PostScript* (an industry standard for a page-description programming language developed by Adobe Systems in 1985) fonts were similar to the original bit-mapped fonts in form but lacked the jagged edges and bumpy curves. Modula, Citizen, and Triplex are examples of 1985 font designs, and they were followed by Variex, Lunatix, Oblong, and Senator by the end of the decade. Although many are more than two decades old, Licko's designs still provide an innovative and contemporary aesthetic.

Laser Printer Technology

Laser printers draw the image on a metal drum with a fine beam of light. The image carries a positive electrostatic charge and attracts dry toner (a mixture of carbon, metal shavings, and plastic dust) to the image area on the drum. A sheet of paper passes a wire with a negative electrostatic charge, which attracts the toner from the drum. The image is adhered to the paper as the sheet passes through a heated fuser unit, fusing the plastic particles and bonding the carbon to the paper.

EMPEROR 8

EMPEROR 10

EMPEROR 15

EMPEROR 19

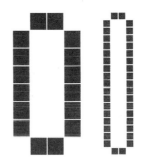

7.12 The Emperor family is based on a one-pixel stem to two-pixel counterform relationship, but the cap height varies.

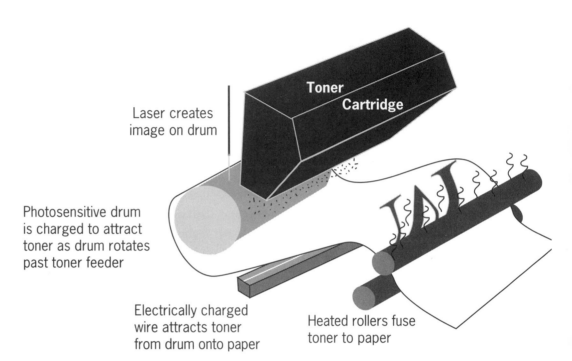

Laser creates
image on drum

**Toner
Cartridge**

Photosensitive drum
is charged to attract
toner as drum rotates
past toner feeder

7.13 Simplified illustration of
laser printing technology.

Electrically charged
wire attracts toner
from drum onto paper

Heated rollers fuse
toner to paper

Original laser printer technology allowed for 300 dpi (300 vertical dots by 300 horizontal dots per square inch = 90,000 dots), a drastic increase in resolution over dot matrix technology. Eliminating the jagged edges on diagonal and curved edges today, laser printers commonly are available in 600, 800, and 1200 dpi versions, so the individual dots in the images and type are not discernible by the naked eye. Myriads of fonts are available in different styles and sizes.

Jeffery Keedy

The industry had braced itself for a tidal wave of poorly proportioned, ugly typeface designs when software applications such as Fontographer (which allows editing and creation of PostScript fonts) became available. Like many others, West Coast teacher and graphic designer *Jeffery Keedy* began to experiment with the creation of new

typefaces based on the PostScript technology, and produced one of the early licensed fonts released by *Émigré* in 1990-91, Keedy Sans. His motivation for the creation of new faces came from the notion that contemporary designs needed contemporary faces to support the visual solution, instead of relying on typefaces and typeface conventions of the past.

In an interview with Rudy VanderLans, published in *Émigré*, issue 15, Keedy discusses the new technology and the expected explosion of new font designs yet to come: "There will never be a font that is as pervasive as Helvetica again, because there are going to be just too many typefaces out there, too many designers wanting to do things that are specific. And what that means is that communication will get a little closer to ideas. Ideas are very specific. Places are specific. Why should every airport sign system on the planet be designed with Helvetica?"

ABCDEFGH
a b c d e f g h
IJKLMNOPQ
i j k l m n o p q
RSTUVWXYZ
r s t u v w x y z
1234567890

7.14 Hard Times Regular, designed by Jeffery Keedy in 1989.

7.15 Keedy Sans Bold, designed by Jeffery Keedy in 1989.

ABCDEFGH
a b c d e f g h
iJKLMNOPQ
i j k l m n o p q
RSTUVWXYZ
r s t u v w x y z
1234567890

Max Kisman

Max Kisman graduated with a degree in graphic design and typography in 1977 from the Rietveld Academy in Amsterdam, the Netherlands. Beginning with the Amiga computer and moving on to the Macintosh, he pioneered digital typographic technology in the mid-1980s for magazine design and typography (*Vinyl Music* magazine, *Language Technology* magazine), poster typography (Paradiso, Amsterdam), and Red Cross stamps for the Dutch postal service. Max Kisman designed a number of fonts for digital application, including Vortex, Traveller, Jacque Slim, and Tegentonen. With an offbeat angularity, some are very condensed and formal, while others are casual and comfortable.

He worked and lived in Barcelona from 1989 to 1992, where he digitized many of his early typefaces for FontShop International in Berlin, Germany. He has been extremely prolific over the past three decades, and currently resides in California, where he works for various clients in the United States and the Netherlands while teaching graphic design and typography.

Kisman's interesting approach to type design continues to be inspired by many different sources. He says, "In a paper bag, I save all kinds of small objects, which somehow make me think of letters or otherwise intriguing symbols. Cardboard hands for glove holders, plastic bread bag clips, hinges, can openers, spark plugs, wooden ice cream sticks or ice cream spoons, nails, file separators, fishing weights, and so on."

The *We Love Your font* is an experimental set of characters derived from Kisman's 1986 TYP/Typografisch Papier contribution "*What*

7.16 Tegentonen, designed by Max Kisman in 1990.

7.17 Vortex, designed by Max Kisman in 1990.

7.18 Traveller Regular, designed by Max Kisman in 1991.

Every Dutch Boy Carries in His Pockets," an alphabet composed of small found objects. This idea for the font was an extension of an idea from a CCA workshop, "A Letter Can Be Anything, Anything Can Be A Letter" in 2003.

Dutch Doubles is a collaborative typographic effort managed by Max Kisman, featured in the book *Double Dutch: The Word of Image*.

LettError

Erik van Blokland and *Just van Rossum* studied at the Royal Academy for Fine and Applied Arts in The Hague. Their study of typeface design, which was encouraged by their teacher Gerrit Noordzij, coincided with the invention of desktop publishing and digital font technology. Their collaboration, branded LettError, started in Berlin, and was based on a philosophy integrating technology and typography.

Their experiments in the generation of randomized fonts through PostScript programming helped contemporary designers realize that it was possible to use technology to move back to the aesthetic of the variables of hand lettering which had been lost with the invention of hot type and phototypesetting. Now, almost two decades later, van Blokland and van Rossum still work both separately and together on various typographic (Beowolf, Instant Types, Trixie, Advert, Kosmik, and Federal), graphic design, and movie projects.

The idea of randomly generated letterforms goes against the classic notion of "invisible" typography—that is, the type is so perfectly formed and set that the reader "sees" only the message at hand and not the typography itself. The idea that the same letterform

Fonts by Max Kisman

Bebedot Black
Bebedot Blonde
Bfrika
Book And
Cattlebrand
Chip 1
Chip 2
Circuit Closed
Circuit Open
FF Cutout
FF Fudoni
Interlace Double
Interlace Single
FF Jacque
Mata Hari Exotique
Mata Hari Hollandaise
Mata Hari Parisienne
Mundenge Rock
FF Network
Nevermind
Pacific Classic Bold
Pacific Classic Light
Pacific Sans Bold
Pacific Sans Light
Pacific Serif Bold
Pacific Serif Light
Pacific Standard Bold
Pacific Standard Light
Quickstep
Quickstep Sans
FF Rosetta
FF Scratch
FF Scratch Outline
Submarine
Traveller
Traveller Bold
Tribe Mono
FF Vortex
We Love Your
Xbats
Zwart Vet

7.19 Dutch Doubles is a collaborative effort managed by Max Kisman, featured in the book *Double Dutch: The Word of Image*.

7.20 We Love Your Font, by Max Kisman, 1986.

7.21 Beowolf 1, designed by Erik van Blokland and Just van Rossum in 1990.

appears slightly differently each time it is printed refers the reader back to the human element of the original written word.

The PostScript Type 1 versions of Beowolf are predictable, whereas the PostScript Type 3 version is completely random. The letterforms change shape as the code is generated in the printer. Beowolf fonts are numbered according to the weight and the amount of distortion—the higher the number, the greater the amount of randomness. Generally speaking, random fonts are memory-intensive and take longer to print.

Neville Brody

British designer and art director *Neville Brody* designed condensed, square, and angular fonts that resonated with the influence of the Russian Constructivists. In

Fact Find! It was not until the last quarter of the 1900s that women designers began to merit public recognition for their creative work in design annuals and historical accounts. Search the Internet for examples of font designs by Jill Bell, Carol Twombly, Teri Marie Kahan, Carol Kemp, Genevieve Cerasoli, Holly Goldsmith, and Barbara Lind. Print out examples for class discussion. Is there a visual trend in the works by these type designers? If so, list some of those characteristics below. If not, describe the differences in the works you selected. Be sure to cite your sources!

_____

_____

_____

_____

_____

_____

_____

_____

http://

http://

http://

Industria (1990) and Arcadia (1990), Brody's characters are more than a strict re-creation of a bygone era—they include contemporary variations of counterforms and some unorthodox shapes that provide an appealing quirkiness. Insignia (1990), Blur (1991), Pop (1991), Gothic (1991), and Harlem (1991) are other fonts designed by Brody.

Matthew Carter

Matthew Carter's career began at the Enschede foundry in the Netherlands, where he learned the art of punch cutting, and spans over four decades through different media and technology. His timeless designs are based on practical solutions to specific design problems, taking into consideration the characteristics and constraints of each medium. Carter's typography has seamlessly integrated aesthetics, functionality, and the technology of the time, resulting in typographic forms that encourage the organization of information. Over the years, his work has significantly influenced our visual language.

Carter's Galliard is an old style face with broad, dark serifs and sturdy strokes. Inspired by the work of Robert Granjon (1513–1589), Galliard is a timeless solution that successfully transitioned from photocomposition technology to digital technology. Although the making of Galliard began around 1965, it was not released until 1978 due to a number of technological difficulties. It has been used for corporate publications, the Bible, and popular packaging applications.

Carter's Bell Centennial replaced Bell Gothic as AT&T worked toward a new identity in the mid-1970s. The font had to be legible at very small sizes (6 point) on both the CRT

Fonts by Matthew Carter

Snell Roundhand
Cascade Script
Gando Ronde
  (with H. J. Hunziker)
Olympian
Auriga
Shelley Script
CRT Gothic
Video
Bell Centennial
Galliard
Georgia
New Baskerville
V&A Titling
Bitstream Charter
Charter
Walker
Tahoma
Verdana
Various Greek, Korean, Hebrew,
  and Indian (Devanagari)
  typefaces

7.22 Industria Inline, designed by Neville Brody in 1990.

typesetting monitors as well as on the highly absorbent newsprint pages used to produce telephone directories. Carter's extensive printing and technology experience paid off; he was able to maintain legibility and printability at that small size.

Walker is a typeface Carter developed for the Walker Art Center in Minneapolis, Minnesota. Internationally known for contemporary visual, performing, and media arts, the museum commissioned the typographic design for an updated aesthetic. The museum intended the font to reflect its mission to attract culturally and ethnically diverse audiences through a new visual identity. The resulting design not only supported the identity of the museum, but also played a primary role in the development of sophisticated signage and exhibition and collateral materials.

Digital Font Technology

Font conflicts seem to be the greatest cause of electronic publishing difficulties. The seemingly infinite number of available fonts means that designers can make a distinguishing and exciting visual impact in compositions without imagery. Using poorly

abcdefghijklmnopqrstuvwxyz 1234567890
ABCDEFGHIJKLMNOPQRSTUVWXYZ

7.23 ITC New Baskerville

abcdefghijklmnopqrstuvwxyz 1234567890
ABCDEFGHIJKLMNOPQRSTUVWXYZ

7.24 Georgia

abcdefghijklmnopqrstuvwxyz 1234567890
ABCDEFGHIJKLMNOPQRSTUVWXYZ

7.25 Tahoma

abcdefghijklmnopqrstuvwxyz 1234567890
ABCDEFGHIJKLMNOPQRSTUVWXYZ

7.26 Verdana

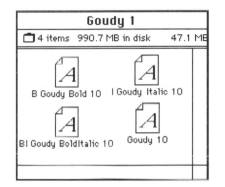

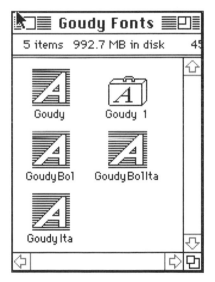

7.27 Goudy font folders in the Macintosh platform are housed within a suitcase, and consist of both printer fonts and screen fonts.

designed fonts or using fonts improperly, however, creates headaches for designers and prepress personnel. The three font formats commonly in use today are PostScript, *TrueType*, and *OpenType*. Of the three formats, PostScript has historically been the preferred format for electronic publishing, while TrueType fonts have been better known for providing great-looking screen rendering for Web design applications. Recent increased support for OpenType makes it a logical choice for reproducing type both on-screen and on paper.

Adobe and the Development of PostScript

In 1984 Adobe Systems was a fledgling company formed by *Chuck Geschke* and *John Warnock*, two engineers from Xerox's Palo Alto Research Center (PARC) Corporation. While at Xerox, the pair had invented a page description language (*PDL*) called Interpress, which was a means of mathematically describing complex forms such as typefaces. When Xerox decided not to commercialize Interpress, Geschke and Warnock left that company and cofounded Adobe Systems. Interpress evolved into PostScript and became available in late 1984, following a similar timeline as the release of the first Apple Macintosh computers. PostScript was device-independent and therefore extremely flexible. A PostScript file could be output to a laser printer at 300 dpi resolution or to an *imagesetter* (an expensive, commercial typesetting device that produces very high-resolution output on paper or film) at a beautifully crisp 2,400 dpi. A manufacturer could license the Adobe PostScript interpreter and build an output device, and anyone could obtain the PostScript specifications and write software that supported it.

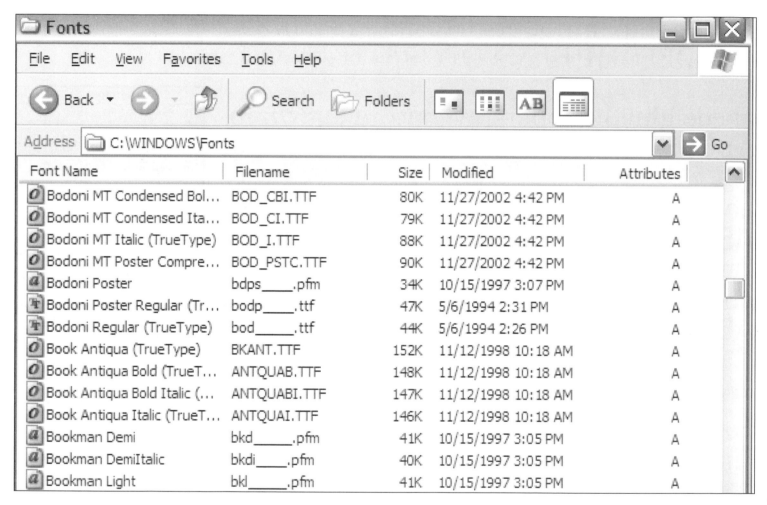

Fonts
File   Edit   View   Favorites   Tools   Help
Back ▾   Search   Folders
Address C:\WINDOWS\Fonts   Go

Font Name	Filename	Size	Modified	Attributes
Bodoni MT Condensed Bol...	BOD_CBI.TTF	80K	11/27/2002 4:42 PM	A
Bodoni MT Condensed Ita...	BOD_CI.TTF	79K	11/27/2002 4:42 PM	A
Bodoni MT Italic (TrueType)	BOD_I.TTF	88K	11/27/2002 4:42 PM	A
Bodoni MT Poster Compre...	BOD_PSTC.TTF	90K	11/27/2002 4:42 PM	A
Bodoni Poster	bdps____.pfm	34K	10/15/1997 3:07 PM	A
Bodoni Poster Regular (Tr...	bodp____.ttf	47K	5/6/1994 2:31 PM	A
Bodoni Regular (TrueType)	bod_____.ttf	44K	5/6/1994 2:26 PM	A
Book Antiqua (TrueType)	BKANT.TTF	152K	11/12/1998 10:18 AM	A
Book Antiqua Bold (TrueT...	ANTQUAB.TTF	148K	11/12/1998 10:18 AM	A
Book Antiqua Bold Italic (...	ANTQUABI.TTF	147K	11/12/1998 10:18 AM	A
Book Antiqua Italic (TrueT...	ANTQUAI.TTF	146K	11/12/1998 10:18 AM	A
Bookman Demi	bkd_____.pfm	41K	10/15/1997 3:05 PM	A
Bookman DemiItalic	bkdi____.pfm	40K	10/15/1997 3:05 PM	A
Bookman Light	bkl_____.pfm	41K	10/15/1997 3:05 PM	A

7.28 The PC Windows operating system houses fonts within one folder under the Windows subdirectory.

Apple computer licensed the PostScript technology for their LaserWriter printers, and the laser printing revolution began. Software manufacturer Aldus developed the first versions of PageMaker, a page-layout program, and the resulting combination of the Apple Macintosh computer, Adobe PostScript font technology, and Aldus' desktop software application proved widely successful. Other manufacturers followed suit, and within a few years, PostScript became the native operating environment and typographic language of most commercial typesetting equipment and many popular graphics programs. PostScript's dominance was undisputed, and Adobe was in complete control of the PostScript technology.

Screen and printer fonts are necessary components for using PostScript fonts in a design project. A screen font gives a computer system the information to display a PostScript font accurately on-screen. Screen fonts are sometimes referred to as *bit-map* (a binary representation in which a bit or set of bits corresponds to some part of an image or font) fonts because of the type of information they contain—72 dpi renderings of some type sizes of a typeface. Monitors typically display images at 72 dpi, so this is the resolution that is displayed.

The printer fonts, or outline fonts as they're sometimes called, have nothing to do with what is on-screen. Printer font files contain outline drawings of every character that is part of a particular font. There are separate printer font files for each font, and these files contain outlines that are vector-based (Sometimes called "object-oriented" graphics; the representation of separate shapes such as lines, polygons, and text, and groups of such objects, as opposed to bit-maps). This means that, like vector graphics produced by a drawing software application such as Adobe Illustrator or Macromedia Freehand (which is also PostScript-based), they can be resized and still remain smooth and clear.

PostScript differs from other PDLs because it treats items on a page as geometric objects. There are three basic versions of PostScript: type 1, type 2, and PostScript type 3. Type 2 PostScript, which was released in 1992, was designed for better support of color printing. PostScript type 3, released in 1997, supports a greater quantity of fonts, has better graphics handling, and includes several features to help speed up PostScript printing.

PostScript Type 1

The outline of each letter contains *hinting* (necessary information for the raster image processor [RIP] for rasterisation of fonts) for use with the relatively coarse pixels of a low-definition 300 dpi printer. This is important in small point sizes, which otherwise would appear heavier on the page. The printer interpreter looks at the character outline, removes any pixels that are more than halfway across the outline boundary, and

adds others that will be less. The hinting information in the PostScript file is also used by Adobe Type Manager (ATM) to provide a smooth display on the screen and to print PostScript fonts on non-PostScript printers. Only one size of QuickDraw screen bit-map is needed.

Multiple Master Font Technology

The *Multiple Master* (MM) format is an extension of the Adobe Type 1 PostScript font format. It allows two design variations to be encoded as opposing ends of a single axis. Thus, any in-between state may be generated by the user on demand. For example, an MM font could have a "weight" axis that has an ultra-light master and an extra-black master, allowing any conceivable variation in between. This is only one possibility; almost any two design extremes could be put on a multiple master, as long as their Bézier control points can be matched up to allow interpolation.

The primary uses to which MM technology has been put are weight (light to bold), width (condensed to extended), and optical size (text to display). A few MM fonts experiment with other forms, such as the existence or type of serifs. All of these adjustments can be done by more primitive means, through the creation of separate fonts, but MM fonts allow typographically aware users to create the precise, typeface desired in a more refined fashion. The release of MM fonts has been slow, since their use requires additional system software in order to generate the variations. Later versions of Adobe PageMaker and QuarkXPress offer Multiple Master support at differing levels, but the lack of consistent systemwide and application-level

Myriad Light SemiCondensed
Myriad Light
Myriad Light SemiExtended

Myriad Condensed
Myriad Semibold Condensed

Myriad Semibold SemiCondensed
Myriad Bold SemiCondensed
Myriad Black SemiCondensed

Myriad Regular
Myriad SemiBold
Myriad Bold
Myriad Black

Myriad SemiExtended
Myriad SemiExtended
Myriad Bold SemiExtended
Myriad Black SemiExtended

7.29 Examples of the first Multiple Master font Myriad, designed by *Carol Twombly* and *Robert Slimbach* in 1992.

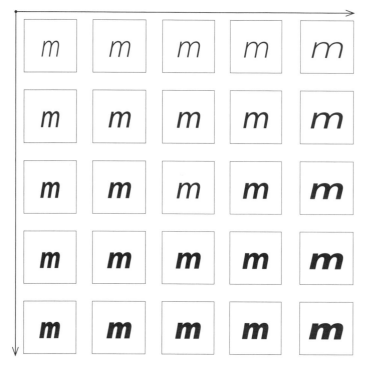

7.30 Multiple Master fonts may be organized as variations on font width (horizontal axis) and font weight (vertical axis).

support for MM fonts has stunted their popularity and availability.

Adobe's first MM font was Myriad—a two-axis font with weight (light to black) on one axis, and width (condensed to expanded) along the other axis. In the case of Myriad, there are four "polar" designs at the "corners" of the design space. The four designs are light condensed, black condensed, light expanded, and black expanded.

PostScript Type 2

As compared to Adobe PostScript Type 1, Type 2 encoding offers smaller sizes and the opportunity for better-quality output and faster performance due to more compact files. This format is used for TrueType fonts.

TrueType

As personal computer operating systems became more sophisticated, both Apple and Microsoft realized that they needed to support scalable font technology at the operating-system level. The combination in the early 1980s of the Apple Macintosh and the Adobe PostScript printing language created a printing and publishing revolution. However, despite the mutual benefits, the alliance was always an uneasy one, and Apple periodically tried to break the PostScript domination of the printed page.

In May, 1991 *TrueType* made its debut on the Macintosh in System 7.0. In 1992, Microsoft introduced TrueType in Windows 3.1. For the first time, through either TrueType or Adobe ATM, Macintosh and Windows users could now see on-screen what the font output would look like at any size. A TrueType font does not require an accompanying bit-mapped screen font, as a PostScript one does, but the greater number of character outline coordinates means that the font files are larger. As time passed, the practical differences began to blur. Support for TrueType was built into many implementations of PostScript Type 2, and is now standard in PostScript Type 3. ATM font rasterizing technology was incorporated into Windows 2000 and Mac OS X.

PostScript Type 3

The Type 3 font format is a way of packaging PostScript descriptions of characters into a font so that the PostScript interpreter can *rasterize* (convert images into bit-map form for display or printing) them. It is easier to create a Type 3 font program than to create the corresponding Type 1 font program. Type 3 font programs have access to the entire PostScript language to do their imaging, including the *image operator* (programming code that creates and returns an image object by flattening or merging the image layers that were provided using the parameters). They can be used for bit-mapped fonts, although that is certainly not a requirement.

The Type 3 font format contains no provisions for "hinting", and as such, Type 3 font programs cannot be of as high a quality at low resolutions as the corresponding Type 1 font program. A separate bit-map must be included for each required size, otherwise the screen display will be jagged. PostScript Type 3 technology is the basis for OpenType fonts.

Both PostScript Type 1 and PostScript Type 3 formats are scalable formats, and both can be run on any PostScript interpreter. However, because of the requirement that a Type 3 font program have a full PostScript interpreter or emulator, Type 3 font programs cannot be understood by Adobe Type Manager (only Type 1 font programs can). Type 3 fonts give as good a definition as Type 1 on 600+ dpi printers and can also use the full range of available gray scales.

OpenType

In 1996, Adobe and Microsoft surprised the entire industry by announcing that they would jointly develop a new font format called *OpenType*. OpenType was intended from the beginning to simplify the use of fonts by being cross-platform compatible—the same font file works on both Macintosh and Windows computers. OpenType is a unification of the Postscript and TrueType font formats. OpenType is believed to be the latest standard in high-quality digital type for both print and Web applications.

No longer confined to the 256-character limit, OpenType fonts offer special features including alternate characters such as swashes, ligatures, old style figures, and small caps. The first OpenType fonts appeared on the market in 2000. Major font foundries such as Adobe, Agfa Monotype, Bitstream, and Linotype now fully support OpenType and are expanding their libraries with OpenType fonts. Adobe has converted the entire Adobe Type Library into OpenType format and offers thousands of OpenType fonts. The ability to use OpenType PostScript fonts requires Mac OS 8.6 or later, or Windows 95 or later. Mac OS X, Windows 2000, and Windows XP all provide native OS-level support for OpenType and do not require the use of ATM or the AdobePS printer driver.

Even though OpenType fonts are marketed as cross-platform compatible, they are offered in two formats: OpenType Postscript (.otf), which is best suited for publishing, and OpenType TrueType (.ttf), which is ideal for Web applications where high screen output quality is critical. Support for OpenType within specific publishing applications is another matter and is the cause of much confusion and consternation. Publishing packages such as QuarkXpress, Adobe InDesign, and Adobe PageMaker, as well as general word-processing programs and font management programs such as Suitcase and Font Reserve, provide varying degrees of support for OpenType. To avoid output difficulties, check your software application and your printer specifications for OpenType compatibility.

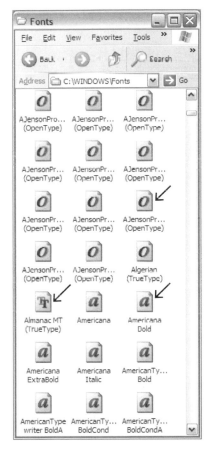

7.31 Different font formats have different icons associated with them. OpenType is indicated by the *o*, TrueType is indicated by the *TT* symbol, and Adobe PostScript fonts are indicated by an *a*. Notice the two different OpenType formats, indicated in parenthesis below the font name.

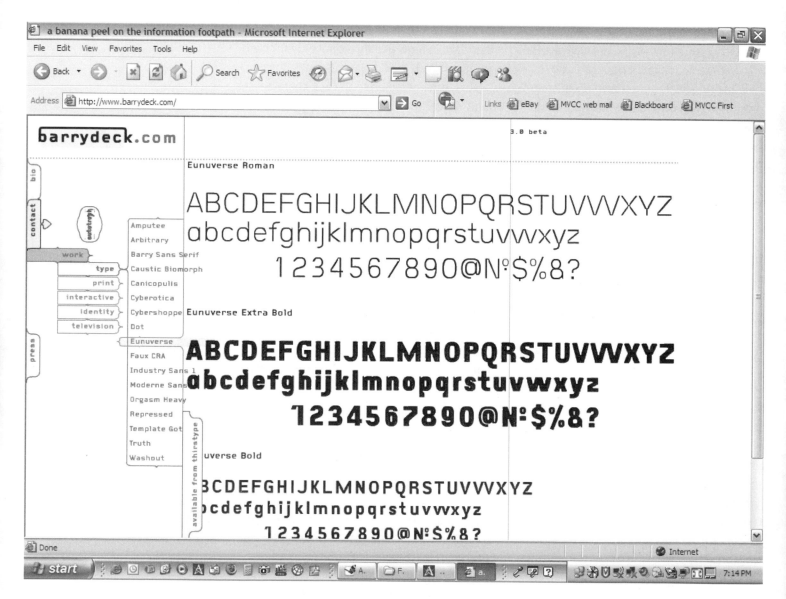

7.32 Font designers such as Barry Deck are
able to provide visual samples and act as their
own retail font distributor, or link to foundries
that distribute their fonts online via the WWW.
This sort of 24/7 access benefits both font
designers and design practitioners.

Chapter Seven Review

Font Availability and Distribution

Since the Renaissance, the culture of typography has been shaped through technology—from hand lettering and calligraphy to mechanical reproduction. Beginning with the introduction of phototypesetting in the 1950s and continuing through the 1980s, the digital revolution expanded font distribution and marketing simultaneously with the progression of the font technology itself. Once only available through large licensed distributors such as Linotype, Agfa Monotype, and International Typeface Corporation, fonts are now readily available from thousands of individual designers and font companies via the World Wide Web. Large corporations such as Adobe and Linotype host extensive sites that allow the download of almost any font twenty-four hours a day, seven days a week. Contemporary type designers, such as Zuzana Licko (Émigré), Just van Rossum and Erik van Blokland (LettError), and *Barry Deck*, have defined their presence in the online world, using current technology to both design and distribute their work globally.

Circle one answer for each definition to indicate the correct key concept term or key player for each. When necessary, determine whether the phrase provided is true or false.

1. Working with the facilities available to him at the time, this designer developed the first issue of *Émigré* magazine in 1983–84.
   a. Max Kisman
   b. Jeffery Keedy
   c. Rudy VanderLans
   d. Barry Deck

2. No longer confined to the 256-character limit, OpenType fonts offer special features including alternate characters such as swashes, ligatures, old style figures, and small caps.
   a. True
   b. False

3. This font format is an extension of the Adobe Type 1 PostScript font format. It allows two design variations to be encoded as opposing ends of a single axis. Thus, any in-between state may be generated by the user on demand.
   a. PostScript Type 2
   b. Multiple Master
   c. PostScript Type 3
   d. OpenType

4. Look closely at the output from a bubble jet printer to see the separate tiny dots that constitute each letter. Each dot on the paper is the result of a tiny pin hitting the inked ribbon against the sheet of paper.
   a. True
   b. False

5. His motivation for the creation of new faces came from the notion that contemporary designs needed contemporary faces to support the visual solution, instead of relying on typefaces and typeface conventions of the past.
   a. Robert Slimbach
   b. Jeffery Keedy
   c. Rudy VanderLans
   d. Barry Deck

6. While at Xerox, Chuck Geschke and John Warnock had invented this, called Interpress, which was a means of mathematically describing complex forms such as typefaces.
   a. DPI
   b. PDL
   c. TTF
   d. PPI

7. No longer confined to the 256-character limit, these fonts offer special features including alternate characters such as swashes, ligatures, old style figures, and small caps.
   a. PostScript Type 1
   b. TrueType
   c. PostScript Type 3
   d. OpenType

8. The PostScript Type 1 versions of Beowolf by Letterror are predictable, whereas the PostScript Type 3 version is completely random. The letterforms change shape as the code is generated in the printer.
   a. True
   b. False

9. Adobe's first Multiple Master font—a two-axis font with weight (light to black) on one axis, and width (condensed to expanded) along the other axis.
   a. Emperor
   b. Verdana
   c. Myriad
   d. Industria Inline

10. These printers draw the image on a metal drum with a fine beam of light. The image carries a positive electrostatic charge and attracts dry toner (a mixture of carbon, metal shavings and plastic dust) to the image area on the drum.
    a. Inkjet printer
    b. Laser printer
    c. Daisy wheel printer
    d. Bubble jet printer

11. This font format contains no provisions for "hinting," and as such, cannot be of as high a quality at low resolutions as the corresponding Type 1 font program.
    a. PostScript Type 3
    b. TrueType
    c. OpenType
    d. PostScrpt Type 2

12. His career began at the Enschede foundry in the Netherlands, where he learned the art of punch cutting, and spans over four decades through different media and technology.
    a. Neville Brody
    b. Eric van Blokland
    c. Rick Valicenti
    d. Matthew Carter

13. According to this designer, "There will never be a font that is as pervasive as Helvetica again, because there are going to be just too many typefaces out there, too many designers wanting to do things that are specific. And what that means is that communication will get a little closer to ideas. Ideas are very specific. Places are specific. Why should every airport sign system on the planet be designed with Helvetica?"
    a. Jeffery Keedy
    b. Carol Twombly
    c. Max Kisman
    d. Matthew Carter

14. Apple Computer licensed the PostScript technology for their ImageWriter printers, and the desktop printing revolution began.
    a. True
    b. False

15. This British designer and art director designed condensed, square, and angular fonts that resonated with the influence of the Russian Constructivists, but they are more than a strict recreation of a bygone era—they include contemporary variations of counterforms and some unorthodox shapes that provide an appealing quirkiness.
    a. Barry Deck
    b. John Warnock
    c. Neville Brody
    d. Charles Bigelow

Character Characteristics

The nomenclature and morphology of type used today evolved primarily from the technological development of writing substrates, writing tools and printing technologies. A complete knowledge of this typographic anatomy provides a foundation for concise and consistent communication with service bureaus, clients, and other designers or art directors. The ability to distinguish one face, font, or family from another is essential to the development of a designer's aesthetic sense. As this typographic lexicon is mastered, the selection of a typeface to communicate meaning and enhance the visual message becomes easier.

8.1 Pieces of type.

Upper- and Lowercase Letterforms

Although writing itself can be traced back to several millennia BCE, to Egyptian hieroglyphics and Sumerian cuneiform inscriptions, modern letterforms have their most immediate heritage in Roman inscriptions from around 50–120 CE, such as the one on the base of Trajan's column in the Roman forum. Early Latin writing was heavily influenced by these chiseled-in-stone letterforms, and over the centuries it evolved into a variety of other shapes, including uncials and the related Carolingian script. It is through this period of the

Key Concepts
base
centered
cicero
concave
convex
descender line
didot
dingbats
display type
em
en
family
flush left
flush right
font
force-justified
italic
justified
kerning
leading
lining figures
lowercase numerals
negative leading
oblique
Old Style figures
phrasing
pica
platform
point
roman
set width
small caps
subscript
superscript
terminal
tied letters
tracking
typeface
uppercase numerals
weight
width

ABCDEFGHIJK
LMNOPQRST
UVWXYZ

8.2 Square capitals.

ABCDEFGHI
JKLMNOPQ
RSTVWXYZ

8.3 Rustic capitals.

ABCDEFGHI
JKLMNOPQ
RSTWXYZ

8.4 Uncials.

abcdefghij
klmnopqr
stuvwxyz

8.5 Half uncials.

abcdefghi
jklmnopq
rstuvwxyz

8.6 Carolingian minuscules.

veramculo meo & Fabu
is praepofuit priapus il
omuuua laua fumptuo

8.7 Humanist script.

nĉto Imperio, finito
me feruo cernuo, &
o. Sopra quelle delit
nia lanacea toga, anc

8.8 Griffo's humanist type.

sixth to tenth centuries that we see the development of the lowercase (minuscule) letter as different from the uppercase (capital or majuscule).

Handwritten articles resembled printed letters until scholars changed the form of writing, using capitals and small letters and writing with more slanted, connecting letters. Gradually writing became more suited to the speed the new writing instruments permitted. The credit for inventing Italian "running hand" or cursive handwriting with its capital and small letters goes to Aldus Mantius of Venice, who departed from the old set forms in 1495. By the end of the sixteenth century, the old Roman capitals and Greek letterforms had been transformed into the twenty-six letters we know today, both upper- and lowercase.

There are stages that can be identified in the evolution from capital or uppercase letters to their lowercase counterparts: square capitals (fourth to eighth centuries), rustic capitals (sixth century), uncials (fifth century), half-uncials (eighth and ninth centuries), Carolingian minuscules (ninth century), black letter (twelfth century), humanist (fifteenth century) and chancery.

The modern Latin alphabet consists of fifty two letters, including upper- and lowercase, plus ten numerals, punctuation marks, and a variety of other symbols such as &, %, and @. Many languages add a variety of accents to the basic letters, and a few also use extra letters and ligatures.

These accented letters can have a number of different functions:

- Modifying the pronunciation of a letter

- Indicating where the stress should fall in a word

- Indicating emphasis in a sentence

8.9 Examples of upper- and lowercase characters, numerals, special characters, and accented characters are shown.

- Indicating pitch or intonation of a word or syllable

- Indicating vowel length

- Distinguishing homophones

Measuring Type

For three hundred years after Gutenberg, no standard system of measurement existed. Type foundries used their own systems of dimension. This meant that type from one house often could not be used successfully by other foundries or printers. Sometimes the name given to a size of type from one foundry was the same as that given to a different type size from another foundry.

Typographic units are different from common measurement units such as centimeters and inches, as the typographic measurements were established before these other systems existed. The first attempt at a standard system of measurement was devised in 1737 by a French type designer, *Pierre Fournier Le Jeune*. His *Table of Proportions* named different sizes of type. Later editions of this book introduced the idea of a family of type, and the use of visually compatible type that could be combined in one printed piece for consistency. He divided one pre-metric French foot into 144 equal parts and called each of these parts a *point*. One of Fournier's

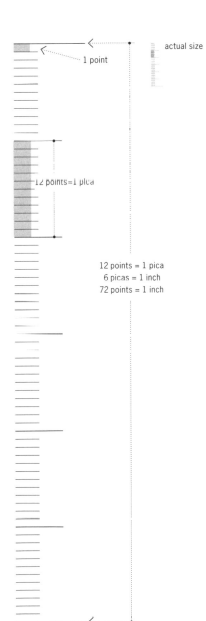

8.10 A pica is divided into 12 points; approximately 6 picas equal 1 inch.

1 point

actual size

12 points=1 pica

12 points = 1 pica
6 picas = 1 inch
72 points = 1 inch

points was equivalent to 0.0137 inch. After Fournier's death, another type designer, *Françoise Ambroise Didot* advocated that Fournier's systems should be based on the legal foot measure of France. The *didot* point equals 0.0148 English inch, and the *cicero*, Didot's equivalent of the pica, measures 0.1776 inch. The Didot system is still used in continental Europe.

Other attempts by English-speaking designers followed the French example, but no consensus of opinion was reached until the late ninteenth century. In 1871, the great fire of Chicago destroyed the premises of Marder, Luse, and Co., one of America's leading type foundries. As a result, a new system was devised to replace the lost matrixes. It was decided to use the *pica* as the main measurement system. This pica was divided into 12 parts called points. In 1898, British type founders adopted the American measurement, and the system became the international standard for English-speaking countries.

Points are used to measure all manner of typographical elements, including the thickness of spaces, the height of type, leading, and the size of rules and borders.

A pica is equivalent to 0.166044 inch, and is divided into twelve points. Although not mathematically precise, 72-point sizes are specified as being equivalent to one inch, and 36-point sizes are half an inch.

The point size measurement of type is determined by the distance from the top of the ascender or the top of the capital letter (whichever is higher) to the bottom of the descender. This area of measurement evolved from the piece of the cast lead type called the *base* or *platform*. Each letterform, regardless of actual size, was cast on the same

Key Players

Françoise Ambroise
 Didot
Pierre Fournier
 Le Jeune

Key Type Anatomy Concepts

apex
arm
ascender
ascender line
baseline
body line
bowl
bracketing
cap height
cap line
counter
cross bar
cross stroke
crotch
descender
descender line
ear
eye
fillet
finial
flag
hairline stroke
leg
ligature
link
loop
serif
shoulder
spine
stem stroke
swash
tail
terminal
vertex
x-height
x-height line

Typographic Measurement Systems Over Time
1 point (Truchet) = 0.188 mm (obsolete today)
1 point (Didot) = 0.3759 mm = 1/72 of a French Royal inch (27.07 mm) = about 1/68 inch
1 point (ATA) = 0.3514598 mm = 0.0138366 inch
1 point (TeX) = 0.3514598035 mm = 1/72.27 inch
1 point (PostScript) = 0.3527777778 mm = 1/72 inch
1 point (l'Imprimérie nationale, IN) = 0.4 mm

8.11 Depending on the specific design of a font, the *ascender line* may be above or below the *cap height line*. Although the point size of a font is estimated by measuring from the tip of the *ascender* to the bottom edge of the *descender*, this is not wholly accurate due to wide variation in the design.

Some of the Languages Written with the Latin Alphabet

Afaan, Afrikaans, Albanian, Aymara, Azeri, Basque, Breton, Catalan, Cheyenne, Cimbrian, Comanche, Cornish, Corsican, Croatian, Czech, Danish, Dutch, English, Esperanto, Estonian, Faroese, Finnish, French, Galician, German, Hausa, Hawaiian, Hungarian, Icelandic, Ido, Indonesian, Interlingua, Irish, Italian, Jèrriais, Kiribati, Kurdish, Latin, Latvian, Lingua Franca Nova, Lithuanian, Lojban, Lombard, Luxembourgish, Malay, Maltese, Manx, Mori, Nahuatl, Navajo, Naxi, Norwegian, Occitan, Oromo, Piedmontese, Polish, Portuguese, Quechua, Romanian, Samoan, Scots, Scottish Gaelic, Slovak, Slovene, Slovio, Spanish, Swahili, Swedish, Tagalog, Tatar, Taiwanese, Turkish, Turkmen, Vietnamese, Volapük, Welsh, Yoruba, Zulu

size base so that all of the letters could fit into the composing stick and neatly align on both the top and bottom.

Type can have different apparent sizes but still be set as the same point size. Different typefaces appear to be larger or smaller than other typefaces of the same point size because of differences in the body height and body width of the individual characters. This dimension is identified by the body line, mean line, or more commonly the *x-height*. Because the legs of the lowercase letter *x* are easy to accurately align with both the mean line (or body line) and the baseline of the set type, it is used as a standard reference.

In order to maintain the same point size, the flexibility in the proportions is in the ascenders and descenders. That is, faces with large x-heights may have shorter ascenders and descenders, while faces with smaller x-heights may have proportionately longer ascenders and descenders.

Distinguishing Font Styles

There are two easily distinguishable styles of font: roman and italic. The *roman* version of a font is based on the perpendicular relationship, or a 90° angle, between the baseline and the strokes of the letterforms. The stress or bias of a roman font is the angle determined by the direction of the thicker stem strokes. Angled or oblique stress in the letterform developed when a flat-tipped pen

or chisel was held at an angle as the letter was drawn or carved. The thickest area of the stroke is the area of maximum stress, and is not always parallel to the main stroke in serif fonts. Many sans serif fonts have stress, although it is less pronounced.

The *italic* version of a font is slanted to the right, often at an angle between 12° and 15°. Although the italic version maintains many visual characteristics of its roman counterpart, it often incorporates additional embellishment such as hooked finials or terminals.

There is a difference between a true italic font and an oblique font. A true italic font is developed by the designer as such, and the letter design refers back to fifteenth-century Italian cursive handwriting. An *oblique* font is a slanted version of its roman counterpart, most commonly seen in sans serif type and in computer-generated variations of popular software applications.

abcdefg
abcdefgh
abcdefg

8.12 The roman version of a font is characterized by the vertical and horizontal strokes. A true italic is a separate but complementary design, while the oblique variation can be generated by altering settings in the computer.

Other font variations are based on the width and weight of the letterforms. The *width* of a character or face is referred to with terms such as *condensed, extended* or *expanded*. The width or set determines how many characters will fit in one line of typeset copy. The same line of type set in a condensed font will take less space than if it were set in a regular or extended font. The variation of width is most common in roman serif fonts and in both roman and italic versions of sans serif fonts. Seldom has a condensed or extended italic font been designed as part of a type family.

The term *weight* refers to the relative blackness of a particular font. The terminology for this changes from one typeface to another, though terms such as *light, book, heavy, bold,* and *extra bold* are often applied. Weight variations appear in both roman and italic serif and sans serif fonts.

Fonts, Faces, and Families

The term *typeface* refers to the upper- and lowercase letters of a given design. The term *font,* however, is a formal term that includes all of the upper- and lowercase letterforms, numerals, symbols, punctuation, accented characters, and small caps that comprise a particular size, style, and weight. The font is a complete selection of all the characters in a specific point size and design, ready for use in a composition or printing project.

A *family* of type includes all of the variations of a type design in all sizes. A family of fonts may include different weight versions of the original face—extra light, light, book, demi, bold, extra bold, heavy, and ultra. A family of fonts may include variations on width as well—condensed,

regular, and extended or expanded. The most comprehensive font family may include sets of fonts based on combinations of weight, width, roman, and italic variations.

Typeface Design

The way that the human eye and brain perceive, process, and interpret visual information provides a sound basis for the foundation of type design. Traditional type designers must explore and understand both aesthetic and technological constraints when designing or altering a font design.

Horizontal and Vertical Proportions of Type

The human brain interprets linear elements positioned horizontally in a composition differently than linear elements positioned vertically. Given the same weight, the vertically oriented line appears thinner than the horizontal line. Since this is a universal phenomenon among human beings, type designers take this into consideration by reducing the thickness of the horizontal strokes of letters, in order to create the appearance of balance and even weight.

Designing Optically Correct Circles, Triangles, and Squares

The basic geometric shapes of circle, triangle, and square are perceived differently by the human eye and brain than one might

Width
Width

8.13 Condensed and regular width variations within the Futura family of type.

Weight
Weight
Weight
Weight
Weight

8.14 Weight variations from Futura Book, Futura, Futura Demi, Futura Bold, and Futura Extra Bold. The heavier the stroke, the more width a letterform occupies.

8.15 Letterform proportions are not always what they seem at first glance. In the letter *T* on the left, Futura Book, the lengths of the two bars are different. The horizontal naturally appears longer to the human eye than the equivalent vertical, so it must be adjusted visually. The *T* on the right is constructed from two equal bars, and the letterform appears top-heavy and unstable.

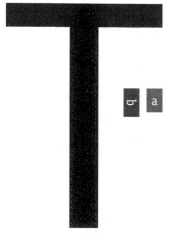

8.16 The weight of the horizontal and vertical strokes often appears equal, but closer inspection reveals the differences used to create visual balance.

8.17 Notice that the curved letterforms extend beyond the baseline and the x-height line to create the illusion of equal height.

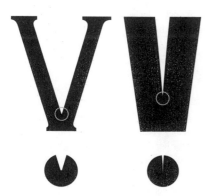

8.18 The intersection of two strokes is often designed to accomodate printing practices. The *vertex* is either opened by spreading the strokes apart, or by extending the white space into the black area so that it does not appear "chunky" or clogged.

think. The four points of an invisible square align along the *baseline* and *cap line* of a font and provide a foundation for uppercase letterforms such as *T, E,* and *L*. The square always appears larger than an equivalent triangle or circle. Because of this, characters that are round, such as an *O* or *C* extend slightly below the baseline and slightly above the cap line. Pointed or triangular letters such as the letter *A* extend slightly above the cap line, and those such as the *V* and *W* extend slightly below the baseline. An understanding of these design concepts affects how the type aligns when it is set or comped correctly, especially in headline type or logotype designs.

Designing Joined Strokes

Where two lines intersect in a letterform, the junction is perceived as heavier than the weights of the two individual strokes. To minimize this effect, which causes the appearance of dark and uneven areas in the character design and subsequent typeset text, the area of the intersection is tapered to adjust the visual amount of the strokes.

When type was produced photographically employing the use of a negative and projected light source, additional considerations made the design of type more complicated. The distortions inherent to the photographic process caused vertices of letters such as *W* and *M* to fill slightly and appear rounded, since it was difficult to accurately project light into the tiny, angled spaces. Those who designed type during the era of phototypesetting learned to extend a thin white line into the areas where the letter strokes joined. This exaggeration of the

8.19 Phototypeset letterforms were extended slightly at the corners in order to appear crisp and clear.

pointed areas allowed the exposed letterform to appear clear, sharp, and pointed, as desired.

The opposite design was required for letterforms with squared-off terminals. When the flash of light exposed a letterform such as an *F* or *E,* the negative required the extension of a small line from the outside corner so that it would appear crisp and sharp instead of rounded.

Type for Use in Different Sizes

Historically, type designers refined three different versions of one font in three slightly different weights to accommodate the variation in point sizes. Four-point type has very different legibility concerns than 36-point headline sizes or 100-point and larger display sizes. To maintain the visual consistency, legibility, and the aesthetic personality of the font, variations on the original design were required. The first was used for 4-point through 14-point sizes, the second was used for 16-point through 36-point sizes, and a third weight was used for sizes larger than 36 points, all of which were separately refined.

8.20 Outline indicates Officina Sans Book set in small caps using the computer software application, while the solid gray area is Officina Sans Book small caps; notice the difference in the stroke weight and letter spacing.

8.21 Outline indicates Minion Pro caption while the solid gray area is Minion Pro Regular. The caption variation is designed for greater legibility at smaller sizes.

8.22 Outline indicates Minion Pro Display while the solid gray area is Minion Pro Regular. Again, notice the difference in stroke weight and in the default letter space designed for use at larger sizes.

8.23 Garmond is a classic face in both the roman and italic styles.

The smallest version often utilized a slightly larger x-height than the version used for larger sizes. This larger x-height improved legibility and allowed for greater detail at the small size. Counterforms, such as the eye on the lowercase *e* were enlarged so that they would not clog or close up on the press. The medium size, ranging from 12 to 36 points, most resembled the original design, since the counters did not require enlarging and the height of the lowercase letterforms could hold the subtle details of the original design without enlarging the x-height. The third variation of the font design requires a great deal of attention in the refinement process, including subtleties in the bracketing of the serifs, weights of the strokes, and optical adjustments to ensure crisp corners and stroke intersections in sizes for wall posters as well as billboards.

Design of an Italic Font

Italic fonts are not merely slanted variations of a roman counterpart. Careful inspection of a true italic font reveals a new translation of the letterforms that incorporates the visual resemblance to a roman variation with the addition of hand-lettered qualities. Many lowercase letters, such as the letter *f*, incorporate a descender while others include swashes and other decorative details not seen in a roman version of the same family. Teardrop terminals are popular in italic fonts, as are the use of Old Style figures.

Other common variations in the letterforms include changes in the shape of the loop on the lowercase *g*, the lowercase *a* appearing as a single bowl form, the lowercase *k* incorporating a loop to replace the arm, lowercase letters *m*, *l*, *i*, and *n* with hooked finials, and lowercase *v*, *x*, *w*, and *y* with teardrop terminals.

Designing Font Variations of Weight and Proportion

The subtleties of each character are reviewed and refined at both lighter and heavier weight variations. Different stroke weights require that the characters be drawn in slightly different proportions than the original to maintain visual harmony and balance, as well as the visual aesthetic relating the fonts to a family. Commonly the counterforms in bolder weights are opened up to maintain legibility in smaller sizes.

At times designers explore the option of adding a stroke (outline) to a letterform to

AaBbCc

AaBbCcc

AaBbCc

AaBbCc

8.24 The top two examples compare Garamond (outline) to Garamond bold, while the bottom two examples compare Garamond semibold (outline) to Garamond bold.

8.25 Artificially changing a standard font design to condensed or extended by stretching and squeezing the letter ruins the stroke weight and proportions of the form as designed. Select a true condensed or extended font instead.

create a bold version when one is not readily available. This is not recommended because it changes the designed proportions of the letterforms, altering the legibility (especially at smaller sizes) and covering up the subtle details in the apices, vertices, and corners of the form. The added stroke often destroys the proportions of the serifs and the bracketing as well, resulting in an undesirable aesthetic.

Just as the regular or book proportions of a font are designed with specific considerations, so are condensed and extended fonts. The condensed and extended variations are changed structurally to accommodate the exaggerated proportions of height to width, to maintain the visual personality of the type family. Designers should be discouraged from stretching type on the computer to create the illusion of a condensed or extended font, as this destroys the subtle design of the typeface.

When a font is mechanically condensed on the computer, the letters are squished, which destroys the optical adjustments and subtlety in the design. The horizontal strokes of the letterforms, originally designed to be thinner than vertical strokes, become thicker, while the vertical strokes become thinner. The bracketing of serifs as well as the length of the serifs are pushed and pulled, just as are the strokes. When a font is mechanically extended on the computer, the thin horizontal strokes become much thinner than originally designed and the weight of the vertical strokes is increased, causing an awkward, uneven appearance. The visual harmony and balance are destroyed.

8.26 At top, the original letterform. In the middle is visual comparison between the original letterform with the bold style of the letterform. At bottom, notice the change in the proportions of the letterform between a true bold variation of the font (outline) as compared to a normal setting with a stroke applied.

$$H_2O$$
$$H_2O$$

$$4^2 = 16$$
$$4^2 = 16$$

8.27 (Left) A visual comparison of a computer-generated subscript (top) and a true subscript font (bottom); notice the diference in weight and proportion between them.

8.28 (Right) A visual comparison of a computer generated superscript (top) and a true superscript font (bottom).

8.29 The crossbar or cross stroke is a horizontal portion of the letterform that connects two main strokes, or extends from a main stroke of the letter.

Lining Figures, Small Caps, Superscript, Subscript, and Dingbats

Uppercase numerals, also called *lining figures*, are numbers within a particular font that match the cap height of the uppercase letters. In addition to the comparable height, these numbers are kerned to match the width of the uppercase letters. *Old Style figures* or *lowercase numerals* are set to the x-height of the font, with ascenders and descenders extending above and below. Lowercase numerals are more widely available in serif fonts than in sans serif fonts.

Small caps are uppercase letterforms set to the dimension of the x-height of any given font. True small caps may be found as part of an expert font set; most popular software applications include a command that allows the generation of a small cap lookalike using the standard uppercase letterform of the selected font. Artificially generated small caps are not of the same weight and proportion of a true small cap.

A *superscript* is a small character written near the cap line of a particular font. Superscripts are used to denote exponents in a scientific or mathematical equation, or the numerators in fractions. A *subscript* is a small character set near the baseline. They are often used to denote molecular combinations of chemical substances or to represent denominators in fraction sets.

Dingbats are sets of decorative swashes, special characters, and symbols. Although some of these symbols are offered in a font set, most dingbat sets are sold as a separate font based on a particular theme or subject area.

Type Anatomy

Just as the human body consists of numerous individually identifiable components, so are letterforms. The primary anatomy of a letterform includes the strokes and cross strokes, the terminals and serifs (or lack thereof), shoulders, arms and legs, links and tails, and so on. Many of these parts are named according to their similarities to their counterparts on the bodies of humans and animals.

Stroke

The weight of the font depends on the type and weight of the stroke. The *hairline stroke* refers to the lighter weight, and the *stem stroke* refers to the heavier weight or main stroke of the letterform. In most sans serif fonts there is a single stroke weight that determines the unique appearance of the

8.30 The link is a portion of the main stroke that connects the two main parts of the lowercase *g*.

8.31 The arms are horizontal or angled strokes that extend in an upward direction at 90° or less from the main stroke.

8.32 The legs are horizontal or angled strokes that extend from the main stroke in a downward direction at 90° or less as seen on the *R* and *K*. The tail is the angled stroke that extends from the *Q*.

8.33 The shoulder is the curvilinear transitional portion of the stroke that connects a somewhat horizontal stroke and a vertical stroke.

particular font, so all strokes that compose the letterform are light or all are heavy.

The *cross bar* is a horizontal stroke that connects two other strokes in a character, as seen in the letters *A* and *H*. Both ends of the crossbar meet and are joined by a stem or hairline stroke. The *cross stroke* is a horizontal stroke that intersects one of the main strokes of a character, but remains free on one end as seen in the *f*, or both ends, as seen in the *t*. Both crossbars and cross strokes are the same width as the hairline stroke of the font, and can be curved, angled, or stepped, depending on the design of the type.

Link

Link is the term for the stroke that connects the bowl and the loop on a lowercase *g*.

Arms and Tails

Arm and *leg* refer to the parts of a letter that extend out from the main stroke that are free on the terminal end. Strokes that extend sideways straight out at a 90° angle or extend upward at less than a 90° angle are arms, as seen on the letters *E* and *Y*. A stroke that extends downward at less than 90° is a *leg*, as seen on the letters *R* and *K*. The capital letter *K* has both an arm and a leg, while the capital letter *Q* has a *tail*.

The Spine and Shoulder

Spine is a term that refers to the double curve found in the main stroke of the uppercase and lowercase *S*. Often the thickest part of the letterform, the term is easy to remember because of its reference to the backbone in human anatomy.

The *shoulder* is the transition area in lowercase letters between the curved part of a

8.34 The spine is the portion of the curved stroke on a letter *S* that reverses from one direction to the opposite direction.

stroke and the vertical part of the same stroke. Shoulders are found on the letters *f*, *h*, *j*, *m*, *n*, and *u*. The weight of this area of the stroke is carefully refined to create a subtle change, and the shape of the shoulder determines the round, oval, or squared-off appearance of the font.

Serifs, Brackets, Terminals, and Finials

A *serif* is the slight extension at the beginning and end of the letter stroke, drawn at a right angle or obliquely across the arm, stem, or tail of a letter. Serifs are thought to have been retained from the days when type was cut into stone with a chisel, although this is debated. Serifs are categorized according to their physical shape. Again, there is great variation in the names and variation of serif shapes among historical examples.

8.35 *Bracketing* (also called the *fillet*). This transitional curve between the stroke and the serif on a letterform is a smooth addition based on the tangents of each of those elements.

Bracketing refers to the curved connecting area between the stroke of the letter and the serif. Bracketing is not essential, but rather is included or left out based on the aesthetic decision of the type designer. The bracket may have differing degrees of weight or thickness. The inclusion or absence of a bracketed serif is one clue to the identification of a face or font. The less common term *fillet* is synonymous with the term *bracket*.

The *terminal* is the ending of a stroke with some sort of self-contained treatment instead of a serif or finial. Author J. Ben Lieberman identifies straight, sheared, acute, grave, convex, concave, flared, hook, tapered, and pointed terminals. The variety of labeling and identification is dependent upon the historical source.

The *finial* is a non-serif ending to the stroke of a letter—for example, a ball, swash, ear, spur, or hook.

Counters and Bowls

The *bowl* is a round stroke that encloses a space and the *counter* is the enclosed space. If the bowl touches a stem stroke, it creates a closed counter as often seen in the letters *a*, *b*, *d*, *g*, *o*, *p*, and *q*. If the bowl does not touch the stem stroke, an open counter

8.36 Beaked serif. The serif terminal of the arm of a letter in the shape of a bird's beak, occurring in such capital letters as *E*, *F*, *K*, and *L*. Sometimes referred to as a half-serif, the beak may extend in two directions from the arm of the letter but only appears at the end of straight strokes.

8.37 Barbed serif. The beaked serif is referred to as a barb when it appears at the end of a curved stroke, as seen on the capital letters *C* and *S*. Like their beaked counterparts, barbs sometimes extend in both directions from the curved stroke.

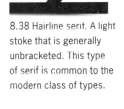

8.38 Hairline serif. A light stroke that is generally unbracketed. This type of serif is common to the modern class of types.

8.39 Spur serif. A serif in certain types of Dutch original (Janson) and on the crossbar of the lowercase *f* or *t* as seen in Goudy Old Style and Erasmus Mediæval.

8.40 Hooked serif. Common in lowercase italic fonts, in such letters as *m*, *n*, and *u*.

8.41 Wedge serif. A wedge-shaped serif seen in fonts such as the Latin Series (Latin Bold, Wide Latin, and Chisel) and in many of the Dutch-English Old Styles on lowercase letters such as *b*, *d*, *h*, and *i*.

8.42 Slab serif. A monotone serif of equal weight as the stem is considered a feature of Egyptian or square serif fonts.

8.43 The lowercase *r* is an interesting form for studying and comparing finials. This is Bodoni, with a ball.

8.44 The lowercase Caslon italic *r* is an example of a teardrop shape. This portion of the letter *r* is sometimes called an ear.

8.45 The *bowl* is the round stroke that encloses the counter.

8.46 The *counter* (sometimes called a counterform) is the internal enclosed or semienclosed space within a letterform.

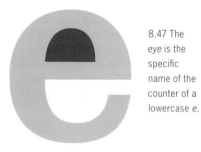

8.47 The *eye* is the specific name of the counter of a lowercase *e*.

8.48 The *swash* and the *flag* are decorative extensions of an arm or stroke that bring attention to a particular character within its typeset context.

results. An open counter may be recognized in many versions of the letters *a*, *c*, *h*, *v*, and *u* regardless of the curved or angled stroke enclosing the space. The term *loop* is the name used to refer to the bowl created in the descender of the lowercase *g* in some fonts.

The term *eye* refers to the counter on the lowercase *e* regardless of whether it is open or closed. The eye is given important consideration in the design and the selection of type for specific applications, since it is often the first area to fill in, or clog, with ink on press.

Apices, Crotches, and Vertices

The *apex* of a letter is formed when two angled strokes come together. The apex usually extends slightly past the cap height so that it appears to be the same height as the other letters. There are pointed, rounded, sheared, hollowed, and flat apices.

Crotch refers to the interior space created by the juncture of two angled strokes as in the *K*, *M*, *N*, *W*, *X*, and *Z*. An acute crotch is based on an angle less than 90°, while an obtuse crotch is created when the strokes meet at an angle greater than 90°.

The *vertex* of a letter is the inverse of the apex; it is the juncture of two downward-slanting strokes. The vertex variations include flat, sheared, pointed, and rounded versions.

Swashes and Flags

A *swash* is a decorative extension of an arm or tail that accents characters, particularly in script fonts such as Bickham Script (designed by Richard Lipton), Arcana Script (Gabriel Martínez Meave), and Balmoral (Martin Wait). Swashes can be twisted or

8.49 Flat apex

8.50 Pointed apex

8.51 Extended apex

8.52 Hollowed apex

8.53 Rounded apex

Took

8.54 A visual comparison of the word took as set in default mode (gray outline), and as tightly kerned by hand (solid black).

Kerning Pairs: Combinations of Capital and Lowercase Letters

Ac Ad Ae Ag Ao Ap Aq At Au
Av Aw Ay
Bb Bi Bk Bl Br Bu By B. B,
Ca Cr C. C,
Da D. D,
Eu Ev
Fa Fe Fi Fo Fr Ft Fu Fy F. F, F; F:
Gu
Hc Ho Hu Hy
Ic Id Iq Io It
Ja Je Jo Ju J. J,
Ke Ko Ku
Lu Ly
Ma Mc Md Me Mo Nu Na Ne Ni
No Nu N. N,
Oa Ob Oh Ok Ol O. O,
Pa Pe Po
Rd Re Ro Rt Ru
Si Sp Su S. S,
Ta Tc Te Ti To Tr Ts Tu Tw Ty
T. T, T; T:
Ua Ug Um Un Up Us U. U,
Va Ve Vi Vo Vr Vu V. V, V; V:
Wd Wi Wm Wr Wt Wu Wy W.
W, W; W:
Xa Xe Xo Xu Xy
Yd Ye Yi Yp Yu Yv Y. Y, Y; Y:

curled and are considered elegant additions. Some decorative fonts offer alternate swash characters, which may be used to draw attention to the beginning of an article or story. Families such as Adobe Garamond Pro (Robert Slimbach) include alternate Latin capitals with swashes.

A *flag* is a small swashlike stroke that appears in a calligraphic font such as black letter. These small flourishes add decoration to the end of the horizontal stokes.

Horizontal Spacing and Measurement

There are two dimensions used to measure horizontal spaces and dashes in typesetting: the em and the en. An *em* is the square of a type size. In 8-point type this dimension equals 8 points. This term is not synonymous with pica; only the em in a 12-point type size measures 12 points. The name for this measurement may stem from the fact that the letter *M* in the Roman alphabet did have a width that filled the full width of a square based on the height. This is not true with condensed fonts, extended fonts, and many contemporary type designs.

In traditional typesetting, an *em quad* is a space the size of an em, used to indent the first line of a paragraph. An *em dash* is used to join two phrases together into one sentence instead of using a conjunction, to insert information that could have been included in parentheses, or to add a final thought or emphasis at the end of a sentence. Occasionally an em dash is used as a replacement for the colon when introducing a list as part of the text.

An *en* measurement is equivalent to one half of the em, and again is named after the space commonly occupied by the width of a

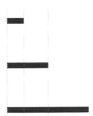

8.55 A visual comparison of the hyphen, en or nut dash, and an em or mutt dash.

Kerning Pairs: Capital Letter Combinations

A' AC AG AO AQ AT AU AV AW AY
BA BE BL BP BR BU BV BW BY
CA CO CR
DA DD DE DI DL DM DN DO DP DR
DU DV DW DY
EC EO
FA FC FG FO F. F,
GE GO GR GU
HO
IC IG IO
JA JO
KO
L' LC LT LV LW LY LG LO LU
M MG MO
NC NG NO
OA OB OD OE OF OH OI OK OL
OM ON OP OR OT OU OV OW OX
OY
PA PE PL PO PP PU PY P. P, P; P:
QU
RC RG RY RT RU RV RW RY
SI SM ST SU
TA TC TO
UA UC UG UO US
VA VC VG VO VS
WA WC WG WO
YA YC YO YS
ZO

Kerning Pairs: Lowercase Letter Combinations

ac ad ae ag ap af at au av
aw ay ap
bl br bu by b. b,
ca ch ck
da dc de dg do dt du dv dw
dy d. d,
ea ei el em en ep er et eu ev
ew ey e. e,
fa fe ff fi fl fo f. f,
ga ge gh gl go gg g. g,
hc hd he hg ho hp ht hu hv hw hy
ic id ie ig io ip it iu iv
ja je jo ju j. j,
ka kc kd ke kg ko
la lc ld le lf lg lo lp lq lu lv lw ly
ma mc md me mg mn mo mp
mt mu mv my
nc nd ne ng no np nt nu nv nw ny
ob of oh oj ok ol om on op or ou
ov ow ox oy o. o,
pa ph pi pl pp pu p. p,
qu t.
ra rd re rg rk rl rm rn ro rq rr
rt rv ry r. r,
sh st su s. s,
td ta te to t. t,
ua uc ud ue ug uo up uq ut
uv uw uy
va vb vc vd ve vg vo vv vy v. v,
wa wx wd we wg wh wo w. w,
xa xe xo
y. y, ya yc yd ye yo

capital letter *N*. An *en dash* is most often used to indicate a range of numbers, such as "pages 17–44." It is also used in dates (December 2002–March 2003), to connect words in a few cases (the London–Paris train), with open compounds (post–World War II), and dates to indicate that something continues (Jane Doe [1950–]). An *en quad* is the white space that measures the same as an en. This white space is also sometimes referred to as a *nut*. This term was used in noisy print shops so that it would not be confused with the em when spoken.

The term *set width* refers to the total width of a letter and its surrounding space. Letter spacing allows the designer to optically space letters in a word or phrase so that the visual texture changes and a different line spacing results. Too much letter space will cause the word or phrase to become illegible. Negative letter space can be used to more effectively communicate a message, but once again, too much causes the word or phrase to become unreadable. In contemporary software applications, letter spacing is referred to as *tracking*.

Tightening the space between letters in a word is called *kerning*. The term comes from the German word "kern" meaning "corner." When a typesetter had to kern lead type, both letters had to be filed down manually, or "cornered," to remove part of the cast lead platform. The letters were then fit into the composing stick and checked for proper letter spacing.

There are certain combinations of letters that should always be kerned. As a general rule, tighter kerning makes it easier for the brain to recognize the letter groups as words, which results in faster and easier reading. The

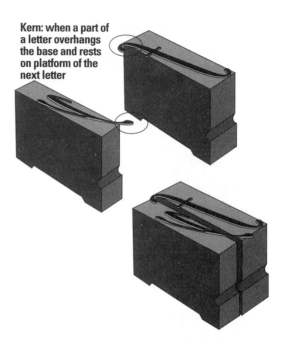

Kern: when a part of a letter overhangs the base and rests on platform of the next letter

8.56 The term *kerning* originates from the cornering, or removal, of the lead base from behind the typeform so that the letters can overlap onto another letter's base for less space between each.

refinement of the letter spacing within words affects the density of the type on the page. The designer or typesetter strives to create an even tone of gray; if one area becomes significantly darker or lighter, then the blocks of text are set too tightly or too loosely. The general rule for spacing is the tight-not-touching (TNT) approach.

The same combination of characters that require kerning in the uppercase version of a font may not be the same as the lowercase combinations, since the shapes are not similar. Type designers know that some character combinations automatically require kerning—for example, any letter set next to an uppercase *F*, *W*, *T*, *V*, or *Y*. It is undesirable to allow letters to actually touch, since this often creates a dark area that attracts too

8.57 Originally ligature forms were cast on one piece of lead (called the body) together with the proper amount of letter space. This avoided the time-consuming practice of trying to hand-kern the delicate letters in the soft lead substrate.

much visual attention, especially in the case of two rounded characters.

Most software applications intended for publishing include preset kerning tables that automatically correct letter spacing whenever kerning pairs appear in the body text of an article. One of these contemporary applications may have two hundred to five hundred sets of kerned characters for each font, depending on the character forms in both uppercase and lowercase, the fastidiousness of the type designer, and the software manufacturer.

The refinement that is now available using popular publishing software is more precise than was possible with traditional hand-set type. Unfortunately, this has created a couple of generations of computer users who do not always understand the details of correct typography well enough to correctly refine the appearance of type on the page. The craft of typesetting has been watered down and the standards lowered with the proliferation of poor-quality typography set by untrained typists. Mastering correct kerning and tracking techniques results in more legible and attractive type solutions.

Ligatures

A ligature is when two or more characters are joined on a single *body* (one piece of lead) of type. The development of ligatures was based on the need to maintain legibility and readability in the closely spaced, hand-lettered manuscripts; ligatures were referred to as *tied letters* in the manuscript era. Although the need to maintain the ligature sequence in some combinations remains, the use of most pairs has been eliminated.

Common ligatures include *f* combinations originally intended to protect the kern of the letter from contact with an ascending character in a line below, as well as the *st* and *ct* combinations. All type that is connected, such as most scripts, is said to be ligated.

Word Space

In addition to the space between letters within each word, the designer must pay

Aliceilaughedisoimuchiat this,ithatishewhaditoiruniback intoithewoodiforifearioftheir hearingiher;iandiwhenishenext peepedioutitheiFish-Footman wasigone,ianditheiothcriwas sittingionitheigroundinearithe door,istaringistupidlyiupiinto theisky.

8.58 A typical practice is to imagine a lowercase *i* between each word in a sentence, phrase, or paragraph for greatest readability. Today's software applications calculate optical word spacing based on the beginning and ending letters of each word.

attention to the space between words, called *word spacing*. The general rule of thumb for word spacing is to visualize the width of a lowercase *i* in the space between each word. This means that the word spacing changes with the use of different fonts and different sizes of fonts.

Spacing type correctly for optimal legibility is one of the most important tasks. Poorly spaced type renders even the best design unreadable, defeating the purpose of the communication. Correct spacing involves aesthetic training and practice, in addition to an acquired intuitive sense that is best developed over time by critiquing and refining your designs. Evaluation of the type you see in your environment leads to a refined typographic sense more quickly.

Vertical Spacing

Leading or *line spacing* refers to the vertical space between stacked lines of type. This term originated with hand-set lead type when a compositor would place thin strips of lead between the lines of type to open the space. This extra space makes it easier for readers to maintain the horizontal movement and flow of their eyes as they read across a page of type, then jump effortlessly to the next line below.

Today, typeset copy is measured from the baseline of one line to the baseline of the next line above or below. This convention is used because it is consistent. Remember that the body height or x-height, the ascender length, and the descender length may vary from font to font and would not provide consistent results.

Some computer software provides the choice between traditional measurement from baseline to baseline and digital measurement

8.59 Wood type with strips of lead used to alter the vertical space between hand-set compositions.

Alice went timidly up to the door, and knocked.

8.60 The vertical space between lines of text is determined by measuring from one baseline to the subsequent baseline.

Alice went timidly up to the door, and knocked.
There's no sort of use in knocking, said the Footman, "and that for two reasons. First, because I'm on the same side of the door as you are; secondly, because they're making such a noise inside, no one could possibly hear you. And certainly there was a most extraordinary noise going on within—a constant howling and sneezing, and every now and then a great crash, as if a dish or kettle had been broken to pieces.

8.61 Garamond 10/6 (negative 4 points of vertical space per line).

Alice went timidly up to the door, and knocked.

"There's no sort of use in knocking," said the Footman, "and that for two reasons. First, because I'm on the same side of the door as you are; secondly, because they're making such a noise inside, no one could possibly hear you." And certainly there was a most extraordinary noise going on within—a constant howling and sneezing, and every now and then a great crash, as if a dish or kettle had been broken to pieces.

8.62 Garamond 10/10.

Alice went timidly up to the door, and knocked.

"There's no sort of use in knocking," said the Footman, "and that for two reasons. First, because I'm on the same side of the door as you are; secondly, because they're making such a noise inside, no one could possibly hear you." And certainly there was a most extraordinary noise going on within—a constant howling and sneezing, and every now and then a great crash, as if a dish or kettle had been broken to pieces.

8.63 Garamond 10/14.

from the center of one line of text to the center of the following line of text. Choosing the digital measurement for leading will cause the paragraph to appear more vertically centered in the type box than choosing the traditional measurement.

In type specification, the first number refers to the point size of the font, while the second number refers to the size of the leading. Ten-point type with two points of vertical space or leading added would be written as 10/12.

Type Alignment

Flush Left

Flush left refers to the alignment of type along an invisible vertical line or margin on the left side of a composition. The term implies that the type is allowed to remain misaligned, or ragged, on the right side. Some people believe that the flush left/ragged right composition is more inviting to the reader, that its somewhat casual appearance encourages reader involvement. Unless there is excessive white space between words, readers don't seem to care, or even to notice, whether they are reading justified or ragged right columns of text. Numerous studies, under a variety of conditions, continue to prove this.

The biggest advantage of unjustified typesetting is the ability to control word spacing. You can have tight, even word spacing in any length line. Not only does consistently tight word spacing look better, it's also an important aspect of efficient and legible typography. Tight word spaces speed up the reading process and allow the reader to absorb thoughts and phrases rather than individual words, which helps to maintain high levels of comprehension.

The disadvantage of unjustified typesetting is that it can be difficult to

Flush left begins at the left margin and ends at a comfortable distance from the right margin.

Centered begins in the middle of the column and ends at a word break near the edges of the column on both the right and left.

Flush right begins at right margin and ends at a word break near the left margin.

Justified aligns the words along the left and right columns by adjusting the word space to accommodate the alignment.

8.64 Explanation of the alignment of type according to standard settings.

"Please, then," said Alice, "how am I to get in?"

"There might be some sense in your knocking," the Footman went on without attending to her, "if we had the door between us. For instance, if you were INSIDE, you might knock, and I could let you out, you know." He was looking up into the sky all the time he was speaking, and this Alice thought decidedly uncivil. "But perhaps he can't help it," she said to herself; "his eyes are so VERY nearly at the top of his head. But at any rate he might answer questions.—How am I to get in?" she repeated, aloud.

"Please, then," said Alice, "how am I to get in?"

"There might be some sense in your knocking," the Footman went on without attending to her, "if we had the door between us. For instance, if you were INSIDE, you might knock, and I could let you out, you know." He was looking up into the sky all the time he was speaking, and this Alice thought decidedly uncivil. "But perhaps he can't help it," she said to herself; "his eyes are so VERY nearly at the top of his head. But at any rate he might answer questions.—How am I to get in?" she repeated, aloud.

"Please, then," said Alice, "how am I to get in?"

"There might be some sense in your knocking," the Footman went on without attending to her, "if we had the door between us. For instance, if you were INSIDE, you might knock, and I could let you out, you know." He was looking up into the sky all the time he was speaking, and this Alice thought decidedly uncivil. "But perhaps he can't help it," she said to herself; "his eyes are so VERY nearly at the top of his head. But at any rate he might answer questions.—How am I to get in?" she repeated, aloud.

8.65 Examples of flush left, centered, and flush right specifications within a column, set in Garamond 10/14.

8.66 Examples of justifed
type specifications within
a column, set in Garamond
10/14. Software applications
provide the option of
justification beginning and
ending the paragraphs with
flush left, centered, flush
right, and force-justified.

"Please, then," said Alice, "how am I to get in?"

"There might be some sense in your knocking," the Footman went on without attending to her, "if we had the door between us. For instance, if you were INSIDE, you might knock, and I could let you out, you know." He was looking up into the sky all the time he was speaking, and this Alice thought decidedly uncivil. "But perhaps he can't help it," she said to herself; "his eyes are so VERY nearly at the top of his head. But at any rate he might answer questions.—How am I to get in?" she repeated, aloud.

"Please, then," said Alice, "how am I to get in?"

"There might be some sense in your knocking," the Footman went on without attending to her, "if we had the door between us. For instance, if you were INSIDE, you might knock, and I could let you out, you know.' He was looking up into the sky all the time he was speaking, and this Alice thought decidedly uncivil. "But perhaps he can't help it," she said to herself; "his eyes are so VERY nearly at the top of his head. But at any rate he might answer questions.—How am I to get in?" she repeated, aloud.

"Please, then," said Alice, "how am I to get in?"

"There might be some sense in your knocking," the Footman went on without attending to her, "if we had the door between us. For instance, if you were INSIDE, you might knock, and I could let you out, you know." He was looking up into the sky all the time he was speaking, and this Alice thought decidedly uncivil. "But perhaps he can't help it,' she said to herself; "his eyes are so VERY nearly at the top of his head. But at any rate he might answer questions.—How am I to get in?" she repeated, aloud.

8.67 *Convex* means curving or bulging outward, while *concave* is just the opposite.

It was, no doubt: only Alice did not like to be told so.

"It's really dreadful," she muttered to herself. "the way all the creatures argue. It's enough to drive one crazy!"

The Footman seemed to think this a good opportunity for repeating his remark. with variations. "I shall sit here," he said, "on and off, for days and days."

"But what am I to do?" said Alice.

"Anything you like," said the Footman, and began whistling.

It was, no doubt: only Alice did not like to be told so.

"It's really dreadful," she muttered to herself. "the way all the creatures argue. It's enough to drive one crazy!"

The Footman seemed to think this a good opportunity for repeating his remark, with variations. "I shall sit here," he said, "on and off, for days and days."

"But what am I to do?" said Alice.

"Anything you like," said the Footman, and began whistling.

produce it as high-quality typography. Very long lines followed by very short ones can cause awkward shapes that are not inviting to the eye. Ideally, unjustified composition should appear to be optically justified. If the right edge of a column describes a shape, it should be *convex* (curving outward)rather than *concave* (curving inward).

In most typesetting situations, the machine logic determines where a line ends. The problem is that logical decisions are not necessarily attractive aesthetic decisions. The person creating the graphic communication needs to carefully review the first set of production proofs and rebreak lines of copy to correct an unattractive set of line endings.

If at all possible, copy should be rewritten to facilitate this process. Unfortunately, the real world rarely provides the graphic communicator the luxury of manually rebreaking lines, let alone the power to request that sentences be rewritten.

Flush Right

Flush right type aligns against the right side of the composition or column width. Just as with flush left text, the designer is able to control the word space for greater legibility. The difficulty is with reading large blocks of text set ragged left; as a reader's eyes scan from the beginning of a line on the left toward the right it is difficult to ascertain the beginning of the next line

of type if it does not align under the first line or above the third. This causes breaks in the reader's mental flow and understanding of the information, slowing down the absorption of the message. Flush right/ragged left type should be used only for small areas of type used to accent a composition—perhaps as a few lines of an address and telephone number.

Justified

Justified type aligns on both the left and the right sides of the column. The major problem with setting justified copy is the risk of creating excessive word spacing inside the column. Many times the computer is presented with remaining space

"Please,   then,"   said
Alice, "how am I to get in?"

"There might be some sense in your
knocking,' the Footman went on
without attending to her, "if we had
the door between us. For instance, if
you were INSIDE, you might knock,
and I could let you out, you know."
He was looking up into the sky all
the time he was speaking, and this
Alice thought decidedly uncivil. "But
perhaps he can't help it," she said to
herself; "his eyes are so VERY nearly
at the top of his head. But at any rate
he might answer questions.—How
am I to get in?" she repeated, aloud.

"Please,iiiiiiiiiiiiiithen,"iiiiiiiiiiiiiisaid
Alice,iiii"howiiiamiiiiIiiiitoiiigetiiiin?"

"Thereiimightibeisomeisenseiniyour
knocking,"iii theii Footmaniiiwentiion
withoutiattendingitoiher, i"ifiweihad
theidooribetweenius.iForiinstance,iif
youiwereiINSIDE,iyouimightiknock,
andiIicouldiletiyouiout,iyouiknow."
Heiwasilookingiupiintoitheiskyiall
theitimeiheiwasispeaking,iandithis
Aliceithoughtidecidedlyiuncivil.i"But
perhapsiheican'tihelpiit,'isheisaidito
herself;i"hisieyesiareisoiVERYinearly
atitheitopiofihisihead.iButiatianyirate
heiimightiianswceriiquestions.—How
am iIitoigetiin?"iisheirepeated,ialoud.

8.68 Examples of *force-justified* specifications within a column, set in Garamond 10/14. Normally, a single lowercase *i* is the correct amount of space between words.

"Please, then," said Alice, "how am I to get in?"

on the line, but not enough to set
another word or a hyphenation
of it. As a result, the word shifts
down to next line, causing the
previous line to be spaced out
with too much space. Short line
measures are especially difficult
to set justified. A look at many
newspaper columns will show you
excessive word space and "rivers"
of white running through the
copy. The longer the line measure,
the less often this problem occurs.

Most desktop publishing
software applications provide
the option of justification by
beginning and ending the
paragraphs flush right, flush
left, centered, or *force-justified*.
The latter is most likely to cause

uncomfortable white spaces and
be the most difficult to read.

Centered

Centered type aligns along a
middle axis in the composition.
Just as with flush right or flush
left text, the designer is able to
control the word space for greater
legibility. However, just as with
flush right paragraphs, it is
difficult for the reader to find the
beginning of the next line of text
and continue reading. Centered
alignment is most effectively
used with small paragraphs, as
in a formal invitation; with short
lists as in a menu; or with large
headlines and mastheads as in
a poster, brochure, magazine, or
newsletter.

Spacing Type and Punctuation in Display Sizes

Headline copy often is the
most important typographic
element in the composition, as it
quickly draws the attention of the
potential reader by summarizing
the content of the ad, brochure,
magazine article, or newspaper
article. If the reader does not
become engaged by the headline,
chances are that the rest of the
copy will go unread.

Display type is type that is
14 points or larger. Because
headlines are set in display-sized
fonts, they can be crowded,
angled, turned upside down,
mirrored, tinted, and decorated
so long as a significant amount of
legibility is maintained. Because
of the larger size of headline type,

8.69 Although the term *display type* often refers to anything above 14 points in size, we often assume something much larger for a headline. The contrast in size establishes the compositional importance or hierarchy that tells the viewer where to look first.

"ARE you
to get in at
all?" said the
Footman.
"That's the first
question, you
know."

"ARE you
to get in at
all?" said the
Footman.
"That's the first
question, you
know."

8.70 Align the vertical edge of the text along the letterforms, and kick the punctuation or quotation marks out to the left for a stronger visual solution. The lines that appear indented due to quotation marks may lend a ragged, unprofessional finish to large text.

"ARE you to get in
at all?" said the
Footman.
"That's the first
question, you know."

8.71 Some fonts have strong vertical strokes and lend themselves to the visual impact needed for display.

special consideration must be paid to the letter spacing, word spacing, leading or line spacing, and phrasing.

Usually headlines are kerned and tracked to a greater extent than body copy. This forces the letters to optically group into stronger visual statements, making them easier to read. Word spacing is also tighter in headlines for greater legibility and visual impact, so the spacing within words and that between words must complement each other. For example, if the word spacing is tight but the letter spacing is normal, then it would be difficult for readers to discern which letters belong to which words in a sentence; both the letter spacing and the word spacing must be changed proportionally to maintain the meaning of the message.

Word spacing is affected by the first and last letters of adjacent words. Because each character is a slightly different shape and proportion, it is necessary to use aesthetic judgment when altering the word spacing in a headline. Although the rule of using the area of a lowercase i works for spacing body copy, this cannot be applied universally in larger fonts since certain characters will have a tendency to appear larger or smaller depending on the font and the surrounding white space.

If one word ends with an l and the next word begins with an i then consider tightening the space between the words to a comfortable optical dimension. If one word ends in a rounded character such as an e and the next word begins with a rounded character such as d then the word space may be slightly larger to accommodate the protruding bowls.

Much experimentation and exploration are required to arrive at the perfect solution. In

the past, letter and word spacing was handled by the typesetter, with the direction of the designer. Now that many designers set their own type in their layouts, they must learn to adjust the subtle differences on their own. The letter spacing and word spacing will vary depending on whether the text is all uppercase, small caps, or mixed upper- and lowercase letters. There are no absolute rules to assist the designer in correctly setting all possible combinations. This is complicated even further by the technology; some are fooled by the assumption that type on the computer screen appears exactly as it will on the printout. Screen fonts are only a close approximation of the printer fonts, so testing is required in the printing process as well.

Line spacing for headlines varies from that used for line spacing body copy. Remember that opening or enlarging the leading between lines of body copy often makes the text more readable, since the viewer's eye can more easily discern the separate lines. When setting headline type solid (the same size type set over the same size leading), often the words appear too far apart and are not grouped comfortably for easy reading and understanding; the words appear to float apart and the reader must assemble them in their mind. This is due to the vertical space automatically allowed for the ascenders and descenders.

Negative leading is the practice of setting type in a smaller vertical space. As an example, 48-point type with 6 additional points of leading would be indicated as 48/54; type set solid would be 48/48; type set with -12 points (negative) leading would be 48/36. Negative leading means that the space of the descenders share the space of the ascenders in

Spacing display text according to the default setting results in distracting spaces and less visual impact.

Spacing display text visually has pleasing results with greater visual impact.

8.72 Combinations of upper- and lowercase type in larger sizes require the designer to pay attention to line space and letter space. The auto-leading setting or solid setting creates a weaker visual statment (top) than the example that has been more tightly spaced (bottom).

SPACING DISPLAY TEXT ACCORDING TO THE DEFAULT SETTING RESULTS IN DISTRACTING SPACES.

SPACING DISPLAY TEXT VISUALLY HAS PLEASING RESULTS WITH GREATER VISUAL IMPACT.

8.73 Using all caps in larger sizes requires the designer to pay attention to line space and letter space. The auto-leading setting or solid setting creates a weaker visual statment (top) than the example that has been more tightly spaced (bottom). The addition of an initial or drop cap also directs the viewer's eye to an important starting position.

It was, no doubt: only Alice did not like to be told so.

It was, no doubt: only Alice did not like to be told so

IT WAS, NO DOUBT: ONLY ALICE DID NOT L

IT WAS, NO DOUBT: ONLY ALICE DID NOT L

8.74 Mixed upper- and lowercase letterforms are easier to read than all caps. The ascenders and the descenders provide more information for the eye and brain to discern the forms and translate the meaning of the message.

It was, no doubt: only Alice did not like to be told so.

"It's really dreadful," she muttered to herself, "the way all the creatures argue. It's enough to drive one crazy!"

IT WAS, NO DOUBT: ONLY ALICE DID NOT LIKE TO BE TOLD SO.

"IT'S REALLY DREADFUL," SHE MUTTERED TO HERSELF, "THE WAY ALL THE CREATURES ARGUE. IT'S ENOUGH TO DRIVE ONE CRAZY!"

IT WAS, NO DOUBT: ONLY ALICE DID NOT LIKE TO BE TOLD SO.

"IT'S REALLY DREADFUL," SHE MUTTERED TO HERSELF, "THE WAY ALL THE CREATURES ARGUE. IT'S ENOUGH TO DRIVE ONE CRAZY!"

8.75 Upper- and lowercase letters are easier to read than all caps, even when there is slightly more leading to open the vertical spacing.

the line below, so the words must be carefully integrated to prevent overlapping.

Phrasing refers to the breaks in the lines of type according to the intended meaning. The phrases should make sense, so the goal is to group descriptive adjectives with the appropriate noun or pronoun; try to keep modifiers on the same line with the word they modify. Poorly phrased headlines may be difficult to read and may change the meaning of the message.

Line breaks must be in logical places, so change the font to support the correct phrasing by trying a condensed version within the same family, or switch from a round serif font to a regular or condensed sans serif font to make the correct fit. Read the phrases out loud with a slight pause at the end of each line to determine if the phrasing is logical and sensible.

Uppercase versus Mixed Upper- and Lowercase Type

Historical sources have proven that a combination of upper- and lowercase letters is more legible or easier to read than the same word or sentence set in all caps. This is due to the fact that uppercase letters are all the same height and a similar width, whereas lowercase

letters vary greatly in shape with their ascenders and descenders. This rule holds true for both body copy and headline copy, with estimates of reading speed being up to 15 percent slower for all caps. The reader is forced to identify the individual letterforms before assembling them into words, whereas mixed upper- and lowercase type allows the brain to recognize entire words at once. This does not mean that all caps should never be used; rather, they work best in limited applications for special emphasis and visual excitement.

Optical Character Alignment in Headlines

The capital letters *A, C, G, J, O, S, T, V, W, X,* and *Y* represent special alignment challenges due to their inherent rounded or angled shapes. If these characters are set flush left, relying on the mechanical settings of the software application, more often than not they appear out of line. Commonly these characters must be set to the left of the alignment of the other letters above and below to make them appear in the correct position.

Different software applications have different ways of allowing optical alignment. One method is to use a soft return (Shift + Enter) at the end of each line of type. Add a

Chapter Eight Review

space at the beginning of each line of type, then highlight the space and change the tracking of the space as necessary to optically align the characters. A negative number shifts the line of type to the left, and a positive number shifts the line of type to the right.

Optical alignment applies to punctuation in headlines. A common example is the inclusion of opening quotes at the beginning of a headline, which causes the type to appear indented from the subsequent lines below. To alleviate the visually irregular margin, use hanging punctuation to vertically align the rest of the lines of type. The quotes become less of a distraction.

Punctuation marks are set in a slightly smaller point size in headlines. This allows the type to remain dominant in the written message, with the punctuation remaining secondary in the visual hierarchy. When the size of quotation marks or apostrophes is reduced in size, the baseline must be shifted to match the baseline or cap line of the original headline copy.

Circle one answer for each definition to indicate the correct key concept term or key player, or key type anatomy concept for each. When necessary, determine whether the phrase provided is true or false.

1. Accented letters can have a number of different functions:
    a. Indicating pitch or intonation of a word or syllable
    b. Indicating vowel length
    c. Distinguishing homophones
    d. All of the above

2. This term refers to the vertical space between stacked lines of type.
    a. Word spacing
    b. Letter spacing
    c. Leading
    d. Set width

3. This dimension is identified by the body line, mean line, or more commonly the _____.
    a. Cap height line
    b. Ascender line
    c. x-height line
    d. Descender line

4. It is the juncture of two downward-slanting strokes. The variations include flat, sheared, pointed, and rounded versions.
    a. Apex
    b. Crotch
    c. Link
    d. Vertex

5. Strokes that extend sideways straight out at a 90° angle or extend upward at less than a 90° angle are _____ as seen on the letters _E_ and _Y_.
    a. Arms
    b. Crossbars
    c. Legs
    d. Tails

6.   The first attempt at a standard system of measurement was devised in 1737 by a French type designer, Pierre
Fournier Le Jeune in his Table of Proportions.
   a.   True
   b.   False

7.   Each letterform, regardless of actual size, was cast on
the same size base so that all of the letters could fit into
the composing stick and neatly align on both the top and
bottom. This base is also called the
   a.   Set width
   b.   Platform
   c.   Font
   d.   Terminal

8.   This is formed when two angled strokes come together.
It usually extends slightly past the cap height so that it
appears to be the same height as the other letters.
   a.   Spine
   b.   Vertex
   c.   Crotch
   d.   Apex

9.   Historical sources have proven that a combination of
upper- and lowercase letters is more legible or easier to
read than the same word or sentence set in all caps.
   a.   True
   b.   False

10.   Tightening the space between letters in a word is
called _____ .
   a.   Tracking
   b.   Kerning
   c.   Letter spacing
   d.   Weighting

11.   Points are used to measure all manner of typographical elements, including the thickness of spaces, the height
of type, leading, and the size of rules and borders.
   a.   True
   b.   False

12.   This is a decorative extension of an arm or tail that
accents characters, particularly in script fonts
   a.   Swash
   b.   Finial
   c.   Terminal
   d.   Apex

13.   This is a formal term that includes all of the upper- and
lowercase letterforms, numerals, symbols, punctuation,
accented characters, and small caps that comprise a
particular size, style, and weight.
   a.   Typeface
   b.   Family
   c.   Font
   d.   Face

14.   The major problem with setting copy this way is the
risk of creating excessive word spacing inside the column.
   a.   Justified
   b.   Flush right
   c.   Centered
   d.   Flush left

15.   Italic fonts are merely slanted variations of a roman
counterpart.
   a.   True
   b.   False

16.   This is a small swashlike stroke that appears in a calligraphic font such as black letter.
   a.   Spine
   b.   Swash
   c.   Flag
   d.   Finial

17.   A pica is equivalent to 0.166044 inch, and is divided
into twelve _____.
   a.   Didots
   b.   Points
   c.   ATAs
   d.   Truchets

18. If the right edge of a column describes a shape, it should be concave (curving outward) rather than convex (curving inward).
    a. True
    b. False

19. This refers to the counter on the lowercase *e* regardless of whether it is open or closed. It is given important consideration in the design and the selection of type for specific applications, since it is often the first area to fill in, or clog, with ink on press.
    a. Apex
    b. Ligature
    c. Eye
    d. Tail

20. This dimension is the square of a type size.
    a. Didot
    b. Em
    c. En quad
    d. Pica

21. The term _____ refers to the upper- and lowercase letters of a given design.
    a. Font
    b. Family
    c. Roman
    d. Typeface

22. The term _____ refers to the relative blackness of a particular font. The terminology for this changes from one typeface to another, though terms such as light, book, heavy, bold, and extra bold are often applied.
    a. Width
    b. Extended
    c. Set width
    d. Weight

23. Link is the term for the stroke that connects the bowl and the loop on a lowercase italic *d*.
    a. True
    b. False

24. This is a round stroke that encloses a space on a letterform. If it touches a stem stroke it creates a closed counter.
    a. Bowl
    b. Shoulder
    c. Eye
    d. Link

25. This is the ending of a stroke with some sort of self-contained treatment. Types of this are categorized as straight, sheared, acute, grave, convex, concave, flared, hook, tapered, and pointed.
    a. Apex
    b. Serif
    c. Descender
    d. Finial

26. The designer must pay attention to the space between words, called _____ .
    a. Tracking
    b. Kerning
    c. Word spacing
    d. Leading

27. These characters are often used to denote molecular combinations of chemical substances or to represent denominators in fractions.
    a. Superscript
    b. Small caps
    c. Display text
    d. Subscript

28. A pica is equivalent to 0.166044 inch, and is divided into twenty points.
    a. True
    b. False

29. Accented letters can have a number of different functions:
    a. Modifying the pronunciation of a letter
    b. Indicating where the stress should fall in a word
    c. Indicating emphasis in a sentence
    d. All of the above

30. Because the legs of the lowercase letter *k* are easy to accurately align with both the mean line (or body line) and the baseline of the set type, it is used as a standard reference.
   a. True
   b. False

31. Strokes that extend sideways straight out at a 90° angle or extend downward at less than a 90° angle are _____as seen on the letters *E* and *Y*.
   a. Arms
   b. Crossbars
   c. Legs
   d. Tails

32. This term refers to the heavier weight or main stroke of the letterform.
   a. Hairline stroke
   b. Crossbar
   c. Stem stroke
   d. Counterform

33. The less common term *fillet* is synonymous with this term.
   a. Finial
   b. Terminal
   c. Bracket
   d. Spine

34. The term set width refers to the total width of a letter and its surrounding space.
   a. True
   b. False

35. This is most often used to indicate a range of numbers, such as "pages 17–44." It is also used in dates (December 2002–March 2003), to connect words in a few cases (the London–Paris train), with open compounds (post–World War II), and dates to indicate that something continues (Jane Doe [1950–])
   a. Em quad
   b. En dash
   c. En quad
   d. Em dash

36. The same combination of characters that require kerning in the uppercase version of a font are the same as the lowercase combinations, since the shapes are similar.
   a. True
   b. False

37. This term refers to the alignment of type along an invisible vertical line or margin on the left side of a composition.
   a. Justified
   b. Flush right
   c. Centered
   d. Flush left

38. Align the vertical edge of the large text along the letterforms, and kick the punctuation or quotation marks out to the left for a stronger visual solution. The lines that appear indented due to quotation marks may lend a ragged, unprofessional finish to large text.
   a. True
   b. False

39. This means that the space of the descenders share the space of the ascenders in the line below, so the words must be carefully integrated to prevent overlapping.
   a. Phrasing
   b. Negative leading
   c. Set solid
   d. Kerning

40. This font is a slanted version of its roman counterpart, most commonly seen in sans serif type and in computer-generated variations of popular software applications.
   a. Italic
   b. Justified
   c. Superscript
   d. Oblique

41. Dingbats are sets of decorative swashes, special characters, and symbols.
   a. True
   b. False

Type Identification and Classification

As the printed word became more prevalent, around the sixteenth century, printers began to develop different styles of type to meet the demands posed by the variety of topics and authors to be published. Originally an integral part of the printing business, type founding evolved into a separate entity when the printers became too busy to cast their own type.

The commercial expansion of goods and services during the Industrial Revolution resulted in wide distribution of manufactured products, and the need for a greater variety of different type styles soon followed. Manufacturers searched for unique identities within the marketplace. Consequently, there was tremendous growth in type foundry work in the nineteenth century. The classic type designs remain for traditional print applications, and new and exotic fonts appeared.

9.1 With the expansion of production of goods and services, the design of fonts multiplied exponentially. Eventually typographers, graphic artists, and designers looked for a means to categorize and organize them into logical groups.

American Type Founders

The American Type Founders (ATF) Company was founded in 1892 and had twenty-six branch plants in cities including New York, Boston, Philadelphia, Havana, Cuba, and Mexico City. But Jersey City was its headquarters, and 300 Communipaw Avenue was the company's central foundry plant. ATF was the dominant American manufacturer of metal type for several decades, from its creation in 1892 via the merger of twenty-three type foundries. Foundries that were incorporated into ATF include Barnhart Brothers & Spindler (1911), Binny & Ronaldson (1892), Boston Type Foundry (1892), Bruce Type Foundry (1901), Central Type Foundry (1893), Farmer, Little & Co. (1892), and Inland Type Foundry (1912).

Faced with competition from composing machines such as the Linotype, profits began to decline in the 1920s, until a bankruptcy threatened in 1933. However, the company continued to manufacture metal type for the next half century.

By 1983, the company had shrunk to six employees, and in 1993 it closed its doors, auctioning off the remaining type and equipment. The printing division became ATF Davidson, and for a while Kingsley/ATF made an attempt to sell digital fonts under the ATF brand.

Early classification systems were too general, employing divisions of roman and italic fonts. As the styles of type proliferated, more complex systems were required to identify the general categories. By the turn of the century, two publications offered type form classifications: *John Southward's Practical Printing* (1898) and *Theodore L. DeVinne's The Practice of Typography: Plain Printing Types* (1900). French typographer *Francis Thibaudeau* devised a system for the historical material of the Peignot foundry (1911–12); *Henry Lewis Bullen* (ATF librarian) developed a similar analytical system for the library of the *American Type Founders*.

In the early twentieth century, academic endeavors to consolidate different strands of historical research and to support the interest in revival of early type styles for contemporary use resulted in revised historical overviews using morphological evolution as the primary organizing structure. D. B. Updike's *Printing Types* (1922), Stanley Morison's *On Type Designs Past and Present* (1926), and Alfred Forbes Johnson's *Type Designs* (1934) are among the influential writings of the time.

Since World War II, the graphic arts and related professions have seen the need to communicate with one another on a global scale. To meet the needs for standardization, many classification systems evolved, but unfortunately there has been little consensus on the adoption of a specific classification system. This may be due in part to the classification demands of different professions: for example, the bibliographer uses one set of characteristics for font recognition, which vary greatly from the characteristics used by the art director in a design firm. The *Vox system* (1954),

The *ATypI system* (1961), the *British Standards system* (1965), and the *DIN system* (1964, 1998) vary in complexity and definition. Even when some degree of consensus is found, there is room for interpretation. Interestingly enough, the ATypI, British Standards, and DIN systems were all influenced by the Vox system, but the resultant systems show diversity in its interpretation.

A simplified system of classification was created by *Alexander Lawson*, who provided a simplified method for type recognition and categorization. The categories within Lawson's system include black letter, Old Style (Venetian, Aldine-French, and Dutch-English), transitional, modern, square serif, sans serif, script-cursive, and display-decorative.

Black Letter

Black letter evolved from handwritten manuscripts from fifteenth-century Germany. Black letter was called "Gothic" by the Europeans, but this was confusing when nineteenth-century Americans named early sans serif fonts "Gothic" as well. The category of black letter fonts includes minor categories of Old English, Textura (Cloister Black and Goudy Text), Gothic-Antique, Rotunda or Round Gothic, and Bastarda (also known as Bartarde). Black letter is used occasionally in the United States, most often in the printing of official-looking certificates, diplomas, liturgical materials, and newspaper mastheads. Goudy Text (Frederic W. Goudy), Linotext (Morris Fuller Benton), Wilhelm Klingspor Gotisch (Rudolph Koch), Agincourt (David Quay), and Clairvaux (Herbert Maring) are readily available digital black letter fonts.

abcdefghijklmnopqrstuvwxyz
ABCDEFGHIJKLMNOPQRSTUVWXYZ

9.2 Olde World Bold.

abcdefghijklmnopqrstuvwxyz
ABCDEFGHIJKLMNOPQRSTUVWXYZ

9.3 Blackletter 686.

abcdefghijklmnopqrstuvwxyz
ABCDEFGHIJKLMNOPQRSTUVWXYZ

9.4 Goudy Old Style Regular.

abcdefghijklmnopqrstuvwxyz
ABCDEFGHIJKLMNOPQRSTUVWXYZ

9.5 Centaur Regular.

9.6 The Old Style faces include heavily bracketed, cupped serifs. Their presence on the page appears heavy but comfortable.

Old Style

The *Old Style* fonts are heavily bracketed, causing the serifs to appear as though they have grown out of the stem strokes. The rounded, cuplike serifs are comfortable and reassuring; the great mass of the letterforms reinforces the sense of stability and strength. Old Style faces are easy to discern because they tend to appear heavy on the printed page. Originally, these faces were designed during the period when all type punches were hand-cut, then cast in lead, so sufficient mass for hand manipulation was essential. The type had to be strong enough to withstand the pressure of the printing press without breaking or chipping, so the greatly bracketed serifs came as much from the practical need for longevity under adverse conditions as they did from aesthetic preference.

Venetian Old Style

Venice emerged as the principal center of printing activity between 1465 CE and 1500 CE because of the city's importance in world trade at the time, and Venetian font styles became well known throughout Europe. Modern cuttings of the fonts developed during this period of time are now called *Venetian Old Style*. There is minimal contrast between the thick and thin strokes of the letterform. The crossbar of the lowercase *e* is slanted. Sometimes, most commonly on the

Old Style Identifying Characteristics

- Minimal variation of thick and thin strokes
- Small, coarse serifs, often with slightly concave bases
- Small x-heights

In the round strokes, the stress is diagonal, or oblique, as their designs mimic the angle at which scribes held their pens.

The tops of lowercase ascenders often exceed the height of the capital characters.

1234567890

The numerals vary in size and have ascenders and descenders. Many contemporary versions of Old Style typefaces do not retain the Old Style figures but, in catering to contemporary taste, use lining, or capital-height figures.

letters *N* and *M*, there are slab serifs extending across the top intersections of the strokes.

In the 1890s William Morris revived the use of Venetian Old Style characteristics in his font Golden Type, used by Kelmscott Press. Although it was adapted from a version of type originally designed and cut by Nicolas Jenson, it appeared heavier. At the turn of the century a bookbinder, T. J. Cobden-Sanderson, established his own press and created an adaptation of Nicolas Jenson's type that he called Dove. This was lighter in weight than Golden Type and was popular for almost twenty years, influencing the revival of Venetian Old Style type.

Modern variations within the Venetian Old Style category include Cloister Old Style (Morris Benton), Centaur (Bruce Rogers), ITC Berkeley, Forum, Kennerley, Goudy Old Style, Deepdene, and Californian (Frederic W. Goudy).

Aldine-French Old Style

Francesco Griffo, one of the most skillful Italian punch cutters of the century, produced type for the infamous publisher and printer, Aldus Mantius. Aldine books were sought after because of their authoritative erudition. Griffo's type designs were copied throughout Europe, particularly in France.

Griffo improved on Venetian Old Style type by emphasizing contrast in the strokes, dropping slab serifs, and straightening the horizontal crossbar of the lowercase letter *e*. During this period in history, British typographers utilized Old Style faces.

Lawson grouped French Old Style faces with Aldine Old Style faces into a single category, *Aldine-French Old Style*, because of their obvious

influence. French adaptations by leading craftsmen such as the Estienne family, Geofroy Tory, Claude Garamond, and Robert Granjon brought the golden age of typography to France. Popular styles of this period include Palatino (Hermann Zapf), Bembo (Stanley Morison), variations on Garamond (such as ITC Garamond, Type Founders Garamond, Linotype Garmond No. 3, Monotype American Garamond, Monotype Garamont, and Intertype Garamond), Granjon (George W. Jones), and a variation of Garamond named Sabon (Jan Tschichold).

Dutch-English Old Style

Holland became an important trade center during the seventeenth century. With the expanded distribution of goods and services, Dutch type styles spread throughout the region. Though considered less refined than the French Old Style type, they were accepted in England. Since England was not important in the type founding trade at this point in time, that country depended on the Dutch type until the 1720s, when William Caslon established a foundry in London.

Colonial America relied on English printing supplies until the late 1700s. This meant that the type cast by Caslon's foundry and its competitors were the only available faces for early American presses. Some historians argue that the Caslon style type should be considered the first true transitional style, since the serifs appear straight-edged and the weights of the strokes contrast greatly. Still, the majority of the lowercase letters show a distinct evolution from the earlier Dutch Old Style versions. In addition to multiple variations on Caslon, another popular version of a *Dutch-English Old Style* face includes Janson

Transitional Style Identifying Characteristics

- A greater contrast between thick and thin strokes.
- Wider, gracefully bracketed serifs with flat bases.

- Larger x-height
- Vertical stress in rounded strokes

- The height of capitals more closely matches that of ascenders
- Numerals are cap height and consistent in size

123Ab

(Miklós Kis, but mistakenly credited to Anton Janson).

Transitional

As implied by the name, *transitional* refers to fonts whose form bridges the gap between the organic Old Style faces and the mechanical-looking structure of the modern fonts. The term denotes a structural style introduced in the late eighteenth century by John Baskerville that followed most Dutch-English Old Style characteristics. Exceptions to these letterform designs were due to the contrast made by a vertically-held broad pen, resulting in vertically stressed letterforms and horizontally balanced curved strokes. Transitional-period faces can be further subdivided categories:

- *Direct line*—significant contrast between thick and thin serifs and thin, more flattened serifs. Typeface examples are Baskerville, Bauer Classic, Bell, Bulmer, Caslon 540, and Scotch Roman.
- *Modified*—less contrast and thicker serifs (also referred to as "new transitional"). Examples include Caslon Antique, Cheltenham, Maximus, and Melior.

Baskerville's technical innovations allowed him to alter the appearance of his type: he had his press built solidly and used a brass plate for a hard impression; he passed the sheets of paper through heated copper cylinders to smooth the printing paper; he maintained wide margins and open leading, introducing a greater amount of white space into the composition than was typical at the time; and he formulated new inks that provided a deeper, richer black.

The transitional category appears to contain the largest number of types, and often is a style that is more difficult to classify. Transitional faces appear more precisely drawn than Old Style faces, with gently thinned hairline stems and tapered, pointed serifs. In many variations the lowercase letter width is slightly extended, creating wide, full counterforms. The italic transitional faces combine elegance, balance, and intricate detail.

Examples of transitional faces, in addition to variations on Baskerville, include faces such as Caledonia (William A. Dwiggins), Bell (Richard Austin), ITC Slimbach (Robert Slimbach), Times Roman and Times New Roman (Stanley

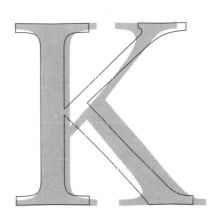

9.7 Baskerville, a transitional style is in gray as compared to Melior in outline, which is also categorized as a transitional-style face. Can you describe the similarities that make these different faces fit into the same category?

AaBbCc
AaBbCc

9.8 Baskerville (top) is considered a direct line transitional face, whereas Melior (bottom) is a modified transitional face.

Modern Style Identifying Characteristics

- Extreme contrast between thick and thin strokes
- Hairline serifs without bracketing

- Small x-height
- Square serif
- Vertical stress in rounded strokes

Morison, Starling Burgess, Victor Lardent), and Century (Lynn Boyd Benton and Theodore L. DeVinne).

Modern Style Typefaces

Within a few decades, the wide acceptance of the transitional types helped to inspire a new sense of typographic style in Europe, especially France and Italy. Typographers, inspired by Baskerville, further rejected the classic Old Style tradition of pen-inspired letters and continued to refine the notion of the perfect letterform. While perhaps not the most readable of styles, *modern* typefaces are the most visually distinct. While transitional designs were based heavily on technological advances, modern designs represent perhaps the first movement toward visual

expression in type. By the end of the century, the popularity of the modern style was established and the printing industry was about to enter a period of unprecedented change.

Françoise Ambroise Didot in France and Giambattista Bodoni in Italy are most well known for type designs that established the modern style. Modern fonts employ a vertical stress and unbracketed serifs. The serifs are clean and crisp, with right angles. Bodoni appears architectural and conservative in appearance with its upright structure. The italic version incorporates beautiful teardrop terminals and sweeping curved strokes. Other examples of modern fonts include ITC Fenice (Aldo Novarese), Linotype Didot (Adrian Frutiger), Caledonia and Electra (William A. Dwiggins), Keppler (Robert Slimbach), and Else (Robert Norton).

Square or Slab Serif

For three and a half centuries, typography and printing had been concerned exclusively with the publishing of books. By the early 1800s, the impact of the Industrial Revolution propelled the printing industry in a new direction. The advent of industrial manufacturing created a need to promote the sale of ready-made goods, and as the technology of industry became more complex, manufacturers required a more literate workforce. In addressing these needs, the commercial or job printer emerged. New print media—magazines and newspapers—proliferated and had great appeal to the masses. Print advertising emerged as an effective way to sell products to large numbers of people.

The impact of technology on printing, paper manufacturing, and mechanical typesetting created a demand for a new style in type design that

Identifying Square Serif or Slab Serif Fonts

- Minimal variation of thick and thin strokes
- Heavy serifs with squared-off ends

- Large x-heights
- Vertical stress in rounded strokes
- Little or no bracketing

was compatible with mass production. The advent of print journalism and advertising demanded types that were not only readable but also bold and distinctive enough to catch the reader's attention.

The square serif typefaces that became popular during this era are often referred to as *slab serif* or Egyptian typefaces. The typical square serif style is often monoline, appearing to be constructed of strokes of the same weight. The letters are based on simple geometric designs; often rounded characters are perfect circles. The x-height is somewhat large in most examples, since a large proportion of the body is consumed by the thick, heavy serifs. Their sturdy structure makes the headline dominant in a composition but detracts from legibility when set in small sizes; the relatively large serifs act as hurdles in the body copy, interrupting smooth reading.

This period is generally considered a step backward in the evolution of type design. The trend toward a more refined aesthetic that began with transitional forms and continued with

modern types was overshadowed by the dictates of mass production and new print media. The design of new types was influenced more by commercial popularity than aesthetic or technological development. This notion of popular appeal is illustrated by the fact that many of these typefaces were given exotic Egyptian-sounding names to exploit the public fascination with the discoveries of ancient Egyptian artifacts.

ITC Officina Serif (Erik Spiekermann, Ole Schäfer), Candida (Jakob Erbar), Egyptienne F, Serifa, Glypha, West (Adrian Frutiger), Lubalin Graph (Herb Lubalin), Memphis (Rudolph Wolf), Stone Informal (Sumner Stone), and Cheltenham (Tony Stan) are examples of fonts in the square serif, slab serif, or Egyptian category.

Sans Serif

The early twentieth century saw continued technological advancement in printing and typesetting, flourishing of advertising and print journalism, and a contemporary movement in type design, influenced by the European Bauhaus and De Stijl design movements. For a new generation of designers and typographers, the typographic character emerged as an expressive design element. Very much a backlash against the typographic excesses of the nineteenth century, the new design direction sought a basic letterform which was suitable for contemporary communication.

Sans serif typefaces abandoned not only the serif but significant variation in stroke weight as well. The x-heights were significantly increased, a practice that has come to exemplify contemporary taste (many twentieth-century revivals of earlier type designs included enlarging the original x-heights).

Sans Serif Characteristics

- Little or no variation between thick and thin strokes
- Lack of serifs
- Larger x-height
- Little or no stress in rounded strokes
- Often squared-off terminals

Script & Cursive Characteristics

- Variation between thick and thin strokes
- Lack of serifs (often replaced by swashes)
- Varying x-heights

Joined letters are characteristic of script fonts

Separate letters are characteristic of cursive fonts

Almost by definition, the Art Deco era translated into sans serif type. The most common modern fonts of this genre include such faces as Avant Garde (Herb Lubalin and Tom Carnase), which is difficult to read at length; a more graceful geometric sans from the 1930s is Futura (Paul Renner) and a more recent Art Deco–style display face is ITC Anna (Daniel Pelavin).

The sans serif movement continued for several decades with the development of immensely popular designs such as Univers (Adrian Frutiger), Helvetica (Max Meidinger), Antique Olive (Roger Excoffon), Kabel (Rudolf Koch), Bell Gothic (Chauncey H. Griffith), and Myriad (Robert Slimbach and Carol Twombly with Fred Brady and Christopher Slye).

Script and Cursive

Script and *cursive* typefaces are those designed to literally represent handwriting or hand-lettering styles. As a general distinction, scripts have linked or joining lowercase letters, similar to handwriting, while cursives appear as unjoined hand lettering.

Script and cursive designs can be calligraphic (appearing to be pen-drawn) and formal, as seen on social printing such as invitations and announcements, or more informal appearing to be brush-drawn. Most designs feature ornate, swashed uppercase characters, making these type styles largely unreadable when set in all caps.

These typefaces began to appear in the late nineteenth century as more and more foundries competed for the commercial printing market. There is a tremendous variety of scripts and cursives available today, most of them designed in the 1930s, at the height of their popularity. From that time through the early 1950s, pen-and-brush

lettering was hugely popular in advertising and commercial printing. Foundries inundated the market with faces in these styles, which were widely used, especially where customers had no budget for lettering artists. Examples of script faces include Linoscript (Morris Fuller Benton), Künstler Script (Hans Bohn), Kaufmann (Max R. Kaufmann), Bickham Script (Richard Lipton), and Snell Roundhand (Matthew Carter). Examples of cursive faces include Giddyup (Laurie Szujewska), Pelican (Arthur Baker), Pepita (Imre Reiner), Charme (Helmut Matheis), Ex Ponto (Jovica Veljovic), and Wiesbaden Swing (Rosemarie Kloos-Rau).

Display and Decorative

For most of type's history, the use of *decorative* characters was applied to the page design of books and usually limited to ornamenting title pages, chapter headings, and initials. In the nineteenth century, though, the proliferation of slab serif typefaces did not ultimately satisfy the insatiable public appetite for distinct and ornate types.

Posters and advertisements relied heavily on large-size type, called *display* type, to attract attention. Because of the size of display type, readability was less important than visual impact. Display type designers incorporated ornamentation to achieve this impact. The designs completely abandoned centuries of aesthetic evolution in favor of nearly any visual trick that might catch the public eye. Types became bolder, incorporated outlines and inlines, were colored or shaded, appeared three-dimensional, or cast shadows. Most of these flamboyant typefaces enjoyed immediate success but were short-lived.

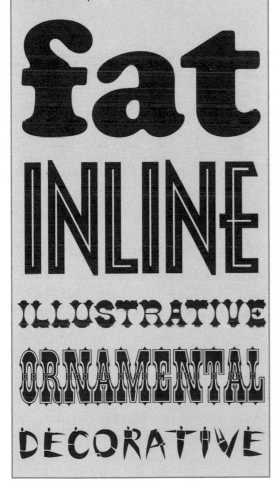

Decorative Display Faces

- Great variation between stroke weight and quality
- Mixed serif and sans serif
- Various x-height in lowercase
- Often all caps

fat

INLINE

ILLUSTRATIVE

ORNAMENTAL

DECORATIVE

The late Victorian era, from 1880 to World War I, was characterized by an ornamental style of art known as Art Nouveau, with organic, asymmetrical, intricate, and flowing lines. The movement produced similarly distinctive and highly decorative typography, which saw a revival during the 1960s.

There are a fair number of digital revivals of Art Nouveau faces, although few are widely used. Some of the more common digital Art Nouveau

typefaces are Arnold Böcklin (O. Weisert), Artistik (unknown), Desdemona (Dickinson Type Foundry [1900], and Jim Spiece [2000]), Galadriel (Alan Meeks), and Victorian (Colin Brignall).

Pepperwood, Rosewood, and Zebrawood (Carl Cosgrove, Carol Twombly, Kim Buker Chansler), Sassafras (Arthur Baker), Bermuda (Garrett Boge and Paul Shaw), Ironwood, Blackoak, Mesquite (Joy Redick), Beesknees (David Farey), Birch (Kim Buker Chansler), Blue Island (Jeremy Tankard), ITC Anna (Daniel Pelavin), Shuriken Boy (Joachim Müller-Lancé), and Umbra (R. Hunter Middleton) are only a few of the decorative faces available in a digital format.

The Search for a Modern Classification System

Online discussions are plagued with requests for information on systems of *type classification*, as the field of type design has exploded since the widespread use of the personal computer in the design industry. Typographic systems established within the last forty years are inadequately equipped to standardize the diverse range of letterforms. This is because existing systems tend to be based on loosely defined categories that have not kept pace with the growth in the industry. Attempts to update them seem to extend the number of categories, and in turn the problems appear to multiply.

There seems to be no simple response to such a complex issue. Typographer *Jonathan Höefler* writes, "A taxonomy for type, if it were comprehensible, adaptable, correctable, expandable, generally accessible yet infinitely refined, would be of immeasurable use to anyone connected with letters. If it chronicled the cultural, aesthetic,

Art Nouveau

Art Deco

9.9 Examples of decorative fonts that derive their style from the Art Nouveau period and the Art Deco period are Arnold Böcklin and Broadway, respectively.

9.10 *Construction* refers to the physical characteristics of the strokes, serifs, crossbars, and so on. Often a visual reference to the tool that may have created the original helps to clarify its specific characteristics.

9.11 *Shape* is the category that is concerned with the relationship between the curvilinear and rectilinear elements—the interaction of shapes such as circles, ovals, squares, and rectangles within the overall whole.

The door led right into a large kitchen, which was full of smoke from one end to the other: the Duchess was sitting on a three-legged stool in the middle, nursing a baby; the cook was leaning over the fire, stirring a large cauldron which seemed to be full of soup.

The door led right into a large kitchen, which was full of smoke from one end to the other: the Duchess was sitting on a three-legged stool in the middle, nursing a baby; the cook was leaning over the fire, stirring a large cauldron which seemed to be full of soup.

Light Medium **Demi Extra Bold**

9.12 *Weight* refers both to the variation of the stroke weight within a family of type, as in light, medium and bold, and to the visual weight, sometimes called *color*, of the typeset text.

technological, and literary influences on type design—instead of postulating a neat progression of styles, implying an uncomplicated evolution—it might attempt a more faithful record of the rich and complex history of typography."

In 1995 *Catherine Dixon* began work on a cataloging program for a photographic lettering archive, the Central Lettering Record, based in London at Central Saint Martin's College of Art and Design. As she continued work on the project, it became evident that no existing typographic nomenclature offered a practical approach to the hybrid forms characteristic of contemporary type design. She studied the possibilities of type classification and the idea of broadening a basic category system, and it was the visualization of that process and the particular use of visual mapping to represent key hierarchical and historical relationships that led to a new, more organic approach to typeform description.

The new descriptive framework for typeforms proposed by Dixon comprises three primary description components: sources, formal attributes, and patterns. The intent of the framework is to provide a system of reference against which typefaces can be examined individually and a description built to the requirements of each. The idea is to arrive at a description that is not centered on an inflexible structure that forces typefaces into a category either visually or conceptually.

Sources describe generic formal influences and usefully draw together broad groupings of typefaces that share underlying similarities in approach or like visual references. These sources identify influences such as decoration or pictorial references, handwriting, ideas of what a roman type is, and so on, according to chronological developments in type from a historical perspective.

Formal attributes describe specific and detailed characteristics of type design and construction. These fall into eight categories:

- ✦ Construction
- ✦ Shape
- ✦ Modeling
- ✦ Terminals
- ✦ Proportion
- ✦ Weight
- ✦ Key characters
- ✦ Decoration

These categories provide the basis for the second portion of the framework, with each category being further subdivided into descriptive listings of more specific characteristics, which allow for more detailed and definitive description.

The *construction* category of formal attributes describes the approach to the assembly or construction of the component parts that make up the characters of a given typeface. These parts are often referred to as "strokes"—particularly when character shapes are derived from handwritten sources. Attributes of stroke and stroke relationships include *continuous*, *broken*, and *interrupted*. Construction attributes also describe alternative approaches to construction (such as modular), reference to tools informing construction of the characters (scissors, calligraphy pen, typewriter, and so on) and a reference to the letterform case (upper- and/or lowercase, single alphabet, and so on).

Attributes of *shape* describe the basic shapes of the Latin alphabet, which are curves and straight lines. Here are listed the factors influencing the appearance of letterform shapes, such as curvature and variability, the treatment of each of these components, and possible variations in their shape. For example, curved lines, which are continuous in traditional letterforms, may be angular, broken, or fractured, and then round, oval, or square in aspect. Stems—the dominant lines in a letterform—may include convex or concave

9.13 An example of Catherine Dixon's taxonomy in use. The sample shown, MT Old English, has been identified through a summary of its visual characteristics.

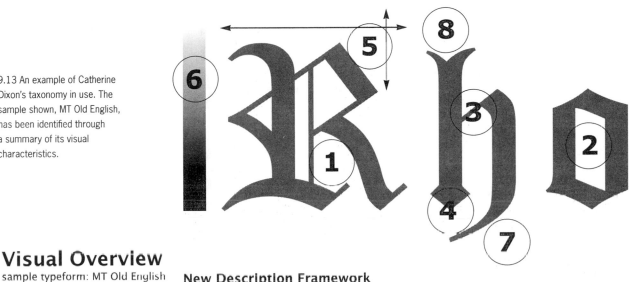

Visual Overview
sample typeform: MT Old English

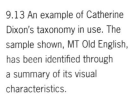

New Description Framework

Summary of **formal attributes**   (specific description component)
Formal attributes describe the physical characteristics of type design and construction. These fall into eight categories:
1 Construction, 2 Shape, 3 Modeling, 4 Terminals, 5 Proportion, 6 Weight, 7 Key characters, 8 Decoration

Patterns
Repeated combinations of sources and formal attributes used throughout type design history. Here these patterns are set out along a time-line from approximate date of introduction

Sources (generic description component)
Sources describe the formal influences underpinning typeface design and include:
decorated/pictorial; handwritten; roman; c 19th vernacular; additional

Timeline entries (approximate dates 1450–2000):
- Curvilinear
- Grecian 3
- Latin & Runic
- Grecians 1 & 2
- Italian & French antique
- Egyptian (slab serif)
- Sans serif: grotesque
- Clarendon/Ionic
- Tuscan
- Fat face
- Old Style
- British taste: late
- Continental taste: late
- British taste: early
- Continental taste: early
- Dutch taste
- Aldine roman
- Humanist roman
- Informality & everyman
- Roundhand (copperplate)
- Italic: secondary roman
- Italic into Italian hand
- Civilité (into Ronde)
- Italic: Old face
- Fraktur
- Italic: Chancery hand
- Schwabacher
- Humanist
- Rotunda
- **Textura**
- Bastarda (generic broken script)
- Decorated/pictorial (encompassing)
- Decorated/pictorial (embellishing)

Handwritten sources

A The new description framework operates on the assumption that the formal character of every typeface can be explained in terms of its specific configuration of the two main description components: sources (generic influences) and formal attributes (specific formal characteristics).

B Reference is also made to the pattern definition listings to see if a given typeform adheres to any of the established configurations of source and formal attributes that recur throughout typeform history. In the case of the sample shown (Monotype Old English) reference is made to the Textura pattern.

C In those instances of description where a pattern is broadly considered appropriate but a given typeform deviates in some way, reference to a pattern is moderated by further reference to the general listings of sources and/or formal attributes.

9.14 (Right) Terminal attributes in Dixon's taxonomy vary according to the type of endiing inherent to the letterform stroke, including decorative spur serifs, traditional serifs, or sans serif options.

9.15 (Below) Summary of the visual characteristics of MT Old English from the previous page, using the typeform descriptive framework.

	Textura
	Sources Handwritten
	Formal Attributes
Construction	approach: broken script
	structural detailing: non-cursive, upright, non-joining characters and possible looping of strokes
	direct reference to tool: broad-edged pen
	character sets: upper- and lowercase, description biased toward lowercase
Shape	overall treatment: some character shapes reflect source/construction influences, emphatically "cut"
	curves: generally angular with square aspect exemplified in an *o* constructed of six straight sides
	stems: (basic) straight with parallel edges
Modeling	as a result of their broken script construction—
	contrast: high/exaggerated
	axis of contrast: inclined
	transition: abrupt
Terminals	baseline/general: handwriting-derived oblique rectangular serifs
	x-height: as above
	ascenders; generally blunt tips, sometimes slightly forked
Proportion	broken script letterforms are generally narrow, in addition to which the large x-height of the Textura results in its letterforms appearing generally tall
	relative internal proportions: ascenders and descenders short
Weight	letterforms black in "color" and generally heavy
Key Characters	*a* double or two-story: closed
	d curled backward
	e with upward-sloping crossbar
	g double or two-story
	h often with right-hand stroke curved inward, possibly descending below the baseline
	p with strokes crossed at baseline
	final *s* similar to the figure 8
Decoration	not applicable

elements and may be parallel, irregular, or flared. Reference may also be made here to specifically named curves (or parts of curves), such as the bowls, as well as the detailing and position of secondary lines, such as crossbars and the overall treatment of counters.

The *modeling* category refers to the contrast in stroke weight, ranging from a consistent weight to a highly exaggerated difference. In addition to the contrast in stroke weight, the stress and the type of transition between the strokes are included.

Terminal attributes describe the variety of terminals and finishing strokes found within letterforms, as well as where and how they have been applied. Descriptions of baseline terminals include those derived from handwriting, the familiar tapered serifs that evolved from Roman inscriptional lettering models, and other variations such as slab serifs, Tuscan (sometimes referred to as forked, spur, or fishtail) serifs, or the sans serif option. Some characters also have

Ah Ah Ah
Ah Ah Ah

9.16 *Proportion* describes the relationship between the components of the letterform—for example, the cap height relative to the x-height.

distinctive terminals to other parts of their forms, which are useful for typeface identification and description. For example, the curve of the top arm of a lowercase *a* can variously be described as tapered, blunt/sheared, lobed (teardrop), or fully rounded.

Proportion describes the letterform in relationship to its use of space. Often these are referred to as the width-to-height relationship and named *condensed, medium,* or *extended.* Another proportional consideration would be the relationship of ascender-to-cap height to x-height.

The formal attribute of *weight* describes the overall visual strength of the forms, as described according to color: light, medium, or black. Type families often include variations of light, medium, and bold.

Key characters identify and describe those characters whose treatment is significant in distinguishing one typeface from another. A basic selection might include a single- or double-story *a* and *g*, an *e* with an oblique or horizontal crossbar, an *f* or *J* sitting on or descending below the baseline, a *Q* with a short tail, long tail, or a tail

bisecting the bowl, and an *R* with a straight or curved leg.

Decoration attributes describe some of the common motifs and treatments used when detailing letterforms. Common motifs include abstract scrolls, medallions, and flourishes or the more pictorial forms of flowers and foliage. Decorative treatments include the use of inline and outline, shadowing, cameos (reversing out), shading, and stenciling.

The third primary description component in Dixon's new descriptive framework is *patterns,* which are defined using the two other basic description components of sources and formal attributes. When a source (or sources) and a particular combination of formal attributes are repeatedly used together in a fixed relationship, the formal result is identified as a pattern. However, while patterns are key to understanding the early centuries of type design, beginning in the late nineteenth century the diversification of form represented within new and original type design practice became so great that it is no longer practical to try to summarize formal trends in this way. More often now, typeforms require description on an individual basis without reference to patterns at all. The resulting type description is based on the premise that all typeforms can be described in terms of their individual combinations of sources and formal attributes.

This prototypical system departs from previous classification systems in that faces no longer need to be pigeonholed into existing categories. Additional description components may be added as required. This taxonomic key allows the designer flexibility in classification by allowing any combination of visual characteristics rather than offering only predetermined groups of identifiers.

ag
ga

9.17 Key characters are the letterforms in a font that provide unique visual clues to assist the viewer in distinguishing one font from another font, such as a double-story *a* and *g* compared to a single-story *a* and *g*.

f f

9.18 The letter *f* is a key character since it can sit on the baseline directly or extend below the baseline as a descender would in a traditional font.

ABCDEFG
ABCDEF
ABCD

9.19 Decorative attributes include special treatments such as inline, abstract scrolls or swashes, and stencil-style aesthetic variations.

Chapter Nine Review

Circle one answer for each definition to indicate the correct key concept term or key player for each. When necessary, determine whether the phrase provided is true or false.

1. Egyptian or slab serif faces are characterized by
   a. Minimal variation of thick and thin strokes with heavy serifs with squared-off ends
   b. Large x-heights and vertical stress in rounded strokes with significant bracketing on serifs
   b. Relatively small ascenders
   d. All of the above

2. This prototypical system departs from previous classification systems in that faces no longer need to be pigeonholed into existing categories. Additional description components may be added as required.
   a. Catherine Dixon's system of classification
   b. Alexander Lawson's system of classification
   c. DIN system
   d. British Standards system

3. These faces appear as unjoined hand lettering, similar to handwriting.
   a. Cursive
   b. Sans serif
   c. Script
   d. Italic

4. In Catherine Dixon's system of classification, these identify influences such as decoration or pictorial references, handwriting, ideas of what a roman type is, and so on, according to chronological developments in type from a historical perspective.
   a. Patterns
   b. Sources
   c. Key characters
   d. Modeling

5. According to Alexander Lawson, these fonts are heavily bracketed, causing the serifs to appear as though they have grown out of the stem strokes. The rounded, cuplike serifs are comfortable and reassuring; the great mass of the letterforms reinforces the sense of stability and strength.
   a. Modern
   b. Venetian Old Style
   c. Transitional
   d. Old Style

6. This category in Catherine Dixon's system refers to the contrast in stroke weight ranging from a consistent weight to a highly exaggerated difference. In addition to the contrast in stroke weight, the stress and the type of transition between the strokes are included.
   a. Patterns
   b. Key characteristics
   c. Terminal attributes
   d. Modeling

7. England became an important trade center during the seventeenth century. With the expanded distribution of goods and services, English type styles spread throughout the region.
   a. True
   b. False

8. This was the dominant American manufacturer of metal type for several decades, from its creation in 1892 via the merger of twenty-three type foundries.
   a. American Type founders
   b. Linotype
   c. Agfa Monotype
   d. British Standards

9. In Catherine Dixon's system of classification, this formal attribute describes the overall visual strength of the forms, as described according to color: light, medium, or black. Type families often include variations of light, medium, and bold.
   a. Contrast
   b. Proportion
   c. Width
   d. Weight

10. Modern style identifying characteristics include
    a. Extreme contrast between thick and thin strokes
    b. Hairline serifs with bracketing and a small x-height
    c. Rounded serifs and vertical stress in rounded strokes
    d. All of the above

11. Transitional period faces can be further subdivided categories:
    a. Direct Line and modified
    b. Modern and direct line
    c. Old Style and modern
    d. Modified and decorative

12. This person wrote, "A taxonomy for type, if it were comprehensible, adaptable, correctable, expandable, generally accessible yet infinitely refined, would be of immeasurable use to anyone connected with letters. If it chronicled the cultural, aesthetic, technological, and literary influences on type design—instead of postulating a neat progression of styles, implying an uncomplicated evolution—it might attempt a more faithful record of the rich and complex history of typography."
    a. Catherine Dixon
    b. Theodore L. DeVinne
    c. Jonathan Höefler
    d. Alexander Lawson

13. This type evolved from handwritten manuscripts from fifteenth-century Germany, and was called "Gothic" by the Europeans.
    a. Aldine-French Old Style
    b. Transitional
    c. Black letter
    d. Modern

14. Alexander Lawson grouped these faces into a single category (Aldine-French Old Style) because of their obvious influence.
    a. Venetian Old Style faces with Aldine Old Style
    a. Dutch Old Style faces with English Old Style
    a. French Old Style faces with Aldine Old Style
    a. French Old Style faces with Dutch Old Style

15. England depended on the Dutch type until the 1720s when William Caslon established a foundry in London.
    a. True
    b. False

16. Charactersitcs of Script and Cursive faces include
    a. Little variation between thick and thin strokes
    b. Lack of serifs which are often replaced by swashes
    c. Similar x-heights
    d. All of the above

17. In the nineteenth century, posters and advertisements relied heavily on large-size type to attract attention. Because of the size of this type, readability was less important than visual impact.
    a. Decorative
    b. Display
    c. Slab serif
    d. Cursive

18. In the 1890s William Morris revived the use of these characteristics in his font Golden Type used by Kelmscott Press.
    a. Black letter
    b. Venetian Old Style
    c. Transitional
    d. Old Style

19. The categories within this system include black letter, Old Style (Venetian, Aldine-French, and Dutch-English), transitional, modern, square serif, sans serif, script-cursive, and display-decorative.
    a. Vox system
    b. Alexander Lawson's system of classification
    c. ATypI system
    d. Catherine Dixon's system of classification

20. These faces have linked or joining lowercase letters, similar to handwriting.
    a. Decorative
    b. Cursive
    c. Script
    d. Italic

21. In Catherine Dixon's system, these describe the variety of terminals and finishing strokes found within letterforms, as well as where and how they have been applied.
    a. Proportion
    b. Key characteristics
    c. Terminal attributes
    d. Modeling

22. Transitional style identifying characteristics include
    a. A greater contrast between thick and thin stokes with wider, gracefully bracketed serifs with flat bases
    b. Larger x-height and vertical stress in rounded strokes
    c. The height of capitals closely matches that of ascenders
    d. All of the above

23. Key characters are the letterforms in a font that provide unique visual clues to assist the viewer in distinguishing one font from another font, such as a double-story *a* and *g* compared to a single-story *a* and *g*.
    a. True
    b. False

24. Sans serif characteristics include
    a. Little or no variation between thick and thin strokes
    b. Lack of serifs, often with squared-off terminals
    c. Little or no stress in rounded strokes
    d. All of the above

25. Black letter was called "Gothic" by the Europeans, but this was confusing when nineteenth-century Americans named early sans serif fonts "Gothic" as well.
    a. True
    b. False

26. In Catherine Dixon's system, this is the category that is concerned with the relationship between the curvilinear and rectilinear elements—the interaction of shapes such as circles, ovals, squares, and rectangles within the overall whole.
    a. Proportion
    b. Key characteristics
    c. Terminal attributes
    d. Shape

Setting Text Type

Of utmost concern to a client is the communication of the client's message in a visual medium. That is, a designer is hired to translate the client's message into a creative, attention-grabbing visual in the form of a brochure, poster, stationery system, or package that will help persuade the target audience to attend the special event, purchase the product, or send a donation. Success of the visual communication may be measured in quantitative terms by determining the number of viewers who take the action the client desires. Success of the visual communication also may be measured in qualitative terms by tracking the longevity of the design's popularity as well as the ease of remembrance by viewers and the attention paid to the quality of the work. In either case, there are several special considerations in the preparation of the final typesetting and mechanical artwork prior to releasing it for print production.

Key Concepts

ampersand
angle brackets
ante meridiem
apostrophe
asterisk
at
backslash
bullet
colon
comma
contrast
curly braces
dagger
dash
double dagger
double prime
ellipsis
exclamation mark
H&J
hyphen
hyphenation
interpunct
interrobang
legibility
minus
number sign
optically corrected
orphan
paraphrasing
parenthesis
period
pipe
post meridiem
prime
quotation mark
readability
semicolon
slash
square brackets
style sheets
tilde
underscore
vertical bar
virgule
widow

Legibility and Readability

Other terms used interchangeably with legibility include discernibility and visibility. *Legibility* means "ablty to be read." Legibly typeset manuscripts exhibit visual characteristics that make them easier for most people to read. Using traditional typesetting conventions increases the probability that those who read the words will be able to clearly decipher the letterforms, grouping them into words, words into sentences, sentences into paragraphs, and so on. The clarity or legibility of visually presented text is affected by factors such as the size of the text, the contrast between similar letters, the quality of printing or display (for example, whether the text is damaged or blurred), the line spacing and word spacing, and the shape and style of individual letters.

The *readability*, of a text is related to its legibility but also depends on non-typesetting-related factors, including vocabulary and writing style. This part of the process is the responsibility of the author or copywriter. Readability in this sense is usually assessed by the age or grade level required for someone to be able to readily understand a written passage.

Legibility also is affected to some extent by the characteristics of the reader and his or her environment, biological age, reading ability, mood, subjective preference for aesthetics (including color, texture, and proportion), amount of interest in the subject of the text, physical position (sitting or standing comfortably), adequate lighting, and amount of visual and auditory distraction in the immediate environment.

Also important is the type of reading matter. Is the reader attempting to decipher a short article in a magazine or concentrate on a novel? Dictionaries, telephone directories, and cookbooks present different sets of legibility and readability concerns as well. Are other modes of communication such as diagrams, charts, icons, symbols, and illustrations necessary, in addition to the written word, to effectively and succinctly communicate?

The reader's experience affects his or her comprehension of the subject matter as much as the content itself does. Many theorists speculate that the typefaces that a reader has grown up with are more comfortable due to learned experience, and therefore preferred typfaces vary for separate generations of readers. According to Zuzana Licko, cofounder of Émigré and internationally known contemporary type designer, "Typefaces are not intrinsically legible. Rather, it is the reader's familiarity with faces that accounts for their legibility. Studies have shown that readers read best what they read most." Based on that line of thought, it would seem that the designers' tendencies to use different font styles in different types of reading materials over the years would impact readers of different generations in different ways. In fact, many of the black letter type styles that are found to be illegible today were once preferred over other choices of humanistic hand in the eleventh century, and again in the fifteenth century. Today's typographic fashion is for fonts with a larger x-height and short ascenders and short descenders. Generally the word spacing is tight.

More recent research into the way that children see and learn letterforms has led to the development of new fonts for use in education. With a design based on visual preferences described by young readers, Sassoon Primary Type was introduced for children by *Adrian Williams* in 1996. It has since proven effective for dyslexic readers, with its longer ascenders

Popular Fonts

There may be some connection between the popular use of these fonts and their perceived or real legibility for a majority of readers. Some of the popularity of fonts such as Times and Helvetica may be due to their use as system fonts for many computers as much as to their readability.

Most popular serif fonts:
Garamond
Caslon
Baskerville
Bodoni
Goudy
Times
Century
Palatino
Sabon
Stone Serif

Most popular sans serif fonts:
Helvetica
Univers
Frutiger
Futura
Franklin Gothic
Optima
Gill Sans
Akzidenz-Grotesk
Avant Garde
Myriad

"There's certainly too much pepper in that soup!" Alice said to herself, as well as she could for sneezing.

There was certainly too much of it in the air. Even the Duchess sneezed occasionally; and as for the baby, it was sneezing and howling alternately without a moment's pause. The only things in the kitchen that did not sneeze, were the cook, and a large cat which was sitting on the hearth and grinning from ear to ear.

There's certainly too much pepper in that soup! Alice said to herself, as well as she could for sneezing.

There was certainly too much of it in the air. Even the Duchess sneezed occasionally; and as for the baby, it was sneezing and howling alternately without a moment's pause. The only things in the kitchen that did not sneeze, were the cook, and a large cat which was sitting on the hearth and grinning from ear to ear.

"There's certainly too much pepper in that soup!" Alice said to herself, as well as she could for sneezing.

There was certainly too much of it in the air. Even the Duchess sneezed occasionally; and as for the baby, it was sneezing and howling alternately without a moment's pause. The only things in the kitchen that did not sneeze, were the cook, and a large cat which was sitting on the hearth and grinning from ear to ear.

10.2 Legibility and readability are affected by the reader's experience, in addition to the qualities of the letterform. At one time, Gothic or black letter fonts were a cultural standard, whereas today the average reader has great difficulty discerning the content of a paragraph set in this font.

and descenders that help readers to define the letterforms more easily, in direct opposition to contemporary trends in typography. The designer's common sense led him to the hypothesis that what suited children could also benefit older students and adults. Next came Sassoon Sans, which deleted the characteristic exit stroke. Other variations are available.

The legibility of typefaces has been measured under strict scientific conditions in terms of factors of distance, speed, comprehension, blink rates, saccadic jump regression, heart rate, and shaking tables. Although many of these studies claim to have the definitive answer on what characteristics are to be used in typesetting for maximal legibility, few address all of the variables controlled by the reader. Once mastered, reading is an automatic process susceptible to influences not consciously known to the reader. In an attempt to prepare the message in a way that will best communicate to the widest range of readers, the designer must always ask, "What, why, for whom, when, and where?" Having answered those questions as accurately as possible, he or she must translate the results into an aesthetic that will maximize the chance for a positive response to the read material.

Font Design Characteristics

Each generation has and will continue to redefine the optimal characteristics of characters for legibility and aesthetics. Internationally recognized authority on print legibility, *Miles Tinker*, defines legibility as "concern for perceiving letters and words, and the reading of continuous textural material." He theorized that the shapes of letters must be clearly discriminated, the characteristic word forms perceived, and continuous text read

AaBbCcDd
EeFfGgHhIi
JjKkLlMm
NnOoPpQq
RrSsTtUuVv
WwXxYyZz

10.3 Sasson One, by Adrian Williams Design Limited, Surrey, England.

AaBbCcDd
EeFfGgHhIi
JjKkLlMm
NnOoPpQq
RrSsTtUuVv
WwXxYyZz

10.4 Sasson Four, by Adrian Williams Design Limited, Surrey, England.

10.5 You decide. Here is a visual comparison between Garamond, Garamond Condensed, and Garamond Condensed Light in the left column, and Futura, Futura Condensed and Futura Condensed Bold in the right column. Which is the easiest for you to read? Which is the most difficult? Why? All examples are set 9/12.

"You don't know much," said the Duchess; "and that's a fact."

Alice did not at all like the tone of this remark, and thought it would be as well to introduce some other subject of conversation. While she was trying to fix on one, the cook took the cauldron of soup off the fire, and at once set to work throwing everything within her reach at the Duchess and the baby —the fire-irons came first; then followed a shower of saucepans, plates, and dishes. The Duchess took no notice of them even when they hit her; and the baby was howling so much already, that it was quite impossible to say whether the blows hurt it or not.

"You don't know much," said the Duchess; "and that's a fact."

Alice did not at all like the tone of this remark, and thought it would be as well to introduce some other subject of conversation. While she was trying to fix on one, the cook took the cauldron of soup off the fire, and at once set to work throwing everything within her reach at the Duchess and the baby —the fire-irons came first; then followed a shower of saucepans, plates, and dishes. The Duchess took no notice of them even when they hit her; and the baby was howling so much already, that it was quite impossible to say whether the blows hurt it or not.

"You don't know much," said the Duchess; "and that's a fact."

Alice did not at all like the tone of this remark, and thought it would be as well to introduce some other subject of conversation. While she was trying to fix on one, the cook took the cauldron of soup off the fire, and at once set to work throwing everything within her reach at the Duchess and the baby —the fire-irons came first; then followed a shower of saucepans, plates, and dishes. The Duchess took no notice of them even when they hit her; and the baby was howling so much already, that it was quite impossible to say whether the blows hurt it or not.

"You don't know much," said the Duchess; "and that's a fact."

Alice did not at all like the tone of this remark, and thought it would be as well to introduce some other subject of conversation. While she was trying to fix on one, the cook took the cauldron of soup off the fire, and at once set to work throwing everything within her reach at the Duchess and the baby —the fire-irons came first; then followed a shower of saucepans, plates, and dishes. The Duchess took no notice of them even when they hit her; and the baby was howling so much already, that it was quite impossible to say whether the blows hurt it or not.

"You don't know much," said the Duchess; "and that's a fact."

Alice did not at all like the tone of this remark, and thought it would be as well to introduce some other subject of conversation. While she was trying to fix on one, the cook took the cauldron of soup off the fire, and at once set to work throwing everything within her reach at the Duchess and the baby —the fire-irons came first; then followed a shower of saucepans, plates, and dishes. The Duchess took no notice of them even when they hit her; and the baby was howling so much already, that it was quite impossible to say whether the blows hurt it or not.

"You don't know much," said the Duchess; "and that's a fact."

Alice did not at all like the tone of this remark, and thought it would be as well to introduce some other subject of conversation. While she was trying to fix on one, the cook took the cauldron of soup off the fire, and at once set to work throwing everything within her reach at the Duchess and the baby —the fire-irons came first; then followed a shower of saucepans, plates, and dishes. The Duchess took no notice of them even when they hit her; and the baby was howling so much already, that it was quite impossible to say whether the blows hurt it or not.

abcdefg

10.6 Visual comparison between type set at 7 points (outline) and enlarged versus type set at 85 points (gray). Notice the slight difference in the ascender and descender lengths, and stroke weights.

accurately, rapidly, and easily with a high level of comprehension. Based on his research, it might be theorized that legible text needs to be large enough and distinct enough that readers may discriminate between individual letters and words. How does that summary translate into specific characteristics to assist designers in making a logical and practical font selection for any given design problem?

American type designer *Edwin Shaar* (Flash, Nuptual Script, Futura Script, Imperial, and Gazette) outlined characteristics of a legible typeface:

- *Alignment of type.* A variation of alignment as small as one or two thousands of an inch is noticeable, so special attention should be paid to the natural alignment of letterforms of a font.

- *Optically corrected face.* **Optical correction** compensates for failure of the eye to differentiate reality from illusion. An example is the need to slightly increase the size of round letters in a font over that of square letters in a font.

- *Uniform letter proportions in a font.* This involves thickness of stroke, length of serif, and evenness of color when seen in a mass.

- *Contrast within a font.* Italic and boldface contrast with the regular weight of roman.

- *Clear symbol identification.* All symbols should be clearly distinguished, so that the numeral *1* cannot be mistaken for the numeral *7* or the capital *I* for the lowercase *l*; neither should *G* become confused with *O* or *Q.* The top half of letterforms should be particularly recognizable.

- *Fitting.* There should be good linkage of one letter to another when composed together.

- *Large x-height.* The x-height should be as large as possible without unduly sacrificing the size of the ascenders and descenders.

- *Printability.* Make sure counters in *b, d, o, p, q, a, e,* and *g* do not trap ink.

- *Familiarity of form.* The typeface should not have strange mannerisms, should offer no distractions, and should appear easy and warm to the reader.

Letterform Proportions

A number of subtleties in the design of letterforms are often overlooked by the lay-person. Involved in understanding the content of the words, sentences, and paragraphs, the reader seldom concerns himself or herself with individual letters unless they are distracting and inhibit the internalization of the communication. In reality, the minute shape differences in a letter of one font compared to the same letter of a different font affect the legibility as well as the aesthetic.

Condensed and Extended Proportions of Letters

Often fonts are designed with an application in mind, and so the relationship of the height, width, and stroke weight is carefully balanced at a given size for a given purpose. Fonts designed for use in newspaper text, for example, are not

Key Players
Edwin Shaar
Martin K. Speckter
Miles Tinker
Adrian Williams

necessarily ideal for use in a telephone directory. Decorative fonts designed for use in display sizes may become illegible at small text sizes, as their intricate components blur and fill in.

In a typeface that is designed as a condensed font, the weight of the stem stroke changes in proportion to the hairline strokes, resulting in a balanced, harmonious solution. This sometimes involves opening up the counters slightly to ensure readability while the horizontal strokes are shortened.

An extended version of a font is one that is wider than the regular face. Again, just like the original font and the condensed counterpart, the proportions of each letter are redesigned with subtle differences to accommodate the new shape. The letterforms are not merely "stretched" to a wider version; rather, each stroke is reconsidered and adjusted in weight and length so that one does not appear too thick and another does not appear too thin.

When fonts are manually stretched on the computer, these designed proportions are ruined, creating areas that are too thick and some that are too thin, which in turn affects the overall aesthetic and legibility of the resulting composition. An awkward and uneven appearance draws attention to the fact that an amateur has manipulated the typography. The rule, then, is to select a condensed font when needed, and an extended font when needed rather than change the proportions of an existing font. Of course, it is acceptable to break the rules once in a while, as long as it is evident that it is done on purpose, as an essential part of the meaning in communication of the message.

Uppercase and Lowercase Letterforms

Most reports on legibility conclude that setting type in all capital letters, as opposed

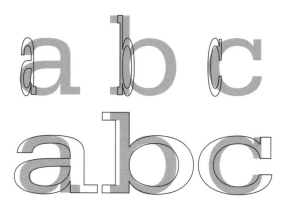

10.7 An example of Serifa set normally (gray), as compared to a computer-condensed variation and a computer-extended variation. Notice how the harmonious proportions of the letterform strokes are destroyed in the stretched versions, making the font less legible. This treatment is amateurish and undesirable.

to setting type in mixed upper- and lowercase letters, makes the text more difficult to discern. The differences in the lowercase letterforms created by contour, ascenders, and descenders provide greater variety for faster recognition. On the other hand, uppercase letterforms are uniform in height and similar in width and visual volume. These similarities mean that the reader must first dissect and then reassemble the internal details of each letter to discern the differences before understanding of meaning is possible. It makes sense to limit the use of all capital letters to short phrases for visual impact, and set larger blocks of copy in mixed upper- and lowercase letters.

Because they are often directed to refrain from setting script and cursive fonts, students may assume it's because of a poor aesthetic. However, that restriction probably resulted from the illegible nature of all caps in a script or cursive font. The curlicues and swashes, in additon to the unusual letterforms, are difficult for the eye to discern from one another.

Setting type in all caps requires up to 50 percent more space than an equivalent phrase in mixed upper- and lowercase. In addition to legibility concerns, added attention is required

"Oh, PLEASE mind what you're doing!" cried Alice, jumping up and down in an agony of terror. "Oh, there goes his PRECIOUS nose"; as an unusually large saucepan flew close by it, and very nearly carried it off.

"If everybody minded their own business," the Duchess said in hoarse growl, "the world would go round a deal faster than it does."

"OH, PLEASE MIND WHAT YOU'RE DOING!" CRIED ALICE, JUMPING UP AND DOWN IN AN AGONY OF TERROR. "OH, THERE GOES HIS PRECIOUS NOSE"; AS AN UNUSUALLY LARGE SAUCEPAN FLEW CLOSE BY IT, AND VERY NEARLY CARRIED IT OFF.

"IF EVERYBODY MINDED THEIR OWN BUSINESS," THE DUCHESS SAID IN HOARSE GROWL, "THE WORLD WOULD GO ROUND A DEAL FASTER THAN IT DOES."

10.8 A visual comparison between sans serif, serif, and script fonts in both upper- and lowercase and all caps. Which is the easiest to read? Which is the most difficult? Why?

"Oh, PLEASE mind what you're doing!" cried Alice, jumping up and down in an agony of terror. "Oh, there goes his PRECIOUS nose"; as an unusually large saucepan flew close by it, and very nearly carried it off.

"If everybody minded their own business," the Duchess said in hoarse growl, "the world would go round a deal faster than it does."

"OH, PLEASE MIND WHAT YOU'RE DOING!" CRIED ALICE, JUMPING UP AND DOWN IN AN AGONY OF TERROR. "OH, THERE GOES HIS PRECIOUS NOSE"; AS AN UNUSUALLY LARGE SAUCEPAN FLEW CLOSE BY IT, AND VERY NEARLY CARRIED IT OFF.

"IF EVERYBODY MINDED THEIR OWN BUSINESS," THE DUCHESS SAID IN HOARSE GROWL, "THE WORLD WOULD GO ROUND A DEAL FASTER THAN IT DOES."

"OH, PLEASE mind what you're doing!" cried Alice, jumping up and down in an agony of terror. "Oh, there goes his precious nose"; as an unusually large saucepan flew close by it, and very nearly carried it off.

"If everybody minded their own business," the Duchess said in hoarse growl, "the world would go round a deal faster than it does."

"OH, PLEASE MIND WHAT YOU'RE DOING!" CRIED ALICE, JUMPING UP AND DOWN IN AN AGONY OF TERROR. "OH, THERE GOES HIS PRECIOUS NOSE"; AS AN UNUSUALLY LARGE SAUCEPAN FLEW CLOSE BY IT, AND VERY NEARLY CARRIED IT OFF.

"IF EVERYBODY MINDED THEIR OWN BUSINESS," THE DUCHESS SAID IN HOARSE GROWL, "THE WORLD WOULD GO ROUND A DEAL FASTER THAN IT DOES."

10.9 A visual comparison between type set in upper- and lowercase and type set in all caps. It is believed that the upper- and lowercase text is easier to read because of the differences in the contours. Does the brain rely more heavily on the differences in the top half of the letterforms or the lower half of the letterforms when deciphering text?

"Oh, PLEASE mind what you're doing!" cried Alice, jumping up and down in an agony of terror. "Oh, there goes his PRECIOUS nose"; as an unusually large saucepan flew close by it, and very nearly carried it off.

"If everybody minded their own business," the Duchess said in hoarse growl, "the world would go round a deal faster than it does."

"OH, PLEASE MIND WHAT YOU'RE DOING!" CRIED ALICE, JUMPING UP AND DOWN IN AN AGONY OF TERROR. "OH, THERE GOES HIS PRECIOUS NOSE"; AS AN UNUSUALLY LARGE SAUCEPAN FLEW CLOSE BY IT, AND VERY NEARLY CARRIED IT OFF.

"IF EVERYBODY MINDED THEIR OWN BUSINESS," THE DUCHESS SAID IN HOARSE GROWL, "THE WORLD WOULD GO ROUND A DEAL FASTER THAN IT DOES."

to determine whether there is sufficient space in the layout; likewise, if there is too much open space in the layout, setting a headline in all caps brings emphasis while occupying the unwanted white space.

Serif and Sans Serif Letterforms

Researchers have concluded that because sans serif letterforms within any given font are more similar to one another, and because serif letterforms within any given font are less similar, serif faces are intrinsically more legible than sans serif faces. However, these studies have not been able to take into account the experience

of the reader, so it is likely that a person who learned to read sans serif typefaces from a young age has little difficulty deciphering the shapes of letters and meanings of words based solely on the serif variation in typeset body copy.

It is possible, however, to compare the visual characteristics and aesthetic of body copy set in serif or sans serif fonts. There is the possibility for monotony in larger quantities of body text set entirely in a sans serif font, as the overall texture of the page results in one tone or texture, with nowhere for the eye to rest. Whether serif or sans serif, provide visual relief by breaking the text with subheads, pull quotes, and sidebars when appropriate for the content.

Letter Spacing, Word Spacing, and Line Spacing

It is nearly impossible to discuss the variables of typesetting independently, since one affects the other. Smaller type requires a shorter line length, while wider line lengths require more leading for easy reading. Remember that some of the decisions regarding "correct" practices for specifying type are founded in scientific discoveries based on tightly controlled circumstances; these rules provide a foundation for making general decisions, but the best solution to any design problem involves so many uncontrollable variables that the designer must finally make a decision based on the desired compositional aesthetic. Correctly set type results in an even visual texture (referred to as color, even though no change in hue is involved). A primary goal is to avoid wide variations in the text color and to strive for an even, consistent quality, avoiding the slipshod appearance associated with a lack of typesetting expertise and practice.

Modern technology has perpetuated the assumption that type designers have built "normal" or naturally occurring letter space into digital fonts. For the most part, this works in smaller text sizes for most text fonts. Attention must be given to the finer details of letter spacing so that the letters are not spaced too far apart; loosely set type combined with standard word spacing makes it more difficult for readers to mentally assemble the groups of letters into words. Legibility depends on the reader being able to quickly glance at the strokes that constitute individual letters and discern the letters' relationship to one another.

"Which would NOT be an advantage," said Alice, who felt very glad to get an opportunity of showing off a little of her knowledge. "Just think of what work it would make with the day and night! You see the earth takes twenty-four hours to turn round on its axis—"

"Talking of axes," said the Duchess, "chop off her head!"

Alice glanced rather anxiously at the cook, to see if she meant to take the hint; but the cook was busily stirring the soup, and seemed not to be listening, so she went on again: "Twenty-four hours, I THINK; or is it twelve? I—"

"Which would NOT be an advantage," said Alice, who felt very glad to get an opportunity of showing off a little of her knowledge. "Just think of what work it would make with the day and night! You see the earth takes twenty-four hours to turn round on its axis—"

"Talking of axes," said the Duchess, "chop off her head!"

Alice glanced rather anxiously at the cook, to see if she meant to take the hint; but the cook was busily stirring the soup, and seemed not to be listening, so she went on again: "Twenty-four hours, I THINK; or is it twelve? I—"

"Which would NOT be an advantage," said Alice, who felt very glad to get an opportunity of showing off a little of her knowledge. "Just think of what work it would make with the day and night! You see the earth takes twenty-four hours to turn round on its axis—"

"Talking of axes," said the Duchess, "chop off her head!"

Alice glanced rather anxiously at the cook, to see if she meant to take the hint; but the cook was busily stirring the soup, and seemed not to be listening, so she went on again: "Twenty-four hours, I THINK; or is it twelve? I—"

"Which would NOT be an advantage," said Alice, who felt very glad to get an opportunity of showing off a little of her knowledge. "Just think of what work it would make with the day and night! You see the earth takes twenty-four hours to turn round on its axis—"

"Talking of axes," said the Duchess, "chop off her head!"

Alice glanced rather anxiously at the cook, to see if she meant to take the hint; but the cook was busily stirring the soup, and seemed not to be listening, so she went on again: "Twenty-four hours, I THINK; or is it twelve? I—"

"Which would NOT be an advantage," said Alice, who felt very glad to get an opportunity of showing off a little of her knowledge. "Just think of what work it would make with the day and night! You see the earth takes twenty-four hours to turn round on its axis—"

"Talking of axes," said the Duchess, "chop off her head!"

Alice glanced rather anxiously at the cook, to see if she meant to take the hint; but the cook was busily stirring the soup, and seemed not to be listening, so she went on again: "Twenty-four hours, I THINK; or is it twelve? I—"

10.10 A visual comparison between type set in 9 point Adobe Garmond Pro with letter spacing and word spacing altered using the tracking feature in the page layout program. From top to bottom, the settings are -100, -50, 0, 50, and 150. Notice how the letter spacing and the word spacing become so similar that it is difficult to see where each word begins and ends.

"Oh, don't bother ME," said the Duchess; "I never could abide figures!" And with that she began nursing her child again, singing a sort of lullaby to it as she did so, and giving it a violent shake at the end of every line:

"Speak roughly to your little boy,
And beat him when he sneezes:
He only does it to annoy,
Because he knows it teases."

CHORUS.

(In which the cook and the baby joined):—

"Wow! wow! wow!"

While the Duchess sang the second verse of the song, she kept tossing the baby violently up and down, and the poor little thing howled so, that Alice could hardly hear the words:—

"I speak severely to my boy,
I beat him when he sneezes;
For he can thoroughly enjoy
The pepper when he pleases!"

CHORUS.

"Wow! wow! wow!"

10.11 A visual comparison between the word spacing that results from type set flush left, justified center, and force-justified. The examples are 9/12 Adobe Garamond Pro.

"Oh, don't bother ME," said the Duchess; "I never could abide figures!"And with that she began nursing her child again, singing a sort of lullaby to it as she did so, and giving it a violent shake at the end of every line:

"Speak roughly to your little boy,
And beat him when he sneezes:
He only does it to annoy,
Because he knows it teases."

CHORUS.

(In which the cook and the baby joined):—

"Wow! wow! wow!"

While the Duchess sang the second verse of the song, she kept tossing the baby violently up and down, and the poor little thing howled so, that Alice could hardly hear the words:—

"I speak severely to my boy,
I beat him when he sneezes;
For he can thoroughly enjoy
The pepper when he pleases!"

CHORUS.

"Wow! wow! wow!"

"Oh, don't bother ME,' said the Duchess; "I never could abide figures!' And with that she began nursing her child again, singing a sort of lullaby to it as she did so, and giving it a violent shake at the end of every line:

"Speak roughly to your little boy,
And beat him when he sneezes:
He only does it to annoy,
Because he knows it teases."

C H O R U S .

(In which the cook and the baby joined):

"Wow!   wow!   wow!"

While the Duchess sang the second verse of the song, she kept tossing the baby violently up and down, and the poor little thing howled so, that Alice could hardly hear the words:—

"I   speak   severely   to   my   boy,
I   beat   him   when   he   sneezes;
For   he   can   thoroughly   enjoy
The   pepper   when   he   pleases!"
C H O R U S .

"Wow!   wow!   wow!"

If there is too much or too little space between the forms, the positions and shapes of strokes are confused with one another and the letter is less easy to identify quickly. Tightly packed letters meld into visual combinations that are not easily recognized, making the words impossible to discern. Coupled with standard word spacing, the combination creates visual lumps that appear to float away from one another, as opposed to a somewhat even visual texture that is easier to view for longer periods of time. Attention to comfortable letter spacing helps the reader differentiate separate words, increasing reading speed and comprehension of the message.

The aesthetic balance is achieved by consideration to comfortable letter spacing and word spacing. One should not be adjusted without adjusting the other, so as to maintain the function of both. The point of correct letter spacing is to provide the reader with a pleasurable reading experience based on even visual texture and easy discernibility of the letterforms so that they can be assembled into words. The goal of correct word spacing it to clearly separate the words from one another, but not to the extent that they no longer visually relate to one another, which makes it difficult for the reader to maintain continuity, speed, and meaning.

Type alignment affects the word spacing. Type set flush left usually assumes proportional letter spacing and word spacing according to the predetermined font characteristics. Forcing text into a justified setting, where both margins are even, causes uneven spacing, especially between words, making it more difficult to read. When several lines of type in a paragraph have large word spaces that align vertically throughout the text, the resulting larger background spaces become dominant "rivers" of white, again detracting from overall legibility. Although altering of the font size can reduce some of these undesirable background areas, it is impossible to eliminate all of them. At this point, the designer must make an aesthetic decision, prioritizing the overall design of the layout with even visual margins over the issue of complete legibility.

Leading

Leading or line spacing (sometimes called interline or interlinear spacing) affects legibility in several ways. Before the introduction of metal spacers (called leads), text was set solid. It was believed to be acceptable for a couple of reasons. First, the ascenders and descenders of classical letterforms and hand-lettered manuscripts were much longer than seen in popular faces used today, providing much more vertical space between lines of type. Second, during the period when these fonts were popular, less of the population was literate enough to read the text; only the clergy and nobles had access to the manuscripts, and they were accustomed to the way the text was assembled because that was how they had always seen it.

The rise of modern type design and technology evolved forms with shorter ascenders and descenders in proportion to the x-height of the letter, requiring more vertical space between lines. Serif fonts are believed to require less leading since the small linear additions increase the horizontal feeling of the letters, leading the eye easily from one form to the next. Sans serif fonts appear to be easier to read when there is slightly more space between the lines to enhance the horizontal flow across the words. A general

10.12 A visual comparison between five examples of 9-point Adobe Garamond Pro with varied leading from -4 points to +14 points of leading.

rule of thumb is to allow 3 points of additional leading per line for sans serif faces; that is, if you select 10-point type, then specify 13 points for the leading, or slightly more, as long as the copy will fit in the designated compositional space.

One industry practice associated with setting text type digitally is that the leading should measure approximately 1.2 times the point size of the type. This figure does not take into account the length of the typeset line, so it may not be the correct leading for all documents. Regardless of its usefulness or uselessness, this is the way that automatic (auto) leading is determined in popular software applications. This means that if the layout is specified as 11 points, the leading is set at 13.2 points. When using the auto leading with type that measures 14 points, the leading measures 16.8 points, while type set at 7 points would result in leading measuring 8.4 points. It is much easier to remember leading specifications in whole or half-number increments than in the odd tenth-of-a-point increments generated by the auto leading setting in most digital environments. It is difficult to see slight differences between the auto leading setting and the next round number line space specification on the computer screen, so it is possible to accidentally mix leading measurements and overlook visual differences until the type file is in its final printed form.

Leading increments are easily controlled throughout the whole document by using *style sheets*. Be sure that the auto leading choice in the preferences in the style sheet designation is turned off and that the actual dimension desired is selected. This is another safe way

9/5 "Here! you may nurse it a bit, if you like!" the Duchess said to Alice, flinging the baby at her as she spoke. "I must go and get ready to play croquet with the Queen," and she hurried out of the room. The cook threw a frying-pan after her as she went out, but it just missed her.

9/9 "Here! you may nurse it a bit, if you like!" the Duchess said to Alice, flinging the baby at her as she spoke. "I must go and get ready to play croquet with the Queen," and she hurried out of the room. The cook threw a frying pan after her as she went out, but it just missed her.

9/12 "Here! you may nurse it a bit, if you like!" the Duchess said to Alice, flinging the baby at her as she spoke. "I must go and get ready to play croquet with the Queen," and she hurried out of the room. The cook threw a frying-pan after her as she went out, but it just missed her.

9/16 "Here! you may nurse it a bit, if you like!" the Duchess said to Alice, flinging the baby at her as she spoke. "I must go and get ready to play croquet with the Queen," and she hurried out of the room. The cook threw a frying-pan after her as she went out, but it just missed her.

9/23 "Here! you may nurse it a bit, if you like!" the Duchess said to Alice, flinging the baby at her as she spoke. "I must go and get ready to play croquet with the Queen," and she hurried out of the room. The cook threw a frying-pan after her as she went out, but it just missed her.

6/7.2   Alice caught the baby with some difficulty, as it was a queer-shaped little creature, and held out its arms and legs in all directions, "just like a star-fish," thought Alice. The poor little thing was snorting like a steam-engine when she caught it, and kept doubling itself up and straightening itself out again, so that altogether, for the first minute or two, it was as much as she could do to hold it.

8/9.6   Alice caught the baby with some difficulty, as it was a queer-shaped little creature, and held out its arms and legs in all directions, "just like a star-fish," thought Alice. The poor little thing was snorting like a steam-engine when she caught it, and kept doubling itself up and straightening itself out again, so that altogether, for the first minute or two, it was as much as she could do to hold it.

10.13 Five examples of type set with auto leading in a commercial publishing software application.

12/14.4   Alice caught the baby with some difficulty, as it was a queer-shaped little creature, and held out its arms and legs in all directions, "just like a star-fish," thought Alice. The poor little thing was snorting like a steam-engine when she caught it, and kept doubling itself up and straightening itself out again, so that altogether, for the first minute or two, it was as much as she could do to hold it.

14/16.8   Alice caught the baby with some difficulty, as it was a queer-shaped little creature, and held out its arms and legs in all directions, "just like a star-fish," thought Alice. The poor little thing was snorting like a steam-engine when she caught it, and kept doubling itself up and straightening itself out again, so that altogether, for the first minute or two, it was as much as she could do to hold it.

18/21.6   Alice caught the baby with some difficulty, as it was a queer-shaped little creature, and held out its arms and legs in all directions, "just like a star-fish," thought Alice. The poor little thing was snorting like a steam-engine when she caught it,

Leading Affects Legibility

Every font has a minimal amount of vertical space built into the digital file so that if text type is specified as "set solid," the ascenders and descenders will not touch. The clearance is tiny, however, and the lack of leading makes the text difficult to read. Solid setting is not advised for long passages, nor for detailed, technical information. The lack of leading is very hard for the eyes and the brain, and it is likely that the information will go unread or that the message will take on negative connotations or interpretation by the reader.

Obviously, text set with negative leading is not recommended for text intended to be read. Special circumstances where the message may be enhanced or more clearly communicated by the special treatment must be carefully and selectively determined.

Seldom does a proportionately large amount of leading affect legibility negatively—at least up to the point where the reader reviews the same line of text more than once because the eye is unable to jump down to the next line easily. Generally, the slightly larger amount of background space allows the reader to clearly distinguish one line from the next. The difficulty with setting type this way is that it requires a great amount of additional space to accommodate a relatively small amount of copy—a luxury seldom affordable in a limited compositional area.

Frequently the space between the lines of type, not necessarily the type design itself, improves the legibility of the message. In other words, 9-point type set with an additional 3 points of leading (9/12) is consistently reported as being easier to read than a larger size with less leading (12/13). Again, the leading depends on other factors such as the line length, letter spacing, word spacing, and characteristics of the font design.

to avoid confusion between the desired setting and the automatic setting in different parts of a document.

One mathematical formula for determining a comfortable amount of leading, which takes into account the length of the typeset line, is as follows: Divide the line length measure in picas by the size of the type in points. Round off the result to the nearest half point. An example using 11-point type set in a 21-pica line length would look like this: 21/11 equals 1.90909090. Round off the result to 2 and specify the type as 11/13. If the type is a smaller point size, such as 10 points, and the column width is slightly longer at 26 picas, the formula provides a result of 26/10, or 2.6. Round off the result to 2.5 points and specify the type as 10/12.5 points. With exception for special circumstances with unusual typefaces, it is seldom necessary to specify increments of less than a half point.

Changes in line spacing can add dramatic effects to an otherwise boring layout; leading sets a rhythmic tone or visual pace for the reader. Leading may be used to communicate the relative speed of the passage of time; it can create the image of confusion, crowded spaces, and noise. Once the correct, traditional methods of letter spacing, word spacing, and line spacing are mastered, explore possibilities to creatively enhance the visual communications you create.

Arrangement of Text Type

The composition often contains elements other than type: illustrations or photographs, lines, fleurons, charts, diagrams, and maps. Added to these are the characteristics of the page (dimensions and horizontal or vertical orientation). Once again, the experience of the reader comes into play, as those who were taught to read using American page sizes find

those easier to read, while those taught using the DIN (Deutsches Institut für Normung, the central authority for standards and industry standards in Germany) dimensions may find European page sizes easier to read. The overall dimensions of the page will inevitably affect the dimensions of the internal columns of type and the amount of type that will fit on the page.

Different studies have reported different comfortable line length dimensions. The general consensus is that line length (or resulting column width) should measure somewhere between 13 and 26 picas. One traditional line length formula recommends the measure in picas be twice the type size in points; that is, if the type is set in 12 points, the line length should measure approximately 24 picas. A second common formula recommends that the line length measure be somewhere between 1.5 and 2.5 alphabets for any given font.

The second formula accommodates differences in the set width of the font, whereas the first does not. Move toward the shorter line length for fonts with smaller x-heights, fonts set in smaller point sizes, thinner condensed fonts, light faces, italic faces, and monoweight sans serif faces. Longer line lengths should be used for fonts with larger x-heights, larger point sizes, and a larger set width seen in bold variations and extended variations.

The column width, coupled with the ability of the human eye to focus on a given area of the page, factors into the readability of the text. In layouts intended to accommodate multiple columns, refrain from using a line length less than 9 picas; this is considered too short, causing increased speed in eye movement that often results in the reader tiring more quickly. In studies conducted in the 1960s, it was determined that the margins should account

Try This! Determine the correct amount of leading for each example using the line length formula: Line length in picas ÷ type size in points equals the recommended leading (rounded off to the nearest half point).

Example: 11-point type in a 33-pica column width? Show your work as 33 ÷ 11 = 3.0, so the type should be set 11/14.

8-point type in a 14-pica column width?

_____

_____

_____

_____

9-point type in a 15-pica column width?

_____

_____

_____

13-point type in a 25-pica column width?

_____

_____

_____

_____

As soon as she had made out the proper way of nursing it (which was to twist it up into a sort of knot, and then keep tight hold of its right ear and left foot, so as to prevent its undoing itself), she carried it out into the open air. "IF I don't take this child away with me," thought Alice, "they're sure to kill it in a day or two: wouldn't it be murder to leave it behind?" She said the last words out loud, and the little thing grunted in reply (it had left off sneezing by this time). "Don't grunt," said Alice; "that's not at all a proper way of expressing yourself."

10.14 A running indent affects a series of lines on either the right or left margin.

    As soon as she had made out the proper way of nursing it (which was to twist it up into a sort of knot, and then keep tight hold of its right ear and left foot, so as to prevent its undoing itself), she carried it out into the open air. "IF I don't take this child away with me," thought Alice, "they're sure to kill it in a day or two: wouldn't it be murder to leave it behind?" She said the last words out loud, and the little thing grunted in reply (it had left off sneezing by this time). "Don't grunt," said Alice; "that's not at all a proper way of expressing yourself."

10.15 A paragraph indent, sometimes called a first line indent, affects a series of lines on either the right or left margin. Standard paragraph indentation is an em space.

As soon as she had made out the proper way of nursing it (which was to twist it up into a sort of knot, and then keep tight hold of its right ear and left foot, so as to prevent its undoing itself), she carried it out into the open air. "IF I don't take this child away with me," thought Alice, "they're sure to kill it in a day or two: wouldn't it be murder to leave it behind?" She said the last words out loud, and the little thing grunted in reply (it had left off sneezing by this time). "Don't grunt," said Alice; "that's not at all a proper way of expressing yourself."

10.16 A hanging indent moves the first line to the left of all other lines in the paragraph.

Alice: As soon as she had made out the proper way of nursing it (which was to twist it up into a sort of knot, and then keep tight hold of its right ear and left foot, so as to prevent its undoing itself), she carried it out into the open air. "IF I don't take this child away with me," thought Alice, "they're sure to kill it in a day or two: wouldn't it be murder to leave it behind?" She said the last words out loud, and the little thing grunted in reply (it had left off sneezing by this time). "Don't grunt," said Alice; "that's not at all a proper way of expressing yourself."

10.17 Commonly used for glossary or definition lists, an indent on point is similar to the hanging indent, but the subsequent lines are indented to the width of the typeset term.

    The baby grunted again, and Alice looked very anxiously into its face to see what was the matter with it. There could be no doubt that it had a VERY turned-up nose, much more like a snout than a real nose; also its eyes were getting extremely small for a baby: altogether Alice did not like the look of the thing at all. "But perhaps it was only sobbing," she thought, and looked into its eyes again, to see if there were any tears.

    The baby grunted again, and Alice looked very anxiously into its face to see what was the matter with it. There could be no doubt that it had a VERY turned-up nose, much more like a snout than a real nose; also its eyes were getting extremely small for a baby: altogether Alice did not like the look of the thing at all. "But perhaps it was only sobbing," she thought, and looked into its eyes again, to see if there were any tears.

10.18 Type set in unusual shapes is a special effect usually reserved for occasions where a photograph or illustration dicates the composition. Skewed type has parallel margins that are not vertical. Using justified settings and adjusting the point size and leading result in the most legible solution.

for close to 50 percent of the total area of the page. A thin vertical column rule helps define the areas of type more clearly when a smaller column space is required to fit text into a given space.

The compositional space dedicated to margins, columns, and column rules affects the aesthetic and visual communication. Pages designed with narrow column margins (sometimes called alleys) often result in a heavy look and appear more serious in tone. Pages accommodating wider columns, broader alleys, and generous leading appear lighter and often are perceived as more inviting to readers.

The most common format for setting text type includes the left alignment of all lines of a paragraph except for the first indented line, with a ragged right margin. Indentation of paragraphs clearly defines the beginning of a thought or a variation on the topic within the article or story. This visual cue has been found to improve the speed of reading. Short-lived trends such as the indentation of alternating lines of text in a paragraph slow the speed of reading. The uneven right side of the column provides a visual clue to the reader that it is time to jump down to the next line, while the even right margin in justified text does not provide an equivalent reminder.

Adjusting the space between paragraphs adds a more professional look to the set type. In the past it was only possible to add space between paragraphs by including a complete blank line, which results in a great deal of wasted space and is not particularly attractive. In modern software applications it is possible to add a few points of additional space between paragraphs, usually using a command such as Space After in the style formatting menu. While many feel that it is redundant to use both a paragraph indent

and additional space between paragraphs as a visual clue signifying the beginning and end of a thought sequence, the aesthetics should play a role in that decision. Perhaps a traditional em indent in a small font requires additional assistance, while the same information set in a different font and larger size may not.

Type set flush right or centered is more time-consuming for readers, as it is more difficult for the human eye to track to the uneven lines of text on the left side of the column. In flush right or justified text, the breaks in the text must make sense in terms of phrases for the reader to understand the communication. Sometimes planning correct breaks in the text requires rewriting or rewording—something as simple as a longer or shorter synonym often solves the problem.

Background Value, Color, and Contrast

Studies as far back as the late 1870s suggested that yellow-tinted papers were the easiest for reading text printed in black ink. No one was quite sure, however, exactly what sort of yellow and what level of tint should be used. By the early 1900s typographers and printers suggested that hard-surfaced, opaque, unglazed handmade papers were most suitable. By 1925, researchers determined that an uncoated, bright white sheet with a clean printing impression, which had no show-through, was preferred. Just as all other preferences change over time, modern practice has established a preference for highly finished papers—either dull or glossy.

Contrast refers to the difference between opposing forces or compositional opposites. Contrast in value or tone, therefore, refers to the difference between the value of the printed type and its background. In printing, the basic color is black, and tones of gray are achieved by the

No, there were no tears. "If you're going to turn into a pig, my dear," said Alice, seriously, "I'll have nothing more to do with you. Mind now!" The poor little thing sobbed again (or grunted, it was impossible to say which), and they went on for some while in silence.

No, there were no tears. "If you're going to turn into a pig, my dear," said Alice, seriously, "I'll have nothing more to do with you. Mind now!" The poor little thing sobbed again (or grunted, it was impossible to say which), and they went on for some while in silence.

No, there were no tears. "If you're going to turn into a pig, my dear," said Alice, seriously, "I'll have nothing more to do with you. Mind now!" The poor little thing sobbed again (or grunted, it was impossible to say which), and they went on for some while in silence.

No, there were no tears. "If you're going to turn into a pig, my dear," said Alice, seriously, "I'll have nothing more to do with you. Mind now!" The poor little thing sobbed again (or grunted, it was impossible to say which), and they went on for some while in silence.

10.19 Visual examples of a serif and sans serif font as black text on a white background (top) and white on a black background. Typographic experts continue to disagree about legibility issues regarding serifs and background values under different circumstances.

10.20–10.37 Examples of black and white type on varying percentages of black backgrounds. The 50 percent black background and lower percentages are relatively easy to read, while higher percentages of black in the background require white type for legibility. The midrange values are least legible, while the high contrast is most legible.

No, there were no tears. "If you're going to turn into a pig, my dear," said Alice, seriously, "I'll have nothing more to do with you. Mind now!" The poor little thing sobbed again (or grunted, it was impossible to say which), and they went on for some while in silence.

No, there were no tears. "If you're going to turn into a pig, my dear," said Alice, seriously, "I'll have nothing more to do with you. Mind now!" The poor little thing sobbed again (or grunted, it was impossible to say which), and they went on for some while in silence.

No, there were no tears. "If you're going to turn into a pig, my dear," said Alice, seriously, "I'll have nothing more to do with you. Mind now!" The poor little thing sobbed again (or grunted, it was impossible to say which), and they went on for some while in silence.

No, there were no tears. "If you're going to turn into a pig, my dear," said Alice, seriously, "I'll have nothing more to do with you. Mind now!" The poor little thing sobbed again (or grunted, it was impossible to say which), and they went on for some while in silence.

No, there were no tears. "If you're going to turn into a pig, my dear," said Alice, seriously, "I'll have nothing more to do with you. Mind now!" The poor little thing sobbed again (or grunted, it was impossible to say which), and they went on for some while in silence.

No, there were no tears. "If you're going to turn into a pig, my dear," said Alice, seriously, "I'll have nothing more to do with you. Mind now!" The poor little thing sobbed again (or grunted, it was impossible to say which), and they went on for some while in silence.

10.20 10% gray background with 100% black type; the top example is 10/12 Times and the bottom example is 10/12 Futura.

10.21 20% gray background with 100% black type; the top example is Times and the bottom example is Futura.

10.22 30% gray background with 100% black type; the top example is 10/12 Times and the bottom example is 10/12 Futura.

No, there were no tears. "If you're going to turn into a pig, my dear," said Alice, seriously, "I'll have nothing more to do with you. Mind now!" The poor little thing sobbed again (or grunted, it was impossible to say which), and they went on for some while in silence.

No, there were no tears. "If you're going to turn into a pig, my dear," said Alice, seriously, "I'll have nothing more to do with you. Mind now!" The poor little thing sobbed again (or grunted, it was impossible to say which), and they went on for some while in silence.

No, there were no tears. "If you're going to turn into a pig, my dear," said Alice, seriously, "I'll have nothing more to do with you. Mind now!" The poor little thing sobbed again (or grunted, it was impossible to say which), and they went on for some while in silence.

10.26 10% black background with white type; the example is 10/12 Times.

10.27 20% black background with white type; the example is 10/12 Times.

10.28 30% black background with white type; the example is 10/12 Times.

No, there were no tears. "If you're going to turn into a pig, my dear," said Alice, seriously, "I'll have nothing more to do with you. Mind now!" The poor little thing sobbed again (or grunted, it was impossible to say which), and they went on for some while in silence.

No, there were no tears. "If you're going to turn into a pig, my dear," said Alice, seriously, "I'll have nothing more to do with you. Mind now!" The poor little thing sobbed again (or grunted, it was impossible to say which), and they went on for some while in silence.

No, there were no tears. "If you're going to turn into a pig, my dear," said Alice, seriously, "I'll have nothing more to do with you. Mind now!" The poor little thing sobbed again (or grunted, it was impossible to say which), and they went on for some while in silence.

No, there were no tears. "If you're going to turn into a pig, my dear," said Alice, seriously, "I'll have nothing more to do with you. Mind now!" The poor little thing sobbed again (or grunted, it was impossible to say which), and they went on for some while in silence.

No, there were no tears. "If you're going to turn into a pig, my dear," said Alice, seriously, "I'll have nothing more to do with you. Mind now!" The poor little thing sobbed again (or grunted, it was impossible to say which), and they went on for some while in silence.

No, there were no tears. "If you're going to turn into a pig, my dear," said Alice, seriously, "I'll have nothing more to do with you. Mind now!" The poor little thing sobbed again (or grunted, it was impossible to say which), and they went on for some while in silence.

10.23 40% black background with black type; the top example is 10/12 Times and the bottom example is 10/12 Futura.

10.24 50% black background with black type; the top example is 10/12 Times and the bottom example is 10/12 Futura.

10.25 60% black background with black type; the top example is 10/12 Times and the bottom example is 10/12 Futura.

No, there were no tears. "If you're going to turn into a pig, my dear," said Alice, seriously, "I'll have nothing more to do with you. Mind now!" The poor little thing sobbed again (or grunted, it was impossible to say which), and they went on for some while in silence.

No, there were no tears. "If you're going to turn into a pig, my dear," said Alice, seriously, "I'll have nothing more to do with you. Mind now!" The poor little thing sobbed again (or grunted, it was impossible to say which), and they went on for some while in silence.

No, there were no tears. "If you're going to turn into a pig, my dear," said Alice, seriously, "I'll have nothing more to do with you. Mind now!" The poor little thing sobbed again (or grunted, it was impossible to say which), and they went on for some while in silence.

10.29 40% black background with white type; the example is 10/12 Times.

10.30 50% black background with white type; the example is 10/12 Times.

10.31 60% black background with white type; the example is 10/12 Times.

No, there were no tears. "If you're going to turn into a pig, my dear," said Alice, seriously, "I'll have nothing more to do with you. Mind now!" The poor little thing sobbed again (or grunted, it was impossible to say which), and they went on for some while in silence.

No, there were no tears. "If you're going to turn into a pig, my dear," said Alice, seriously, "I'll have nothing more to do with you. Mind now!" The poor little thing sobbed again (or grunted, it was impossible to say which), and they went on for some while in silence.

No, there were no tears. "If you're going to turn into a pig, my dear," said Alice, seriously, "I'll have nothing more to do with you. Mind now!" The poor little thing sobbed again (or grunted, it was impossible to say which), and they went on for some while in silence.

No, there were no tears. "If you're going to turn into a pig, my dear," said Alice, seriously, "I'll have nothing more to do with you. Mind now!" The poor little thing sobbed again (or grunted, it was impossible to say which), and they went on for some while in silence.

No, there were no tears. "If you're going to turn into a pig, my dear," said Alice, seriously, "I'll have nothing more to do with you. Mind now!" The poor little thing sobbed again (or grunted, it was impossible to say which), and they went on for some while in silence.

No, there were no tears. "If you're going to turn into a pig, my dear," said Alice, seriously, "I'll have nothing more to do with you. Mind now!" The poor little thing sobbed again (or grunted, it was impossible to say which), and they went on for some while in silence.

10.32 70% black background with black type; the top example is 10/12 Times and the bottom example is 10/12 Futura.

10.33 80% black background with black type; the top example is 10/12 Times and the bottom example is 10/12 Futura.

10.34 90% black background with black type; the top example is 10/12 Times and the bottom example is 10/12 Futura.

No, there were no tears. "If you're going to turn into a pig, my dear," said Alice, seriously, "I'll have nothing more to do with you. Mind now!" The poor little thing sobbed again (or grunted, it was impossible to say which), and they went on for some while in silence.

No, there were no tears. "If you're going to turn into a pig, my dear," said Alice, seriously, "I'll have nothing more to do with you. Mind now!" The poor little thing sobbed again (or grunted, it was impossible to say which), and they went on for some while in silence.

No, there were no tears. "If you're going to turn into a pig, my dear," said Alice, seriously, "I'll have nothing more to do with you. Mind now!" The poor little thing sobbed again (or grunted, it was impossible to say which), and they went on for some while in silence.

10.35 70% black background with white type; the example is 10/12 Times.

10.36 80% black background with white type; the example is 10/12 Times.

10.37 90% black background with white type; the example is 10/12 Times.

use of very small black dots. The size of the dot and the distance between the dots determine the resulting gray tone. Gray values are commonly specified in 10 percent increments from white (0 percent) to black (100 percent).

Designers and typographers realized a long time ago that reading white type on a black background is more difficult than reading black type on a white background. In small quantities, white type on a black background can be an attractive addition for providing emphasis. The only thing worse for legibility than printing large tracts of white body copy on a black background is printing the text in a complementary color scheme, such as green on a red background which can make the text unreadable for color-blind people, or in a combination of red and black. Even though both red and black are different colors, they are of equal value or intensity, so red type does not read well on a black background, or vice versa. Individuals with vision impairments may not be able to discern the difference.

Hot, fluorescent colors may be overwhelming to readers' eyes, especially in brightly lit environments. Attempting to read text printed on such bright colors may result in more blinking and after-images. Complementary colors (orange and blue, red and green, and yellow and violet) appear to vibrate when placed next to each other, making it nearly impossible for most people to read the text on a page in these combinations. The use of this phenomenon was widespread throughout the 1960s in the Op Art movement. Needless to say, this effect is not recommended for important messages meant to be read by a broad target audience.

While color is an effective tool for providing emphasis, it is highly influential in determining the legibility of a typeset message. Remember

No, there were no tears. "If you're going to turn into a pig, my dear," said Alice, seriously, "I'll have nothing more to do with you. Mind now!" The poor little thing sobbed again (or grunted, it was impossible to say which), and they went on for some while in silence.

No, there were no tears. "If you're going to turn into a pig, my dear," said Alice, seriously, "I'll have nothing more to do with you. Mind now!" The poor little thing sobbed again (or grunted, it was impossible to say which), and they went on for some while in silence.

No, there were no tears. "If you're going to turn into a pig, my dear," said Alice, seriously, "I'll have nothing more to do with you. Mind now!" The poor little thing sobbed again (or grunted, it was impossible to say which), and they went on for some while in silence.

No, there were no tears. "If you're going to turn into a pig, my dear," said Alice, seriously, "I'll have nothing more to do with you. Mind now!" The poor little thing sobbed again (or grunted, it was impossible to say which), and they went on for some while in silence.

10.38 10% gray background with 50% black type; the top example is 10/12 Times and the bottom example is 10/12 Futura.

10.39 20% gray background with 50% black type; the top example is 10/12 Times and the bottom example is 10/12 Futura.

No, there were no tears. "If you're going to turn into a pig, my dear," said Alice, seriously, "I'll have nothing more to do with you. Mind now!" The poor little thing sobbed again (or grunted, it was impossible to say which), and they went on for some while in silence.

No, there were no tears. "If you're going to turn into a pig, my dear," said Alice, seriously, "I'll have nothing more to do with you. Mind now!" The poor little thing sobbed again (or grunted, it was impossible to say which), and they went on for some while in silence.

10.40 10% black type with white background; the example is 10/12 Times.

10.41 20% black type with a white background; the example is 10/12 Times.

No, there were no tears. "If you're going to turn into a pig, my dear," said Alice, seriously, "I'll have nothing more to do with you. Mind now!" The poor little thing sobbed again (or grunted, it was impossible to say which), and they went on for some while in silence.

No, there were no tears. "If you're going to turn into a pig, my dear," said Alice, seriously, "I'll have nothing more to do with you. Mind now!" The poor little thing sobbed again (or grunted, it was impossible to say which), and they went on for some while in silence.

No, there were no tears. "If you're going to turn into a pig, my dear," said Alice, seriously, "I'll have nothing more to do with you. Mind now!" The poor little thing sobbed again (or grunted, it was impossible to say which), and they went on for some while in silence.

No, there were no tears. "If you're going to turn into a pig, my dear," said Alice, seriously, "I'll have nothing more to do with you. Mind now!" The poor little thing sobbed again (or grunted, it was impossible to say which), and they went on for some while in silence.

No, there were no tears. "If you're going to turn into a pig, my dear," said Alice, seriously, "I'll have nothing more to do with you. Mind now!" The poor little thing sobbed again (or grunted, it was impossible to say which), and they went on for some while in silence.

No, there were no tears. "If you're going to turn into a pig, my dear," said Alice, seriously, "I'll have nothing more to do with you. Mind now!" The poor little thing sobbed again (or grunted, it was impossible to say which), and they went on for some while in silence.

10.42 30% gray background with 50% black type; the top example is 10/12 Times and the bottom example is 10/12 Futura.

10.43 40% gray background with 50% black type; the top example is 10/12 Times and the bottom example is 10/12 Futura.

10.44 60% gray background with 50% black type; the top example is 10/12 Times and the bottom example is 10/12 Futura.

No, there were no tears. "If you're going to turn into a pig, my dear," said Alice, seriously, "I'll have nothing more to do with you. Mind now!" The poor little thing sobbed again (or grunted, it was impossible to say which), and they went on for some while in silence.

No, there were no tears. "If you're going to turn into a pig, my dear," said Alice, seriously, "I'll have nothing more to do with you. Mind now!" The poor little thing sobbed again (or grunted, it was impossible to say which), and they went on for some while in silence.

No, there were no tears. "If you're going to turn into a pig, my dear," said Alice, seriously, "I'll have nothing more to do with you. Mind now!" The poor little thing sobbed again (or grunted, it was impossible to say which), and they went on for some while in silence.

10.48 30% black type with white background; the example is 10/12 Times.

10.49 40% black type with a white background; the example is 10/12 Times.

10.50 50% black type with white background; the example is 10/12 Times.

No, there were no tears. "If you're going to turn into a pig, my dear," said Alice, seriously, "I'll have nothing more to do with you. Mind now!" The poor little thing sobbed again (or grunted, it was impossible to say which), and they went on for some while in silence.

No, there were no tears. "If you're going to turn into a pig, my dear," said Alice, seriously, "I'll have nothing more to do with you. Mind now!" The poor little thing sobbed again (or grunted, it was impossible to say which), and they went on for some while in silence.

No, there were no tears. "If you're going to turn into a pig, my dear," said Alice, seriously, "I'll have nothing more to do with you. Mind now!" The poor little thing sobbed again (or grunted, it was impossible to say which), and they went on for some while in silence.

10.38–10.53 Examples of 50 percent black type on varying percentages of black backgrounds, and varying percentages of black type on white backgrounds. The high contrast is most legible.

No, there were no tears. "If you're going to turn into a pig, my dear," said Alice, seriously, "I'll have nothing more to do with you. Mind now!" The poor little thing sobbed again (or grunted, it was impossible to say which), and they went on for some while in silence.

No, there were no tears. "If you're going to turn into a pig, my dear," said Alice, seriously, "I'll have nothing more to do with you. Mind now!" The poor little thing sobbed again (or grunted, it was impossible to say which), and they went on for some while in silence.

No, there were no tears. "If you're going to turn into a pig, my dear," said Alice, seriously, "I'll have nothing more to do with you. Mind now!" The poor little thing sobbed again (or grunted, it was impossible to say which), and they went on for some while in silence.

10.45 70% gray background with 50% black type; the top example is 10/12 Times and the bottom example is 10/12 Futura.

10.46 80% gray background with 50% black type; the top example is 10/12 Times and the bottom example is 10/12 Futura.

10.47 90% gray background with 50% black type; the top example is 10/12 Times and the bottom example is 10/12 Futura.

No, there were no tears. "If you're going to turn into a pig, my dear," said Alice, seriously, "I'll have nothing more to do with you. Mind now!" The poor little thing sobbed again (or grunted, it was impossible to say which), and they went on for some while in silence.

No, there were no tears. "If you're going to turn into a pig, my dear," said Alice, seriously, "I'll have nothing more to do with you. Mind now!" The poor little thing sobbed again (or grunted, it was impossible to say which), and they went on for some while in silence.

No, there were no tears. "If you're going to turn into a pig, my dear," said Alice, seriously, "I'll have nothing more to do with you. Mind now!" The poor little thing sobbed again (or grunted, it was impossible to say which), and they went on for some while in silence.

10.51 60% black type with white background; the example is 10/12 Times.

10.52 70% black type with a white background; the example is 10/12 Times.

10.53 80% black type with white background; the example is 10/12 Times.

So she set the little creature down, and felt quite relieved to see it trot away quietly into the wood. "If it had grown up," she said to herself, "it would have made a dreadfully ugly child: but it makes rather a handsome pig, I think."

So she set the little creature down, and felt quite relieved to see it trot away quietly into the wood. "If it had grown up," she said to herself, "it would have made a dreadfully ugly child: but it makes rather a handsome pig, I think."

10.54 Far left: Flush left, aligned with the top of the text box.

10.55 Left: Flush left, aligned with the top of the text box and indented on the left and right.

10.56 Right: Centered and aligned with the top of the text box.

So she set the little creature down, and felt quite relieved to see it trot away quietly into the wood. "If it had grown up," she said to herself, "it would have made a dreadfully ugly child: but it makes rather a handsome pig, I think."

So she set the little creature down, and felt quite relieved to see it trot away quietly into the wood. "If it had grown up," she said to herself, "it would have made a dreadfully ugly child: but it makes rather a handsome pig, I think."

So she set the little creature down, and felt quite relieved to see it trot away quietly into the wood. "If it had grown up," she said to herself, "it would have made a dreadfully ugly child: but it makes rather a handsome pig, I think."

10.57 Far left: Flush left, centered within the text box.

10.58 Left: Flush left, centered within the text box and indented on the left and right.

10.59 Right: Centered vertically and horizontally within the text box.

So she set the little creature down, and felt quite relieved to see it trot away quietly into the wood. "If it had grown up," she said to herself, "it would have made a dreadfully ugly child: but it makes rather a handsome pig, I think."

So she set the little creature down, and felt quite relieved to see it trot away quietly into the wood. "If it had grown up," she said to herself, "it would have made a dreadfully ugly child: but it makes rather a handsome pig, I think."

So she set the little creature down, and felt quite relieved to see it trot away quietly into the wood. "If it had grown up," she said to herself, "it would have made a dreadfully ugly child: but it makes rather a handsome pig, I think."

10.60 Far left: Flush left, aligned with the bottom of the text box.

10.61 Left: Flush left, aligned with the bottom of the text box and indented on the left and right.

10.62 Right: Centered and aligned with the bottom of the text box.

So she set the little creature down, and felt quite relieved to see it trot away quietly into the wood. "If it had grown up," she said to herself, "it would have made a dreadfully ugly child: but it makes rather a handsome pig, I think."

So she set the little creature down, and felt quite relieved to see it trot away quietly into the wood. "If it had grown up," she said to herself, "it would have made a dreadfully ugly child: but it makes rather a handsome pig, I think."

So she set the little creature down, and felt quite relieved to see it trot away quietly into the wood. "If it had grown up," she said to herself, "it would have made a dreadfully ugly child: but it makes rather a handsome pig, I think."

10.63 Far left: Flush left, vertically justified within the text box.

10.64 Left: Flush left, vertically justified within the text box and indented on the left and right.

10.65 Right: Vertically justified and horizontally centered within the text box.

that color varies greatly depending on the characteristics of the environment in which it is viewed. For example, perception of a color varies depending on the characteristics of the colors or values that color is placed next to in a composition; colored inks are affected by the color and value of the paper on which they are printed. Just as color in our offices, homes, clothes, furniture, and accessories affect our mood and outlook, so does color affect a reader's perception of the content he or she is about to read or has just read. Because color can have such a negative impact with overuse, it is best to err on the side of caution.

Type Enclosed by Boxes and Bars

Type set within the confines of a shape creates additional compositional consideration. More often than not, the type should be centered vertically and horizontally within the defined space, the shape of the typeset text should mimic the contour of the enclosure, and any text that is outside of the callout or pullquote should be set equidistant from all sides. By balancing the borders enclosing the text, and balancing the size and proportion of the box to the size and proportion of the selected font, awkward negative or background shapes can be avoided. When the internal and external margins do not balance, the reader becomes distracted by the interaction of the compositional elements, as opposed to concentrating on the message.

Single Spaces Following Punctuation

A practice of typing double spaces following punctuation ending a sentence or question evolved from the era of typewriters. Typewritten manuscripts used monospaced fonts in which all of the characters, regardless of their physical characteristics, occupied the same set width. The

two spaces following a period, question mark, or exclamation point provided a visual pause that accentuated the end of the idea.

Since modern digital fonts are variably spaced, taking into account the visual characteristics of each letterform, the additional space is no longer necessary. Two spaces create a proportionally larger amount of white space that may result in white rivers running vertically through the blocks of text, instead of the smooth, even gray texture that is desirable.

Use the Find/Change command (usually located under the Edit menu) in any contemporary word processing or desktop publishing software application. Search for double spacing following punctuation marks, and replace them with a single space. This small effort will add a level of professionalism to the final composition.

Typesetting Abbreviations

The abbreviations AM (*ante meridiem*, meaning the period of time between midnight and noon) and PM (*post meridiem*, meaning the period of time between noon and midnight) following the hour indicate the time of day. The abbreviations BCE (before common era) and CE (common era) in reference to historical time periods, are other common abbreviations. Over time the preference for setting these abbreviations in all uppercase without or without periods, or in all lowercase with or without periods has changed. It is best to refer to the appropriate style manual (commonly A.P.A, C.B.E., Chicago, or M.L.A.) for up-to-date guidance.

For hours and minutes, consider shifting the baseline of the colon used to separate the two so that it is centered vertically between the baseline and the cap height of the numerals, as opposed

9:00 AM
9:00 PM
9:00 A.M.
9:00 P.M.

9:00 AM
9:00 PM
9:00 A.M.
9:00 P.M.

9:00 am
9:00 pm
9:00 a.m.
9:00 p.m.

10.66 Correctly typeset the abbreviations for ante meridiem and post meridiem using preferences indicated in an appropriate style manual. Shown are (top) all caps with and without periods, small caps (middle) with and without periods, and lowercase (bottom) with and without periods.

In 1962 *Martin K. Speckter* introduced the *Interrobang*, which was created to fill a gap in the American English punctuation system. Previously writers used the cumbersome and unattractive combination of the question mark and exclamation mark sequentially, to punctuate statements in which neither the question mark nor the exclamation point alone exactly communicated the intonation and emphasis: "Who forgot to feed the dog this morning?"

to leaving the colon aligned with the baseline at the bottom of the numerals. This shift is not noticeable to most people in text sizes but is obvious in large display text.

Other common rules for abbreviations include:

- In the United Kingdom no period is used if the last letter of the abbreviation is also the final letter of word, as in Mr, Dr, Lieut or Lt.

- Abbreviations following Canadian conventions generally omit periods for all abbreviations consisting of all uppercase or ending in uppercase (TV, MiG, YMCA), except place-names, personal names, degrees, and legal references.

- Hyphenate an abbreviation if the original was hyphenated (Lt.-Gov. for Lieutenant-Governor; but note that the Canadian style does not hyphenate that combination any longer).

- Acronyms are usually full caps (NATO) unless they are formed from company names (Stelco, Inco, Alcoa).

- Close up *ampersands* (R&D, S&L) in abbreviations so that there is not any additional space between the letters and the ampersand.

- Do not begin a sentence with an abbreviation that is a partial word (Fig. 1, though courtesy titles such as Dr. are okay), a number (14C), or lowercase (t-square).

- In the case of plural abbreviations, add an s (Drs., IOUs). If it is a single letter, or is lowercase, or would be confusing, or uses periods, add an 's (A's, SOS's, Ph.D.'s). Measures do not change (mi., ft.). Some plurals are irregular (pp., ff., cc.), so it may be best to look up special abbreviations in a style guide appropriate for the subject.

- In the case of possessive abbreviations, in the singular form add 's (FDR's); for plurals, add apostrophe only following the s in the plural word (RNs' but Oakland A's winning streak).

Using Bullets to Emphasize Listed Information

Setting a *bullet* at the beginning of each point in a list brings attention to the individual points. The size of the bullet or other dingbat should be relatively small as compared to the size of the typeset text so as to emphasize the beginning of a new thought, but not so large as to distract from the overall communication of the message. More often than not, a bullet in the same size as the text is too large; do not hesitate to reduce this by one or two points, and adjust the vertical location up slightly using the baseline shift command in the software application.

Bullets should be set in a hanging indent format. That is, the bullet should be set to the left of the left margin of the typeset text so that they do not cause the first line to indent. If bullets (as well as parentheses and dashes) are used with copy that is set in all caps, they should be shifted up one or two points, since they are designed to align along the center of the x-height of a font.

Prime Marks, Quotation Marks, and Apostrophes

Direct quotations from a written or spoken source are incorporated into someone else's written text through the use of double *quotation marks*.

- Use a set of quotation marks to enclose each direct quotation included in your writing.

Table of Names and Uses for Punctuation Marks

'	**apostrophe**	A punctuation mark in English; it marks omissions, forms the possessive, and, in special cases, forms plurals. It is a diacritic mark in some languages written in the Latin alphabet.
( )	**parentheses**	Enclose an explanatory or qualifying word, clause, or sentence inserted into a passage with which it has not necessarily any grammatical connection. Also called round brackets or round braces.
[ ]	**square brackets**	Used to set off an interruption within a direct quotation; to insert a clarifying word or phrase into a quotation; to change an uppercase letter to a lowercase one (often used in a quotation of a poem); or to mark a mistake of spelling or grammar that occurs in the original quotation.
{ }	**curly brackets** or **braces**	Sometimes used in prose to indicate a series of equal choices: "Select your entree (spaghetti, lasagne, ravioli) and place your order with the waitress." In mathematics, curly braces are used to delimit sets.
< >	**angle brackets** or **chevrons**	Used to enclose highlighted material. Some dictionaries use angle brackets to enclose short excerpts illustrating the usage of words. True angle brackets are not available on a typical computer keyboard, so the < (less than) and > (greater than) symbols are used if the true glyph is not available using an ASCII key combination.
:	**colon**	Used as a punctuation mark after a word introducing a quotation, an explanation, an example, or a series, and often after the salutation of a business letter. May be used as a mathematical symbol between numbers or groups of numbers in expressions of time (2:30) and ratios (1:2).
,	**comma**	Used to indicate a separation of ideas or elements within the structure of a sentence.
—	**figure dash**	So named because it is the same width as the number set in a font. Used to separate numeral sequences, as in a telephone number: for example, 555-5555.
—	**em dash**	Used to indicate a parenthetical statement.
–	**en dash**	Used in the separation of a compound adjective or to indicate the range or connection between two groups of information, for example 3:00–5:00.
—	**quotation dash** or **horizontal bar**	Used to introduce quoted material; this is interchangeable with the em dash.
...	**ellipsis**	A three-dot symbol used to show an incomplete statement. An ellipsis can also be used to indicate a pause in speech, or be used at the end of a sentence to indicate a trailing off into silence.

Table of Names and Uses for Punctuation Marks continued

¡ !	**exclamation mark**	Used to indicate a tone of surprised emphasis. Some languages, such as Spanish, require the upside-down exclamation mark at the beginning of the sentence to indicate the tone of the communication before reaching the end of the message. Sometimes called a screamer or a bang.
.	**full stop** or **period**	Commonly placed at the end of several different types of sentences in several languages, including English. Also called a full point.
–	**hyphen** or **minus** or **soft hyphen**	Used both to join words and to separate syllables. In mathematics it is a symbol used to indicate the operation of subtraction.
‽	**interrobang**	English-language punctuation mark intended to combine the functions of a question mark and an exclamation point. The typographical character resembles those marks superimposed over each other. Few fonts include this character as part of the standard character set.
¿ ?	**question mark**	Used at the end of the sentence to indicate the rising tone in the speaker's voice that elicits a response from the listener(s). In some languages, such as Spanish, an upside-down question mark prepares the reader before reaching the end of the sentence.
' '	**single quotation marks**	Used in pairs to set off a speech, quotation, or phrase. Single quotes are British and double quotes are American. Available in straight variations, as on a typewriter, or in curly versions, as professionally typeset.
" "	**double quotation marks**	Used in pairs to set off speech, a quotation, or a phrase. The pair consists of an opening quotation mark and a closing quotation mark. May be used to call attention to ironic or apologetic words; ironic quotes are sometimes called scare, sneer, or distance quotes. These are available in straight variations, as on a typewriter, or in curly versions, as professionally typeset. Also called quotes or inverted commas.
;	**semicolon**	Used as a stronger division than a comma, to make meaning clear in a sentence where commas are already being used for other purposes. It is used to join two sentences slightly more closely than they would be joined if separated by a period. It often replaces a conjunction such as *and* or *but*.
/	**slash** or **forward slash**	Most common use is to replace the hyphen to make clear a strong joint between words or phrases. In mathematical applications, it can indicate a division operation, or separate the numerator from the denominator in a fraction. Before the use of decimals came about in the United Kingdom, it was used to separate pounds, shillings, and pence values. In programming, it is used to separate directory or names in Unix file paths and in URLs. Also called a diagonal, separatrix, shilling mark, stroke, virgule, or slant.

Table of Names and Uses for Punctuation Marks continued

•	**bullet**	Used to introduce items in a list.
\	**backslash**	Used in computing environments. In the Japanese equivalent of ASCII, the code point that would be used for backslash is instead a yen mark (¥). Sometimes called a reverse solidus.
·	**interpunct**	Small, vertically centered dot used for interword separation in ancient Latin script.
&	**ampersand**	Logogram representing the word *and*.
*	**asterisk**	Used to indicate a footnote.
†	**dagger**	Used to indicate a second footnote. In European time tables the symbol is used to denote Sundays (representing the Christian Cross) and holidays. Also called an obelisk or obelus.
‡	**double dagger**	Used to indicate a third footnote.
@	commercial **at**	Symbolic abbreviation for the word *at*. Its formal name comes from its commercial use in invoices. Used as part of an e-mail address, for example, jdoe@domainname.com. Also known as the *at* symbol.
#	**number sign**	Used to replace the letters *No.* as an abbreviation for the word *number*. Also called a pound sign, hash mark, or octothorpe.
'	**prime**	Has a number of mathematical applications, the most popular being to represent the *foot* as a unit of measurement, or minutes in latitude or longitude. Also used for the transliteration (mapping) of one language to another. Should not be confused with the apostrophe.
"	**double prime**	Has a number of mathematical applications, the most popular of which is to represent the *inch* as a unit of measurement, or seconds in latitude or longitude. Should not be confused with quotation marks.
~	**tilde**	In languages, a tilde is a diacritic mark placed over a letter to indicate a change in pronunciation, such as nasalization. Also called a swung dash.
_	**underscore**	Used as a diacritic mark in some African and Native American languages. In English it is a character left over from the typewriter era. Prior to the advent of word processing, using the underscore character was the only method of underlining words.
|	**vertical bar** or **pipe**	Name of the ASCII character at position 124. Primary use is in programming and in mathematics, however, more recently it has become popular for use on Web pages to divide or separate the names of links.

This sign, called the "at" symbol in English, is most commonly seen in UNIX programming and in Internet e-mail addresses. In other cultures @ has a number of different names: in Italian it's known as *chiocciolina* and in French, *petit escargo*—both translating to "little snail." In Germany @ is *klammeraffe* or spider monkey, while the Dutch refer to it as *api*, from *apestaart*, meaning "monkey's tail."

In Finland it's a cat's tail and is named *miau*; In Norway it's a spiral-shaped cinnamon cake called *kanel-bolle* and in Israel it's called a *shtrudel*. Denmark's version of @ is a *snabel*, meaning "A with trunk" while the Spanish call the @ symbol an *arroba* which is a unit of measure weighing approximately 25 pounds.

- use a capital letter with the first word of a direct quotation of a whole sentence. Do not use a capital letter with the first word of a direct quotation of part of a sentence.

- If the quotation is interrupted and then continues in your sentence, do not capitalize the second part of the quotation.

- Use a set of quotation marks to indicate titles of short or minor works, such as songs, short stories, essays, short poems, one-act plays, and other literary works that are shorter than a three-act play or a complete book.

- Use a set of quotation marks to indicate titles of parts of larger works, such as chapters in books; articles in newspapers, magazines, journals, or other periodical publications; and episodes of television and radio series.

- Use quotation marks to indicate words used ironically, with reservations, or in some unusual way (sometimes called scare quotes).

Indirect quotations refer to the content of the original author's words but include only a newly phrased version without using the exact words, called *paraphrasing*. Paraphrasing does not mean changing only one or two words while maintaining the original sentence structure, but rather means that the meaning is maintained in a newly worded interpretation. In these cases, double quotation marks are not used.

Single quotation marks are used when a quotation is enclosed within another quotation—that is, when a second party is directly quoting the exact words of a third party.

The apostrophe has three uses: to form possessives of nouns, to show the omission of letters (as in contractions), and to indicate certain plurals of lowercase letters.

Prime marks, located along the right side of the keyboard, represent the measurements of feet and inches, or minutes and seconds.

Adding and Omitting Quoted Content Correctly

The *ellipsis* (three consecutive dots) often is typed as three periods. Closer inspection reveals that the points in a true ellipsis are more closely spaced than three periods. Using three periods instead of the ellipsis creates a larger white area in the text than is visually advisable, resulting in a relatively large white space between the two connecting thoughts. Ellipsis points are used within a quotation when some of the exact words of the original author are omitted.

Square brackets are used to enclose information that is added to clarify meaning within a direct quotation, indicating which words are added for clarification. Often this technique is used when the direct quotation uses pronouns as the subject and one needs to identify the pronoun to make the quotation understandable to the reader in the new context.

Using a Virgule

The *virgule*, often called the *slant bar* or *slash* by computer users, has four specific uses in punctuation.

- A virgule separates parts of an extended date, for example: "the 1994/95 basketball season."

- A virgule represents the word *per* in measurements, for example, "Light travels at a speed of 186,000 mi/sec" (meaning miles per second).

- A virgule stands for the word *or* in the expression *and/or*. (Though not considered standard, it sometimes stands for the word *or* in other expressions also, for example, s/he, him/her).

- A virgule with space on either side separates lines of poetry that are quoted in run-on fashion in the text, for example, "Mary had a little lamb / Its fleece was white as snow / And everywhere that Mary went / The lamb was sure to go."

Hyphenation and Justification

Hyphenation and justification in typesetting refer to the decisions that are made by the computer about how to end a line of type when the line length or column width is filled with characters. This decision-making process is often controlled by industry-standard defaults, since less experienced designers often ignore the possibilities for altering the program's settings.

When the alignment settings are specified as flush left/ragged right text, the options for allowing hyphenation are fairly simple. When the end of the line is reached and a word is too long to fit, the computer determines where to break the word. If the hyphenation command is turned off, the word moves in its entirety to the next line, sometimes leaving an uncomfortably large white space. More complicated variations on hyphenation settings may include the compression of word spaces and/or letter spaces, or the slight alteration of character widths.

In type set with justified margins, the options become slightly more complicated, and without the alteration of default settings by the designer, numerous hyphens in consecutive lines may result. The same options are available as with flush left type, with the addition of several others. Hyphenation can be determined according to an electronic dictionary or an algorithm, and the number of hyphens allowable

in subsequent lines may be defined. Algorithmic hyphenation decisions are made according to a mathematical formula that analyzes the structure of the word in question. Although these often make a decision at a faster speed than hyphenation settings that force the computer to search a dictionary, they are not as reliable.

Particular *H&J* settings vary in different software applications. The average hyphenation zone (the amount of space for hyphenation decisions at the end of a typeset line) in longer lines of text, such as in book layouts, is greater than that of type set in shorter line lengths, as found in newspapers, magazines, and newsletter-type publications.

Hyphenation is at times a necessary evil, since it slows reading speed and impedes quick comprehension of the printed content. Multiple hyphens in a document or paragraph detract from the compositional aesthetic. A trial-and-error approach to determining the correct settings for hyphenation and justification options may prove the best solution, since so many variables (type alignment, type size, font selection) interact in the composition. Here are a few considerations when proofing typeset text:

- Never hyphenate the last word in a sentence.

- Never allow the hyphenation of a word at the end of a column that wraps up to the beginning of the next column of text.

- Never double-hyphenate a word (that is, do not hyphenate part of a compound word that already includes hyphenation).

- Never hyphenate an acronym; this usually only occurs from the automatic hyphenation and justification settings when the acronym has the same spelling as a real word (found in the hyphenation dictionary).

And she began thinking over other children she knew, who might do very well as pigs, and was just saying to herself, "if one only knew the right way to change them—" when she was a little startled by seeing the Cheshire Cat sitting on a bough of a tree a few yards off.

The Cat only grinned when it saw Alice. It looked good-natured, she thought: still it had VERY long claws and a great many teeth, so she felt that it ought to be treated with re-spect.

10.67 Do not allow a hyphen in the last word of a sentence.

Widows and Orphans

The last line of a paragraph is called a *widow* if it is particularly short as compared to the overall line length of the typeset paragraph. This leaves a large, open white space that appears as a blank line between the paragraphs, drawing unwanted and unnecessary attention to a single paragraph in the article. Experiment with hyphenation in earlier lines of text to eliminate the last line altogether, or to increase the length of the line. Kerning and tracking may be slightly altered to alleviate the problem as well. Rewriting the sentence using a synonym or two may decrease or increase the line length enough that the proper aesthetic is restored.

The term *orphan* refers to short segments of a paragraph (usually one to three lines) that are separated by a column break. Orphans are most effectively minimized by adjusting hyphenation or by editorial changes in the manuscript. Contemporary word processing and desktop publishing software applications allow the typesetter or designer to alter the possibilities for orphans; for example, one can select an option to keep all lines in a paragraph together, or specify that at least two or three lines of a paragraph be kept together. Particular lines, especially headings and subheadings, can be set to stay with the paragraph that follows, so that they cannot be orphaned at the bottom of a column or page. These settings often result in greatly varying column lengths, so a decision must be made as to which settings are least offensive.

"Cheshire Puss," she began, rather timidly, as she did not at all know whether it would like the name: how- ever, it only grinned a little wider. "Come, it's pleased so far,' thought Alice, and she went on. "Would you tell me,

10.68 Do not allow a hyphen in the last word in a column of type; instead, adjust the column length or the type size to eliminate the awkward break.

"Cheshire Puss," she began, rather timidly, as she did not at all know whether it would like the name: how- ever, it only grinned a little wider. "Come, it's pleased so far," thought Alice, and she went on. "Would you tell me, please, which way I ought to go from here?"

And she began thinking over other children she knew, who might do very well as pigs, and was just saying to herself, "if one only knew the right way to change them—" when she was a little startled by seeing the Cheshire Cat sitting on a bough of a tree a few yards off.

The Cat only grinned when it saw Alice. It looked good-natured, she thought: still it had VERY long claws and a great many teeth, so she felt that it ought to be treated with respect.

10.69 Do not allow a hyphen in a word that is already hyphenated.

Chapter Ten Review

Circle one answer for each definition to indicate the correct key concept term or key player for each. When necessary, determine whether the phrase provided is true or false.

1. Bullets should be set in a running indent format.
   a. True
   b. False

2. This is a term for indirect quotations which refer to the content of the original author's words but include only a newly phrased version without using the exact word.
   a. Paraphrasing
   b. Optically corrected
   c. Ante meridiem
   d. Double quotation

3. Particular H&J settings vary in different software applications.
   a. True
   b. False

4. This is a symbolic abbreviation for the word *at*. Its formal name comes from its commercial use in invoices. Also, it is used as part of an e-mail address.
   a. ®
   b. ¿
   c. @
   d. &

5. This person defines legibility as, "concern for perceiving letters and words, and the reading of continuous textural material."
   a. Martin K. Speckter
   b. Edwin Shaar
   c. Miles Tinker
   d. Adrian Williams

6. An ellipsis are always typed as three periods.
   a. True
   b. False

7. This term means "ablity to be read."
   a. Ampersand
   b. Legibility
   c. Interrobang
   d. Readability

8. Use a set of single quotation marks to indicate titles of parts of larger works, such as chapters in books; articles in newspapers, magazines, journals, or other periodical publications; and episodes of television and radio series.
   a. True
   b. False

9. This term refers to short segments of a paragraph (usually one to three lines) that are separated by a column break.
   a. Virgule
   b. Hyphenation
   c. Widow
   d. Orphan

10. The most common format for setting text type includes the right alignment of all lines of a paragraph except for the first indented line, with a ragged leftt margin.
    a. True
    b. False

11. This often depends on non-typesetting-related factors, including vocabulary and writing style and is the responsibility of the author or copywriter. It is usually assessed by the age or grade level required for someone to be able to readily understand a written passage.
    a. Legibility
    b. Hyphenation
    c. Readability
    d. Underscore

12. This should not be confused with the apostrophe. It has a number of mathematical applications, the most popular being to represent the foot as a unit of measurement, or minutes in latitude or longitude.
    a. ′
    b. `
    c. ˘
    d. ′

13. Used in the separation of a compound adjective or to indicate the range or connection between two groups of information, for example 3:00–5:00.
    a. Em dash
    b. Figure dash
    c. En dash
    d. Quotation dash

14. An American type designer who outlined characteristics of a legible typeface.
    a. Martin K. Speckter
    b. Edwin Shaar
    c. Miles Tinker
    d. Adrian Williams

15. Type set flush right or centered is more time-consuming for readers as it is more difficult for the human eye to track to the uneven lines of text on the left side of the column.
    a. True
    b. False

16. This is used as a stronger division than a comma, to make meaning clear in a sentence where commas are already being used for other purposes. It is used to join two sentences slightly more closely than they would be joined if separated by a period.
    a. /
    b. ;
    c. :
    d. …

17. This term refers to the difference between opposing forces or compositional opposites.
    a. Justification
    b. Contrast
    c. Readability
    d. Colon

18. A running indent affects a series of lines on either the right or left margin.
    a. True
    b. False

19. Automatic (auto) leading is approximately 1.2 times the point size of the type in most popular desktop publishing software applications. The correct auto leading setting for 15 point text is
    a. 16.7 points
    b. 18 points
    c. 15.2 points
    d. 21 points

20. This version of a font is one that is wider than the regular face.
    a. Condensed
    b. Compressed
    c. Extended
    d. Extra bold

21. Always type two spaces following a period or question mark at the end of sentence or question.
    a. True
    b. False

22. Use these to indicate words used ironically, with reservations, or in some unusual way.
    a. Pipe
    b. Single quotations
    c. Prime marks
    d. Double quotations

Selecting and Combining Fonts Creatively

The thousands of fonts available provide a myriad of visual possibilities for contemporary designers, often resulting in the time-consuming, even daunting task of matching the intended message with the most appropriate visual characteristics. While experimentation often leads to interesting solutions, extreme complexity may compromise readability and legibility, perhaps even being detrimental to the marketing of the product, service, or event. Clearly define the problem, identify the intended audience for your message, and then select the appropriate compositional possibilities for further development and exploration.

Key Concepts
connotative evaluation
denotation
hierarchy
resonance
reverse or reversal
target audience

Font Selection Considerations

Base the selection of your font, or combination of fonts, on the characteristics of the audience you intend to reach, called the *target audience*. Clearly defining the target audience and researching the characteristics of the demographic will ensure that your message is well received.

For example, children and senior citizens have different but specific requirements for readability and legibility. Both audiences require relatively large, distinctly formed letters. Because children are learning to identify individual letters, the differences between upper and lowercase forms must be easily discernible. For an older population (those 65 and up), 12- or 14-point type appears to be more appropriate. Avoid typefaces that are light and small. Instead use medium and bold type

Try This! List the names of your five favorite fonts. Below each, identify its most important visual characteristic(s). What type of business (restaurant, financial institution, clothing retail, toy outlet, gourmet specialty, art and crafts, etc.) would this font represent appropriately?

_____

_____

_____

_____

_____

_____

_____

_____

_____

_____

_____

_____

_____

_____

_____

_____

weights which are easier to read. For young children (or beginning readers of any age), a larger type size, around 14 points is considered a comfortable size.

Text selection for print and Internet applications to serve older eyes is a growing issue. The number of Americans over the age of sixty-five will double to approximately 65 million by the year 2030, and many of them will have some age-related visual impairment. As a general rule of thumb, use an 11- or 12-point type size for readers in the forty-to-sixty five age range. (Of course, 11-point Bodoni is not the same visual size as 11-point Courier, so your judgment is necessary in the selection process.)

Spacing is an important feature of text design. Most elderly readers (and young readers as well) find it easier to read text with more spacing between words, letters, and lines. Avoid bizarre or decorative fonts that may confuse the reader. More recent research has indicated that using a sans serif face instead of a serif face afforded a 4 percent improvement among older readers.

Along with larger type sizes and a font that provides adequate spacing between letters and words, use paragraph indents to help elderly readers navigate from one line to another.

Typographic Personality: Denotation, Connotation, and Resonance

It is improbable that there is only one appropriate type solution for each problem. In fact, there are so many well-designed choices that the difficulty is to narrow the choices of which face or faces are best.

To simplify the process of selecting the correct style or combination of styles, it is important to clearly identify your primary

$$X x X x X x X x$$

11.1 Although all of the fonts above are 42 points, the x-height varies greatly. Understanding the wide range in size is necessary to make a reasonable judgment about the appropriate visual requirements for any job.

intent. Establish a list of characteristics that the solution will need to communicate, then begin searching for inspirational examples to guide your visualization and sketching process. Find a balance between stylistic attributes and legibility to achieve the most successful results.

Following the problem clarification, determine the personality of the desired solution and select typefaces that complement that feeling. Learn to make typographic choices based on your own knowledge, experience, and intuitive judgment. Analyze the aesthetic sensibility of each choice as it relates (or does not relate) to the intended mood of the design problem. Is the intent serious, entertaining, contemporary, whimsical, frightening, romantic, or melancholy?

Designers make font selections based on visual characteristics. Staid, historical designs convey a sense of stability and credibility, while many contemporary digital faces communicate activity and indicate direction. Bodoni radiates elegance, clarity, and tradition. New Century Schoolbook is a pragmatic, easy-to-read face, as is Helvetica, but the former conveys more character. Classic scripts communicate upscaleness and formality, while Mistral and Harding are unrefined and textured examples for casual solutions.

The *denotation* of a specific font is an analytical description of its serifs and bracketing, terminal formation, stroke direction, and stroke weight. The physical description provides a definition of the visual characteristics based on observation. The *connotative evaluation* of the font refers to the subjective associations assigned to the visual characteristics. This includes thoughts and feelings and visual reminders that the viewer associates with the particular aesthetic. Designers select fonts for specific applications based on the connotative aspects but must be able to address the denotative attributes during discussion and critique of the solution with colleagues and clients.

The *resonance* of a font refers to the visual cues and classification of the visual characteristics according to the connotative associations. How do you determine which fonts communicate romance, historical events, contemporary locations, or futuristic technology? How do fonts convey a sense that one product is a hygiene necessity, and another a romantic indulgence? Use resonant cues to effectively communicate your message, or to contrast meaning with satire when appropriate.

Determining Compositional Importance

The elements with a typographic message should be organized according to importance. Ranking the different components of the message is referred to as a *hierarchy*. The importance of each of the elements is carefully weighed and ranked. Hierarchies communicate what is most important, what is second in importance, and so on by the size, weight, and arrangement of the elements in the composition. Once the message is divided into logical groups of information, then the visual treatment for each group can be determined with respect to the whole composition and communication.

Spacing and Grouping Type

Differences in leading or line spacing are one way to bring emphasis to one or more lines or phrases in a typographic composition. Equal leading is used for blocks of type of equal importance in the composition. The introduction of more space surrounding a line or phrase of text brings greater attention by separating it from the rest of the group.

Letter spacing is another way to bring attention to one area of a typographic composition. Regular or normal letter spacing creates a visual texture and supports a particular rhythm as the reader perceives and interprets the typographic message. Changing the visual texture of the type slows or stops this rhythm and causes the reader to pay additional attention to certain words.

Altering the alignment visually separates one group of type from another. If the largest proportion of text type is aligned flush left/ ragged right and one word, sentence, or phrase is aligned flush right, then the contrast will bring the reader's attention to the portion of the composition that is different from the rest.

Weight

Light, book, regular, bold, and extra bold are relatively common weight variations for traditional fonts. The greater the contrast in weight for selected portions of the composition, the greater the difference in the hierarchy. Commonly, readers associate the lighter weights with body text, as they create an even texture against the compositional ground area. The darker, bolder variations are traditionally reserved for short passages, headlines, and subheads, since large amounts of these weights can become difficult to read.

"That depends a good deal on where you want to get to," said the Cat.
"I don't much care where—" said Alice.
"Then it doesn't matter which way you go," said the Cat.
"—so long as I get somewhere," Alice added as an explanation.
"Oh, you're sure to do that," said the Cat, "if you only walk long enough."

"That depends a good deal on where you want to get to," said the Cat.
"I don't much care where—" said Alice.
"Then it doesn't matter which way you go," said the Cat.

"—so long as I get somewhere,"

Alice added as an explanation.
"Oh, you're sure to do that," said the Cat, "if you only walk long enough."

"That depends a good deal on where you want to get to," said the Cat.
"I don't much care where—" said Alice.
"Then it doesn't matter which way you go," said the Cat.
"—so long as I get
s o m e w h e r e ,"
Alice added as an explanation.
"Oh, you're sure to do that," said the Cat, "if you only walk long enough."

"That depends a good deal on where you want to get to," said the Cat.
"I don't much care where—" said Alice.
"Then it doesn't matter which way you go," said the Cat.
"—so long as I get somewhere,"
Alice added as an explanation.
"Oh, you're sure to do that," said the Cat, "if you only walk long enough."

11.2 Set the text with equal leading on each line and traditional em space indents. Then it is easy to compare ways to emphasize one phrase by altering leading, letter spacing, or alignment.

Alice felt that this could not be denied, so she tried another question. "What sort of people live about here?"

"In that direction," the Cat said, waving its right paw round, "lives a Hatter: and in that direction," waving the other paw, "lives a March Hare. Visit either you like: they're both mad."

"But I don't want to go among mad people," Alice remarked.

Alice felt that this could not be denied, so she tried another question. "What sort of people live about here?"

"In THAT direction," the Cat said, waving its right paw round, "lives a Hatter: and in THAT direction," waving the other paw, "lives a March Hare. Visit either you like: they're both mad."

"But I don't want to go among mad people," Alice remarked.

Alice felt that this could not be denied, so she tried another question. "What sort of people live about here?"

"In **that** direction," the Cat said, waving its right paw round, "lives a Hatter: and in **that** direction," waving the other paw, "lives a March Hare. Visit either you like: they're both mad."

"But I don't want to go among mad people," Alice remarked.

Alice felt that this could not be denied, so she tried another question. "What sort of people live about here?"

"In *that* direction," the Cat said, waving its right paw round, "lives a Hatter: and in *that* direction," waving the other paw, "lives a March Hare. Visit either you like: they're both mad."

"But I don't want to go among mad people," Alice remarked.

11.3 The visual hierarchy can manifest itself in a variety of ways: all caps, bold, or the more subtle italic variations.

Size

Contrast in the size of type brings visual interest and importance to one area of a typographic composition. Often used for emphasis to indicate the importance of a particular heading or phrase within the greater composition, size can be used to illustrate the volume of an onomatopoeia or emphasize one character's voice in a story. Contrast in size is one of the most easily understood visual treatments for emphasizing portions of a composition.

11.4 A combination of scale and proportion is used to create this graphic of a sneeze.

Proportion

Emphasis in a message can be controlled by the proportions of the individual fonts selected to communicate the meaning of the typographic composition. Proportions of a font can be varied by selecting different weights within the same family, or by selecting one font that is condensed to contrast with one that is extended. Given that all other variables are the same in the composition (size, alignment, weight, and so on), changing the proportion of the forms is an interesting way to bring attention to some areas of the composition.

Value and Texture

Traditional setting of text for large areas of reading, as in a story or article, should be fairly direct and easily understood. The use of the same font for all body text sets a precedent and

"OH you can't help that," said the Cat: "we're all mad here. I'm mad. You're mad."

"Oh, you can't help that," said the Cat: "we're all mad here. I'm mad. You're mad."

"Oh, you can't help that," said the Cat: "we're all mad here. I'm mad. You're mad."

11.5 The important phrase can be larger than the rest of the text to make it more important. An initial or drop cap sets the first character or two apart and indicates where the reader should begin. Determine whether the leading should remain the same as the bulk of the text for a crowded effect, or be altered to accommodate the larger text.

"Oh, you can't help that," said the Cat: "we're all mad here. I'm mad. You're mad."

"Oh, you can't help that," said the Cat: "we're all mad here. I'm mad. You're mad."

"Oh, you can't help that," said the Cat: "we're all mad here. I'm mad. You're mad."

"'Oh, you can't help that," said the Cat: "**we're all mad here**. I'm mad. You're mad."

"Oh, you can't help that," said the Cat: "**we're all mad here.** I'm mad. You're mad."

11.6 The proportion of letterforms is a ratio between the height and width of the shape and the stroke weight. Alter one or the other, or both for the most emphasis.

'You must be,' said the Cat, 'or you wouldn't have come here.'

Alice didn't think that proved it at all; however, she went on, 'And how do you know that you're mad?'

'To begin with,' said the Cat, 'a dog's not mad. You grant that?'

'I suppose so,' said Alice.

'Well, then,' the Cat went on, 'you see, a dog growls when it's angry, and wags its tail when it's pleased. Now I growl when I'm pleased, and wag my tail when I'm angry. Therefore I'm mad.'

'I call it purring, not growling,' said Alice.

'Call it what you like,' said the Cat. 'Do you play croquet with the Queen to-day?'

'I should like it very much,' said Alice, 'but I haven't been invited yet.'

'You'll see me there,' said the Cat, and vanished.

11.7

'You must be,' said the Cat, 'or you wouldn't have come here.'

Alice didn't think that proved it at all; however, she went on, 'And how do you know that you're mad?'

'To begin with,' said the Cat, 'a dog's not mad. You grant that?'

'I suppose so,' said Alice.

'Well, then,' the Cat went on, 'you see, a dog growls when it's angry, and wags its tail when it's pleased. Now I growl when I'm pleased, and wag my tail when I'm angry. Therefore I'm mad.'

'I call it purring, not growling,' said Alice.

'Call it what you like,' said the Cat. 'Do you play croquet with the Queen to-day?'

'I should like it very much,' said Alice, 'but I haven't been invited yet.'

'You'll see me there,' said the Cat, and vanished.

11.8

'You must be,' said the Cat, 'or you wouldn't have come here.'

Alice didn't think that proved it at all; however, she went on, 'And how do you know that you're mad?'

'To begin with,' said the Cat, 'a dog's not mad. You grant that?'

'I suppose so,' said Alice.

'Well, then,' the Cat went on, 'you see, a dog growls when it's angry, and wags its tail when it's pleased. Now I growl when I'm pleased, and wag my tail when I'm angry. Therefore I'm mad.'

'I call it purring, not growling,' said Alice.

'Call it what you like,' said the Cat. 'Do you play croquet with the Queen to-day?'

'I should like it very much,' said Alice, 'but I haven't been invited yet.'

'You'll see me there,' said the Cat, and vanished.

11.9

11.7–11.12 A visual comparison of value and texture in typeset body text.

11.7 This text shows a consistent value and texture.

11.8 Semibold indicates the characters' voices.

11.9 The characters' voices are separated, using semibold italic for the Cat and semibold for Alice.

11.10 The characters' voices are separated from the narrative text by using italic, which creates a different visual texture.

11.11 All of the text is italic, which creates a consistent visual texture; however, semibold italic subtly emphasizes the characters' voices.

11.12 All of the text is set in a variation of italic—the narrative text is medium weight, the Cat's voice is bold, and Alice's voice is semibold. What is the hierarchy? Who or what is the most important and least important?

'You must be,' said the Cat, 'or you wouldn't have come here.'

Alice didn't think that proved it at all; however, she went on, 'And how do you know that you're mad?'

'To begin with,' said the Cat, 'a dog's not mad. You grant that?'

'I suppose so,' said Alice.

'Well, then,' the Cat went on, 'you see, a dog growls when it's angry, and wags its tail when it's pleased. Now I growl when I'm pleased, and wag my tail when I'm angry. Therefore I'm mad.'

'I call it purring, not growling,' said Alice.

'Call it what you like,' said the Cat. 'Do you play croquet with the Queen to-day?'

'I should like it very much,' said Alice, 'but I haven't been invited yet.'

'You'll see me there,' said the Cat, and vanished.

11.10

'You must be,' said the Cat, 'or you wouldn't have come here.'

Alice didn't think that proved it at all; however, she went on, 'And how do you know that you're mad?'

'To begin with,' said the Cat, 'a dog's not mad. You grant that?'

'I suppose so,' said Alice.

'Well, then,' the Cat went on, 'you see, a dog growls when it's angry, and wags its tail when it's pleased. Now I growl when I'm pleased, and wag my tail when I'm angry. Therefore I'm mad.'

'I call it purring, not growling,' said Alice.

'Call it what you like,' said the Cat. 'Do you play croquet with the Queen to-day?'

'I should like it very much,' said Alice, 'but I haven't been invited yet.'

'You'll see me there,' said the Cat, and vanished.

11.11

'You must be,' said the Cat, 'or you wouldn't have come here.'

Alice didn't think that proved it at all; however, she went on, 'And how do you know that you're mad?'

'To begin with,' said the Cat, 'a dog's not mad. You grant that?'

'I suppose so,' said Alice.

'Well, then,' the Cat went on, 'you see, a dog growls when it's angry, and wags its tail when it's pleased. Now I growl when I'm pleased, and wag my tail when I'm angry. Therefore I'm mad.'

'I call it purring, not growling,' said Alice.

'Call it what you like,' said the Cat. 'Do you play croquet with the Queen to-day?'

'I should like it very much,' said Alice, 'but I haven't been invited yet.'

'You'll see me there,' said the Cat, and vanished.

11.12

Study each of the examples and assign characteristics to each, writng as many as possible on the line next to the font. The list on the right side of the page may provide ideas to get you started, but do not hesitate to add your own descriptors as well.

Determine which fonts you might use for various applications. Would you use the font to develop a logotype for a bank, a toy store, or an automotive center? How about a men's or women's clothing outlet or an Italian restaurant?

AaBbCcDdEeFfGgHhIiJjKk

AABBCCDDEEFFGGHHIIJJKK

AaBbCcDdEeFfGgHhIiJjKk

AaBbCcDdEeFfGgHhIiJjKk

AaBbCcDdEeFfGgHhIiJjKk

AaBbCcDdEeFfGgHhIiJjKk

AaBbCcDdEeFfGgHhIiJjKk

AaBbCcDdEeFfGgHhIiJjKk

AABBCCDDEEFFGGHHIIJJKK

AaBbCcDdEeFfGgHhIiJjKk

AaBbCcDdEeFfGgHhIiJjKk

AaBbCcDdEeFfGgHhIiJjKk

Typographic Personalities

organized
classic
ecumenical
upscale
unrefined
fast
cluttered
historical
generic
weak
gregarious
refined
melancholy
automotive
hard
formal
digital
feminine
independent
appliances
secular
food
whimsical
romantic
home and garden
inexpensive
awkward
active
soft
traditional
social
corporate
contemporary
commercial
slow
clothing
entertaining
masculine
casual
static
practical
strong
upbeat

Alice was not much surprised at this, she was getting so used to queer things happening. While she was looking at the place where it had been, it suddenly appeared again.

"By-the-bye, what became of the baby?" said the Cat. "I'd nearly forgotten to ask."

"It turned into a pig," Alice quietly said, just as if it had come back in a natural way.

"I thought it would," said the Cat, and vanished again.

Alice was not much surprised at this, she was getting so used to queer things happening. While she was looking at the place where it had been, it suddenly appeared again. "By-the-bye, what became of the baby?" said the Cat. "I'd nearly forgotten to ask."

"It turned into a pig," Alice quietly said, just as if it had come back in a natural way.

"I thought it would," said the Cat, and vanished again.

11.13 Try changing the value of the background area to bring emphasis to one or more words in a block of text.

a pattern that allows the reader to develop a rhythm and cadence to his or her reading and an understanding of the material presented. The contrast of the dark letterforms against a light background allows for little interference in deciphering and understanding the composition.

Altering the font throughout the message changes the visual texture and slows the reader, as the cadence of his or her thoughts is broken in the deciphering process. Font variation can be used purposely, to emphasize the meaning of the message, but should be done sparingly.

Emphasizing one or more words or phrases can be done by changing the background value; this technique is especially effective when larger text is separated from the story as a sidebar or a pull quote.

Positive and Negative

Incorporation of both positive (black on white) and negative (white on black) areas in a typographic composition is an effective way to create visual contrast and excitement. It is the designer's responsibility to find compositional balance and a visually pleasing solution when combining the positive and negative areas.

Placing white type and imagery on a black background is referred to as a *reverse* or *reversal* in the printing industry. This technique raises some concerns that must be addressed at the design stage of the project so that they do not become a problem during the production phase.

During the printing process there is a tendency for the larger black area to spread into the smaller white area, especially when text type is set on a black background, making the small, thin text appear even thinner. In some cases, the black area will completely

Alice waited a little, half expecting to see it again, but it did not appear, and after a minute or two she walked on in the direction in which the March Hare was said to live. "I've seen hatters before," she said to herself; "the March Hare will be much the most interesting, and perhaps as this is May it won't be raving mad—at least not so mad as it was in March." As she said this, she looked up, and there was the Cat again, sitting on a branch of a tree. **"Did you say pig, or fig?"** "Did you say pig, or fig?" said the Cat. "I said pig," replied Alice; "and I wish you wouldn't keep appearing and vanishing so suddenly: you make one quite giddy."

Alice waited a little, half expecting to see it again, but it did not appear, and after a minute or two she walked on in the direction in which the March Hare was said to live. "I've seen hatters before," she said to herself; "the March Hare will be much the most interesting, and perhaps as this is May it won't be raving mad—at least not so mad as it was in March." As she said this, she looked up, and there was the Cat again, sitting on a branch of a tree. **"Did you say pig, or fig?"** "Did you say pig, or fig?" said the Cat. "I said pig," replied Alice; "and I wish you wouldn't keep appearing and vanishing so suddenly: you make one quite giddy."

11.14 Adding a color or light value to the background area of text, for emphasis, is particularly effective in pull quotes. The rectangular area defines and separates interesting and/or important information, moving it up in hierarchical importance. Once the background area becomes nearly as dark as the quote, the type must be reversed (light on dark) instead of overprinted.

fill the small counterforms, making the final message illegible. Characters set close together may appear joined, and pinched type will appear to break apart. This can become exaggerated to the extent that the message is illegible when printed on an absorbent stock such as newsprint.

Adjusting the imagesetter exposure is one way to minimize the encroachment of the black ground area into the white typography.

An even better solution would be to select a typeface that has even, somewhat bold strokes, as opposed to a decorative or script font with subtle details and thin strokes. If it is necessary to select a font with contrast in the thick and thin strokes, then consider using a semibold weight variation to enlarge the width of the thinner strokes.

Varying Position and Orientation

When type is set on the page, it is viewed in relation to the edges of the format area. Does the type hang from the top edge of the format? Does it sit contentedly in the middle of the page, fall down one side or the other, or huddle in a corner?

Once the first line of the message is positioned in the format, the others must follow in a logical manner, so as not to confuse the meaning of the communication.

Varying the orientation of the message or a portion of the message can direct the viewer's attention to one area instead of another, again establishing a hierarchy of importance. The standard assumption is to position the most important text at the top of the page in a horizontal orientation. Don't hesitate to experiment with the vertical and diagonal orientation of text in the composition as well.

Vertical text can be stacked, with one letter above another, but this is not recommended. It tends to look amateurish, since the letters are of different widths and a Western viewer's eyes and brain often find it difficult to decipher the message. In areas of the world where the primary language is traditionally written from the top to the bottom of the page, however, such as Japan and China, and the characters are of a similar weight and width, this stacking technique is less of an issue.

11.15 The reversed text at the top balances with the larger black area of the hand graphic and the descriptive text reversed from the black bar at the bottom of the graphic. The black bar at the bottom encloses the script text and holds the graphic together visually as one message.

11.16 The reversed text and the building graphic appear as architectural elements rising above the inferred horizon line. The division of positive and negative space provides visual contrast and emphasizes the difference between sky and ground in a more literal translation.

11.17 Text is reversed from a concave quadrilateral form, conveying the impression of a rocklike element sitting on the moon's surface. The contrast is further emphasized by the difference in the proportion of the letterforms between the tall, thin letters in "Moonrock" and the short, bold letterforms in "Fashions."

11.18 Again, the contrast between the two primary typographic components is emphasized by the different proportions of the letterforms and the positive areas versus the negative areas.

11.19 Reversed type works best when it is relatively large, bold, and simple.

v
e
r
t
i
c
a
l

V
E
R
T
I
C
A
L

vertical

VERTICAL

VERTICAL

vertical

11.20 Vertically stacked type creates an unusual margin that is difficult to read. Contrary to what one might assume, the centered, vertically stacked type does not create a symmetrical profile, since the individual letterforms are not all symmetrical.

11.21 A more desirable solution is to rotate the text 90° so that it is easier to read. Make the text face the composition: if it is on the left margin it reads from the bottom to the top; when it is against the right margin, orient it so that it reads from top to bottom.

FRESHWATER

The long,
pointed
bill aids
in fishing.

11.22 Large type set sideways against the left margin causes the viewer to read into the composition.

The most practical variation of the vertical type is to turn the whole word or phrase sideways, so that it reads into the composition. Remember to use a special arrangement or effect sparingly, so as to maintain its visual emphasis and importance in the hierarchy.

Diagonal orientation within the composition follows the same rules as vertical orientation. Positioning the text letter by letter diagonally across the format makes it more difficult to decipher than does tilting the whole word or phrase at the desired angle. The most logical and meaningful orientation is from the top left to the bottom right of the composition; however, this is only a suggestion and not a hard-and-fast rule.

Developing shapes with typeset text is another way of bringing visual interest to a composition. Text can be set along a path that is shaped to form the silhouette of a representational or abstract shape. Only the imagination limits the possibilities for setting text in shapes with most popular, vector-based drawing and layout programs. The difficulty is to find an effective solution that takes into consideration reasonable letter spacing and word spacing.

Text can be set inside a shape so that the overall contour gives the impression of the meaning of the story or passage. This is more difficult to fit correctly, and often requires the skills of a creative copywriter and comprehensive thesaurus, so that individual words can be changed to fill the area more accurately. In addition, the text must be justified to fill the whole shape evenly, and the type size and leading may require subtle finessing to avoid rivers in the background areas between the words.

11.23 Diagonally stacked type is more difficult to read than text set in one horizontal line and rotated to the desired angle. Notice that the single line of text can be larger, even though it is letter spaced, than the stacked type in the same amount of horizontal space.

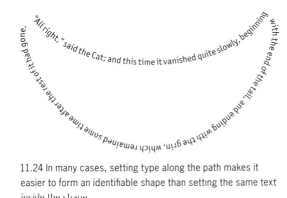

11.24 In many cases, setting type along the path makes it easier to form an identifiable shape than setting the same text inside the shape.

"All right,"   said
the Cat; and this time it vanished quite
slowly, beginning with the end of
the tail, and ending with the
grin, which remained some
time after the rest of
it had gone.

"All right,"   said
the Cat; and this time it vanished quite
slowly, beginning with the end of
the tail, and ending with the
grin, which remained some
time after the rest of it
had gone.

"All
right,"
said the
Cat; and this
time it vanished
quite slowly, beginning with the end of
the tail, and ending with the grin,
which remained some time after
the rest of it had gone.

11.25 Without the dotted line for indication, it would be difficult to know that the intended shape is a cat's smile. Slightly changing the orientation of the shape contour by tilting it eliminates the large space in the middle of the sentence that is created when the corners of the mouth turn upward. It is almost impossible for the reader to get the complete message on the first reading.

"Well! I've often seen a cat without a grin," thought Alice; "but a grin without a cat! It's the most curious thing I ever saw in my life!"

"Well! I've often seen a cat without a grin," thought Alice; "but a grin without a cat! It's the most curious thing I ever saw in my life!"

"Well! I've often seen a cat without a grin," thought Alice; "but a grin without a cat! It's the most curious thing I ever saw in my life!"

"Well! I've often seen a cat without a grin," thought Alice; "but a grin without a cat! It's the most curious thing I ever saw in my life!"

11.26 Outline type becomes a great deal more difficult to read than the traditional solid black text; it should be reserved for minimal use on special occasions

11.27 Outline type is slightly more legible when it is filled than when it is empty. The type is also easier to read when the stroke color or value is similar to the fill color or value.

11.28 For some reason a number of software developers thought that it would be a positive move to include drop shadow features in popular programs, so students seem to think it is a good idea to use the feature liberally. In most cases the message becomes muddy and the meaning is not enhanced. Be sure that special effects support and enhance the message.

Varying Font Structure and Style

Creating visual variation in a composition can be done by selecting variations within one family, or by contrast through the use of different typefaces. A number of options for variation are italic versus roman, script versus roman, sans serif versus serif, uppercase versus lowercase, light versus bold, and condensed or extended versus regular width.

Hand-rendered type in the form of gracefully flowing calligraphy or a textured spontaneous scrawl contrasts with typeset text, since it retains the imperfect human qualities of the creator. Some hand-rendered type conveys a sense of immediacy, timeliness, and individuality, while other calligraphic forms of Chancery and Gothic lettering imply a personalization, formality, or elevated social standing or rank.

A number of modern faces are designed to give the appearance of hand-generated typography through the incorporation of brush-stroke-like textures and irregular outlines. However, the regularity created as each form is repeated in different words makes it clear that it is a commercial product, not a one-of-a-kind solution.

Special effects may be added to fonts, but just because something is possible does not necessarily make it a good idea. Outline, inline, and shadowed typefaces have their place in special circumstances, but the combination of these effects or characteristics can result in a muddy, illegible message.

11.29 (Left) Italic and roman variations of the same face.

11.30 (Right) Condensed and regular widths of the same face.

11.31 (Left) Script font and roman font mixed.

11.32 (Right) Condensed and extended widths of two different serif faces.

11.33 (Left) Light and bold stroke variations of the same face.

11.34 (Right) Sans serif and slab serif combined.

Chapter Eleven Review

Circle one answer for each definition to indicate the correct key concept term for each. When necessary, determine whether the phrase provided is true or false.

1. _____ of a font can be varied by selecting different weights within the same family, or by selecting one font that is condensed to contrast with one that is extended.
   a. Sizes
   b. Values
   c. Proportions
   d. Textures

2. Vertical text can be stacked, with one letter above another, but this is not recommended.
   a. True
   b. False

3. This refers to the visual cues and classification of the visual characteristics according to the connotative associations of a font.
   a. Resonance
   b. Connotative evaluation
   c. Hierarchy
   d. Denotation

4. Placing white type and imagery on a black background is referred to as this in the printing industry.
   a. Resonance
   b. Reversal
   c. Hierarchy
   d. Denotation

5. The _____ of the font refers to the subjective associations assigned to the visual characteristics. This includes thoughts and feelings and visual reminders that the viewer associates with the particular aesthetic.
   a. Resonance
   b. Connotative evaluation
   c. Hierarchy
   d. Denotation

6. As a general rule of thumb, use an 8- or 10-point type size for readers in the forty-to-sixty-five age range.
   a. True
   b. False

7. The elements with a typographic message should be organized according to importance. Ranking the different components of the message is referred to as this term.
   a. Reversal
   b. Size
   c. Hierarchy
   d. Proportion

8. Diagonal orientation within the composition follows the same rules as vertical orientation.
   a. True
   b. False

9. Base the selection of your font, or combination of fonts, on the characteristics of the audience you intend to reach, called the intended audience.
   a. True
   b. False

10. The _____ of a specific font is an analytical description of its serifs and bracketing, terminal formation, stroke direction, and stroke weight.
    a. Resonance
    b. Connotative evaluation
    c. Hierarchy
    d. Denotation

11. Often used for emphasis to indicate the importance of a particular heading or phrase within the greater composition, this can be used to illustrate the volume of an onomatopoeia or emphasize one character's voice in a story.
    a. Resonance
    b. Size
    c. Hierarchy
    d. Value and texture

Organizing Typographic Compositions

Organization of the elements within the compositional format is the primary task of the designer. Which element is most important? What size should it be? What color best communicates the message? What size is the final composition? How will this composition be distributed? What are the advantages and disadvantages of each proposed concept?

In order to find the best possible solution to a design problem, it makes sense to start by creating a plan based on logical research and practical information. Approaching the task at hand well versed in the relevant technical information can help minimize the frustration of finding that the concepts you had in mind won't work.

Key Concepts

accordian fold
alleys
barrel fold
bleed
body text
bullet
byline
call out
caption
credit
dingbat
drop cap
envelope converter
folio
foot margin
footer
form
French fold
gate fold
gripper
gutter
hanging caps
header
headlines
head margin
initial caps
ISO
list
masthead
parallel fold
pull quote
raised cap
ream
rolled fold
runover
short fold
sidebar
signature
simple fold
spread
subhead
table

Basic Page Layout Considerations

The first step in determining the correct layout for a new design is to refer to the goals and constraints established at the beginning of the project.

Paper

A primary factor driving the solution is the printing budget. A significant part of a project's final cost derives from the quantity and quality of the paper stock specified by the designer and the number of colors used to print the job. Obviously, the more economical the use of paper, the lower-quality the paper, and the smaller the number of ink colors, the less expensive the printed piece will be.

Paper averages close to 30 percent of the cost of a print project, so its definitely useful to take a closer look at it, especially if you work on a tight budget. If you are flexible when it comes to your paper choice, consider your printer's house sheets. Since printers buy those in bulk, they are readily available and you will usually get a good price.

Paper manufactured and sold in North America is measured in inches, while paper manufactured and distributed in other parts of the world follows the _ISO_ (International Standards Organization) dimensions, which are metric. In the United States, sheet sizes are commonly based on multiples of 8½″ × 11″. Larger sheet sizes are based on the 8½″ × 11″ multiple with slight adjustment to allow for the press requirements (grippers, color bars and bleed areas); for example, a 23″ × 35″ sheet of paper results in sixteen trimmed 8½″ × 11″ single pages, or one sixteen-page section of an 8½″ × 11″ book or periodical (called a _signature_).

North American Paper Sheet Sizes

Inches	Millimeters
8½″ × 11″	216 × 279
11″ × 17″	279 × 432
17½″ × 22½″	445 × 572
19″ × 25″	483 × 635
25″ × 35″	584 × 889
25″× 38″	635 × 965

In the ISO system there are five different series of sizes: A, RA, SR, B, and C. Within each of these categories, a sheet is twice the size of the next smaller sheet and half of the next larger sheet. The starting sheet size is A0 which measures 841 × 1189 mm (33⅛″×46¾″), which is equivalent to 1 square meter. The A series is used for most general printing applications, such as stationery, flyers, and newsletters.

A standard newsletter size would consist of one or more sheets of 11″ × 17″ paper with no allowance for type or imagery to _bleed_ (or extend beyond the predetermined margins of the trimmed page). This size job, in black ink, could be reproduced on a photocopier for relatively short runs, or on a small press by a local quick-print establishment to meet strict budget constraints. If the design requires a bleed on one or more edges, then the final size of the printed piece is trimmed down to a smaller dimension, and any trim is waste that must be thrown out or recycled.

The term _basis weight_ (also called _ream weight_) refers to the weight, measured in pounds, of a ream of cut paper. A _ream_ equals 500 sheets of the basic size of paper. The difficulty lies in the fact that the basic size of the sheet is different for different grades of paper.

Type of Paper	Basic Sheet Size
Bond, ledger, and writing	17″ × 22″
Uncoated book and text	25″ × 38″
Coated book	25″ × 38″
Bristol (lightweight card stock)	22½″ × 28½″
Kraft, tag, and newsprint	24″ × 36″

One of the most important factors in selecting a paper is its basis weight. Papers are classified into *bond, text, book,* and *cover weights*—categories that immediately give us some indication of their purpose. A 20 lb. bond will work for photocopied flyers, but isn't heavy enough to prevent show through if offset-printed on both sides. A 60 lb. text or book-weight paper is well suited to a two-sided print job, but lacks the rigidity necessary for a business card. Cover weights are ideal for business cards, but may require scoring if there's folding involved. Because of the variety in sheet dimensions, paper grades that share the same basis weight look and

Paper Grade	Approximate Equivalent
16 lb. bond	40 lb. text
20 lb. bond	50 lb. text
24 lb. bond	60 lb. text
28 lb. bond	70 lb. text
90 lb. bond	50 lb. cover
100 lb. bond	55 lb. cover
110 lb. bond	60 lb. cover
120 lb. bond	65 lb. cover

feel different—65 lb. text-weight paper is much lighter and thinner than 65 lb. cover stock.

Paper is manufactured in large continuous rolls. As the paper fibers move through the multiple stages, the fibers align along the length of the roll parallel to the edges resulting in a *grain*. Paper scores, folds, and tears more easily with the grain than against the grain. Depending on the size, shape, and orientation of the final printed piece, the printer will order the cut sheets of paper as grain long (long edge running with the length of the paper roll) or grain short (with the short side cut parallel to the length.

Paper is available in either coated or uncoated finishes. *Coated* papers are often specified as matte or *dull-coated, gloss-coated,* or *cast-coated.* The technical terms for these are *uncalendered,* referring to an unpolished coated surface, *machine calendered,* which has a gloss surface on the coated sheet, and *supercalendered,* which results in a high-gloss, shiny surface.

Uncoated papers are available in a number of different surface finishes, the most common of which are *smooth, linen, laid,* and *cockle.* Today these textures usually are embossed into the surface of the sheet during the manufacturing process.

For image and photographic reproduction, a smooth-finish, uncoated or coated text-weight stock is a good choice. A linen-finish paper is more suitable for stationery where image reproduction isn't a factor and its tactile characteristics can be appreciated by those who handle it.

Colored paper can enhance a one-color job, serving as background color, but it can also affect the appearance of printed text and

Key Paper and Envelope Concepts

A-style envelope
baronial envelope
basis weight
bond weight
booklet envelope
book weight
calendered
cast-coated
catalog envelope
coated
cockle
coin envelope
commercial envelope
cover weight
dull-coated
gloss-coated
grain
index
kraft
laid
linen
machine-calendered
metal clasp
newsprint
OE
OS
official envelope
policy envelope
ream weight
remittance envelope
smooth
supercalendered
text weight
ticket envelope
uncalendered
uncoated
wallet flap
window envelope

Paper Type	Availability	Standard Sheet Sizes	Weight	Uses
Bond	Available in a wide range of neutral and pastel colors	8½″ × 11″; 8½″ × 14″; 11″ × 17″ (4-page 8½″× 11" newsletter); 17″ × 22″; 17″ × 28″; 19″ × 24″; 23″ × 35″; rolls	16, 20, 24 lb.	Flyers, forms, photocopies, newsletters
Writing	Available in a range of colors and surface finishes with matching envelopes, text weights, and cover weights	8½″ × 11″; 11″ × 17″ ; 22½″ × 35″; 23″ × 35″; 25″ × 38″	24, 28 lb.	Stationery
Uncoated Book	Available in a variety of colors; slightly thicker and more opaque than bond or writing papers	8½″ × 11″; 8½″ × 14″; 17½″ × 22½″; 23″ ×29″; 22½″ × 35″; 23″ × 35″; 25″×38″; 35″×45″; 38″×50"; rolls	30, 32, 35, 40, 45,50, 60, 65, 70, 80 lb.	Books, direct mail, newsletters, catalogs
Text	Available in a range of colors, weights, and surface finishes with matching envelopes and cover weights	8½″ × 11″; 17½″ × 22½″; 23″ × 35″; 25″ × 38″; 26″ × 40″	60, 65, 70, 80, 100 lb.	Letterhead, newsletters, annual reports, invitations, posters, brochures, direct mail, books
Coated Book	Specialty runs in a variety of colors, but the matching cover weight is typically available in white and off-white or cream	19″ × 25″; 23″ × 29″; 23″ × 35″; 25″ × 38″; 35″ × 45″; 38″×50″	40, 45, 50, 60, 70, 80, 100 lb.	Periodicals, catalogs, books, direct mail, annual reports
Cover	Heavier, durable counterpart intended to coordinate with text, book, and writing papers in a variety of coated and uncoated finishes	20″ × 26″; 23″ × 35″; 35″ × 38″; 26″ × 40″	60, 65, 80, 100, 120, 130 lb.	Business cards, report covers, menus, invitations, tickets, postcards, pocket folders, greeting cards
Index/Bristol	Available in a range of colors and uncoated finishes	22″ × 28″; 22½″ × 28½″; 23″ × 35″; 24″ × 36″; 25½″ × 30½″; 28″ × 44″	67, 90, 100, 110, 125, 140, 150, 175 lb.	Postcards, file folders, index cards, small boxes, tickets, clothing tags
Newsprint	Inexpensive, lightweight absorbent stock available in white and manila	Sheets by special order; rolls	30 lb.	Newspapers, tabloids
Kraft	Inexpensive, durable, and strong; available in brown and manila	Rolls	30, 40, 50 lb.	Bags, envelopes

images. Blue ink, for instance, will appear dark green when printed on ochre-colored stock. Dark green images and text on ochre paper is a look that may not work for every client.

Another factor to consider is how the final printed piece will be distributed. If the design is intended for mailing, then the postal service requirements must be taken into account; there are several possible levels of service, so ask for the most recent information.

There are common names for the types of standard folds, including the four-page *simple fold*, four-page *short fold*, six-page *accordion fold*, six-page *barrel* or *rolled fold*, eight-page *gate fold*, eight-page *French fold*, and eight-page *parallel fold*. Each single page or sheet is counted as 2 pages since both the front and the back are used.

Some of the multiple-page folds require additional material on some panels to accommodate the fold (for example, the center pages of a gate fold will be approximately ⅛˝ wider than the two outside pages) so be sure to make an accurate full-size mock-up or comp, and consult with your printer for exact specifications. At that time your printing representative can alert you to any possible difficulties with the design during production, and help determine the correct sheet size and trim size.

Envelopes

Most publications, including newsletters and brochures, can be designed for distribution with or without an envelope, whereas stationery, some periodicals, and annual reports require an envelope for mailing purposes. Envelopes are available in

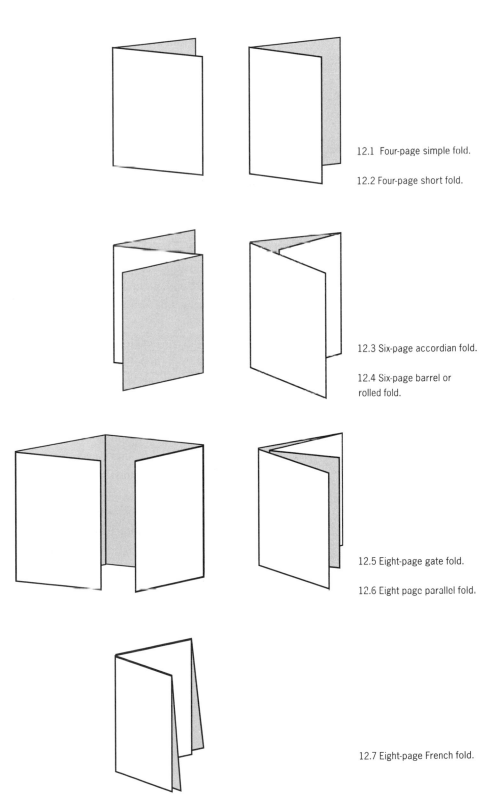

12.1 Four-page simple fold.

12.2 Four-page short fold.

12.3 Six-page accordian fold.

12.4 Six-page barrel or rolled fold.

12.5 Eight-page gate fold.

12.6 Eight page parallel fold.

12.7 Eight-page French fold.

12.8 Commercial/Official.

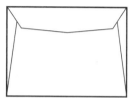

12.9 Booklet.

12.10 Window.

12.11 Remittance.

12.12 Policy.

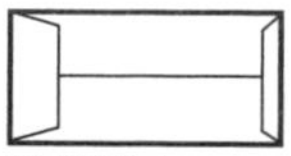

12.13 Coin.

standard sizes that are determined by their use: common types are *commercial, official, booklet, ticket, window, remittance, policy, catalog, metal clasp, A-style* or *baronial, wallet flap,* business announcement, and *coin.* The most popular styles are commercial/official, booklet and window. Commercial (sizes no. 5 through no. 6¾) and official (sizes no. 7 through no. 14) envelopes commonly include a gummed flap, while booklet style envelopes are available with or without a gummed flap depending on the size.

Envelope closures are designated as either *OE* (open-end), with an opening along one short-dimension side, or *OS* (open-side), with the opening along one long dimension of the envelope. Open-end envelopes are commonly used for hand insertion of the contents while open-side envelopes can be used for hand insertion or automated insertion of the contents.

Window envelopes are similar in size to many commercial and official envelopes. In the standard size, the glassine or open window measures 4¾˝ × 1⅛˝ and is placed ⅞˝ from the left edge and ⅝˝ from the bottom edge of the envelope front. No. 8⅝ window envelopes have slightly different specifications with the window positioned ⅝˝ from the left edge and ¹³⁄₁₆˝ from the bottom edge. These are designed for mailing invoices, statements, checks, and receipts printed on a standard format so the mailing address shows through the window. This eliminates the work of addressing both the envelope and its contents.

Commercial/Official Envelope	Size
No. 5	3¹⁄₁₆˝ × 5½˝
No. 6	3⅜˝ × 6˝
No. 6¼	3½˝ × 6˝
No. 6½	3⁹⁄₁₆˝ × 6½˝
No. 6¾	3⅝˝ × 6½˝
No. 7	3¾˝ × 6¾˝
No. 7½	3¾˝ × 7⅝˝
No. 7¾ Monarch	3⅞˝ × 7½˝
Data card	3½˝ × 7⅝˝
No. 8 ⅝ Check	3⅝˝ × 8⅝˝
No. 9	3⅞˝ × 8⅞˝
No. 10	4⅛˝ × 9½˝
No 10½	4½˝ × 9½˝
No. 11	4½˝ × 10⅜˝
No. 12	4¾˝ × 11˝
No. 14	5˝ × 11½˝

Booklet Envelope	Size
No. 2½	4½˝ × 5⅞˝
No. 3	4¾˝ × 6½˝
No. 4¼	5˝ × 7½˝
No. 5	5½˝ × 8½˝
No. 6	5¾˝ × 8⅞˝
No. 7	6¼˝ × 9⅝˝
No. 7¼	7˝ × 10˝
No. 7½	7½˝ × 10½˝
No. 8	8˝ × 11⅛˝
No. 9	8¾˝ × 11½˝
No. 10	9½˝ × 12⅝˝
No. 13	10˝ × 13˝

Window Envelope	Size
No. 6¾	3⅝″ × 6½″
No. 7	3¾″ × 6¾″
No. 7¾ Monarch	3⅞″ × 7½″
No. 8⅝ Check	3⅝″ × 8⅝″
No. 9	3⅞″ × 8⅞″
No. 10	4⅛″ × 9½″
No. 11	4½″ × 10⅜″
No. 12	4¾″ × 11″
No. 14	5″ × 11½″

Envelopes are manufactured by envelope *converters* that cut, fold, glue, and assemble them. Envelopes may be converted and sold by paper mills using their own paper stock, or they may be printed by a commercial printer and then converted as special-order items. Premade envelopes from the mill are much less expensive than specialty envelopes ordered through a commercial printer.

Special-order envelopes from the commercial printer include those with complicated designs and/or multiple color printing on one or both sides. Unless the production run is a minimum of five thousand, they are often prohibitively costly. The larger the order, the lower the cost per unit.

Printing on premade envelopes is confined to a small graphic and return address located on the front, positioned in the top left corner. Printing presses require a minimum of ⅜″ margin for the *gripper* (the part of the printing press that holds the sheet of paper), and postal regulations have become strict, requiring the majority of the face open for addressing and automated processing of individual pieces.

Typical Layout Considerations

According to Robert Bringhurst (American author, poet, book designer, typographer, historian and linguist), "If a text calls for Renaissance type it calls for Renaissance typography as well. This usually means Renaissance page proportions and margins and the absence of a boldface." This is a specific example, but generally speaking, the layout of type on a page is meant to enhance and support the meaning of the message by subtly, almost invisibly, transporting the reader into a specific visual context.

Fortunately, there is no single rule or set of rules for designing a publication—if there were, all solutions would appear equally exciting or equally boring and none would provide an individual identity for the client. Unfortunately, the lack of standard specifications makes design a more complicated process than it would be if there were such absolute and finite choices.

Basic considerations for the design of a publication include the selection of typefaces for different components within the publication (headings, body text, subheadings, sidebars, and so on) based on general guidelines for legibility, readability, and printability; the compositional arrangement as dictated by the hierarchy of importance and the quantity of information; and the method of distribution (e.g., passed out via literature holders in public spaces or mailed). A number of these considerations are determined by the designer in cooperation

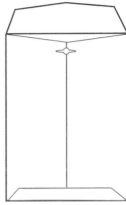
12.14 Catalog w/metal clasp.

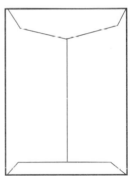
12.15 Catalog.

12.16 A-style or baronial.

12.17 Business announcement.

12.18 Wallet flap.

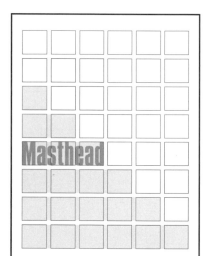

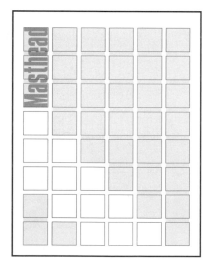

12.19 Use the grid units to help determine the correct size and position of both image and type elements in a composition. The grid areas may be used individually or in combination.

with the client and the art director, based on the budget and schedule.

Establishing a Grid

The most common place to start developing a composition for publication is to establish a grid, which subdivides the format into small units intended to help the designer determine the location and size of the compositional components. Grids are especially important in the design of periodicals (magazines, newsletters, tabloids, catalogs, and newspapers) to speed the layout process and create a consistent, uniform appearance from one issue to the next, even if multiple graphic artists are assigned to the project.

The practical development and use of a grid for controlling typographic layouts came from Switzerland following World War II, as seen in historical examples from the late 1940s. This compositional trend was characterized by somewhat strict rules for page layout based on the notion that the designs remain objective in the presentation of the subject content. Some of the first writing on the subject of organizing compositions using a grid was by Josef Müller-Brockman in 1961; his *The Graphic Artist and His Design Problems* included a brief description of a grid system. In 1981 his *Grid Systems in Graphic Design* presented American designers with detailed explanations and visual examples of working grids in the Swiss style (also known as the International Style).

Although employed with much less rigor and formality than only two decades ago, the grid is still a useful tool in logically organizing text and imagery within the compositional format. Most modern software applications have automated the development of grids

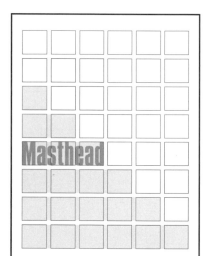

12.20 The grid units should match the lines of text on the page. Many popular software applications allow a "lock to grid" or "align with grid" function for use with an accurate, formal grid.

for page layout, making it much easier for today's designer to explore various layout possibilities.

A grid subdivides the page into smaller units by first establishing a number of vertical columns. These columns are subdivided into a number of smaller units that establish the dimensions for the smallest unit of type or image. In a formal system, the depth of each field is based on a number of lines of text (including leading), and this dimension is also equal to the width of an individual column. Column width should be determined not only by the personal style or aesthetic of the designer, but also by practical considerations of line length, with legibility and readability in mind (too short and the reader cannot settle into a meaningful rhythm; too long and the reader finds it strenuous to focus on a single line for the whole length).

Contemporary Western applications of the grid seldom organize the information into such a formal configuration; it is unclear whether the designers do not know the formal aspects of composition using a grid system or simply choose to work in a less confining compositional structure.

While the grid determines the basic dimensions of spaces in order to build visual relationships in the composition, there are numerous possible compositional combinations. The greater the number of columns and modules on a single page, the more active the resulting composition will be. The fewer the number of columns and modules, the more static and calm the resulting composition will be.

Margins, Gutters, and Alleys

The grid area is surrounded by margins, since there is often a $\frac{1}{16}''$ to $\frac{1}{4}''$ discrepancy along different sides of the trimmed and/or bound page. Without any margins, it is likely that a portion of the text will be cut off, rendering the subject matter incomplete and most likely destroying its meaning. Well-designed and proportioned margins frame the content of each page and provide a comfortable amount of white space to rest the eyes. Historical models of book design have based margin dimensions on mathematical calculations and principles such as the golden section, but more often than not, contemporary margins are determined by the designer in consultation with the printer, taking into account technical constraints.

The margin at the top of the page is called the *head margin* (or head space); the one at the bottom of the page is a called the *foot margin* (or foot space). Often a running head (*header*) or running foot (*footer*) is placed in this space to remind the reader of the chapter

or section name consecutively. According to contemporary trends, the head margin is usually the largest, to allow for a balanced, enclosed composition that does not appear top-heavy, with the smallest margins being the space between the columns (called the intercolumn space or *alleys*).

In a single-page layout, often the side margins (or thumb spaces) are equal to the foot margin, whereas in a *spread* (two or more consecutive pages that face each other in a publication) the interior margin (called the *gutter*), is reduced to up to half the dimension of the outside page margins so that the page contents read together as one coherent message.

Mastheads, Headlines, and Subheads

The *masthead* is the unusual decorative type that names the periodical or newsletter. The masthead may be the largest and boldest element, often incorporating some sort of imagery. The masthead is an area of the publication that both allows and demands a designer's creativity, since it is such a large component of the overall aesthetic and meaning of the piece.

Headlines and *subheads* introduce the primary and secondary levels of information within the story, article, or book. The headlines are more important within the information hierarchy than the subheads, and commonly are set in larger and bolder type. Headlines, also called *heads* or *headings*, should be easy to read and clearly stand out from the body copy. Subheads are helpful in organizing information for the reader and indicate a category of information that is more focused or more specific to one area of the main topic. Subheads may be set in the

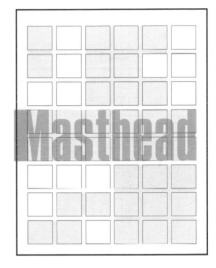

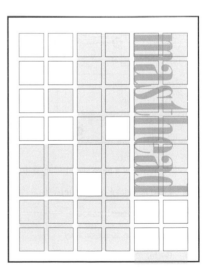

12.21 A grid system should not limit the creativity in your layout, but rather assist in helping to build visual relationships of size and alignment. Explore variations in position, size, and orientation in the layout.

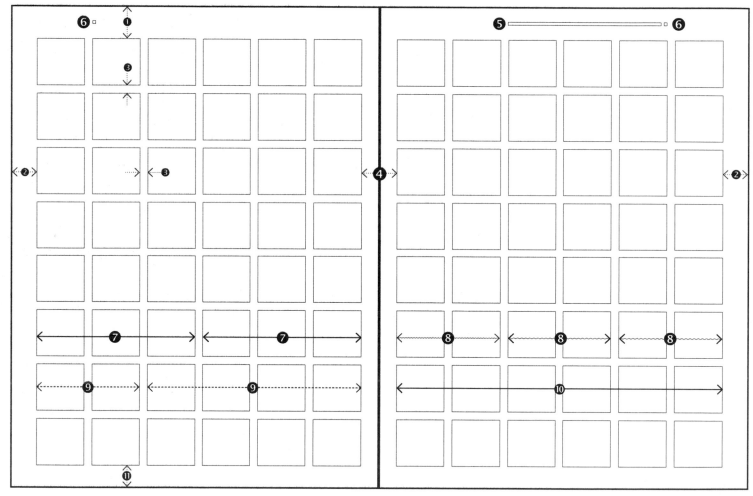

12.22 Anatomy of a page layout using a grid.

❶ Head margin or head space

❷ Margin or thumb space

❸ Intercolumn space or alley

❹ Gutter

❺ Running head (header) in head margin

❻ Folio or page number

❼ Two-column layout

❽ Three-column layout

❾ Two-column layout

❿ One-column layout

⓫ Foot margin or foot space

same font as the headlines but usually are a smaller size and/or a semibold or regular stroke weight instead of a bold weight.

Headers and Footers

Running heads (headers) and/or running feet (footers) appear on every page of the publication, with the exception of the front page of a newsletter or the first page in each chapter of a book. Designed to be incorporated into either the head margin or foot margin of the publication, respectively, these elements are relatively small in comparison to the other page elements. The

header or footer may include the title of the publication (book or periodical), the *folio* (page number) in multiple-page documents, and/or the section or chapter name.

Body Copy

Well-designed body copy or body text establishes the look and tone of the printed piece, communicating the character of the message. Since the majority of the whole story, article, or book is set in the *body text* font, it should be carefully selected for legibility and readability. Often the body copy is started with an initial cap or drop cap to mark the starting point for the reader. Another variation is to begin the article or chapter with a few lines or words in all caps or small caps to draw the reader into the story. These special treatments are not used on every paragraph of the story, only on the first paragraph of the story.

Limit the number of faces in a publication; determine the quantity of visual changes based on the quantity of text and the number of chapters or sections. When faces are selected it will provide more practical visual interest if the fonts represent a meaningful hierarchy; that is, select one font for the body text, one font for headlines and subheads, one font for sidebar information, and one for pull quotes. For more complicated text, restrain font use to italic and bold variations within the same family.

Callouts and Pull Quotes

Information that is emphasized within the typeset text by a bold font is a *callout*; this highlights certain information within the text. Information that is separated from the typeset text, often inset with a background color or value and rules in a larger size is a *pull quote*; this provides insight into or an overview of the main point of the article or story. Pull quotes can be in a different font or a larger size; they can also be offset by decorative rules or flourishes. Callouts and pull quotes bring variety and visual interest to the page layout.

Tables, Lists, and Forms

Tabular settings are used to organize information in lists, tables and forms.

SHE THOUGHT IT MUST BE THE RIGHT HOUSE, BECAUSE THE CHIMNEYS WERE SHAPED LIKE EARS AND THE ROOF WAS THATCHED WITH FUR.

12.23 A pull quote highlights an important issue or characters in an article or story while adding visual interest to the composition. This element should be sized in terms of grid units, just as other compositional elements are.

Tables

A *table* is information organized into rows and columns so that the data in each area of the cells have a meaningful relationship to the data above, below, and beside it. A table may include rules to divide the rows and columns. The organization of the text can be done with more subtle visual cues, first and foremost tabular spaces between columns of text and leading between rows of text. If rule lines are a necessary component of the design, use a fine weight such as .25 point. Experiment with dotted or dashed rules to make the rule even lighter in texture and presence on the page.

Lists

A *list* is a group of related terms or information sometimes organized in

Experiment with using a six-column grid for a two-page magazine spread. Include a headline, a minimum of three photographs or illustrations with credit and captions, an author's byline, and a three-column by six-row data table. Using a pencil, draw boxes with an *x* from corner to corner to indicate the spaces occupied by images. Use lines to indicate lines of text and small, neat scribbles to show the credit, caption, and byline text. Take notes to remind yourself of positive and negative areas of each composition.

Layout Thumbnails Using a Grid

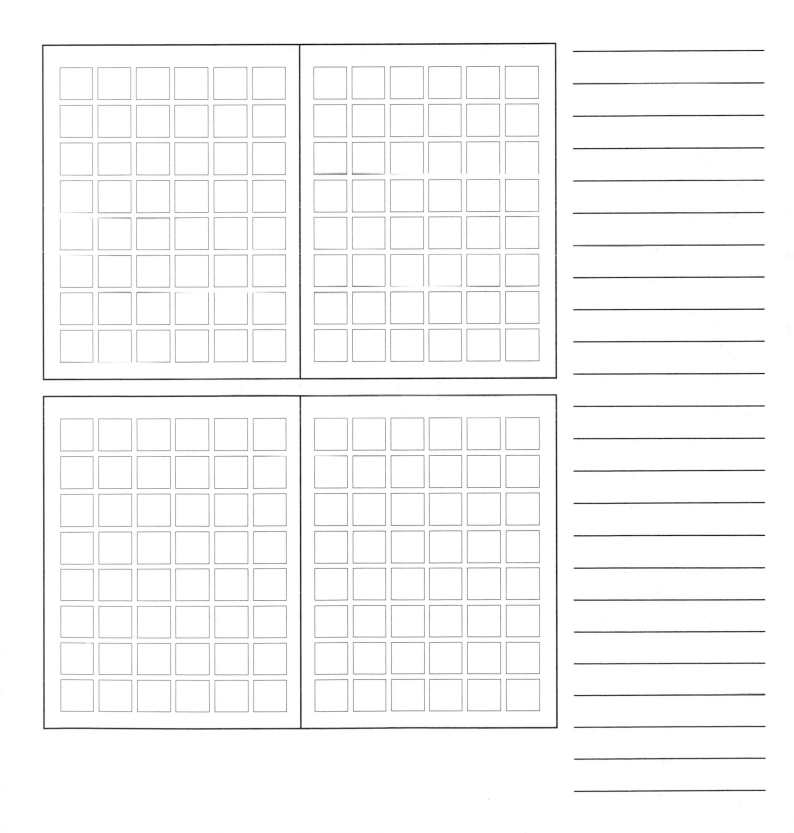

hierarchial order. Often lists utilize a *bullet* (a small geometric shape, usually a circle) or *dingbat* (a small decorative image) to indicate each separate item in the list. Occasionally a list begins with a name or glossary term followed by a dash. The bulleted item is set in from the left margin a pica or two from the bullet, and the descriptive text follows. A *runover* is the text of the description that follows onto subsequent lines and should be set so that it aligns with the first letter of the first line of descriptive text. Specified like a hanging indent in most contemporary software applications, this type layout allows the term or name to be set apart from the definition or description.

A small column width makes it impossible to take advantage of indented text, as the additional inset creates a very short line and interrupts the reader's rhythm and interpretation of meaning.

Forms

In a *form* the type of information to be collected is listed in some manner, followed by a space or line to be filled in by the user. Forms range in complexity. As the amount of information and complexity of information increase, so must the designer's awareness and consideration. The construction and layout of a form must allow an appropriate amount of space for the user to fill in the blank areas; information should be grouped logically and in an orderly manner, without extraneous items and unnecessary rules. Some forms must maintain margins and columns so that the information can be automatically processed, so consultation with technological experts and software vendors

Alice	Small, blond, naive girl wearing a blue-and-white checked frock with a white apron; she is the key character and experiences a number of strange subordinate characters and unusual physical phenomena throughout the story.
Mad Hatter	Although well dressed, he seems to have an issue with offering food and beverage that does not exist, and wears a large top hat. Perhaps "mad" does not refer to his disposition, but his state of mind.
March Hare	Also well dressed, especially for a small rodent, he seems to be consistently late for appointments, and somewhat nervous.
Dormouse	Small, somewhat cute rodent who is excessively tired throughout most of the story.

12.24 A hanging indent may be used to clarify the term or subject when runover text is involved. A tab may be set at the same position as the indented text for a more concise appearance. The hanging indent is effective for lists, such as a glossary.

Tea Party Attendees
Alice
March Hare
Mad Hatter
Dormouse

Tea Party Attendees
- Alice
- March Hare
- Mad Hatter
- Dormouse

Tea Party Attendees
➢ Alice
➢ March Hare
➢ Mad Hatter
➢ Dormouse

12.25 A list item often becomes clearer to the reader when it is offset by a bullet (middle example) or a dingbat (bottom example).

Tea Party Attendees	Cups of Tea	Pieces of Cake
Alice	1	1
March Hare	2	0
Mad Hatter	5	2
Dormouse	0	3

12.26 Although text can be organized in a tablelike structure without horizontal or vertical guides, it is more difficult for the reader to align the information visually and understand the meaning of the data.

Tea Party Attendees	Cups of Tea	Pieces of Cake
Alice	1	1
March Hare	2	0
Mad Hatter	5	2
Dormouse	0	3

12.27 Horizontal and vertical guides assist the reader to understand the meaning of the data but are often too heavy and amateurish-looking.

Tea Party Attendees	Cups of Tea	Pieces of Cake
Alice	1	1
March Hare	2	0
Mad Hatter	5	2
Dormouse	0	3

12.28 Horizontal and vertical guides can be made using background shades and thin decorative rules; this example emphasizes the vertical columns of information.

Tea Party Attendees	Cups of Tea	Pieces of Cake
Alice	1	1
March Hare	2	0
Mad Hatter	5	2
Dormouse	0	3

12.29 Horizontal and vertical guides can be made using background shades; this example emphasizes the horizontal rows of information.

March Hare: "Have some wine!"

Alice: "I don't see any wine."

March Hare: "There isn't any."

Alice: "Then it wasn't very civil of you to offer it."

March Hare: "It wasn't very civil of you to sit down without being invited."

Alice: "I didn't know it was YOUR table... it's laid for a great many more than three."

Mad Hatter: "Your hair wants cutting."

Alice: "You should learn not to make personal remarks, it's very rude."

Mad Hatter: "Why is a raven like a writing-desk?"

Alice: "I believe I can guess that."

March Hare: "Do you mean that you think you can find out the answer to it?"

Alice: "Exactly so."

March Hare: "Then you should say what you mean."

Alice: "I do, at least—at least I mean what I say—that's the same thing, you know."

Mad Hatter: "Not the same thing a bit! You might just as well say that 'I see what I eat' is the same thing as 'I eat what I see'!"

12.30 A hanging indent may be used to clarify the term or subject when runover text is involved. This text example is set as a play script, separating the list of cast members from the lines they speak.

may be required to create an accurate and usable form design.

A standard rule of thumb is to allow approximately 20 points of leading between lines of a form that will be filled with handwritten answers. A much smaller space forces the user to cram information into it, often resulting in illegible responses. Font weight can be used to develop a visual hierarchy, often eliminating the need for rule lines that may cause visual clutter.

Captions, Bylines, and Credits

Small type such as captions, bylines, and credits may seem insignificant to

Employment Application

We are an equal opportunity employer.

Position Applied For: _____   **Date of Application:** _____

Name: _____
LAST   FIRST   MIDDLE

Address: _____
STREET   CITY   STATE   ZIP

Phone: _____ **Mobile/FAX:** _____ **Soc. Sec. No.:** _____

Date available to start: _____

Type of employment desired: ☐ Full-Time ☐ Part-Time ☐ Temporary

Have you been convicted of a crime in the past?   ☐ YES   ☐ NO

If Yes, please explain: _____

Have you ever been employed here before?   ☐ YES   ☐ NO

Are you legally eligible for employment in this country? ☐ YES   ☐ NO

If you are under 18, do you have a work permit?   ☐ YES   ☐ NO

Work Experience

FROM	TO	EMPLOYER		PHONE
JOB TITLE		ADDRESS		
Immediate supervisor and title		Nature of the work and responsibilities		
Reason for Leaving		Hourly Rate Salary		
FROM	TO	EMPLOYER		PHONE
JOB TITLE		ADDRESS		
Immediate supervisor and title		Nature of the work and responsibilities		
Reason for Leaving		Hourly Rate Salary		
FROM	TO	EMPLOYER		PHONE
JOB TITLE		ADDRESS		
Immediate supervisor and title		Nature of the work and responsibilities		
Reason for Leaving		Hourly Rate Salary		

12.31 An example of a typical, generic employment application. Is there an appropriate amount of space to fill in the blanks neatly? What suggestions can you make for improvement, in terms of both functionality and aesthetic?

Title/name MR. SHORTNAME
Street address PO BOX 6987
City/State ITTA BENA, MISSISSIPPI
Zip code 38941
Telephone number (662) 888-7777

12.32 A form with less than 20 points of leading makes it almost impossible to complete with readable handwriting.

Title/name MR. SHORTNAME

Street address PO BOX 6987

City/State ITTA BENA, MISSISSIPPI

Zip code 38941

Telephone number (662) 888-7777

12.33 A form with at least 20 points of leading is easier to complete with readable handwriting.

Title/name MR. SHORTNAME

Street address PO BOX 6987

City/State ITTA BENA, MISSISSIPPI

Zip code 38941

Telephone number (662) 888-7777

12.34 A form with at 24 points of leading and a guideline is easier to complete with readable handwriting.

MR. THOMAS SHORTNAME
TITLE/NAME
PO BOX 6987
STREET ADDRESS
ITTA BENA, MISSISSIPPI
CITY/STATE
38941
ZIP CODE
(662) 888-7777
TELEPHONE NUMBER

12.35 A form with more than 20 points of leading is easier to complete, making it likely that the handwriting will be legible enough to avoid transcription mistakes. The small type below the line leaves more room to write.

Drop cap

Photo credit

Sidebar

Byline

12.36 (Left) Examples of a drop cap, photo credit, sidebar, and author's byline as it might appear in a single-page layout, using a grid for sizing and alignment.

12.37 Photograph with photo credit.

inexperienced designers, however the quality and placement of this important information often reveal the typographic sophistication of the designer. The small type must be judiciously oriented and placed so that it is clearly visible and legible without being disruptive and distracting. These small references are another element in the visual hierarchy and should work together with the other page elements in the communication.

Captions

Captions are the small type below or beside an image or illustration; they explain the content and context of the subject. Most captions are set in a small point size and different face than the other text on the page, so as to eliminate any confusion with other text elements on the page. There are four different types of captions: narrative, identifier, essay, and pull-quote. *Narrative captions* are longer, since they are used to explain the content and/or context of the photo or illustration. *Identifier captions* are short descriptive sentences or phrases containing only the most basic information necessary to understand the image. *Essay captions* are long, descriptive, storylike explanations that tell as much or more of the story line as the body text. Often essay captions accompany photographic essays in a journalistic style, so there is no written story

*S*he had not gone much farther before she came in sight of the house of the March Hare: she thought it must be the right house, because the chimneys were shaped like ears and the roof was thatched with fur. It was so large a house, that she did not like to go nearer till she had nibbled some more of the lefthand bit of mushroom, and raised herself to about two feet high: even then she walked up towards it rather timidly, saying to herself, "Suppose it should be raving mad after all! I almost wish I'd gone to see the Hatter instead!"

*T*here was a table set out under a tree in front of the house, and the March Hare and the Hatter were having tea at it: a Dormouse was sitting between them, fast asleep, and the other two were using it as a cushion, resting their elbows on it, and talking over its head. "Very uncomfortable for the Dormouse," thought Alice; "only, as it's asleep, I suppose it doesn't mind."

12.38 These examples of a raised cap and a drop cap. These indicate where the story begins by drawing attention to the first letter of the first sentence.

line set in body copy. *Pull-quote captions* are statements taken from the body text and used as a description for the photograph or illustration.

Bylines

The *byline* contains the name of the author or authors responsible for writing the story, article, or book. These do not follow any standardized rules for size or placement in the composition, but typically appear at the beginning of the story just above or below the headline. The byline may be typeset as a sidebar or at the end of the article, sometimes accompanied by a short biography of the writer. In newspapers, the byline commonly follows the article head, often with the author's name and profession affiliation, since most newspapers pick up articles from multiple sources.

Credits

Photographic and illustration credits vary widely according to the design of the publication or periodical and according to the contractual agreement with the photographer, designer, or illustrator who created the imagery. Some publication images are accompanied by very small type running along the bottom or right side of the image; some publications include the credit in the caption text; some publications and books group the credits for all images at the end of the publication or textbook.

Sidebars

A *sidebar* consists of information that is secondary to the main topic of the section, subsection, or chapter. The information relates to and supports the information in

*T*he table was a large one, but the three were all crowded together at one corner of it: "No room! No room!" they cried out when they saw Alice coming. "There's PLENTY of room!" said Alice indignantly, and she sat down in a large arm-chair at one end of the table.

12.39 Example of a hanging cap.

the main story line, often providing a more in-depth explanation that assists readers in reaching a deeper understanding of the topic. The information in the sidebar is not essential to understanding the main content, but may clarify a point of view different than that featured in the main article.

Sidebars are separated from the main text by their placement and typographic treatment. A sidebar may be enclosed in a box or decorative rule; a background color or value may draw additional attention to the fact that this information is separate content. A sidebar may be set in a different face—most commonly a condensed or lightweight variation of the face used for headings and subheadings in longer publications, where numerous sidebars may appear. In a newsletter, where there may be only one sidebar per issue, the designer may choose a more decorative font and more elaborate design.

Initial Caps

Initial caps are large, somewhat decorative letterforms used to call attention to the beginning of an article, story, or chapter. Variations on the initial cap include stand-up or raised caps, drop caps (sometimes called inset caps), and hanging caps.

The *stand-up* or *raised cap* is larger than the typeset body text, and its baseline aligns with the baseline of the first line of text at the beginning of the story. The size of this raised

Chapter Twelve Review

letter is usually based on a multiple of the typeset dimension—that is, two or three lines tall. Special attention must be paid to the letter spacing before and after a stand-up cap so that it maintains proper association with the rest of the letters in the word.

A *drop cap*, like the raised cap, is sized as a multiple of the lines of text, often three or four lines in height. The difference is that the inset or drop cap's baseline aligns with the second, third, or fourth line of text. Often the subsequent lines of text require additional mortising, or word spacing, immediately next to the large letterform, so that they are not read as part of a word beginning with that letter. The cap line of the drop cap aligns with the cap line of the first line of text in the story. Letters with angled strokes, such as *A*, *V*, or *W* may require special mortising to avoid a relatively large, trapped, white space next to the character. The most pleasing solution is for the subsequent lines of type to create a visual angle that complements the angle of the side stroke on the drop cap.

Hanging caps are large initial caps that often combine characteristics of the raised cap and the drop cap. A hanging cap may be typeset so that it extends above the cap line of the first line of text and drops to the baseline of the second, third, or fourth line of text. The unique characteristic of a hanging cap is that all subsequent lines of text are inset so that they align vertically with the second character of the first line of text; the hanging cap is set out in the left margin by itself, just like the first line of a hanging indentation, or the bullet indicating an element in a list.

Circle one answer for each definition to indicate the correct key concept term for each. When necessary, determine whether the phrase provided is true or false.

1. This term refers to information that is separated from the typeset text, often inset with a background color or value and rules in a larger size.
   a. Drop cap
   b. Callout
   c. Masthead
   d. Pull quote

2. The term *basis weight* refers to the weight, measured in pounds, of a ream of cut paper.
   a. True
   b. False

3. This interior margin is reduced to up to half the dimension of the outside page margins so that the page contents read together as one coherent message.
   a. Alley
   b. Footer
   c. Gutter
   d. Thumb space

4. This establishes the look and tone of the printed piece, communicating the character of the message. Since the majority of the whole story, article, or book is set in this, it should be carefully selected for legibility and readability.
   a. Masthead
   b. Folio
   c. Running head
   d. Body text

5. Envelopes are manufactured by
   a. Robert Bringhurst
   b. A printer
   c. Converters
   d. Dingbats

6.   This is the term for information organized into rows and columns so that the data in each area of the cells have a meaningful relationship to the data above, below, and beside it.
    a.   Table
    b.   Callout
    c.   Form
    d.   List

7.   Some publication images are accompanied by very small type running along the bottom or right side of the image; some publications include this in the caption text; some publications and books group these for all images at the end of the publication or textbook.
    a.   Credit
    b.   Masthead
    c.   Ream
    d.   Byline

8.   A standard rule of thumb is to allow approximately 37 points of leading between lines of a form that will be filled with handwritten answers.
    a.   True
    b.   False

9.   Paper is manufactured in large continuous rolls. As the paper fibers move through the multiple stages, the fibers align along the length of the roll parallel to the edges resulting in a _____ .
    a.   Bleed
    b.   Grain
    c.   Ream
    d.   Runover

10. Paper weight is easy to determine since all reams manufactured in North America are 8 1/2″ × 11″ with 500 sheets of paper in a package.
    a.   True
    b.   False

11. Often these utilize a *bullet* or *dingbat* to indicate each separate item.
    a.   Bleed
    b.   List
    c.   Caption
    d.   Table

12. These are large, somewhat decorative letterforms used to call attention to the beginning of an article, story, or chapter.
    a.   Byline
    b.   Pull quote
    c.   Callout
    d.   Initial cap

13. These papers are available in a number of different surface finishes, the most common of which are smooth, linen, laid, and cockle.
    a.   Newsprint
    b.   Uncoated
    c.   Kraft
    d.   Matte-coated

14. This may be typeset so that it extends above the cap line of the first line of text and drops to the baseline of the second, third, or fourth line of text. The unique characteristic of a this is that all subsequent lines of text are inset so that they align vertically with the second character of the first line of text.
    a.   Drop Cap
    b.   Hanging cap
    c.   Raised cap
    d.   Initial cap

15. These are the small type below or beside an image or illustration; they explain the content and context of the subject.
    a.   Byline
    b.   Credit
    c.   Caption
    d.   Signature

Academy Engraved

abcdefghijklmnopqrstuvwxyz
ABCDEFGHIJKLM
NOPQRSTUVWXYZ
1234567890?!$%&*:;"

6/9 Alice was beginning to get very tired of sitting by her sister on the bank, and of having nothing to do: once or twice she had peeped into the book her sister was reading, but it had no pictures or conversations in it, "and what is the use of a book," thought Alice, "without pictures or conversation?"

8/12 Alice was beginning to get very tired of sitting by her sister on the bank, and of having nothing to do: once or twice she had peeped into the book her sister was reading, but it had no pictures or conversations in it, "and what is the use of a book," thought Alice, "without pictures or conversation?"

11/14 Alice was beginning to get very tired of sitting by her sister on the bank, and of having nothing to do: once or twice she had peeped into the book her sister was reading, but it had no pictures or conversations in it, "and what is the use of a book," thought Alice, "without pictures or conversation?"

14/15 Alice was beginning to get very tired of sitting by her sister on the bank, and of having nothing to do: once or twice she had peeped into the book her sister was reading, but it had no pictures or conversations in it, "and what is the use of a book," thought Alice, "without pictures or conversation?"

18/20 Alice was beginning to get very tired of sitting by her sister on the bank, and of having nothing to do: once or twice she had peeped into the book her sister was reading, but it had no pictures or conversations in it, "and what is the use of a book," thought Alice, "without pictures or

Academy Engraved

Academy Engraved, designed by Vince Whitlock in 1989, was based upon the elegant Caslon typeface. The refined forms of this roman-style face communicate a noble, classic feel.

Try combining the inline capital letters as initials with other fonts.

Agency FB

abcdefghijklmnopqrstuvwxyz

ABCDEFGHIJKLMNOPQRSTUVWXYZ

1234567890?!@#$%^&*

Agency FB

This font was originally designed by Morris Fuller Benton as ATF Agency Gothic in 1932 for use as a titling font. In 1990, David Berlow was inspired by the squared forms of the narrow, monotone capitals. He designed a lowercase and added a bold variation to produce Agency FB, also known as Font Bureau Agency.

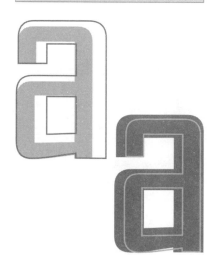

14/15 So she was considering in her own mind (as well as she could, for the hot day made her feel very sleepy and stupid), whether the pleasure of making a daisy-chain would be worth the trouble of getting up and picking the daisies, when suddenly a White Rabbit with pink eyes ran close by her.

18/20 So she was considering in her own mind (as well as she could, for the hot day made her feel very sleepy and stupid), whether the pleasure of making a daisy-chain would be worth the trouble of getting up and picking the daisies, when suddenly a White Rabbit with pink eyes ran close by her.

21/23 So she was considering in her own mind (as well as she could, for the hot day made her feel very sleepy and stupid), whether the

6/9 So she was considering in her own mind (as well as she could, for the hot day made her feel very sleepy and stupid), whether the pleasure of making a daisy-chain would be worth the trouble of getting up and picking the daisies, when suddenly a White Rabbit with pink eyes ran close by her.

7/10 So she was considering in her own mind (as well as she could, for the hot day made her feel very sleepy and stupid), whether the pleasure of making a daisy-chain would be worth the trouble of getting up and picking the daisies, when suddenly a White Rabbit with pink eyes ran close by her.

8/12 So she was considering in her own mind (as well as she could, for the hot day made her feel very sleepy and stupid), whether the pleasure of making a daisy-chain would be worth the trouble of getting up and picking the daisies, when suddenly a White Rabbit with pink eyes ran close by her.

11/14 So she was considering in her own mind (as well as she could, for the hot day made her feel very sleepy and stupid), whether the pleasure of making a daisy-chain would be worth the trouble of getting up and picking the daisies, when suddenly a White Rabbit with pink eyes ran close by her.

ALGERIAN

ABCDEFGHIJKLM
NOPQRSTUVWXYZ
1234567890?!$%&*:;"

12/14   THERE WAS NOTHING SO VERY REMARKABLE IN THAT; NOR DID ALICE THINK IT SO VERY MUCH OUT OF THE WAY TO HEAR THE RABBIT SAY TO ITSELF, "OH DEAR! OH DEAR! I SHALL BE LATE!" (WHEN SHE THOUGHT IT OVER AFTERWARDS, IT OCCURRED TO HER THAT SHE OUGHT TO HAVE WONDERED AT THIS, BUT AT THE TIME IT ALL SEEMED QUITE NATURAL);

15/17   THERE WAS NOTHING SO VERY REMARKABLE IN THAT; NOR DID ALICE THINK IT SO VERY MUCH OUT OF THE WAY TO HEAR THE RABBIT SAY TO ITSELF, "OH DEAR! OH DEAR! I SHALL BE LATE!" (WHEN SHE THOUGHT IT OVER AFTERWARDS, IT OCCURRED TO HER THAT SHE OUGHT TO HAVE WONDERED AT THIS, BUT AT THE TIME IT ALL SEEMED QUITE NATURAL);

21/23   THERE WAS NOTHING SO VERY REMARKABLE IN THAT; NOR DID ALICE THINK IT SO VERY MUCH OUT OF THE WAY TO HEAR THE RABBIT SAY TO ITSELF, "OH DEAR! OH DEAR! I SHALL BE LATE!"(WHEN SHE THOUGHT IT OVER

Algerian

In 1988 type designer Phillip Kelly created this font, which is reminiscent of woodcut type from the Victorian era. Variations on this alphabet of all capital letters includes many alternate characters.

ITC American Typewriter Medium

abcdefghijklmnopqrstuvwxyz
ABCDEFGHIJKLM
NOPQRSTUVWXYZ
1234567890?!$%&*:;"

ITC American Typewriter

ITC American Typewriter, designed by Joel Kaden and Tony Stan in 1974, is a compromise between the original version and the expectations of the digital age. ITC American Typewriter retains the typical typewriter alphabet forms—bulbous serif design, large x-height, and curvaceous numerals—lending the font a hint of nostalgia.

The family includes light, light alternate, medium, medium alternate, **bold**, **bold alternate**, light condensed, light condensed alternate, condensed, condensed alternate, **bold condensed**, and **bold condensed alternate**. The digital ITC version is not monospaced as the original typewriter version was.

6/9   but when the Rabbit actually TOOK A WATCH OUT OF ITS WAISTCOAT-POCKET, and looked at it, and then hurried on, Alice started to her feet, for it flashed across her mind that she had never before seen a rabbit with either a waistcoat-pocket, or a watch to take out of it, and burning with curiosity, she ran across the field after it, and fortunately was just in time to see it pop down a large rabbit-hole under the hedge.

8/12   but when the Rabbit actually TOOK A WATCH OUT OF ITS WAISTCOAT-POCKET, and looked at it, and then hurried on, Alice started to her feet, for it flashed across her mind that she had never before seen a rabbit with either a waistcoat-pocket, or a watch to take out of it, and burning with curiosity, she ran across the field after it, and fortunately was just in time to see it pop down a large rabbit-hole under the hedge.

11/14   but when the Rabbit actually TOOK A WATCH OUT OF ITS WAISTCOAT-POCKET, and looked at it, and then hurried on, Alice started to her feet, for it flashed across her mind that she had never before seen a rabbit with either a waistcoat-pocket, or a watch to take out of it, and burning with curiosity, she ran across the field after it, and fortunately was just in time to see it pop down a large rabbit-hole under the hedge.

14/16   but when the Rabbit actually TOOK A WATCH OUT OF ITS WAISTCOAT-POCKET, and looked at it, and then hurried on, Alice started to her feet, for it flashed across her mind that she had never before seen a rabbit with either a waistcoat-pocket, or a watch to take out of it, and burning with curiosity, she ran across the field after it, and

ITC Americana

abcdefghijklmnopqrstuvwxyz
ABCDEFGHIJKLM
NOPQRSTUVWXYZ
1234567890?!$%&*:;"

6/9 In another moment down went Alice after it, never once considering how in the world she was to get out again.
The rabbit-hole went straight on like a tunnel for some way, and then dipped suddenly down, so suddenly that Alice had not a moment to think about stopping herself before she found herself falling down a very deep well.

8/12 In another moment down went Alice after it, never once considering how in the world she was to get out again.
The rabbit-hole went straight on like a tunnel for some way, and then dipped suddenly down, so suddenly that Alice had not a moment to think about stopping herself before she found herself falling down a very deep well.

11/14 In another moment down went Alice after it, never once considering how in the world she was to get out again.

14/16 In another moment down went Alice after it, never once considering how in the world she was to get out again.
The rabbit-hole went straight on like a tunnel for some way, and then dipped suddenly down, so suddenly that Alice had not a moment to think about stopping herself before she found herself falling down a very deep well.

20/22 In another moment down went Alice after it, never once considering how in the world she was to get out again.
The rabbit-hole went straight on like a tunnerl for some way, and then dipped suddenly down, so suddenly

ITC Americana

Designed by Richard Isbell in 1965, Americana was inspired by the upcoming U.S. Bicentennial. The most distinguishing feature of Americana is its extremely large x-height. The letter proportions are very wide, with short ascenders and descenders. Americana works well for short texts, such as headlines. The broad width of the characters makes it necessary to set a longer line length.

Andale Mono Regular

abcdefghijklmnopqrstuvwxyz

ABCDEFGHIJKLM

NOPQRSTUVWXYZ

1234567890?!$%&*:;"

Andale Mono

Andale is a monospace digital font designed by Steve Matteson and owned by Agfa Monotype. It is distributed by Microsoft with Internet Explorer.

The font was designed to meet the demands of low-resolution imaging while maintaining legibility. The design is currently included with many software products and supports character sets for Hebrew, Arabic, Thai, Greek, Cyrillic, and several other languages.

6/9   Either the well was very deep, or she fell very slowly, for she had plenty of time as she went down to look about her and to wonder what was going to happen next. First, she tried to look down and make out what she was coming to, but it was too dark to see anything; then she looked at the sides of the well, and noticed that they were filled with cupboards and book-shelves;

8/12   Either the well was very deep, or she fell very slowly, for she had plenty of time as she went down to look about her and to wonder what was going to happen next. First, she tried to look down and make out what she was coming to, but it was too dark to see anything; then she looked at the sides of the well, and noticed that they were filled with cupboards and book-shelves;

11/14   Either the well was very deep, or she fell very slowly, for she had plenty of time as she went down

14/16   Either the well was very deep, or she fell very slowly, for she had plenty of time as she went down to look about her and to wonder what was going to happen next. First, she tried to look down and make out what she was coming to, but it was too dark to see anything; then she looked at the sides of the well, and noticed that they were filled with cupboards and book-shelves;

20/20   Either the well was very deep, or she fell very slowly, for she had plenty of time as she went down

Arnold Böcklin

abcdefghijklmnopqrstuvwxyz
ABCDEFGHIJKLM
NOPQRSTUVWXYZ
1234567890?!§$%&*.,"

6/9 "Well!" thought Alice to herself, "after such a fall as this, I shall think nothing of tumbling down stairs! How brave they'll all think me at home! Why, I wouldn't say anything about it, even if I fell off the top of the house!" (Which was very likely true.)

8/12 "Well!" thought Alice to herself, "after such a fall as this, I shall think nothing of tumbling down stairs! How brave they'll all think me at home! Why, I wouldn't say anything about it, even if I fell off the top of the house!" (Which was very likely true.)

11/14 "Well!" thought Alice to herself, "after such a fall as this, I shall think nothing of tumbling down stairs! How brave they'll all think me at home! Why, I wouldn't say anything about it, even if I fell off the top of the house!" (Which was very likely true.)

14/16 "Well!" thought Alice to herself, "after such a fall as this, I shall think nothing of tumbling down stairs! How brave they'll all think me at home! Why, I wouldn't say anything about it, even if I fell off the top of the house!" (Which was very likely true.)

18/20 "Well!" thought Alice to herself, "after such a fall as this, I shall think nothing of tumbling down stairs! How brave they'll all think me at home! Why, I wouldn't say anything about it, even if I fell off the top of the house!" (Which was very likely true.)

Arnold Böcklin Standard

Arnold Böcklin was designed by Otto Weisert in 1904 at the height of the Art Nouveau period. Traces of the floral forms of the Jugendstil are seen in this typeface. Alphabets of this style were intended for use at larger point sizes, as on posters. A decorative feel was much more important than legibility during this era, and Arnold Böcklin was important in book cover design of the time.

Attic Antique

abcdefghijklmnopqrstuvwxyz

ABCDEFGHIJKLM
NOPQRSTUVWXYZ
1234567890?!$%&*:;"

Attic Antique

Attic Antique was designed in
1993 by Brian Willson, founder of
Three Islands Press. Early in the
1990s, Willson began tinkering
with type design, resulting
in a number of now-familiar
handwriting, text, and offbeat
fonts including Attic Antique,
Treefrog, and Marydale. Willson's
design niche is authentic old
penmanship, and he has designed
the antique handwriting faces
Emily Austin, Houston Pen, Lamar
Pen, Schooner Script, and Texas
Hero.

6/9   Down, down, down. Would
the fall NEVER come to an end! "I
wonder how many miles I've fallen by this
time?" she said aloud. "I must be getting
somewhere near the centre of the earth. Let
me see: that would be four thousand miles
down, I think—" (for, you see, Alice had
learnt several things of this sort in her
lessons in the schoolroom, and though
this was not a VERY good opportunity for
showing off her knowledge, as there was no
one to listen to her, still it was good practice
to say it over) "—yes, that's about 8/11

Down, down, down.
Would the fall NEVER
come to an end! "I
wonder how many miles
I've fallen by this time?"
she said aloud. "I must
be getting somewhere
near the centre of the
earth. Let me see: that
would be four thousand
miles down, I think—"
(for, you see, Alice had
learnt several things of
this sort in her lessons
in the schoolroom, and
though this was not a
VERY good opportunity
for showing off her
knowledge, as there was
no one to listen to her,
still it was good practice
to say it over) "—yes,
that's about the right
distance—but then I
wonder what Latitude
or Longitude I've got
to?" (Alice had no idea
what Latitude was, or
Longitude either, but
thought they were nice
grand words to say.)

18/11.5   Down, down, down.
Would the fall NEVER
come to an end! "I wonder
how many miles I've
fallen by this time?" she
said aloud. "I must be
getting somewhere near
the centre of the earth.
Let me see: that would be
four thousand miles down,
I think—" (for, you see,
Alice had learnt several
things of this sort in her
lessons in the schoolroom,
and though this was not
a VERY good opportunity
for showing off her
knowledge, as there was
no one to listen to her,
still it was good practice
to say it over) "—yes,
that's about the right
distance—but then I
wonder what Latitude
or Longitude I've got
to? (Alice had no idea
what Latitude was, or
Longitude either, but
thought they were nice

ITC Avant Garde Gothic Book

abcdefghijklmnopqrstuvwxyz

ABCDEFGHIJKLM

NOPQRSTUVWXYZ

1234567890?!$%&*:;"

6/9 Down, down, down. There was nothing else to do, so Alice soon began talking again. "Dinah'll miss me very much to-night, I should think!" (Dinah was the cat.) "I hope they'll remember her saucer of milk at tea-time. Dinah my dear! I wish you were down here with me! There are no mice in the air, I'm afraid, but you might catch a bat, and that's very like a mouse, you know. But do cats eat bats, I wonder?"

8/12 Down, down, down. There was nothing else to do, so Alice soon began talking again. "Dinah'll miss me very much to-night, I should think!" (Dinah was the cat.) "I hope they'll remember her saucer of milk at tea-time. Dinah my dear! I wish you were down here with me! There are no mice in the air, I'm afraid, but you might catch a bat, and that's very like a mouse, you know. But do cats eat bats, I wonder?"

11/14 Down, down, down. There was nothing else to do, so Alice soon began talking again. "Dinah'll miss me very much to-night, I should think" (Dinah was the

14/16 Down, down, down. There was nothing else to do, so Alice soon began talking again. "Dinah'll miss me very much to-night, I should think!" (Dinah was the cat.) "I hope they'll remember her saucer of milk at tea-time. Dinah my dear! I wish you were down here with me! There are no mice in the air, I'm afraid, but you might catch a bat, and that's very like a mouse, you know. But do cats eat bats, I wonder?"

18/21 Down, down, down. There was nothing else to do, so Alice soon began talking again. "Dinah'll miss me very much to-night, I should think!" (Dinah was

Avant Garde Gothic

Avant Garde is constructed from perfect circles and vertical strokes. Originally designed by Herb Lubalin for the nameplate of the magazine *Avant Garde*, it was later developed into a complete font with the assistance of Tom Carnase in 1970. This font has come in and out of style over the past three and a half decades, and remains a staple digital font on both the Macintosh and PC platforms today.

Balmoral Script

abcdefghijklmnopqrstuvwxyz

ABCDEFGHIJKLM
NOPQRSTUVWXYZ
1234567890?!$%&:;*

Balmoral Script

Created by British designer Martin Wait in 1978, Balmoral is a florid, formal script face appropriate for short passages and small items such as an initial or drop cap.

11/14   *And here Alice began to get rather sleepy, and went on saying to herself, in a dreamy sort of way, "Do cats eat bats? Do cats eat bats?" and sometimes, "Do bats eat cats?" For, you see, as she couldn't answer either question, it didn't much matter which way she put it. She felt that she was dozing off, and had just begun to dream that she was walking hand in hand with Dinah, and saying to her very earnestly, "Now, Dinah, tell me the truth: did you ever eat a bat?" When suddenly, thump! thump! down she came upon a heap of sticks and dry leaves, and the fall was over.*

14/15   *And here Alice began to get rather sleepy, and went on saying to herself, in a dreamy sort of way, "Do cats eat bats? Do cats eat bats?" and sometimes, "Do bats eat cats?" For, you see, as she couldn't answer either question, it didn't much matter which way she put it. She felt that she was dozing off, and had just begun to dream that she was walking hand in hand with Dinah, and saying to her very earnestly, "Now, Dinah, tell me the truth: did you ever eat a bat?" When suddenly, thump! thump! down she came upon a heap of sticks and dry leaves, and the fall was over.*

25/26   *And here Alice began to get rather sleepy, and went on saying to herself, in a dreamy sort of way, "Do cats eat bats? Do cats eat bats?" and sometimes, "Do bats eat cats?" for, you see, as she couldn't answer either question, it didn't much matter which way she put it. She felt that she was dozing off, and had just begun to dream that she was walking hand in hand with Dinah, and saying to her very earnestly, "Now, Dinah, tell me the truth: did you ever eat a bat?" When suddenly, thump! thump! down she came upon a heap of sticks and dry leaves, and the fall was over.*

Baskerville Old Face

abcdefghijklmnopqrstuvwxyz
ABCDEFGHIJKLM
NOPQRSTUVWXYZ
1234567890?!$%&*:;"

6/9 Alice was not a bit hurt, and she jumped up on to her feet in a moment: she looked up, but it was all dark overhead; before her was another long passage, and the White Rabbit was still in sight, hurrying down it. There was not a moment to be lost: away went Alice like the wind, and was just in time to hear it say, as it turned a corner, "Oh my ears and whiskers, how late it's getting!" She was close behind it when she turned the corner, but the Rabbit was no longer to be seen: she found herself in a long, low hall, which was lit up by a row of lamps hanging from the roof.

8/12 Alice was not a bit hurt, and she jumped up on to her feet in a moment: she looked up, but it was all dark overhead; before her was another long passage, and the White Rabbit was still in sight, hurrying down it. There was not a moment to be lost: away went Alice like the wind, and was just in time to hear it say, as it turned a corner, "Oh my ears and whiskers, how late it's getting!" She was close behind it when she turned the corner, but the Rabbit was no longer to be seen: she found herself in a long, low hall, which was lit up by a row of lamps hanging from the roof.

11/14 Alice was not a bit hurt, and she jumped up on to her feet in a moment: she looked up, but it was all dark overhead; before her was another long passage, and the White Rabbit was still in sight, hurrying down it. There was not a moment to be lost: away went Alice like the wind, and was just in time to hear it say, as

14/16 Alice was not a bit hurt, and she jumped up on to her feet in a moment: she looked up, but it was all dark overhead; before her was another long passage, and the White Rabbit was still in sight, hurrying down it. There was not a moment to be lost: away went Alice like the wind, and was just in time to hear it say, as it turned a corner, "Oh my ears and whiskers, how late it's getting!" She was close behind it when she turned the corner, but the Rabbit was no longer to be seen: she found herself in a long, low hall, which was lit up by a row of lamps hanging from the roof.

18/20 Alice was not a bit hurt, and she jumped up on to her feet in a moment: she looked up, but it was all dark overhead; before her was another long passage, and the

ITC New Baskerville

abcdefghijklmnopqrstuvwxyz
ABCDEFGHIJKLM
NOPQRSTUVWXYZ
1234567890?!$%&*:;"

Baskerville

Before Baskerville, the standard English type of the early eigteenth century was Caslon—a traditional font that dated back to Aldus Manutius (fifteenth century). The eighteenth century printer John Baskerville was known for technological improvements in existing fonts, inks, and presses that produced a clearer, blacker type than any of his contemporaries could manage. Unfortunately, critics maintained that his type "hurt the eye" and would be "responsible for blinding the nation." It was a commercial failure and wasn't revived until the early twentieth century.

6/9   There were doors all round the hall, but they were all locked; and when Alice had been all the way down one side and up the other, trying every door, she walked sadly down the middle, wondering how she was ever to get out again.

8/11   There were doors all round the hall, but they were all locked; and when Alice had been all the way down one side and up the other, trying every door, she walked sadly down the middle, wondering how she was ever to get out again.

11/14   There were doors all round the hall, but they were all locked; and when Alice had been all the way down one side and up the other, trying every door, she walked sadly down the middle, wondering how she was ever to get out again.

14/16   There were doors all round the hall, but they were all locked; and when Alice had been all the way down one side and up the other, trying every door, she walked sadly down the middle, wondering how she was ever to get out again.

18/20   There were doors all round the hall, but they were all locked; and when Alice had been all the way down one side and up the other, trying every door, she walked sadly down the middle, wondering how she was ever to get out again.

Basketcase

abcdefghijklmnopqrstuvwxyz
ABCDEFGHIJKLM
NOPQRSTUVWXYZ
1234567890?!$ &:;"

8/10 Suddenly she came upon a little three-legged table, all made of solid glass; there was nothing on it except a tiny golden key, and Alice's first thought was that it might belong to one of the doors of the hall; but, alas! either the locks were too large, or the key was too small, but at any rate it would not open any of them. However, on the second time round, she came upon a low curtain she had not noticed before, and behind it was a little door about fifteen inches high: she tried the little golden key in the lock, and to her great delight it fitted!

11/12 Suddenly she came upon a little three-legged table, all made of solid glass; there was nothing on it except a tiny golden key, and Alice's first thought was that it might belong to one of the doors of the hall; but, alas! either the locks were too large,

17/15 Suddenly she came upon a little three-legged table, all made of solid glass; there was nothing on it except a tiny golden key, and Alice's first thought was that it might belong to one of the doors of the hall; but, alas! either the locks were too large, or the key was too small, but at any rate it would not open any of them. However, on the second time round, she came upon a low curtain she had not noticed before, and behind it was a little door about fifteen inches high: she tried the little golden key in the lock, and to her great delight it fitted!

Basketcase

This shareware grunge font is often found on Internet sites featuring scary and creepy topics. Although each character has the appearance of a washed-out inkblot, there is a visual resemblance to Times New Roman Bold. Obviously it is only for use in short passages and headlines, as seeing a whole book set in this would send you to your optometrist, psychiatrist, or both.

Beckett

abcdefghijklmnopqrstuvwxyz
ABCDEFGHIJKLM
NOPQRSTUVWXYZ
1234567890?!\$%&*.."
;

Beckett

Reminiscent of classic Gothic faces, Beckett is a TrueType font that—unlike most such faces—includes both upper- and lowercases and a full punctuation set. It's based on printing styles of old-fashioned Germanic text, yet is simplified enough to be readable by contemporary eyes. The lowercase set is condensed, making it easier to copy-fit longer titles and passages than most digital variations of calligraphic typefaces allow.

Think twice before using it for body text, as its floridity is confusing and the kerning isn't perfect.

Alice opened the door and found that it led into a small passage, not much larger than a rat-hole: she knelt down and looked along the passage into the loveliest garden you ever saw. How she longed to get out of that dark hall, and wander about among those beds of bright flowers and those cool fountains, but she could not even get her head though the doorway; "and even if my head would go through," thought poor Alice, "it would be of very little use without my shoulders. Oh, how I wish I could shut up like a telescope! I think I could, if I only know how to begin." For, you see, so many out-of-the-way things had happened lately, that Alice had begun to think that very few things indeed were really impossible.

Bell Gothic Standard

abcdefghijklmnopqrstuvwxyz
ABCDEFGHIJKLM
NOPQRSTUVWXYZ
1234567890?!$%&*:;"

ABCDEFGHIJKLMNOPQRSTUVWXYZ
ABCDEFGHIJKLMNOPQRSTUVWXYZ
ABCDEFGHIJKLMNOPQRSTUVWXYZ

6/9   There seemed to be no use in waiting by the little door, so she went back to the table, half hoping she might find another key on it, or at any rate a book of rules for shutting people up like telescopes: this time she found a little bottle on it, ("which certainly was not here before," said Alice) and round the neck of the bottle was a paper label, with the words "DRINK ME" beautifully printed on it in large letters.

8/12   There seemed to be no use in waiting by the little door, so she went back to the table, half hoping she might find another key on it, or at any rate a book of rules for shutting people up like telescopes: this time she found a little bottle on it, ("which certainly was not here before," said Alice) and round the neck of the bottle was a paper label, with the words "DRINK ME" beautifully printed on it in large letters.

11/14   There seemed to be no use in waiting by the little door, so she went back to the table, half hoping she might find another key on it, or at any rate a book of rules for shutting people up like telescopes: this time she found a little bottle on it, ("which certainly was not here before," said Alice) and round the neck of the bottle was a paper label, with the words "DRINK ME" beautifully printed on it in large letters.

14/15   There seemed to be no use in waiting by the little door, so she went back to the table, half hoping she might find another key on it, or at any rate a book of rules for shutting people up like telescopes: this time she found a little

Bell Gothic Standard
Chauncey H. Griffith was commissioned by the American Telephone and Telegraph company to design a typeface that would be particularly suited to the small, compressed text and inferior-quality newsprint paper of its telephone books. Griffith, already experienced with the design of newsprint fonts, was interested in legibility issues. In 1922 Griffith created the Legibility Group, which contained particularly legible fonts expressly designed for newspapers. Bell Gothic has all the typical characteristics that optimize a font's legibility. The modern heir of Bell Gothic is Bell Centennial, designed by Matthew Carter in 1974 in celebration of the Bell Company's 100th birthday.

Belwe Medium

abcdefghijklmnopqrstuvwxyz
ABCDEFGHIJKLM
NOPQRSTUVWXYZ
1234567890?!$%&*:;"

Belwe

Designed by Georg Belwe in 1926, this font maintains readability in relatively small sizes despite the quirky "flag" extensions of the v, w, and y. Two of the most pronounced identifying characteristics are the tight loop on the 2 and the g in addition to the reverse curve of the shoulder on the f. It is available in different weights.

6/9   It was all very well to say "Drink me," but the wise little Alice was not going to do THAT in a hurry. "No, I'll look first," she said, "and see whether it's marked 'poison' or not"; for she had read several nice little histories about children who had got burnt, and eaten up by wild beasts and other unpleasant things, all because they WOULD not remember the simple rules their friends had taught them: such as, that a red-hot poker will burn you if you hold it too long; and that if you cut your finger VERY deeply with a knife, it usually bleeds; and she had never forgotten that, if you drink much from a bottle marked "poison," it is almost certain to disagree with you, sooner or later.

8/10   It was all very well to say "Drink me," but the wise little Alice was not going to do THAT in a hurry. "No, I'll look first," she said, "and see whether it's marked 'poison' or not";for she had read several nice little histories about children who had got burnt, and eaten up by wild beasts and other unpleasant things, all because they WOULD not remember the simple rules their friends had taught them: such as, that a red-hot poker will burn you if you hold it too long; and that if you cut your finger VERY deeply with a knife, it usually bleeds; and she had never forgotten that, if you drink much from a bottle marked "poison," it is almost certain to disagree with

It was all very well to say "Drink me," but the wise little Alice was not going to do THAT in a hurry. "No, I'll look first," she said, "and see whether it's marked 'poison' or not"; for she had read several nice little histories about children who had got burnt, and eaten up by wild beasts and other unpleasant things, all because they WOULD not remember the simple rules their friends had taught them: such as, that a red-hot poker will burn you if you hold it too long; and that if you cut your finger VERY deeply with a knife, it usually bleeds; and she had never forgotten that, if you drink much from a bottle marked "poison," it is almost certain to disagree with you, sooner or later.

Bembo Regular

abcdefghijklmnopqrstuvwxyz
ABCDEFGHIJKLM
NOPQRSTUVWXYZ
1234567890?!$%&★:;"

6/9   However, this bottle was NOT marked "poison," so Alice ventured to taste it, and finding it very nice (it had, in fact, a sort of mixed flavour of cherry-tart, custard, pine-apple, roast turkey, toffee, and hot buttered toast), she very soon finished it off.

8/12   However, this bottle was NOT marked "poison," so Alice ventured to taste it, and finding it very nice (it had, in fact, a sort of mixed flavour of cherry-tart, custard, pine-apple, roast turkey, toffee, and hot buttered toast), she very soon finished it off.

11/14   However, this bottle was NOT marked "poison," so Alice ventured to taste it, and finding it very nice, (it had, in fact, a sort of mixed flavour of cherry-tart, custard, pine-apple, roast turkey, toffee, and hot buttered toast), she very soon finished it off.

14/15   However, this bottle was NOT marked "poison," so Alice

18/20   However, this bottle was NOT marked "poison," so Alice ventured to taste it, and finding it very nice (it had, in fact, a sort of mixed flavour of cherry-tart, custard, pine-apple, roast turkey, toffee, and hot buttered toast), she very soon finished it off.

23/24   However, this bottle was NOT marked "poison," so Alice ventured to taste it, and finding it very nice (it had, in fact, a sort of mixed flavour of cherry-tart, custard, pine-

Bembo

This classic font was designed by Francesco Griffo as commissioned by Cardinal Bembo in 1495, for Aldus Mantius' publication of *De Aetna*. Identifying characteristics are the relatively small x-height, the short, flat bowl on the lowercase *a*, and the graceful tail on the uppercase *R*. It is available in roman and italic variations as well as in different weights.

ITC Benguiat Book

abcdefghijklmnopqrstuvwxyz
ABCDEFGHIJKLM
NOPQRSTUVWXYZ
1234567890?!$%&*:;"

Benguiat

This font is characterized by the harshness of the sharp, piercing serifs. Designed by Edward Benguiat in 1977, the arched crossbars on the uppercase letterforms as well as the slightly flared terminals combine to communicate a less serious compositional feeling reminiscent of Art Nouveau faces.

Benguiat is well known for his work with Herb Lubalin on *U&lc* for the International Typeface Corporation, as well as for logotypes for the *New York Times*, *Playboy*, *Reader's Digest*, *Sports Illustrated*, *Esquire*, and *Look* magazines.

6/9 "What a curious feeling!" said Alice; "I must be shutting up like a telescope."

8/11 "What a curious feeling!" said Alice; "I must be shutting up like a telescope."

11/13 "What a curious feeling!" said Alice; "I must be shutting up like a telescope."

14/15 "What a curious feeling!" said Alice; "I must be shutting up like a telescope."

18/20 "What a curious feeling!" said Alice; "I must be shutting up like a telescope."

W hat a curious feeling!" said Alice; "I must be shutting up like a telescope."

Berkeley Old Style Book

abcdefghijklmnopqrstuvwxyz
ABCDEFGHIJKLM
NOPQRSTUVWXYZ
1234567890?!$%&*:;"

6/9   And so it was indeed: she was now only ten inches high, and her face brightened up at the thought that she was now the right size for going through the little door into that lovely garden. First, however, she waited for a few minutes to see if she was going to shrink any further: she felt a little nervous about this; "for it might end, you know," said Alice to herself, "in my going out altogether, like a candle. I wonder what I should be like then?" And she tried to fancy what the flame of a candle is like after the candle is blown out, for she could not remember ever having seen such a thing.

8/10   And so it was indeed: she was now only ten inches high, and her face brightened up at the thought that she was now the right size for going through the little door into that lovely garden. First, however, she waited for a few minutes to see if she was going to shrink any further: she felt a little nervous about this; "for it might end, you know," said Alice to herself, "in my going out altogether, like a candle. I wonder what I should be like then?" And she tried to fancy what the flame of a candle is like after the candle is blown out, for she could not remember ever having seen such a thing.

11/14   And so it was indeed: she was now only ten inches high, and her face brightened up at the thought

14/16   And so it was indeed: she was now only ten inches high, and her face brightened up at the thought that she was now the right size for going through the little door into that lovely garden. First, however, she waited for a few minutes to see if she was going to shrink any further: she felt a little nervous about this; "for it might end, you know," said Alice to herself, "in my going out altogether, like a candle. I wonder what I should be like then?" And she tried to fancy what the flame of a candle is like after the candle is blown out, for she could not remember ever having seen such a thing.

18/22   And so it was indeed: she was now only ten inches high, and her face brightened up at the thought that she was now the

Berkeley Old Style

ITC Berkeley Old Style is based on the California Old Style of Frederick Goudy, which he designed in 1940 for the University Press. Monotype released this font in 1956 under the name Californian. It was redesigned by Tony Stan in 1983 and released as Berkeley Old Style. Stan is also known for designing ITC American Typewriter (with Joel Kaden), ITC Garamond, ITC Cheltenham, and ITC Century.

The variations include oldstyle book, *old style book italic*, old style medium, *old style italic*, **old style bold**, ***old style bold italic***, **old style black** and ***old style black italic***.

Berlin Sans &
Berlin Sans Demi

abcdefghijklmnopqrstuvwxyz
ABCDEFGHIJKLM
NOPQRSTUVWXYZ
1234567890?!$%&*•,"

Berlin Sans

Originally a sans serif font designed by Lucian Bernhard (born Emil Kahn) and released by Bauer Type foundry under the name *Negro*, the contemporary version is by Matthew Butterick and David Berlow, 1994. They expanded this single font into a series of four weights, all complete with expert character sets, plus a dingbat font.

6/9   After a while, finding that nothing more happened, she decided on going into the garden at once; but, alas for poor Alice! when she got to the door, she found she had forgotten the little golden key, and when she went back to the table for it, she found she could not possibly reach it: she could see it quite plainly through the glass, and she tried her best to climb up one of the legs of the table, but it was too slippery; and when she had tired herself out with trying, the poor little thing sat down and cried.

8/11   After a while, finding that nothing more happened, she decided on going into the garden at once; but, alas for poor Alice! when she got to the door, she found she had forgotten the little golden key, and when she went back to the table for it, she found she could not possibly reach it: she could see it quite plainly through the glass, and she tried her best to climb up one of the legs of the table, but it was too slippery; and when she had tired herself out with trying, the poor little thing sat down and cried.

11/14   After a while, finding that nothing more happened, she decided on going into the garden at once; but, alas for poor Alice! when she got to the door, she

14/15   After a while, finding that nothing more happened, she decided on going into the garden at once; but, alas for poor Alice! when she got to the door, she found she had forgotten the little golden key, and when she went back to the table for it, she found she could not possibly reach it: she could see it quite plainly through the glass, and she tried her best to climb up one of the legs of the table, but it was too slippery; and when she had tired herself out with trying, the poor little thing sat down and cried.

18/20   After a while, finding that nothing more happened, she decided on going into the garden at once; but, alas for poor Alice! when she got to the door, she found she had

Bernhard Modern

abcdefghijklmnopqrstuvwxyz
ABCDEFGHIJKLM
NOPQRSTUVWXYZ
1234567890?!$%&*:;"

6/9 "Come, there's no use in crying like that!" said Alice to herself, rather sharply; "I advise you to leave off this minute!" She generally gave herself very good advice (though she very seldom followed it), and sometimes she scolded herself so severely as to bring tears into her eyes; and once she remembered trying to box her own ears for having cheated herself in a game of croquet she was playing against herself, for this curious child was very fond of pretending to be two people. "But it's no use now," thought poor Alice, "to pretend to be two people! Why, there's hardly enough of me left to make ONE respectable person!"

8/11 "Come, there's no use in crying like that!" said Alice to herself, rather sharply; "I advise you to leave off this minute!" She generally gave herself very good advice (though she very seldom followed it), and sometimes she scolded herself so severely as to bring tears into her eyes; and once she remembered trying to box her own ears for having cheated herself in a game of croquet she was playing against herself, for this curious child was very fond of pretending to be two people. "But it's no use now," thought poor Alice, "to pretend to be two people! Why, there's hardly enough of me left to make ONE respectable person!"

11/14 "Come, there's no use in crying like that!" said Alice to herself, rather sharply; "I advise you to leave off this minute!"

14/15 "Come, there's no use in crying like that!" said Alice to herself, rather sharply; "I advise you to leave off this minute!" She generally gave herself very good advice (though she very seldom followed it), and sometimes she scolded herself so severely as to bring tears into her eyes; and once she remembered trying to box her own ears for having cheated herself in a game of croquet she was playing against herself, for this curious child was very fond of pretending to be two people. "But it's no use now," thought poor Alice, "to pretend to be two people! Why, there's hardly enough of me left to make ONE respectable person!"

18/20 "Come, there's no use in crying like that!" said Alice to herself, rather sharply; "I advise you to leave off this minute!" She generally gave herself very good advice (though she very seldom

Bernhard Modern

Bernhard Modern, designed by Lucian Bernhard in 1937, is a version of the engravers' old styles popular at the time. It remains popular today, more that sixty years after its initial release. It is easily recognizable by its small x-height, which contrasts with the relatively tall cap height. The serifs and terminals are slightly curved and join the flared main stroke of the letterform or numeral.

ITC Blackadder

abcdefghijklmnopqrstuvwxyz

ABCDEFGHIJKLM

NOPQRSTUVWXYZ

1234567890 ?!$%.&.:;""

ITC Blackadder

British designer Bob Anderton designed ITC Blackadder, Lino Cut, and ITC Mithras. ITC Blackadder was modeled on the signature of sixteenth-century British insurrectionist Guy Fawkes and other handwritten letterforms. Anderton captured the scrolls and curlicues of the era, as well as the texture of the quill pen on the handmade paper or parchment.

6/9
She ate a little bit, and said anxiously to herself, "Which way? Which way?", holding her hand on the top of her head to feel which way it was growing, and she was quite surprised to find that she remained the same size: to be sure, this generally happens when one eats cake, but Alice had got so much into the way of expecting nothing but out-of-the-way things to happen, that it seemed quite dull and stupid for life to go on in the common way. So she set to work, and very soon finished off the cake.

8/11
She ate a little bit, and said anxiously to herself, "Which way? Which way?", holding her hand on the top of her head to feel which way it was growing, and she was quite surprised to find that she remained the same size: to be sure, this generally happens when one eats cake, but Alice had got so much into the way of expecting nothing but out-of-the-way things to happen, that it seemed quite dull and stupid for life to go on in the common way. So she set to work, and very soon finished off the cake.

11/14
She ate a little bit, and said anxiously to herself, "Which way? Which way?", holding her hand on the top of her head to feel which way it was growing, and she was quite surprised to find that she remained the same size: to be sure, this generally

14/14
She ate a little bit, and said anxiously to herself, "Which way? Which way?", holding her hand on the top of her head to feel which way it was growing, and she was quite surprised to find that she remained the same size: to be sure, this generally happens when one eats cake, but Alice had got so much into the way of expecting nothing but out-of-the-way things to happen, that it seemed quite dull and stupid for life to go on in the common way. So she set to work, and very soon finished off the cake.

20/19
She ate a little bit, and said anxiously to herself, "Which way? Which way?", holding her hand on the top of her head to feel which way it was growing, and she was quite surprised to find that she remained the same size: to be sure, this generally happens when one eats cake, but

Blackoak

abcdefghijklmnopqrstuvwxyz
ABCDEFGHIJKLM
NOPQRSTUVWXYZ
1234567890?!$%&*:;"

Curiouser and ouriouser!" cried Alice (she was so much surprised, that for the moment she quite forgot how to speak good English); "now I'm opening out like the largest telescope that ever was! Good-bye, feet!" (for when she looked down at her feet, they seemed to be almost out of sight, they were getting so far off). "Oh, my poor little feet, I wonder who will put on your shoes and stockings for you now, dears? I'm sure I shan't be able! I shall be a great deal too far off to trouble myself about you: you must manage the best way you can; —but I must be kind to them," thought Alice, "or perhaps they won't walk the way I want to go! Let me see: I'll give them a new pair of boots every Christmas."

Blackoak

Created by Joy Redick in 1990, Blackoak is best specified for use in headlines in large and very large point sizes. This hefty alphabet in slab serif style is reminiscent of advertising wood type from the Victorian era. The figures were flattened and stretched for emphasis.

Prolific in the early 1990s, designer Joy Redick created Blackoak, Ironwood, Juniper, Mesquite, Willow, and Woodtype Ornaments (with Barbara Lind).

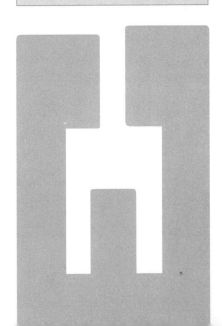

Bodoni

abcdefghijklmnopqrstuvwxyz

abcdefghijklmnopqrstuvwxyz

ABCDEFGHIJKLM
NOPQRSTUVWXYZ
1234567890?!$%&*:;"

Bodoni

Originally designed by Giambattista Bodoni around 1767, this font (also called Didone) is considered modern in style . In the early 1900s, Morris Fuller Benton revived Bodoni with his version, ATF Bodoni, in 1911, which is considered the first accurate revival of a historical face for general printing and design applications.

Numerous versions have come about from a variety of designers and foundries and often include book and italic styles, in book and bold weights. The strong vertical emphasis and the contrast between the fine and thick lines makes Bodoni's legibility better in larger print with generous leading.

6/9   And she went on planning to herself how she would manage it. "They must go by the carrier," she thought; "and how funny it'll seem, sending presents to one's own feet! And how odd the directions will look!

ALICE'S RIGHT FOOT, ESQ.
HEARTHRUG,
NEAR THE FENDER,
(WITH ALICE'S LOVE).

Oh dear, what nonsense I'm talking!"

8/12   And she went on planning to herself how she would manage it. "They must go by the carrier," she thought; "and how funny it'll seem, sending presents to one's own feet! And how odd the directions will look!

ALICE'S RIGHT FOOT, ESQ.
HEARTHRUG,
NEAR THE FENDER,
(WITH ALICE'S LOVE).

Oh dear, what nonsense I'm talking!"

18/20   And she went on planning to herself how she would manage it. "They must go by the carrier," she thought; "and how funny it'll seem, sending presents to one's own feet! And how odd the directions will look!

ALICE'S RIGHT FOOT, ESQ.
HEARTHRUG,
NEAR THE FENDER,
(WITH ALICE'S LOVE).

Oh dear, what nonsense I'm talking!"

Bodoni Poster

abcdefghijklmnopqrstuvwxyz
ABCDEFGHIJKLM
NOPQRSTUVWXYZ
1234567890?!$$%&*:;"

6/9   Just then her head struck against the roof of the hall: in fact she was now more than nine feet high, and she at once took up the little golden key and hurried off to the garden door.

8/12   Just then her head struck against the roof of the hall: in fact she was now more than nine feet high, and she at once took up the little golden key and hurried off to the garden door.

11/14   Just then her head struck against the roof of the hall: in fact she was now more than nine feet high, and she at once took up the little golden key and hurried off to the garden door.

14/15   Just then her head struck against the roof of the hall: in fact

20/21   Just then her head struck against the roof of the hall: in fact she was now more than nine feet high, and she at once took up the little golden key and hurried off to the garden door.

20/21   Just then her head struck against the roof of the hall: in fact she was now more than nine feet

Bodoni Poster

Designed by Chauncey H. Griffith in 1929, it has little resemblance to the original font designed by Giambattista Bodoni at the end of the eighteenth century, with exception of the contrasting thick and thin strokes and vertical emphasis. The thin vertical counterforms are emphasized by the round, somewhat flattened circular contours. The proportional contrast between these two elements fits Bodoni Poster into a group of fat-face fonts popular in display sizes. The ball terminals and curvaceous strokes communicate a feeling of cheerfulness.

Book Antiqua

abcdefghijklmnopqrstuvwxyz

abcdefghijklmnopqrstuvwxyz

abcdefghijklmnopqrstuvwxyz

ABCDEFGHIJKLM
NOPQRSTUVWXYZ
1234567890?!$%&*:;"

Book Antiqua

Book Antiqua is an AGFA Monotype font similar to Palatino, URW Palladio, and Zapf Calligraphic. Its popularity has blossomed since its inclusion in Microsoft Office software packages. See the comparison between Book Antiqua (gray) and Palatino (outline), below.

a a a

6/9   Poor Alice! It was as much as she could do, lying down on one side, to look through into the garden with one eye; but to get through was more hopeless than ever: she sat down and began to cry again.

8/12   Poor Alice! It was as much as she could do, lying down on one side, to look through into the garden with one eye; but to get through was more hopeless than ever: she sat down and began to cry again.

11/14   Poor Alice! It was as much as she could do, lying down on one side, to look through into the garden with one eye; but to get through was more hopeless than ever: she sat down and began to cry again.

14/15   Poor Alice! It was as much as she could do, lying down on one side, to look through into the garden with one eye; but to get through was more hopeless than ever: she sat down and began to cry again.

18/20   Poor Alice! It was as much as she could do, lying down on one side, to look through into the garden with one eye; but to get through was more hopeless than ever: she sat down and began to

Bookman Old Style

abcdefghijklmnopqrstuvwxyz

ABCDEFGHIJKLM
NOPQRSTUVWXYZ
1234567890?!$%&*:;"

6/9   "You ought to be ashamed of yourself," said Alice, "a great girl like you" (she might well say this), "to go on crying in this way! Stop this moment, I tell you!" But she went on all the same, shedding gallons of tears, until there was a large pool all round her, about four inches deep and reaching half down the hall."

8/12   "You ought to be ashamed of yourself," said Alice, "a great girl like you" (she might well say this), "to go on crying in this way! Stop this moment, I tell you!" But she went on all the same, shedding gallons of tears, until there was a large pool all round her, about four inches deep and reaching half down the hall.

11/14   "You ought to be ashamed of yourself," said Alice, "a great girl like you" (she might well say this), "to go on crying in this way! Stop this moment, I tell you!" But she went on all the same, shedding gallons of tears, until

14/16   "You ought to be ashamed of yourself," said Alice, "a great girl like you" (she might well say this), "to go on crying in this way! Stop this moment, I tell you!" But she went on all the same, shedding gallons of tears, until there was a large pool all round her, about four inches deep and reaching half down the hall.

Bookman Old Style

The Bookman font, designed with a large x-height and wide set width, is originally credited to Wadsworth A. Parker around the turn of the twentieth century. The contemporary redesign is attributed to Edward Benguiat, 1975, for ITC.

19/23   "You ought to be ashamed of yourself," said Alice, "a great girl like you" (she might well say this), "to go on crying in this way! Stop this moment, I tell you!" But she went on all the same, shedding gallons of tears, until there was a large pool all round her, about four inches deep and reaching half down the hall.

ITC Bookman Light

abcdefghijklmnopqrstuvwxyz
ABCDEFGHIJKLM
NOPQRSTUVWXYZ
1234567890?!$%&*:;"

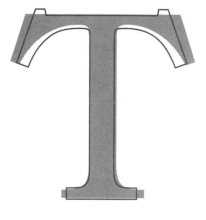

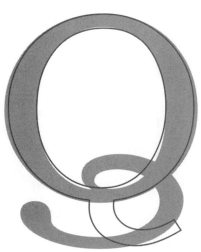

6/9 After a time she heard a little pattering of feet in the distance, and she hastily dried her eyes to see what was coming. It was the White Rabbit returning, splendidly dressed, with a pair of white kid gloves in one hand and a large fan in the other: he came trotting along in a great hurry, muttering to himself as he came, "Oh! the Duchess, the Duchess! Oh! won't she be savage if I've kept her waiting!" Alice felt so desperate that she was ready to ask help of any one; so, when the Rabbit came near her, she began, in a low, timid voice, "If you please, sir—" The Rabbit started violently, dropped the white kid gloves and the fan, and skurried away into the darkness as hard as he could go.

8/12 After a time she heard a little pattering of feet in the distance, and she hastily dried her eyes to see what was coming. It was the White Rabbit returning, splendidly dressed, with a pair of white kid gloves in one hand and a large fan in the other: he came trotting along in a great hurry, muttering to himself as he came, "Oh! the Duchess, the Duchess! Oh! won't she be savage if I've kept her waiting!" Alice felt so desperate that she was ready to ask help of any one; so, when the Rabbit came near her, she began, in a low, timid voice, "If you please, sir—"

11/14 After a time she heard a little pattering of feet in the distance, and she hastily dried her eyes to see what was coming. It was the White Rabbit returning, splendidly dressed, with a pair of white kid gloves in one hand and a large fan in the other: he came trotting along in a great hurry, muttering to himself as he came, "Oh! the Duchess, the Duchess! Oh! won't she be savage if I've kept her waiting!" Alice felt so desperate that she was ready to ask help of any one; so, when the Rabbit came near her, she began, in a low, timid voice, "If you please, sir—" The Rabbit started violently, dropped the white kid gloves and the fan, and skurried away into the darkness as hard as he could go.

14/15 After a time she heard a little pattering of feet in the distance, and she hastily dried her eyes to see what was coming. It was the White Rabbit returning, splendidly dressed, with a pair of white kid gloves in one hand and a large fan

Broadway

abcdefghijklmnopqrstuvwxyz

ABCDEFGHIJKLM
NOPQRSTUVWXYZ
1234567890?!$%&*:;""

Alice took up the fan and gloves, and, as the hall was very hot, she kept fanning herself all the time she went on talking: "Dear, dear! How queer everything is today! And yesterday things went on just as usual. I wonder if I've been changed in the night? Let me think: was I the same when I got up this morning? I almost think I can remember feeling a little different. But if I'm not the same, the next question is, Who in the world am I? Ah, THAT's the great puzzle!" And she began thinking over all the children she knew that were of the same age as herself, to see if she could have been changed for any of them.

Broadway

Indicative of the decorative spirit of the 1920s, Broadway is attributed to Morris Fuller Benton in 1925. It is popularly used in theater playbills as well as advertisements by hairdressers and beauty salons. The contrast in stroke weight makes it eye-catching when used in large headlines and signage applications.

Calcite Pro

abcdefghijklmnopqrstuvwxyz
ABCDEFGHIJKLM
NOPQRSTUVWXYZ
1234567890?!$%&*:;

Calcite Pro

This contemporary sans serif font was designed by Akira Kobayashi for Adobe. Although the variation in stroke weight is reminiscent of historical chancery scripts, the contemporary flare makes it an attractive change for compositions requiring visual interest, direction, and motion.

Like all of the Adobe Professional fonts, Calcite is available in a number of variations including *regular*, **bold**, and **black**.

6/9
"I'm sure those are not the right words," said poor Alice, and her eyes filled with tears again as she went on, "I must be Mabel after all, and I shall have to go and live in that poky little house, and have next to no toys to play with, and oh! ever so many lessons to learn! No, I've made up my mind about it; if I'm Mabel, I'll stay down here! It'll be no use their putting their heads down and saying 'Come up again, dear!' "

8/11
"I'm sure those are not the right words," said poor Alice, and her eyes filled with tears again as she went on, "I must be Mabel after all, and I shall have to go and live in that poky little house, and have next to no toys to play with, and oh! ever so many lessons to learn! No, I've made up my mind about it; if I'm Mabel, I'll stay down here! It'll be no use their putting their heads down and saying 'Come up again, dear!' "

11/14
"I'm sure those are not the right words," said poor Alice, and her eyes filled with tears again as she went on, "I

14/16
"I'm sure those are not the right words," said poor Alice, and her eyes filled with tears again as she went on, "I must be Mabel after all, and I shall have to go and live in that poky little house, and have next to no toys to play with, and oh! ever so many lessons to learn! No, I've made up my mind about it; if I'm Mabel, I'll stay down here! It'll be no use their putting their heads down and saying, 'Come up again, dear!' "

18/18
"I'm sure those are not the right words," said poor Alice, and her eyes filled with tears again as she went on, "I must be Mabel after all, and I shall have to go and live

New Caledonia

abcdefghijklmnopqrstuvwxyz
ABCDEFGHIJKLM
NOPQRSTUVWXYZ
1234567890?!$%&*:;"

6/9 I shall only look up and say "Who am I then? Tell me that first, and then, if I like being that person, I'll come up: if not, I'll stay down here till I'm somebody else—but, oh dear!" cried Alice, with a sudden burst of tears, "I do wish they WOULD put their heads down! I am so VERY tired of being all alone here!"

8/12 I shall only look up and say "Who am I then? Tell me that first, and then, if I like being that person, I'll come up: if not, I'll stay down here till I'm somebody else—but, oh dear!" cried Alice, with a sudden burst of tears, "I do wish they WOULD put their heads down! I am so VERY tired of being all alone here!"

11/14 I shall only look up and say "Who am I then? Tell me that first, and then, if I like being that person, I'll come up: if not, I'll stay down here till I'm somebody else"—but, oh dear!" cried Alice, with a sudden burst of tears, "I do wish they WOULD put their heads down! I am so VERY

14/16 I shall only look up and say "Who am I then? Tell me that first, and then, if I like being that person, I'll come up: if not, I'll stay down here till I'm somebody else—but, oh dear!" cried Alice, with a sudden burst of tears, "I do wish they WOULD put their heads down! I am so VERY tired of being all alone here!"

18/20 I shall only look up and say "Who am I then? Tell me that first, and then, if I like being that person, I'll come up: if not, I'll stay down here till I'm somebody else"—but, oh dear!" cried Alice, with a sudden burst of tears, "I do wish they WOULD put their heads down!

New Caledonia

Known as Cornelia, this font was designed by William A. Dwiggins in 1939 for the Mergenthaler typesetting machine factory in Berlin. Dwiggins created the design as a rework of Scotch Roman which was designed for Mergenthaler Linotype in New York. Linotype again reworked the typeface in 1982 and released it as New Caledonia. This large typeface family is perfect for large amounts of text due to the fine weight differences it allows. It is available in medium, *italic*, semibold, *semibold italic*, **bold**, ***bold italic***, **black,** and ***black italic*** styles.

Caslon 3 Roman

abcdefghijklmnopqrstuvwxyz
ABCDEFGHIJKLM
NOPQRSTUVWXYZ
1234567890?!$%&*:;"

Caslon

The original 1725 version of this font was designed by William Caslon (1692–1766). The Caslon font was long known as the script of kings, although on the other side of the political spectrum, the Americans used it as well for the Declaration of Independence.

Since its inception in the eighteenth century, it has been reworked over and over by a variety of designers. Caslon 540 is attributed to the ATF from 1902; and Caslon 3, a slightly bolder face, also came from ATF in 1905.

6/9   As she said this she looked down at her hands, and was surprised to see that she had put on one of the Rabbit's little white kid gloves while she was talking. "How CAN I have done that?" she thought. "I must be growing small again."

8/11   As she said this she looked down at her hands, and was surprised to see that she had put on one of the Rabbit's little white kid gloves while she was talking. "How CAN I have done that?" she thought. "I must be growing small again."

12/14   As she said this she looked down at her hands, and was surprised to see that she had put on one of the Rabbit's little white kid gloves while she was talking. "How CAN I have done that?" she thought. "I must be growing small again."

14/16   As she said this she looked down at her hands, and was surprised to see that

18/20   As she said this she looked down at her hands, and was surprised to see that she had put on one of the Rabbit's little white kid gloves while she was talking. "How CAN I have done that?" she thought. "I must be growing small again."

24/22   As she said this she looked down at her hands, and was surprised to see that she had put on one of the Rabbit's little white kid gloves

Caslon 540 Roman

abcdefghijklmnopqrstuvwxyz

ABCDEFGHIJKLM

NOPQRSTUVWXYZ

1234567890?!$%&-*:;"

6/9   She got up and went to the table to measure herself by it, and found that, as nearly as she could guess, she was now about two feet high, and was going on shrinking rapidly: she soon found out that the cause of this was the fan she was holding, and she dropped it hastily, just in time to avoid shrinking away altogether.

8/12   She got up and went to the table to measure herself by it, and found that, as nearly as she could guess, she was now about two feet high, and was going on shrinking rapidly: she soon found out that the cause of this was the fan she was holding, and she dropped it hastily, just in time to avoid shrinking away altogether.

11/14   She got up and went to the table to measure herself by it, and found that, as nearly as she could guess, she was now about two feet high, and was going on shrinking rapidly: she soon found out that the cause of this was the fan she was holding, and she dropped it hastily, just in time to avoid shrinking away altogether.

14/16   She got up and went to the table to measure herself by it, and found that, as nearly as she could guess, she was now about two feet high, and was going on shrinking rapidly: she soon found out that the cause of this was the fan she was holding, and she dropped it hastily, just in time to avoid shrinking away altogether.

19/22   She got up and went to the table to measure herself by it, and found that, as nearly as she could guess, she was now about two feet high, and was going on shrinking rapidly: she soon found out that the cause of this was the fan she was holding, and she dropped it hastily, just in time to avoid shrinking away altogether.

Linotype Centennial

abcdefghijklmnopqrstuvwxyz

abcdefghijklmnopqrstuvwxyz

abcdefghijklmnopqrstuvwxyz

abcdefghijklmnopqrstuvwxyz

ABCDEFGHIJKLM
NOPQRSTUVWXYZ
1234567890?!$%&*:;"

Linotype Centennial

Linotype Centennial was designed by Adrian Frutiger in 1986 for the celebration of Linotype's 100th anniversary. The typeface is a tribute to the Benton brothers, who designed Century, a similar typeface for the ATF at the end of the nineteenth century. Linotype's Centennial is available in eight weights.

8/11   Just then she heard something splashing about in the pool a little way off, and she swam nearer to make out what it was: at first she thought it must be a walrus or hippopotamus, but then she remembered how small she was now, and she soon made out that it was only a mouse that had slipped in like herself.

11/14   Just then she heard something splashing about in the pool a little way off, and she swam nearer to make out what it

15/18   Just then she heard something splashing about in the pool a little way off, and she swam nearer to make out what it was: at first she thought it must be a walrus or hippopotamus, but then she remembered how small she was now, and she soon made out that it was only a mouse that had slipped in like herself.

Century Old Style

abcdefghijklmnopqrstuvwxyz
ABCDEFGHIJKLM
NOPQRSTUVWXYZ
1234567890?!$%&*:,"

6/9   "Would it be of any use, now," thought Alice, "to speak to this mouse? Everything is so out-of-the-way down here, that I should think very likely it can talk: at any rate, there's no harm in trying." So she began: "O Mouse, do you know the way out of this pool? I am very tired of swimming about here, O Mouse!" (Alice thought this must be the right way of speaking to a mouse: she had never done such a thing before, but she remembered having seen in her brother's Latin Grammar, "A mouse—of a mouse—to a mouse—a mouse—O mouse!") The Mouse looked at her rather inquisitively, and seemed to her to wink with one of its little eyes, but it said nothing.

8/12   "Would it be of any use, now," thought Alice, "to speak to this mouse? Everything is so out-of-the-way down here, that I should "think very likely it can talk: at any rate, there's no harm in trying." So she began: "O Mouse, do you know the way out of this pool? I am very tired of swimming about here, O Mouse!" (Alice thought this must be the right way of speaking to a mouse: she had never done such a thing before, but she remembered having seen in her brother's Latin Grammar, "A mouse—of a mouse—to a mouse—a mouse—O mouse!") The Mouse looked at her rather inquisitively, and seemed to her to wink with one of its little eyes, but it said nothing.

11/14   "Would it be of any use, now," thought Alice, "to speak to this mouse? Everything is so out-of-the-way down here, that I should think very likely it can talk: at any rate, there's no harm in trying." So she began: "O Mouse, do

14/16   "Would it be of any use, now," thought Alice, "to speak to this mouse? Everything is so out-of-the-way down here, that I should think very likely it can talk: at any rate, there's no harm in trying." So she began: "O Mouse, do you know the way out of this pool? I am very tired of swimming about here, O Mouse!" (Alice thought this must be the right way of speaking to a mouse: she had never done such a thing before, but she remembered having seen in her brother's Latin Grammar, "A mouse—of a mouse—to a mouse—a mouse—O mouse!") The Mouse looked at her rather inquisitively, and seemed to her to wink with one of its little eyes, but it said nothing.

New Century Schoolbook

abcdefghijklmnopqrstuvwxyz
ABCDEFGHIJKLM
NOPQRSTUVWXYZ
1234567890?!$%&*:;"

Century Old Style and New Century Schoolbook

Century Old Style was finished in 1894 by Linn Boyd Benton; it had been a new text typeface for the *Century* magazine. Morris Fuller Benton revived it in 1906, and New Century Schoolbook was designed by Morris Fuller Benton in 1919.

The Century family of fonts is indicative of the neo-Renaissance aesthetic that became prevalent in typography at the end of the ninteenth century.

6/9   "Perhaps it doesn't understand English," thought Alice; "I daresay it's a French mouse, come over with William the Conqueror." (For, with all her knowledge of history, Alice had no very clear notion how long ago anything had happened.) So she began again: "Ou est ma chatte?" which was the first sentence in her French lesson-book. The Mouse gave a sudden leap out of the water, and seemed to quiver all over with fright. "Oh, I beg your pardon!" cried Alice hastily, afraid that she had hurt the poor animal's feelings. "I quite forgot you didn't like cats."

8/11   "Perhaps it doesn't understand English," thought Alice; "I daresay it's a French mouse, come over with William the Conqueror." (For, with all her knowledge of history, Alice had no very clear notion how long ago anything had happened.) So she began again: "Ou est ma chatte?" which was the first sentence in her French lesson-book. The Mouse gave a sudden leap out of the water, and seemed to quiver all over with fright. "Oh, I beg your pardon!" cried Alice hastily, afraid that she had hurt the poor animal's feelings. "I quite forgot you didn't like cats."

11/14   "Perhaps it doesn't understand English," thought Alice; "I daresay it's a French mouse, come over with William the Conqueror." (For, with all her knowledge of history, Alice had no very clear notion how long ago anything had happened.) So she began again: "Ou est ma chatte?" which was the first sentence in her French lesson-book. The Mouse gave a sudden leap out of the water, and seemed to quiver all over with fright. "Oh, I beg your pardon!" cried Alice hastily, afraid that she had hurt the poor animal's feelings. "I quite forgot you didn't like cats."

14/16   "Perhaps it doesn't understand English," thought Alice; "I daresay it's a French mouse, come over with William the Conqueror." (For, with all her knowledge of history, Alice had no very clear notion how long ago anything had happened.) So she began again: "Ou est ma chatte?" which was the first sentence in

ITC Cheltenham

abcdefghijklmnopqrstuvwxyz
ABCDEFGHIJKLM
NOPQRSTUVWXYZ
1234567890?!$%&*:;"

6/9 "Well, perhaps not," said Alice in a soothing tone: "don't be angry about it. And yet I wish I could show you our cat Dinah. I think you'd take a fancy to cats if you could only see her. She is such a dear quiet thing," Alice went on, half to herself, as she swam lazily about in the pool, "and she sits purring so nicely by the fire, licking her paws and washing her face—and she is such a nice soft thing to nurse—and she's such a capital one for catching mice—oh, I beg your pardon!" cried Alice again, for this time the Mouse was bristling all over, and she felt certain it must be really offended. "We won't talk about her any more if you'd rather not."

8/12 "Well, perhaps not," said Alice in a soothing tone: "don't be angry about it. And yet I wish I could show you our cat Dinah: I think you'd take a fancy to cats if you could only see her. She is such a dear quiet thing," Alice went on, half to herself, as she swam lazily about in the pool, "and she sits purring so nicely by the fire, licking her paws and washing her face—and she is such a nice soft thing to nurse—and she's such a capital one for catching mice—oh, I beg your pardon!" cried Alice again, for this time the Mouse was bristling all over, and she felt certain it must be really offended. "We won't talk about her any more if you'd rather

11/14 "Well, perhaps not," said Alice in a soothing tone: "don't be angry about it. And yet I wish I could show you our cat Dinah: I think you'd take a fancy to cats if you could only see her. She is such a dear quiet thing," Alice went on, half to herself, as she swam lazily about in the pool, "and she sits purring so nicely by the fire, licking her paws and washing her face—and she is such a nice soft thing to nurse—and she's such a capital one for catching mice—oh, I beg your pardon!" cried Alice again, for this time the Mouse was bristling all over, and she felt certain it must be really offended. "We won't talk about her any more if you'd rather not."

14/16 "Well, perhaps not," said Alice in a soothing tone: "don't be angry about it. And yet I wish I could show you our cat Dinah: I think you'd take a fancy to cats if you could only see her. She is such a dear quiet thing," Alice went on, half to herself, as she swam

ITC Cheltenham

Designer Tony Stan reworked a turn-of-the-century font originally designed by architect Bertram Grosvenor Goodhue. Although typefaces from that period were often thin, Cheltenham was created as an alternative to the norm; the original Cheltenham was designed with long ascenders and short descenders as a result of legibility studies from the period, indicating that the eye identifies letters by scanning their tops. Tony Stan's ITC Cheltenham mixes a heavier stroke weight with condensed letterform proportions and a large x-height, resulting in a legible text type.

Berthold City Medium

abcdefghijklmnopqrstuvwxyz
ABCDEFGHIJKLM
NOPQRSTUVWXYZ
1234567890?!$%&*:;"

Berthold City Medium

Designed by Georg Trump in 1930 for the Weber foundry in Stuttgart, City has a contemporary feeling, with a 90° relationship between even vertical and horizontal strokes connected by both curved and angled corners. The large slab serifs stabilize the font, giving it visual strength and presence. His designs were originally categorized with others in the style of "new typography," but later his own unique style evolved in later designs.

Georg Trump fought in both world wars and spent much of the rest of his life as a teacher, instructing students in the art of graphics and typography.

6/9   "We indeed!" cried the Mouse, who was trembling down to the end of his tail. "As if I would talk on such a subject! Our family always HATED cats: nasty, low, vulgar things! Don't let me hear the name again!"

8/11   "We indeed!" cried the Mouse, who was trembling down to the end of his tail. "As if I would talk on such a subject! Our family always HATED cats: nasty, low, vulgar things! Don't let me hear the name again!"

11/14   "We indeed!" cried the Mouse, who was trembling down to the end of his tail. "As if I would talk on such a subject! Our family always HATED cats: nasty, low, vulgar things! Don't let me hear the name again!"

14/16   "We indeed!" cried the Mouse, who was trembling down to the end of his tail. "As if

18/20   "We indeed!" cried the Mouse, who was trembling down to the end of his tail. "As if I would talk on such a subject! Our family always HATED cats: nasty, low, vulgar things! Don't let me hear the name again!"

24/24   "We indeed!" cried the Mouse, who was trembling down to the end of his tail. "As if I would talk on such a subject! Our family always HATED cats: nasty,

Clarendon

abcdefghijklmnopqrstuvwxyz
ABCDEFGHIJKLM
NOPQRSTUVWXYZ
1234567890?!$%&*:;"

6/9 "I won't indeed!" said Alice, in a great hurry to change the subject of conversation. "Are you—are you fond—of—of dogs?" The Mouse did not answer, so Alice went on eagerly: "There is such a nice little dog near our house I should like to show you! A little bright-eyed terrier, you know, with oh, such long curly brown hair! And it'll fetch things when you throw them, and it'll sit up and beg for its dinner, and all sorts of things—I can't remember half of them—and it belongs to a farmer, you know, and he says it's so useful, it's worth a hundred pounds! He says it kills all the rats and—oh dear!" cried Alice in a sorrowful tone, "I'm afraid I've offended it again!" For the Mouse was swimming away from her as hard as it could go, and making quite a commotion in the pool as it went.

8/12 "I won't indeed!" said Alice, in a great hurry to change the subject of conversation. "Are you—are you fond—of—of dogs?" The Mouse did not answer, so Alice went on eagerly: "There is such a nice little dog near our house I should like to show you! A little bright-eyed terrier, you know, with oh, such long curly brown hair! And it'll fetch things when you throw them, and it'll sit up and beg for its dinner, and all sorts of things—I can't remember half of them—and it belongs to a farmer, you know, and he says it's so useful, it's worth a hundred

11/14 "I won't indeed!" said Alice, in a great hurry to change the subject of conversation. "Are you—are you fond—of—of dogs?" The Mouse did not answer, so Alice went on eagerly: "There is such a nice little dog near our house I should like to show you! A little bright-eyed terrier, you know, with oh, such long curly brown hair! And it'll fetch things when you throw them, and it'll sit up and beg for its dinner, and all sorts of things—I can't remember half of them—and it belongs to a farmer, you know, and he says it's so useful, it's worth a hundred pounds! He says it kills all the rats and—oh dear!" cried Alice in a sorrowful tone, "I'm afraid I've offended it again!" For the Mouse was swimming away from her as hard as it could go, and making quite a commotion in the pool as it went.

Clarendon

Clarendon was created by graphic artist and teacher Hermann Eidenbenz in 1953, and was inspired by some of the first slab serif fonts that appeared at the beginning of industrialization in Great Britain in the 1820s. Clarendon was one of the names for this new typographic style, which was known in Europe as English Egyptienne. Clarendon's clear, objective, and timeless forms have never lost their contemporary feel. In small point sizes Clarendon is still a legible font, and in larger print its individual style attracts attention which makes it a common solution for retail signage applications.

ITC Clearface Regular

abcdefghijklmnopqrstuvwxyz
ABCDEFGHIJKLM
NOPQRSTUVWXYZ
1234567890?!$%&*:;"

ITC Clearface

The original version of this font was designed by Morris Fuller Benton in 1910 and was named Clearface Gothic.

The contemporary version was designed by Victor Caruso in 1978. The variation in stroke weight with the large serifs makes the font legible in different sizes. It is available in regular, *italic*, **bold**, ***bold italic***, **heavy**, ***heavy italic***, **black**, and ***black italic*** style variations.

6/9   So she called softly after it, "Mouse dear! Do come back again, and we won't talk about cats or dogs either, if you don't like them!" When the Mouse heard this, it turned round and swam slowly back to her: its face was quite pale (with passion, Alice thought), and it said in a low trembling voice, "Let us get to the shore, and then I'll tell you my history, and you'll understand why it is I hate cats and dogs."

8/11   So she called softly after it, "Mouse dear! Do come back again, and we won't talk about cats or dogs either, if you don't like them!" When the Mouse heard this, it turned round and swam slowly back to her: its face was quite pale (with passion, Alice thought), and it said in a low trembling voice, "Let us get to the shore, and then I'll tell you my history, and you'll understand why it is I hate cats and dogs."

11/14   So she called softly after it, "Mouse dear! Do come back again, and we won't talk about cats or dogs either, if you don't like them!" When the Mouse heard this, it turned round and swam slowly back to her: its face was quite pale

14/16   So she called softly after it, "Mouse dear! Do come back again, and we won't talk about cats or dogs either, if you don't like them!" When the Mouse heard this, it turned round and swam slowly back to her: its face was quite pale (with passion, Alice thought), and it said in a low trembling voice, "Let us get to the shore, and then I'll tell you my history, and you'll understand why it is I hate cats and dogs."

18/20   So she called softly after it, "Mouse dear! Do come back again, and we won't talk about cats or dogs either, if you don't like them!" When the Mouse heard this, it turned round and swam slowly back to her: its face

Compacta

abcdefghijklmnopqrstuvwxyz

ABCDEFGHIJKLMNOPQRSTUVWXYZ

1234567890?!$%&*·.,"

6/9 CHAPTER III: A CAUCUS-RACE AND A LONG TALE They were indeed a queer-looking party that assembled on the bank—the birds with draggled feathers, the animals with their fur clinging close to them, and all dripping wet, cross, and uncomfortable.

8/11 CHAPTER III: A CAUCUS-RACE AND A LONG TALE They were indeed a queer-looking party that assembled on the bank—the birds with draggled feathers, the animals with their fur clinging close to them, and all dripping wet, cross, and uncomfortable.

11/14 CHAPTER III: A CAUCUS-RACE AND A LONG TALE They were indeed a queer-looking party that assembled on the bank—the birds with draggled feathers, the animals with their fur clinging close to them, and all dripping wet, cross, and uncomfortable.

14/16 CHAPTER III: A CAUCUS-RACE AND A LONG TALE They were indeed a queer-looking party that assembled on the bank—the birds with draggled feathers, the animals with their fur clinging close to them, and all dripping wet, cross, and

18/20 CHAPTER III: A CAUCUS-RACE AND A LONG TALE They were indeed a queer-looking party that assembled on the bank—the birds with draggled feathers, the animals with their fur clinging close to them, and all dripping wet, cross, and uncomfortable.

30/30 CHAPTER III: A CAUCUS-RACE AND A LONG TALE They were indeed a queer-looking party that assembled on the bank—the birds with draggled feathers, the animals with their fur clinging close to them, and all dripping wet, cross, and uncomfortable.

Compacta

Designed by Fred Lambert between 1963 and 1965. Compacta has strong verticals that are impressive when used as a large headline or title to contrast with the body text. The font variations include light, light compressed, regular, italic, bold italic, black, and black poster.

Cooper Black

abcdefghijklmnopqrstuvwxyz
ABCDEFGHIJKLM
NOPQRSTUVWXYZ
1234567890?!$%&*:;"

Cooper Black

Oswald Bruce Cooper designed the extra-bold roman face Cooper Black in 1920. He based the newer design on the forms of his typeface Cooper Old Style, which appeared with Barnhart Bros. & Spindler Type Founders in Chicago a year earlier. Cooper Black was produced by Barnhart in 1922 and acquired in 1924 by Schriftguß AG in Dresden, where it was later completed with a matching italic. Cooper Black has a sturdy presence and may be found on storefronts in almost any city worldwide. The rounded outer contours create forms that appear soft and friendly.

6/9   At last the Mouse, who seemed to be a person of authority among them, called out, "Sit down, all of you, and listen to me! I'll soon make you dry enough!" They all sat down at once, in a large ring, with the Mouse in the middle. Alice kept her eyes anxiously fixed on it, for she felt sure she would catch a bad cold if she did not get dry very soon.

8/11   At last the Mouse, who seemed to be a person of authority among them, called out, "Sit down, all of you, and listen to me! I'll soon make you dry enough!" They all sat down at once, in a large ring, with the Mouse in the middle. Alice kept her eyes anxiously fixed on it, for she felt sure she would catch a bad cold if she did not get dry very soon.

11/13   At last the Mouse, who seemed to be a person of authority among them, called out, "Sit down, all of you, and listen to me! I'll soon make you dry enough!" They all sat down at once, in a large ring,

14/16   At last the Mouse, who seemed to be a person of authority among them, called out, "Sit down, all of you, and listen to me! I'll soon make you dry enough!" They all sat down at once, in a large ring, with the Mouse in the middle. Alice kept her eyes anxiously fixed on it, for she felt sure she would catch a bad cold if she did not get dry very soon.

18/19   At last the Mouse, who seemed to be a person of authority among them, called out, "Sit down, all of you, and listen to me! I'll soon make you dry enough!" They all sat down at once, in a large ring, with the Mouse in

COPPERPLATE GOTHIC

ABCDEFGHIJKLM
NOPQRSTUVWXYZ
1234567890?!$%&*:;"

Copperplate Gothic

Although the original design of Copperplate Gothic was drawn by Frederic W. Goudy at the turn of the twentieth century, the subsequent variations in weight and style were created by Clarence C. Marder. The wide, square font is legible at small sizes and is attractive in large display sizes as well.

6/9
"AHEM!" SAID THE MOUSE WITH AN IMPORTANT AIR, "ARE YOU ALL READY? THIS IS THE DRIEST THING I KNOW. SILENCE ALL ROUND, IF YOU PLEASE! 'WILLIAM THE CONQUEROR, WHOSE CAUSE WAS FAVOURED BY THE POPE, WAS SOON SUBMITTED TO BY THE ENGLISH, WHO WANTED LEADERS, AND HAD BEEN OF LATE MUCH ACCUSTOMED TO USURPATION AND CONQUEST. EDWIN AND MORCAR, THE EARLS OF MERCIA AND NORTHUMBRIA—' "

8/11
"AHEM!" SAID THE MOUSE WITH AN IMPORTANT AIR, "ARE YOU ALL READY? THIS IS THE DRIEST THING I KNOW. SILENCE ALL ROUND, IF YOU PLEASE! 'WILLIAM THE CONQUEROR, WHOSE CAUSE WAS FAVOURED BY THE POPE, WAS SOON SUBMITTED TO BY THE ENGLISH, WHO WANTED LEADERS, AND HAD BEEN OF LATE MUCH ACCUSTOMED TO USURPATION AND CONQUEST. EDWIN AND MORCAR, THE EARLS OF

11/14
"AHEM!" SAID THE MOUSE WITH AN IMPORTANT AIR, "ARE YOU ALL READY? THIS IS THE DRIEST THING I KNOW. SILENCE ALL ROUND, IF YOU PLEASE! 'WILLIAM THE CONQUEROR, WHOSE CAUSE WAS FAVOURED BY THE POPE, WAS SOON SUBMITTED TO BY THE ENGLISH, WHO WANTED LEADERS, AND HAD BEEN OF LATE MUCH ACCUSTOMED TO USURPATION AND CONQUEST. EDWIN AND MORCAR, THE EARLS OF MERCIA AND NORTHUMBRIA—' "

14/16
"AHEM!" SAID THE MOUSE WITH AN IMPORTANT AIR, "ARE YOU ALL READY? THIS IS THE DRIEST THING I KNOW. SILENCE ALL ROUND, IF YOU PLEASE! 'WILLIAM THE CONQUEROR, WHOSE CAUSE WAS FAVOURED BY THE POPE, WAS SOON SUBMITTED TO BY THE ENGLISH, WHO WANTED

18/18
"AHEM!" SAID THE MOUSE WITH AN IMPORTANT AIR, "ARE YOU ALL READY? THIS IS THE DRIEST THING I KNOW. SILENCE ALL ROUND, IF YOU PLEASE! 'WILLIAM THE CONQUEROR, WHOSE CAUSE WAS FAVOURED BY THE POPE, WAS SOON SUBMITTED TO BY THE ENGLISH, WHO WANTED LEADERS, AND HAD BEEN OF LATE MUCH ACCUSTOMED TO USURPATION AND CONQUEST. EDWIN AND MORCAR, THE EARLS OF MERCIA AND NORTHUMBRIA—' "

24/22
"AHEM!" SAID THE MOUSE WITH AN IMPORTANT AIR, "ARE YOU ALL READY? THIS IS THE DRIEST THING I KNOW. SILENCE ALL ROUND,

Courier Standard

abcdefghijklmnopqrstuvwxyz
ABCDEFGHIJKLM
NOPQRSTUVWXYZ
1234567890?!$%&*:;"

Courier Standard

This monospaced Adobe font was originally designed by Howard Kettler for IBM typewriters. Later it was redesigned by by Adrian Frutiger for the IBM Selectric Typewriters.

6/9   "Ugh!" said the Lory, with a shiver.
 "I beg your pardon!" said the Mouse, frowning, but very politely: "Did you speak?"
 "Not I!" said the Lory hastily.

8/11   "Ugh!" said the Lory, with a shiver.
 "I beg your pardon!" said the Mouse, frowning, but very politely: "Did you speak?"
 "Not I!" said the Lory hastily.

11/14   "Ugh!" said the Lory, with a shiver.
 "I beg your pardon!" said the Mouse, frown-

14/16   "Ugh!" said the Lory, with a shiver.
 "I beg your pardon!" said the Mouse, frowning, but very politely: "Did you speak?"
 "Not I!" said the Lory hastily.

18/20   "Ugh!" said the Lory, with a shiver.
 "I beg your pardon!" said the Mouse, frowning, but very politely: "Did you speak?"
 "Not I!" said the Lory hastily.

24/22   "Ugh!" said the Lory, with a shiver.
 "I beg your pardon!" said the Mouse, frowning, but very politely: "Did you speak?"

Data Seventy

abcdefghijklmnopqrstuvwxyz
ABCDEFGHIJKLM
NOPQRSTUVWXYZ
1234567890?!$%&*:;"

18/20 The Mouse did not notice this question, but hurriedly went on," '—found it advisable to go with Edgar Atheling to meet William and offer him the crown. William's conduct at first was moderate. But the insolence of his Normans—' How are you getting on now, my dear?" it continued, turning to Alice as it spoke.

27/22 The Mouse did not notice this question, but hurriedly went on,"" — found it advisable to go with Edgar Atheling to meet William and

11/14 The Mouse did not notice this question, but hurriedly went on, " '—found it advisable to go with Edgar Atheling to meet William and offer him the crown. William's conduct at first was moderate. But the insolence of his Normans—' How are you getting on now, my dear?" it continued, turning to Alice as it spoke.

14/16 The Mouse did not notice this question, but hurriedly went on, " '—found it advisable to go with Edgar Atheling to meet William and offer him the crown. William's conduct at first was moderate. But the insolence of his Normans—' How are you getting on now, my dear?"

Data Seventy

British designer Bob Newman created this font in 1970. At that time, this font envoked the image of a futuristic, computer-generated message. Although the font is "retro" at this point in time, the contrasting vertical stroke widths transitioned by curvilinear elements provide a friendly and fun compositional element in headlines.

6/9 The Mouse did not notice this question, but hurriedly went on," '—found it advisable to go with Edgar Atheling to meet William and offer him the crown. William's conduct at first was moderate. But the insolence of his Normans—' How are you getting on now, my dear?" it continued, turning to Alice as it spoke.

8/12 The Mouse did not notice this question, but hurriedly went on," '—found it advisable to go with Edgar Atheling to meet William and offer him the crown. William's conduct at first was moderate. But the insolence of his Normans—' How are you getting on now, my dear?" it continued, turning to Alice as it spoke.

ECCENTRIC

ABCDEFGHIJKLM
NOPQRSTUVWXYZ
1234567890?!;!#$()+{}:?

Eccentric

Although the original font foundry is unknown, the font design is attributed to Gustav F. Schroeder, from 1881. This narrow, all-caps font is referred to as "high-waisted" since the crossbars are placed within the top quarter of the height of the letterforms. The thin monoline font is whimsical and lighthearted.

W HAT I WAS GOING TO SAY," SAID THE DODO IN AN OFFENDED TONE, "WAS, THAT THE BEST THING TO GET US DRY WOULD BE A CAUCUS-RACE."

"WHAT IS A CAUCUS-RACE?" SAID ALICE; NOT THAT SHE WANTED MUCH TO KNOW, BUT THE DODO HAD PAUSED AS IF IT THOUGHT THAT SOMEBODY OUGHT TO SPEAK, AND NO ONE ELSE SEEMED INCLINED TO SAY ANYTHING.

"WHY," SAID THE DODO, "THE BEST WAY TO EXPLAIN IT IS TO DO IT." (AND, AS YOU MIGHT LIKE TO TRY THE THING YOURSELF, SOME WINTER DAY, I WILL TELL YOU

ITC Eras Medium

abcdefghijklmnopqrstuvwxyz
ABCDEFGHIJKLM
NOPQRSTUVWXYZ
1234567890?!$%&*:;"

11/14 ""But who is to give the prizes?" quite a chorus of voices asked.
"Why, SHE, of course," said the Dodo, pointing to Alice with one finger; and the whole party at once crowded round her, calling out in a confused way, "Prizes! Prizes!"

14/16 "But who is to give the prizes?" quite a chorus of voices asked.

"Why, SHE, of course," said the Dodo, pointing to Alice with one finger; and the whole party at once crowded round her, calling out in a confused way, "Prizes! Prizes!"

18/20 "But who is to give the prizes?" quite a chorus of voices asked.

"Why, SHE, of course," said the Dodo, pointing to Alice with one finger; and the whole party at once crowded round her, calling out in a confused way, "Prizes! Prizes!"

24/24 "But who is to give the prizes?" quite a chorus of voices asked.
"Why, SHE, of course," said the

Eras

Eras was a 1961 collaborative creation by French designers Albert Boton and Albert Hollenstein. It is a sans serif typeface distinguished by its unusual slight forward slant and subtle variations in stroke weight. ITC Eras is an open and airy typeface inspired by both Greek stone-cut lapidary letters and Roman capitals.

6/9 "But who is to give the prizes?" quite a chorus of voices asked.
"Why, SHE, of course," said the Dodo, pointing to Alice with one finger; and the whole party at once crowded round her, calling out in a confused way, "Prizes! Prizes!"

8/12 "But who is to give the prizes?" quite a chorus of voices asked.
"Why, SHE, of course," said the Dodo, pointing to Alice with one finger; and the whole party at once crowded round her, calling out in a confused way, "Prizes! Prizes!"

Eurostile Medium

abcdefghijklmnopqrstuvwxyz
ABCDEFGHIJKLM
NOPQRSTUVWXYZ
1234567890?!$%&*:;"

Eurostile

Eurostile is the work of Italian designer Aldo Novarese from 1962. It is based on an earlier font by Novarese and his colleague A. Butti, named Microgramma. The Eurostile font family has eleven weights and styles, from roman to bold and condensed to extended.

6/9 Alice had no idea what to do, and in despair she put her hand in her pocket, and pulled out a box of comfits (luckily the salt water had not got into it), and handed them round as prizes. There was exactly one a-piece all round.

8/11 Alice had no idea what to do, and in despair she put her hand in her pocket, and pulled out a box of comfits (luckily the salt water had not got into it), and handed them round as prizes. There was exactly one a-piece all round.

11/14 Alice had no idea what to do, and in despair she put her hand in her pocket, and pulled out a box of comfits (luckily the salt water had not got into it), and handed them round as prizes. There was exactly one a-piece all round.

14/16 Alice had no idea what to do, and in despair she put her hand in her pocket, and pulled out a box of comfits (luckily the salt water had not got into it), and handed them round as prizes. There was exactly one a-piece all round.

18/20 Alice had no idea what to do, and in despair she put her hand in her pocket, and pulled out a box of comfits (luckily the salt water had not got into it), and handed them round as prizes. There was exactly one a-piece all round.

ITC Fenice Regular

ABCDEFGHIJKLM
NOPQRSTUVWXYZ
1234567890?!$%&*:;"

11/14 Alice thought the whole thing very absurd, but they all looked so grave that she did not dare to laugh; and, as she could not think of anything to say, she simply bowed, and took the thimble, looking as solemn as she could.

14/16 Alice thought the whole thing very absurd, but they all looked so grave that she did not dare to laugh; and, as she could not think of anything to say, she simply bowed, and took the thimble, looking as solemn as she could.

18/20 Alice thought the whole thing very absurd, but they all looked so grave that she did not dare to laugh; and, as she could not think of anything to say, she simply bowed, and took the thimble, looking as solemn as she could.

18/20 Alice thought the whole thing very absurd, but they all looked so grave that she did not dare to laugh; and, as she could not think of anything to say, she simply bowed, and took the thimble, looking as solemn as she

Fenice

Designed by Aldo Novarese in 1980, Fenice (pronounced *fe-NEE-chay*) was influenced by the traditional designs of Didot, Bodoni, and Ibarra. Somewhat narrow, it is a good choice for fitting larger quanitites of type into a limited amount of space. The great contrast between the thick vertical strokes and the thin horizontal strokes makes it more difficult to decipher in smaller sizes, since the thin horizontal strokes appear to dissolve or disappear.

6/9 Alice thought the whole thing very absurd, but they all looked so grave that she did not dare to laugh; and, as she could not think of anything to say, she simply bowed, and took the thimble, looking as solemn as she could.

8/12 Alice thought the whole thing very absurd, but they all looked so grave that she did not dare to laugh; and, as she could not think of anything to say, she simply bowed, and took the thimble, looking as solemn as she could.

ITC Franklin Gothic

abcdefghijklmnopqrstuvwxyz

ABCDEFGHIJKLM

NOPQRSTUVWXYZ

1234567890?!$%&*:;"

Franklin Gothic

Morris Fuller Benton designed the Franklin Gothic Type family between 1903 and 1912. Much of his inspiration came from the grotesque designs out of Europe, such as Berthold's Akzidenz and Stemple's Reform fonts.

In 1980, Victor Caruso redrew the original Franklin Gothic and designed several more weights. In 1991, David Berlow added several condensed and compressed weights.The variety of weights and styles makes this font continue as a favorite in the industry. The existing ITC Franklin Gothic family is a collaborative design that has evolved over the last century.

6/9   The next thing was to eat the comfits: this caused some noise and confusion, as the large birds complained that they could not taste theirs, and the small ones choked and had to be patted on the back. However, it was over at last, and they sat down again in a ring, and begged the Mouse to tell them something more.

8/11   The next thing was to eat the comfits: this caused some noise and confusion, as the large birds complained that they could not taste theirs, and the small ones choked and had to be patted on the back. However, it was over at last, and they sat down again in a ring, and begged the Mouse to tell them something more.

11/14   The next thing was to eat the comfits: this caused some noise and confusion, as the large birds complained that they could not taste theirs, and the small ones choked and had to be patted on the back However, it was over at last, and they sat down again in a ring, and begged the Mouse

14/16   The next thing was to eat the comfits: this caused some noise and confusion, as the large birds complained that they could not taste theirs, and the small ones choked and had to be patted on the back. However, it was over at last, and they sat down again in a ring, and begged the Mouse to tell them something more.

18/20   The next thing was to eat the comfits: this caused some noise and confusion, as the large birds complained that they could not taste theirs, and the small ones choked and had to be patted on the back. However, it was over at last, and they sat down again in a

Friz Quadrata

abcdefghijklmnopqrstuvwxyz
ABCDEFGHIJKLM
NOPQRSTUVWXYZ
1234567890?!$%&*:;"

6/9   "It IS a long tail, certainly," said Alice, looking down with wonder at the Mouse's tail; "but why do you call it sad?" And she kept on puzzling about it while the Mouse was speaking, so that her idea of the tale was something like this:—

8/11   "It IS a long tail, certainly," said Alice, looking down with wonder at the Mouse's tail; "but why do you call it sad?" And she kept on puzzling about it while the Mouse was speaking, so that her idea of the tale was something like this:—

11/14   "It IS a long tail, certainly," said Alice, looking down with wonder at the Mouse's tail; "but why do you call it sad?" And she kept on puzzling about it while the Mouse was speaking, so that her idea of the tale was something like this:—

14/16   "It IS a long tail, certainly," said Alice, looking down with wonder at the Mouse's tail; "but why

do you call it sad?" And she kept on puzzling about it while the Mouse was speaking, so that her idea of the tale was something like this:—

25/23   "It IS a long tail, certainly," said Alice, looking down with wonder at the Mouse's tail; "but why do you call it sad?" And she kept on puzzling about it while the Mouse was speaking, so that her idea of the tale was something like this:—

Friz Quadrata

This is another example of a collaborative design that has evolved over time. The original version was designed by Swiss designer Ernst Friz in 1965. The bold variation was designed by Victor Caruso, and then in 1992 French designer Thierry Puyfoulhoux designed italic variations in style to complement and complete the family.

It is characterized by a slight change in stroke weight and the open counterforms on the lowercase letters a, b, d, p, and q and numbers 6 and 9. Several of the capital letterforms have small serifs that extend only on the left top, and only on the bottom right strokes.

Garish Monde

abcdefghijklmnopqrstuvwxyz
ABCDEFGHIJKLM
NOPQRSTUVWXYZ
1234567890?!$%&*:;"

Garish Monde

Garish Monde is a fractured variation of classic Garamond, including upper- and lowercase, punctuation, and ligatures. The designer, Bernard Haber, took an existing digitized Garamond, made semirandom vertical cuts in the letterforms, and then rearranged the pieces. As he writes in the Read Me file: "The origins of this font are a sample sheet of an American Type Founders Garamond font printed in 1934, an unusually tart bottle of French table wine, and a relaxing evening discussing literary deconstructionist theory with some very confused friends of mine from the University."

"I wish I had our Dinah here, I know I do!" said Alice aloud, addressing nobody in particular. "She'd soon fetch it back!"

"And who is Dinah, if I might venture to ask the question?" said the Lory.

Alice replied eagerly, for she was always ready to talk about her pet: "Dinah's our cat. And she's such a capital one for catching mice you can't think! And oh, I wish you could see her after the birds! Why, she'll eat a little bird as soon as look at it!"

Georgia

abcdefghijklmnopqrstuvwxyz
ABCDEFGHIJKLM
NOPQRSTUVWXYZ
1234567890?!$%&*:;"

6/9 This speech caused a remarkable sensation among the party. Some of the birds hurried off at once: one old Magpie began wrapping itself up very carefully, remarking, "I really must be getting home; the night-air doesn't suit my throat!" and a Canary called out in a trembling voice to its children, "Come away, my dears! It's high time you were all in bed!" On various pretexts they all moved off, and Alice was soon left alone.

8/12 This speech caused a remarkable sensation among the party. Some of the birds hurried off at once: one old Magpie began wrapping itself up very carefully, remarking, "I really must be getting home; the night-air doesn't suit my throat!" and a Canary called out in a trembling voice to its children, "Come away, my dears! It's high time you were all in bed!" On various pretexts they all moved off, and Alice was soon left alone.

11/14 This speech caused a remarkable sensation among the party. Some of the birds hurried off at once: one old Magpie began wrapping itself up very carefully, remarking, "I really must be getting home; the night-air doesn't suit my

14/16 This speech caused a remarkable sensation among the party. Some of the birds hurried off at once: one old Magpie began wrapping itself up very carefully, remarking, "I really must be getting home; the night-air doesn't suit my throat!" and a Canary called out in a trembling voice to its children, "Come away, my dears! It's high time you were all in bed!" On various pretexts they all moved off, and Alice was soon left alone.

18/20 This speech caused a remarkable sensation among the party. Some of the birds hurried off at once: one old Magpie began wrapping itself up very carefully, remarking, "I really must be getting home; the night-air doesn't suit my

Georgia

This Microsoft Corporation font was designed by Matthew Carter and "hinted" by Tom Rickner (from Agfa Monotype) for release in 1997. This font was designed for legibility in the low-resolution computer screen environment. Georgia maintains a sense of class and friendliness, in both Web and print publishing applications.

The italic variation of Georgia is a true italic, not merely a computer-generated oblique version of the roman, as are so many italicized digital fonts. This can be seen easily in the variations of the lowercase letters, such as the two-story roman *a* and *g*, that become one-story in the italic style variation.

Gill Sans

abcdefghijklmnopqrstuvwxyz
ABCDEFGHIJKLM
NOPQRSTUVWXYZ
1234567890?!$%&*:;"

6/9 "I wish I hadn't mentioned Dinah!" she said to herself in a melancholy tone. "Nobody seems to like her, down here, and I'm sure she's the best cat in the world! Oh, my dear Dinah! I wonder if I shall ever see you any more!" And here poor Alice began to cry again, for she felt very lonely and low-spirited. In a little while, however, she again heard a little pattering of footsteps in the distance, and she looked up eagerly, half hoping that the Mouse had changed his mind, and was coming back to finish his story.

8/11 "I wish I hadn't mentioned Dinah!" she said to herself in a melancholy tone. "Nobody seems to like her, down here, and I'm sure she's the best cat in the world! Oh, my dear Dinah! I wonder if I shall ever see you any more!" And here poor Alice began to cry again, for she felt very lonely and low-spirited. In a little while, however, she again heard a little pattering of footsteps in the distance, and she looked up eagerly, half hoping that the Mouse had changed his mind, and was coming back to finish his story.

11/14 "I wish I hadn't mentioned Dinah!" she said to herself in a melancholy tone. "Nobody seems to like her,

14/16 "I wish I hadn't mentioned Dinah!" she said to herself in a melancholy tone. "Nobody seems to like her, down here, and I'm sure she's the best cat in the world! Oh, my dear Dinah! I wonder if I shall ever see you any more!" And here poor Alice began to cry again, for she felt very lonely and low-spirited. In a little while, however, she again heard a little pattering of footsteps in the distance, and she looked up eagerly, half hoping that the Mouse had changed his mind, and was coming back to finish his story.

22/22 "I wish I hadn't mentioned Dinah!" she said to herself in a melancholy tone. "Nobody seems to like her, down here, and I'm sure she's the best cat in the world! Oh, my dear Dinah! I wonder if I shall ever see you any more!" And here poor Alice began to cry again, for she felt very lonely and low-spirited. In a little while, however, she again heard a little pattering of footsteps in the

Goudy

abcdefghijklmnopqrstuvwxyz

ABCDEFGHIJKLM
NOPQRSTUVWXYZ
1234567890?!$%&*.;"

6/9

CHAPTER IV: THE RABBIT SENDS IN A LITTLE BILL
It was the White Rabbit, trotting slowly back again, and looking anxiously about as it went, as if it had lost something; and she heard it muttering to itself "The Duchess! The Duchess! Oh my dear paws! Oh my fur and whiskers! She'll get me executed, as sure as ferrets are ferrets! Where CAN I have dropped them, I wonder?"

8/12

CHAPTER IV: THE RABBIT SENDS IN A LITTLE BILL
It was the White Rabbit, trotting slowly back again, and looking anxiously about as it went, as if it had lost something; and she heard it muttering to itself "The Duchess! The Duchess! Oh my dear paws! Oh my fur and whiskers! She'll get me executed, as sure as ferrets are ferrets! Where CAN I have dropped them, I wonder?"

11/14

CHAPTER IV: THE RABBIT SENDS IN A LITTLE BILL
It was the White Rabbit, trotting slowly back again, and looking anxiously about as it went, as if it had lost something; and she heard it muttering to itself "The Duchess! The Duchess! Oh my dear paws! Oh my fur and whiskers! She'll get me executed, as sure as ferrets are ferrets! Where CAN I have dropped them, I wonder?"

14/16

CHAPTER IV: THE RABBIT SENDS IN A LITTLE BILL
It was the White Rabbit, trotting slowly back again, and looking anxiously about as it went, as if it had lost something; and she heard it muttering to itself "The Duchess! The Duchess! Oh my dear paws! Oh my fur and whiskers! She'll get me executed, as sure as ferrets are ferrets! Where CAN I have dropped them, I wonder?"

18/20

CHAPTER IV: THE RABBIT SENDS IN A LITTLE BILL
It was the White Rabbit, trotting slowly back again, and looking anxiously about as it went, as if it had lost something; and she

Goudy Sans

abcdefghijklmnopqrstuvwxyz
ABCDEFGHIJKLM
NOPQRSTUVWXYZ
1234567890?!$%&*.;"

6/9   Alice guessed in a moment that it was looking for the fan and the pair of white kid gloves, and she very good-naturedly began hunting about for them, but they were nowhere to be seen—everything seemed to have changed since her swim in the pool, and the great hall, with the glass table and the little door, had vanished completely.

8/11   Alice guessed in a moment that it was looking for the fan and the pair of white kid gloves, and she very good-naturedly began hunting about for them, but they were nowhere to be seen—everything seemed to have changed since her swim in the pool, and the great hall, with the glass table and the little door, had vanished completely.

11/14   Alice guessed in a moment that it was looking for the fan and the pair of white kid gloves, and she very good-naturedly began hunting about for them, but they were nowhere to be seen—everything seemed to have changed since her swim

14/16   Alice guessed in a moment that it was looking for the fan and the pair of white kid gloves, and she very good-naturedly began hunting about for them, but they were nowhere to be seen—everything seemed to have changed since her swim in the pool, and the great hall, with the glass table and the little door, had vanished completely.

18/20   Alice guessed in a moment that it was looking for the fan and the pair of white kid gloves, and she very good-naturedly began hunting about for them, but they were nowhere to be seen—

Goudy and Goudy Sans

Recognizable characteristics in Goudy's fonts include the upward pointing ear of the *g*, the diamond-shaped dots over the *i* and *j*, and the round, upward expansion of the horizontal strokes at the base of the *E* and *L*. The original Goudy Old Style was completed for the ATF in 1915–16, while the italic variation came a year later. Goudy Bold and Extra Bold were drawn by Morris Fuller Benton a few years after that.

Goudy designed three weights of this friendly-looking sans serif font from 1922 to 1929. Goudy imparted personality to the sans serif by adding a slight curve to the terminals and strokes. Some capital letterforms include a decorative slab serif, and some alternate uncial forms are available as well. Goudy Sans was drawn at the same time as geometric sans serifs, such as Futura, were growing in popularity.

Hobo Medium

abcdefghijklmnopqrstuvwxyz
ABCDEFGHIJKLM
NOPQRSTUVWXYZ
1234567890?!$%&*:;,"

Hobo

This whimsical font was designed by Morris Fuller Benton in 1910. The curvilinear strokes, indicative of the Art Nouveau style of the time, meld into one another while many terminals fade into a curvilinear swash. The weight of the design and lack of descenders makes the font difficult to read in small sizes.

8/12   Very soon the Rabbit noticed Alice, as she went hunting about, and called out to her in an angry tone, "Why, Mary Ann, what ARE you doing out here? Run home this moment, and fetch me a pair of gloves and a fan! Quick, now!" And Alice was so much frightened that she ran off at once in the direction it pointed to, without trying to explain the mistake it had made.

11/14   Very soon the Rabbit noticed Alice, as she went hunting about, and called out to her in an angry tone, "Why, Mary Ann, what ARE you doing out here? Run home this moment, and fetch me a pair of gloves and a fan! Quick, now!" And Alice was so much frightened that she ran off at once in the direction it pointed to, without trying to explain the mistake it had made.

14/16   Very soon the Rabbit noticed Alice, as she went hunting about, and called out to her in an angry tone, "Why, Mary Ann,

18/22   Very soon the Rabbit noticed Alice, as she went hunting about, and called out to her in an angry tone, "Why, Mary Ann, what ARE you doing out here? Run home this moment, and fetch me a pair of gloves and a fan! Quick, now!" And Alice was so much frightened that she ran off at once in the direction it pointed to, without trying to explain the mistake it had made.

Impact

abcdefghijklmnopqrstuvwxyz

ABCDEFGHIJKLM
NOPQRSTUVWXYZ
1234567890?!$%&*:;"

Impact

This 1965 Grotesque-style font was designed by Geoffrey Lee for the Stephenson Blake foundry. The heavy, condensed, sans serif display font is very similar to Helvetica Inserat and makes eye-catching headlines. A closer inspection of the details of the design reveal a subtle thinning of the stroke weight on the horizontal axis and at the intersection of curvilinear strokes, which add character and definition.

He took me for his housemaid," she said to herself as she ran. "How surprised he'll be when he finds out who I am! But I'd better take him his fan and gloves—that is, if I can find them." As she said this, she came upon a neat little house, on the door of which was a bright brass plate with the name "W. RABBIT" engraved upon it. She went in without knocking, and hurried upstairs, in great fear lest she should meet the real Mary Ann, and be turned out of the house before she had found the fan and gloves.

Imprint Shadow

abcdefghijklmnopqrstuvwxyz
ABCDEFGHIJKLM
NOPQRSTUVWXYZ
1234567890?!$%&*:;"

14/16.5 "How queer it seems," Alice said to herself, "to be going messages for a rabbit! I suppose Dinah'll be sending me on messages next!" And she began fancying the sort of thing that would happen: " 'Miss Alice! Come here directly, and get ready for your walk!' 'Coming in a minute, nurse! But I've got to see that the mouse doesn't get out.' Only I don't think," Alice went on, "that they'd let Dinah stop in the house if it began ordering people about like that!"

18/23 "How queer it seems," Alice said to herself, "to be going messages for a rabbit! I suppose Dinah'll be sending me on messages next!" And she began fancying the sort of thing

8/12 "How queer it seems," Alice said to herself, "to be going messages for a rabbit! I suppose Dinah'll be sending me on messages next!" And she began fancying the sort of thing that would happen: " 'Miss Alice! Come here directly, and get ready for your walk!' 'Coming in a minute, nurse! But I've got to see that the mouse doesn't get out.' Only I don't think," Alice went on, "that they'd let Dinah stop in the house if it began ordering people about like that!"

11/14 "How queer it seems," Alice said to herself, "to be going messages for a rabbit! I suppose Dinah'll be sending me on messages next!" And she began fancying the sort of thing that would happen: " 'Miss Alice! Come here directly, and get ready for your walk!' 'Coming in a minute, nurse! But I've got to see that the mouse doesn't get out.' Only I don't think," Alice went on, "that they'd let Dinah stop in the house if it began ordering people about like that?"

Imprint

Imprint is a classic Old Style font with a number of variations, including bold, bold italic, shadow, and expert sets. Imprint Shadow is a bold inline variation.

The font family is the result of a 1912 collaborative effort by Gerald Meynell with J. H. Mason, Ernest Jackson and Edward Johnston. The large x-height font, modeled after Caslon, was commissioned as the text face for *The Imprint*, a short-lived magazine about fine printing and typography.

6/9 "How queer it seems," Alice said to herself, "to be going messages for a rabbit! I suppose Dinah'll be sending me on messages next!" And she began fancying the sort of thing that would happen: " 'Miss Alice! Come here directly, and get ready for your walk!' 'Coming in a minute, nurse! But I've got to see that the mouse doesn't get out.' Only I don't think," Alice went on, "that they'd let Dinah stop in the house if it began ordering people about like that!"

Janson Text 55

abcdefghijklmnopqrstuvwxyz
ABCDEFGHIJKLM
NOPQRSTUVWXYZ
1234567890?!$%&*:;"

Janson

This font was not cut by the seventeenth-century Dutch punch cutter Anton Janson but rather by Hungarian punch cutter Miklós Kis in about 1685. Some of the Kis punches and matrices made their way to D. Stempel AG in Frankfurt in 1919, and it was discovered at that point that the font had been wrongly attributed.

Linotype Janson was cut in 1954 under the supervision of Hermann Zapf, while Horst Heiderhoff led the Linotype Design Studio in the most recent expansion of Janson in 1985. It now includes eight variations in weight and style from which to choose.

6/9   It did so indeed, and much sooner than she had expected: before she had drunk half the bottle, she found her head pressing against the ceiling, and had to stoop to save her neck from being broken. She hastily put down the bottle, saying to herself "That's quite enough—I hope I shan't grow

8/12   It did so indeed, and much sooner than she had expected: before she had drunk half the bottle, she found her head pressing against the ceiling, and had to stoop to save her neck from being broken. She hastily put down the bottle, saying to herself "That's quite enough—I hope I shan't grow any more—As it is, I can't get out at the door—I do wish I hadn't drunk quite so much!"

11/14   It did so indeed, and much sooner than she had expected: before she had drunk half the bottle, she found her head pressing against the ceiling, and had to stoop to save her neck from being broken. She hastily put down the bottle, saying to herself "That's quite enough—I hope I shan't grow any more—As it is, I can't get out at the door—I do wish I hadn't drunk quite so much!"

14/16   It did so indeed, and much sooner than she had expected: before she had drunk half the bottle, she found her head pressing against the ceiling, and had to stoop to save her neck from being broken. She hastily put down the bottle, saying to herself "That's quite enough—I hope I shan't grow any more—As it is, I can't get out at the door—I do wish I hadn't drunk quite so much!"

18/20   It did so indeed, and much sooner than she had expected: before she had drunk half the bottle, she found her head pressing against the ceiling, and had to stoop to save her neck from being broken. She hastily put down the bottle, saying to herself

Jimbo

abcdefghijklmnopqrstuvwxyz
ABCDEFGHIJKLM
NOPQRSTUVWXYZ
1234567890?!$%&*:;"

8/12   Luckily for Alice, the little magic bottle had now had its full effect, and she grew no larger: still it was very uncomfortable, and, as there seemed to be no sort of chance of her ever getting out of the room again, no wonder she felt unhappy.

11/14   Luckily for Alice, the little magic bottle had now had its full effect, and she grew no larger: still it was very uncomfortable, and, as there seemed to be no sort of chance of her ever getting out of the room again, no wonder she felt unhappy.

14/16   Luckily for Alice, the little magic bottle had now had its full effect, and she grew no larger: still it was very

18/20   Luckily for Alice, the little magic bottle had now had its full effect, and she grew no larger: still it was very uncomfortable, and, as there seemed to be no sort of chance of her ever getting out of the room again, no wonder she felt unhappy.

24/24   Luckily for Alice, the little magic bottle had now had its full effect, and she grew no larger: still it was very uncomfortable, and, as there seemed to be no sort of chance of her ever getting out of the room again, no wonder she felt unhappy.

La Bamba

abcdefghijklmnopqrstuvwxyz
ABCDEFGHIJKLM
NOPQRSTUVWXYZ
1234567890?!$%&*:;"

La Bamba

British designer David Quay created this casual, wedge-serif font in 1992. The complete lowercase and uppercase sets were inspired by examples from the 1950s.

6/9 "But then," thought Alice, "shall I NEVER get any older than I am now? That'll be a comfort, one way—never to be an old woman—but then—always to have lessons to learn! Oh, I shouldn't like THAT!"

8/11 "But then," thought Alice, "shall I NEVER get any older than I am now? That'll be a comfort, one way—never to be an old woman—but then—always to have lessons to learn! Oh, I shouldn't like THAT!"

11/14 "But then," thought Alice, "shall I NEVER get any older than I am now? That'll be a comfort, one way—never to be an old woman—but then— always to have lessons to learn! Oh, I shouldn't like THAT!"

14/16 "But then," thought Alice, "shall I NEVER get any older than I am now? That'll be a comfort, one way—never

18/20 "But then," thought Alice, "shall I NEVER get any older than I am now? That'll be a comfort, one way—never to be an old woman— but then—always to have lessons to learn! Oh, I shouldn't like THAT!"

24/24 "But then," thought Alice, "shall I NEVER get any older than I am now? That'll be a comfort, one way—never to be an old woman—but then— always to have lessons to

Letter Gothic

abcdefghijklmnopqrstuvwxyz

ABCDEFGHIJKLM
NOPQRSTUVWXYZ
1234567890?!$%&*:;"

18/20 "Oh, you foolish Alice!" she answered herself. "How can you learn lessons in here? Why, there's hardly room for YOU, and no room at all for any lesson-books!"

24/26 "Oh, you foolish Alice!" she answered herself. "How can you learn lessons in here? Why, there's hardly room for

11/14 "Oh, you foolish Alice!" she answered herself. "How can you learn lessons in here? Why, there's hardly room for YOU, and no room at all for any lesson-books!"

15/18 "Oh, you foolish Alice!" she answered herself. "How can you learn lessons in here? Why, there's hardly room for YOU, and no room at all for any lesson-books!"

Letter Gothic

This monospaced, sans serif font was designed by Roger Roberson for IBM sometime in the late 1950s or early 1960s. Reportedly inspired by Optima, the typeface original drawings included flared stems. Intended for use on an IBM Selectric typewriter, Letter Gothic is a good choice for tabular material, or to invoke a period look in compositions.

6/9 "Oh, you foolish Alice!" she answered herself. "How can you learn lessons in here? Why, there's hardly room for YOU, and no room at all for any lesson-books!"

8/12 "Oh, you foolish Alice!" she answered herself. "How can you learn lessons in here? Why, there's hardly room for YOU, and no room at all for any lesson-books!"

Lubalin Graph

abcdefghijklmnopqrstuvwxyz

ABCDEFGHIJKLM
NOPQRSTUVWXYZ
1234567890?!$%&*:;"

Lubalin Graph

Named for its designer, Herb Lubalin designed this font in 1974. It was drawn by Tony DiSpigna and Joe Sundwall, based on Lubalin's earlier design of Avant Garde. The geometric forms and monoline strokes are embellished with slab serifs for a friendly, stable aesthetic.

6/9   "Mary Ann! Mary Ann!" said the voice. "Fetch me my gloves this moment!" Then came a little pattering of feet on the stairs. Alice knew it was the Rabbit coming to look for her, and she trembled till she shook the house, quite forgetting that she was now about a thousand times as large as the Rabbit, and had no reason to be afraid of it.

8/11   "Mary Ann! Mary Ann!" said the voice. "Fetch me my gloves this moment!" Then came a little pattering of feet on the stairs. Alice knew it was the Rabbit coming to look for her, and she trembled

11/14   "Mary Ann! Mary Ann!" said the voice. "Fetch me my gloves this moment!" Then came a little pattering of feet on the stairs. Alice knew it was the Rabbit coming to look for her, and she trembled till she shook the house, quite forgetting that she was now about a thousand times as large as the Rabbit, and had no reason to be afraid of it.

14/16   "Mary Ann! Mary Ann!" said the voice. "Fetch me my gloves this moment!" Then

18/20   "Mary Ann! Mary Ann!" said the voice. "Fetch me my gloves this moment!" Then came a little pattering of feet on the stairs. Alice knew it was the Rabbit coming to look for her, and she trembled till she shook the house, quite forgetting that she was now about a thousand times as large as the Rabbit, and had no reason to be afraid of it.

Lucida

abcdefghijklmnopqrstuvwxyz
ABCDEFGHIJKLM
NOPQRSTUVWXYZ
1234567890?!$%&*:;"

6/9 Presently the Rabbit came up to the door, and tried to open it; but, as the door opened inwards, and Alice's elbow was pressed hard against it, that attempt proved a failure. Alice heard it say to itself "Then I'll go round and get in at the window."

8/11 Presently the Rabbit came up to the door, and tried to open it; but, as the door opened inwards, and Alice's elbow was pressed hard against it, that attempt proved a failure. Alice heard it say to itself "Then I'll go round and get in at the window."

11/14 Presently the Rabbit came up to the door, and tried to open it; but, as the door opened inwards, and Alice's elbow was pressed hard against it, that attempt proved a failure. Alice heard it say to itself "Then I'll go round and get in at the window."

14/16 Presently the Rabbit came up to the door, and tried to open it; but, as the door opened inwards, and Alice's elbow was pressed hard against it, that attempt proved a failure. Alice heard it say to itself "Then I'll go round and get in at the window."

Lucida

Designed by Chris Holmes and Charles Bigelow, Lucida comes in a variety of weights and styles in both serif and sans serif styles.

24/24 Presently the Rabbit came up to the door, and tried to open it; but, as the door opened inwards, and Alice's elbow was pressed hard against it, that attempt proved a failure. Alice heard it say to itself "Then I'll go round and get in at the window."

Madrone

abcdefghijklm
nopqrstuvwxyz
ABCDEFGHIJKLM
NOPQRSTUVWXYZ
1234567890?!$%&*:;"

Madrone

Designed by Barbara Lind in 1991, Adobe Madrone was digitized from proofs in the woodtype collection at the National Museum of American History in Washington, D.C. A fat-face roman similar to Bodoni Poster, Madrone is typical of popular early-nineteenth-century styles. The extreme horizontal proportions of the letterforms, combined with the very short ascenders and descenders, make it possible to set the leading at a negative number without causing vertical overlap.

THAT YOU WON'T, " thought Alice, and, after waiting till she fancied she heard the Rabbit just under the window, she suddenly spread out her hand, and made a snatch in the air. She did not get hold of anything, but she heard a little shriek and a fall, and a crash of broken glass, from which she concluded that it was just possible it had fallen into a cucumber-frame, or something of the sort.

Magneto Bold

abcdefghijklmnopqrstuvwxyz
ABCDEFGHIJKLM
NOPQRSTUVWXYZ
1234567890?!$%&*:;"

Magneto

This decorative script was designed in 1995 by illustrator, designer, and author Leslie Cabarga. Magneto is a retro font, reminiscent of automobile advertising and logotypes from earlier in the twentieth century.

8/11 Next came an angry voice—the Rabbit's—"Pat! Pat! Where are you?" And then a voice she had never heard before, "Sure then I'm here! Digging for apples, yer honour!"

"Digging for apples, indeed!" said the Rabbit angrily. "Here! Come and help me out of THIS!" (Sounds of more broken glass.)

11/14 Next came an angry voice—the Rabbit's—"Pat! Pat! Where are you?" And then a voice she had never heard before, "Sure then I'm here! Digging for apples, yer honour!"

18/20 Next came an angry voice—the Rabbit's—"Pat! Pat! Where are you?" And then a voice she had never heard before, "Sure then I'm here! Digging for apples, yer honour!"

"Digging for apples, indeed!" said the Rabbit angrily. "Here! Come and help me out of THIS!" (Sounds of more broken glass.)

24/24 Next came an angry voice—the Rabbit's—"Pat! Pat! Where are you?" And then a voice she had never heard before, "Sure then I'm here! Digging for apples, yer honour!"

"Digging for apples, indeed!" said the Rabbit angrily.

Maiandra

abcdefghijklmnopqrstuvwxyz
ABCDEFGHIJKLM
NOPQRSTUVWXYZ
1234567890?!$%&*:;"

Maiandra

This Agfa Monotype font was designed by American designer Dennis Pasternak in 1994. The Maiandra family includes six style and weight variations. The curvilinear strokes with slightly flared terminals create a comfortable, conversational tone in any composition.

6/8 "Now tell me, Pat, what's that in the window?"
"Sure, it's an arm, yer honour!" (He pronounced it "arrum.")
"An arm, you goose! Who ever saw one that size? Why, it fills the whole window!"
"Sure, it does, yer honour: but it's an arm for all that."
"Well, it's got no business there, at any rate: go and take it away!"

8/10 "Now tell me, Pat, what's that in the window?"
"Sure, it's an arm, yer honour!" (He pronounced it "arrum.")
"An arm, you goose! Who ever saw one that size? Why, it fills the whole window!"

10/12 "Now tell me, Pat, what's that in the window?"
"Sure, it's an arm, yer honour!" (He pronounced it "arrum.")
"An arm, you goose! Who ever saw one that size? Why, it fills the whole window!"
"Sure, it does, yer honour: but it's an arm for all that."
"Well, it's got no business there, at any rate: go and take it away!"

13.5/15 "Now tell me, Pat, what's that in the window?"
"Sure, it's an arm, yer honour!" (He pronounced it "arrum.")
"An arm, you goose! Who ever saw one that size? Why, it

21/21 "Now tell me, Pat, what's that in the window?"
"Sure, it's an arm, yer honour!" (He pronounced it "arrum.")
"An arm, you goose! Who ever saw one that size? Why, it fills the whole window!"
"Sure, it does, yer honour: but it's an arm for all that."
"Well, it's got no business there, at any rate: go and take it away!"

ITC MATISSE

ABCDEFGHIJKLM
NOPQRSTUVWXYZ
1234567890?!$%&*:;"

THERE WAS A LONG SILENCE AFTER THIS, AND ALICE COULD ONLY HEAR WHISPERS NOW AND THEN; SUCH AS, "SURE, I DON'T LIKE IT, YER HONOUR, AT ALL, AT ALL!" "DO AS I TELL YOU, YOU COWARD!" AND AT LAST SHE SPREAD OUT HER HAND AGAIN, AND MADE ANOTHER SNATCH IN THE AIR. THIS TIME THERE WERE TWO LITTLE SHRIEKS, AND MORE SOUNDS OF BROKEN GLASS.

Matisse

This Agfa Monotype font was designed by Gregory Grey in 1995 for use in an editorial layout for *Madame Figaro*, a supplement to the Paris newspaper *Figaro*. This offbeat display font was cut from paper using an X-Acto knife, then the cutouts were scanned into a computer. The great contrast in proportion between the letterforms in this all-caps font creates visual interest but make large blocks of text difficult to decipher.

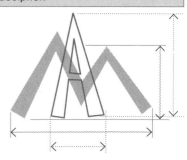

Mekanik

abcdefghijklmnopqrstuvwxyz
ABCDEFGHIJKLMNOPQRSTUVWXYZ
1234567890 ?!$%&*.:;"

11/14   She waited for some time without hearing anything more: at last came a rumbling of little cartwheels, and the sound of a good many voices all talking together: she made out the words: "Where's the other ladder?——Why, I hadn't to bring but one; Bill's got the other——Bill! fetch it here, lad!——Here, put 'em up at this corner——No, tie 'em together first——they don't reach half high enough yet——Oh! they'll do well enough; don't be particular—— Here, Bill! catch hold of this rope——Will the roof bear?——Mind that loose slate——Oh, it's coming down! Heads below!" (a loud crash)——"Now, who did that?——It was Bill, I fancy——Who's to go down the chimney?——Nay, I shan't! YOU do it!——That I won't, then!——Bill's to go down——Here, Bill! the master says you're to go down the chimney!"

14/16   She waited for some time without hearing anything more: at last came a rumbling of little cartwheels, and the sound of a good many voices all talking together: she made out the words: "Where's the other ladder?——Why, I hadn't to bring but one; Bill's got the other——Bill! fetch it here,

21/21   She waited for some time without hearing anything more: at last came a rumbling of little cartwheels, and the sound of a good many voices all talking together: she made out the words: "Where's the other ladder?——Why, I hadn't to bring but one; Bill's got the other——Bill! fetch it here, lad!——Here, put 'em up at this corner——No, tie 'em together first——they don't reach half high enough yet——Oh! they'll do well enough; don't be particular—— Here, Bill! catch hold of this rope——Will the roof bear?——Mind that loose slate——Oh, it's coming down! Heads below!" (a loud crash)——"Now, who did that?——It was Bill, I fancy——Who's to go down the chimney?——Nay, I shan't! YOU do it!——That I won't, then!——Bill's to go down——Here, Bill! the master says you're to go down

Melior Medium

abcdefghijklmnopqrstuvwxyz
ABCDEFGHIJKLM
NOPQRSTUVWXYZ
1234567890?!$%&*:;"

14/16 "Oh! So Bill's got to come down the chimney, has he?" said Alice to herself. "Why, they seem to put everything upon Bill! I wouldn't be in Bill's place for a good deal: this fireplace is narrow, to be sure; but I THINK I can kick a little!"

18/20 "Oh! So Bill's got to come down the chimney, has he?" said Alice to herself. "Why, they seem to put everything upon Bill! I wouldn't be in Bill's place for a good deal: this fireplace is narrow, to be sure; but I THINK I can kick a little!"

24/24 "Oh! So Bill's got to come down the chimney, has he?" said Alice to herself. "Why, they seem to put everything upon Bill! I wouldn't be in Bill's place for a good deal: this fireplace is narrow, to be sure; but I

Melior

This versatile and highly legible font was designed by Hermann Zapf in 1952. There are four variations in weight and style: Melior Medium, *Melior Medium Italic*, **Melior Bold**, and ***Melior Bold Italic***.

8/12 "Oh! So Bill's got to come down the chimney, has he?" said Alice to herself. "Why, they seem to put everything upon Bill! I wouldn't be in Bill's place for a good deal: this fireplace is narrow, to be sure; but I THINK I can kick a little!"

11/14 "Oh! So Bill's got to come down the chimney, has he?" said Alice to herself. "Why, they seem to put everything upon Bill! I wouldn't be in Bill's place for a good deal: this fireplace is narrow, to be sure; but I THINK I can

MESQUITE

ABCDEFGHIJKLMNOPQRSTUVWXYZ
1234567890?!$%&*:;"

SHE DREW HER FOOT AS FAR DOWN THE CHIMNEY AS SHE COULD, AND WAITED TILL SHE HEARD A LITTLE ANIMAL (SHE COULDN'T GUESS OF WHAT SORT IT WAS) SCRATCHING AND SCRAMBLING ABOUT IN THE CHIMNEY CLOSE ABOVE HER: THEN, SAYING TO HERSELF, "THIS IS BILL," SHE GAVE ONE SHARP KICK, AND WAITED TO SEE WHAT WOULD HAPPEN

Adobe Minion Pro

abcdefghijklmnopqrstuvwxyz

ABCDEFGHIJKLM

NOPQRSTUVWXYZ

1234567890?!$%&*.;"

11/14   Last came a little feeble, squeaking voice. ("That's Bill," thought Alice.) "Well, I hardly know—No more, thank ye; I'm better now—but I'm a deal too flustered to tell you—all I know is, something comes at me like a Jack-in-the-box, and up I goes like a sky-rocket!"

"So you did, old fellow!" said the others.

14/16   Last came a little feeble, squeaking voice. ("That's Bill," thought Alice.) "Well, I hardly know—No more, thank ye; I'm better now—but I'm a deal too flustered to tell you—all I know is, something comes at me like a Jack-in-the-box, and up I goes like a sky-rocket!"

"So you did, old fellow!" said the others.

18/20   Last came a little feeble, squeaking voice. ("That's Bill," thought Alice.) "Well, I hardly know—No more, thank ye; I'm better now—but I'm a deal too flustered to tell you—all I know is, something comes at me like a Jack-in-the-box, and up I goes like a sky-rocket!"

"So you did, old fellow!" said the others.

Adobe Minion Pro

Designed by Robert Slimbach, this Adobe original was first released in 1990. Later editions soon followed, which included Greek and Cyrillic support as well as the incorporation of OpenType technology.

The design is bound to be a classic in the digital realm as it embodies a number of characteristics associated with traditional Renaissance fonts. The complete family contains three weights and two widths, each with optical size variants, ligatures, small caps, oldstyle figures, swashes, and other added glyphs.

6/9   Last came a little feeble, squeaking voice ("That's Bill," thought Alice) "Well, I hardly know—No more, thank ye; I'm better now—but I'm a deal too flustered to tell you—all I know is, something comes at me like a Jack-in-the-box, and up I goes like a sky-rocket!"

"So you did, old fellow!" said the others.

Mistral

abcdefghijklmnopqrstuvwxyz

ABCDEFGHIJKLM
NOPQRSTUVWXYZ

6/9 "We must burn the house down!" said the Rabbit's voice; and Alice called out as loud as she could, "If you do, I'll set Dinah at you!"

8/11 "We must burn the house down!" said the Rabbit's voice; and Alice called out as loud as she could, "If you do, I'll set Dinah at you!"

11/14 "We must burn the house down!" said the Rabbit's voice; and Alice called out as loud as she could, "If you do, I'll set Dinah at you!"

14/16 "We must burn the house down!" said the Rabbit's voice; and Alice called out as loud as she could, "If you do, I'll set Dinah at you!"

18/20 "We must burn the house down!" said the Rabbit's voice; and

24/30 "We must burn the house down!" said the Rabbit's voice; and Alice called out as loud as she could, "If you do, I'll set Dinah at you!"

30/30 "We must burn the house down!" said the Rabbit's voice; and Alice called out as loud as she could, "If you do, I'll set Dinah at you!"

Mistral

Mistral was designed by Roger Excoffon for the Olive foundry in 1953. This unique brush script was named for the strong, cold winds of southern France, and is based on the designer's handwriting. It is a true script, since the letters are designed to connect.

Modern No. 20

abcdefghijklmnopqrstuvwxyz
ABCDEFGHIJKLM
NOPQRSTUVWXYZ
1234567890?!$%&*.;"

6/9 There was a dead silence instantly, and Alice thought to herself, "I wonder what they WILL do next! If they had any sense, they'd take the roof off." After a minute or two, they began moving about again, and Alice heard the Rabbit say, "A barrowful will do, to begin with."

8/12 There was a dead silence instantly, and Alice thought to herself, "I wonder what they WILL do next! If they had any sense, they'd take the roof off." After a minute or two, they began moving about again, and Alice heard the Rabbit say, "A barrowful will do, to begin with."

11/14 There was a dead silence instantly, and Alice thought to herself, "I wonder what they WILL do next! If they had any sense, they'd take the roof off." After a minute or two, they began moving about again, and Alice heard the Rabbit say, "A barrowful will do, to begin with."

14/16 There was a dead silence instantly, and Alice thought to herself, "I wonder what they WILL do next! If they had any sense, they'd take the roof off." After a minute or two, they began moving about again, and Alice heard the Rabbit say, "A barrowful will do, to begin with."

18/20 There was a dead silence instantly, and Alice thought to herself, "I wonder what they WILL do next! If they had any sense, they'd take the roof off." After a minute or two, they began moving about again, and Alice heard the Rabbit say, "A barrowful will do, to begin with."

24/24 There was a dead silence instantly, and Alice thought to herself, "I wonder what they WILL do next! If they had any sense, they'd take the roof off." After a minute or two, they began moving about

MOJO

ABCDEFGHIJKLMNOPQRSTUVWXYZ
1234567890?!$%&*:;"

Mojo

Jim Parkinson designed this font in 1960, and it was popularized during that decade for psychedelic rock-concert posters. The style reflects characteristics from the Art Nouveau period: each letter flows into a rectangular contour, and the upper- and lowercase forms are mixed to create the single set of primarily all caps.

Setting larger blocks of type justified forces the word spacing to open slightly and increases legibility in most lines.

24/24

"A BARROWFUL OF WHAT?" THOUGHT ALICE; BUT SHE HAD NOT LONG TO DOUBT, FOR THE NEXT MOMENT A SHOWER OF LITTLE PEBBLES CAME RATTLING IN AT THE WINDOW, AND SOME OF THEM HIT HER IN THE FACE. "I'LL PUT A STOP TO THIS," SHE SAID TO HERSELF, AND SHOUTED OUT, "YOU'D BETTER NOT DO THAT AGAIN!" WHICH PRODUCED ANOTHER DEAD SILENCE.

Adobe Myriad Pro

abcdefghijklmnopqrstuvwxyz
ABCDEFGHIJKLM
NOPQRSTUVWXYZ
1234567890?!$%&*:;"

18/20 Alice noticed with some surprise that the pebbles were all turning into little cakes as they lay on the floor, and a bright idea came into her head. "If I eat one of these cakes," she thought, "it's sure to make SOME change in my size; and as it can't possibly make me larger, it must make me smaller, I suppose."

24/24 Alice noticed with some surprise that the pebbles were all turning into little cakes as they

11/14 Alice noticed with some surprise that the pebbles were all turning into little cakes as they lay on the floor, and a bright idea came into her head. "If I eat one of these cakes," she thought, "it's sure to make SOME change in my size; and as it can't possibly make me larger, it must make me smaller, I suppose."

14/16 Alice noticed with some surprise that the pebbles were all turning into little cakes as they lay on the floor, and a bright idea came into her head. "If I eat one of these cakes," she thought, "it's sure to make SOME change in

Myriad

This Adobe family, released in 1992, was a collaborative effort by designers Carol Twombly, Christopher Slye, Fred Brady, and Robert Slimbach. The sans serif family includes Greek and Cyrillic glyphs, as well as Old Style figures and a true italic. The full Myriad Pro family consists of condensed, normal, and extended widths in a full range of weights.

6/9 Alice noticed with some surprise that the pebbles were all turning into little cakes as they lay on the floor, and a bright idea came into her head. "If I eat one of these cakes," she thought, "it's sure to make SOME change in my size; and as it can't possibly make me larger, it must make me smaller, I suppose."

8/12 Alice noticed with some surprise that the pebbles were all turning into little cakes as they lay on the floor, and a bright idea came into her head. "If I

MYTHOS

ABCDEFGHIJKLM
NOPQRSTUVWXYZ

Mythos

This Adobe font was designed by Min Wang and Jim Wasco. Fascinated by mythology from around the world, they found inspiration in images of legendary beasts from various cultures.

SO SHE SWALLOWED ONE OF THE CAKES, AND WAS DELIGHTED TO FIND THAT SHE BEGAN SHRINKING DIRECTLY. AS SOON AS SHE WAS SMALL ENOUGH TO GET THROUGH THE DOOR, SHE RAN OUT OF THE HOUSE, AND FOUND QUITE A CROWD OF LITTLE ANIMALS AND BIRDS WAITING OUTSIDE. THE POOR LITTLE LIZARD, BILL, WAS IN THE MIDDLE, BEING HELD UP BY TWO GUINEA-PIGS, WHO WERE GIVING IT SOMETHING OUT OF A BOTTLE. THEY ALL MADE A RUSH AT ALICE THE MOMENT SHE APPEARED; BUT SHE RAN OFF AS HARD AS SHE COULD, AND SOON FOUND HERSELF SAFE IN A THICK WOOD.

Niagara Solid &
Niagara Engraved

abcdefghijklmnopqrstuvwxyz
ABCDEFGHIJKLMNOPQRSTUVWXYZ
1234567890?!$%&*:;"
abcdefghijklmnopqrstuvwxyz
ABCDEFGHIJKLMNOPQRSTUVWXYZ

It sounded an excellent plan, no doubt, and very neatly and simply arranged; the only difficulty was, that she had not the smallest idea how to set about it; and while she was peering about anxiously among the trees, a little sharp bark just over her head made her look up in a great hurry.

Niagara

Rhode Island School of Design graduate Tobias Frere-Jones designed this family, which consists of ten styles. The condensed fonts are reminiscent of the crisp styles available in the 1930s and 1940s.

The designer's wide range of experiences and sources of inspiration in his relatively short career to date have helped him produce numerous fonts, including Armada, Asphalt, Benton Gothic, Benton Modern, Benton Sans, Cafeteria, Citadel, Epitaph, Fuller Modern, Garage Gothic, Grand Central, Griffith Gothic, Hightower, Interstate, Niagara, Nobel, Pietro, Pilsner, Poynter Gothic Text, Poynter Old Style Display, Poynter Old Style Text, Reactor FB, Reiner Script, and Stereo.

Novarese

abcdefghijklmnopqrstuvwxyz

abcdefghijklmnopqrstuvwxyz

ABCDEFGHIJKLM
NOPQRSTUVWXYZ
1234567890?!$%&*:;"

Novarese

Designed by Aldo Novarese for Switzerland's Haas foundry, the International Typeface Corporation licensed it in 1980. Novarese is an aesthetic blend of the old classic forms and proportions, with the new large x-height, low contrast between thick and thin strokes, and wide range of weights. The italic is unusual with its cursive lowercase and upright roman capitals. Novarese is a well-balanced and relatively wide text font.

Novarese
Novarese
Novarese
Novarese

6/9"   An enormous puppy was looking down at her with large round eyes, and feebly stretching out one paw, trying to touch her. "*Poor little thing!*" said Alice, in a coaxing tone, and she tried hard to whistle to it; but she was terribly frightened all the time at the thought that it might be hungry, in which case it would be very likely to eat her up in spite of all her coaxing.

8/12   An enormous puppy was looking down at her with large round eyes, and feebly stretching out one paw, trying to touch her. "*Poor little thing!*" said Alice, in a coaxing tone, and she tried hard to whistle to it; but she was terribly frightened all the time at the thought that it might be hungry, in which case it would be very likely to eat her up in spite of all her coaxing.

11/14   An enormous puppy was looking down at her with large round eyes, and feebly stretch-

14/16   An enormous puppy was looking down at her with large round eyes, and feebly stretching out one paw, trying to touch her. "*Poor little thing!*" said Alice, in a coaxing tone, and she tried hard to whistle to it; but she was terribly frightened all the time at the thought that it might be hungry, in which case it would be very likely to eat her up in spite of all her coaxing.

18/20   An enormous puppy was looking down at her with large round eyes, and feebly stretching out one

Nueva

abcdefghijklmnopqrstuvwxyz

ABCDEFGHIJKLM
NOPQRSTUVWXYZ
1234567890?!$%&*:;"

8/12   Hardly knowing what she did, she picked up a little bit of stick, and held it out to the puppy; whereupon the puppy jumped into the air off all its feet at once, with a yelp of delight, and rushed at the stick, and made believe to worry it; then Alice dodged behind a great thistle, to keep herself from being run over; and the moment she appeared on the other side, the puppy made another rush at the stick, and tumbled head over heels in its hurry to get hold of it;

11/14   Hardly knowing what she did, she picked up a little bit of stick, and held it out to the puppy; whereupon the puppy jumped into the air off all its feet at once, with a yelp of delight, and rushed at the stick, and made believe to worry it; then Alice dodged behind a great thistle, to keep herself from being run over; and the moment she appeared on the other side, the puppy made another rush at the stick, and tumbled head over heels in its hurry to get hold of it;

14/16   Hardly knowing what she did, she picked up a little bit of stick, and held it out to the puppy; whereupon the puppy jumped into the air off all its feet at once, with a yelp of delight, and rushed at the stick, and made believe to worry it; then Alice dodged behind a great thistle, to keep herself from being run over; and the moment she appeared on the other side, the puppy made another rush at the stick, and tumbled head over

Nueva

This 1994 Adobe Multiple Master font by Carol Twombly has eighteen variations in style and weight. In addition to the wide variety of designs, the multiple master configuration allows alteration along two axes, resulting in a great range of possible weight and width variations that can be used in display work, 16 points and above in size.

6/9   Hardly knowing what she did, she picked up a little bit of stick, and held it out to the puppy; whereupon the puppy jumped into the air off all its feet at once, with a yelp of delight, and rushed at the stick, and made believe to worry it; then Alice dodged behind a great thistle, to keep herself from being run over; and the moment she appeared on the other side, the puppy made another rush at the stick, and tumbled head over heels in its hurry to get hold of it;

Optima

abcdefghijklmnopqrstuvwxyz
ABCDEFGHIJKLM
NOPQRSTUVWXYZ
1234567890?!$%&*:;"

Optima

Approximately eight years in the making, Optima was designed by Hermann Zapf and released in 1958. In 1950, Zapf made his first sketches from letters on grave plates dating back to 1530 while visiting a church in Florence. The classically proportioned sans serif forms are designed according to the golden section proportions. In 1952, after careful legibility testing, the first drawings were finished, and this design became one of Zapf's most popular designs.

6/9　　　　"And yet what a dear little puppy it was!" said Alice, as she leant against a buttercup to rest herself, and fanned herself with one of the leaves: "I should have liked teaching it tricks very much, if—if I'd only been the right size to do it! Oh dear! I'd nearly forgotten that I've got to grow up again! Let me see—how IS it to be managed? I suppose I ought to eat or drink something or other; but the great question is, what?"

8/12　　　　"And yet what a dear little puppy it was!" said Alice, as she leant against a buttercup to rest herself, and fanned herself with one of the leaves: "I should have liked teaching it tricks very much, if—if I'd only been the right size to do it! Oh dear! I'd nearly forgotten that I've got to grow up again! Let me see—how IS it to be managed? I suppose I ought to eat or drink something or other; but the great question is, what?"

11/14　　　　"And yet what a dear little puppy it was!" said Alice, as she leant against a buttercup to rest herself, and fanned herself with one of the leaves: "I should have liked teaching it tricks very much, if—if I'd only been the right size to do it! Oh dear! I'd nearly forgotten that I've got to grow up again! Let me see—how IS it to be managed? I suppose I ought to eat or drink something or

18/20　　"And yet what a dear little puppy it was!" said Alice, as she leant against a buttercup to rest herself, and fanned herself with one of the leaves: "I should have liked teaching it tricks very much, if—if I'd only been the right size to do it! Oh dear! I'd nearly forgotten that I've got to grow up again! Let me see—how IS it to be managed? I suppose I ought to eat or drink something or other; but the great question is, what?"

Linotype Palatino

abcdefghijklmnopqrstuvwxyz
ABCDEFGHIJKLM
NOPQRSTUVWXYZ
1234567890?!$%&*:;"

8/11   The great question certainly was, what? Alice looked all round her at the flowers and the blades of grass, but she did not see anything that looked like the right thing to eat or drink under the circumstances. There was a large mushroom growing near her, about the same height as herself; and when she had looked under it, and on both sides of it, and behind it, it occurred to her that she might as well look and see what was on the top of it.

14/16   The great question certainly was, what? Alice looked all round her at the flowers and the blades of grass, but she did not see nything that looked like the right thing to eat or drink under the circumstances. There was a large mushroom growing near her, about the same height as herself; and when she had looked under it, and on both sides of it, and behind it, it occurred to her that she might as well

18/20   The great question certainly was, what? Alice looked all round her at the flowers and the blades of grass, but she did not see anything that looked like the right thing to eat or drink under the circumstances. There was a large mushroom growing near her, about the same height as herself; and when she had looked under it, and on both sides of it, and behind it, it occurred to her that she might as well look and see what was on the top of it.

Palatino

This popular font, based on classical Italian Renaissance forms, was designed by Hermann Zapf in 1950. It consists of eighteen different variations in weight and style.

Zapf gave careful consideration to the fact that at first the design would be printed under post–World War II conditions on inferior paper; for this reason he matched open counterforms with carefully weighted strokes. Zapf named the font after Giambattista Palatino, a master of calligraphy from the time of Leonardo da Vinci. This classic design has remained popular for use in both text and display applications.

Park Avenue

abcdefghijklmnopqrstuvwxyz
ABCDEFGHIJKLM
NOPQRSTUVWXYZ
1234567890?!$%&*;;""

6/9 She stretched herself up on tiptoe, and peeped over the edge of the mushroom, and her eyes immediately met those of a large caterpillar, that was sitting on the top with its arms folded, quietly smoking a long hookah, and taking not the smallest notice of her or of anything else.

8/12 She stretched herself up on tiptoe, and peeped over the edge of the mushroom, and her eyes immediately met those of a large caterpillar, that was sitting on the top with its arms folded, quietly smoking a long hookah, and taking not the smallest notice of her or of anything else.

11/14 She stretched herself up on tiptoe, and peeped over the edge of the mushroom, and her eyes immediately met those of a large caterpillar, that was sitting on the top with its arms folded, quietly smoking a long hookah, and taking not the smallest notice of her or of anything else.

14/16 She stretched herself up on tiptoe, and peeped over the edge of the mushroom, and her eyes

18/20 She stretched herself up on tiptoe, and peeped over the edge of the mushroom, and her eyes immediately met those of a large caterpillar, that was sitting on the top with its arms folded, quietly smoking a long hookah, and taking not the smallest notice of her or of anything else.

29/27 She stretched herself up on tiptoe, and peeped over the edge of the mushroom, and her eyes immediately met those of a large caterpillar, that was sitting on the top with its arms folded, quietly smoking a long hookah, and taking not the smallest notice of her or of anything else.

Perpetua

abcdefghijklmnopqrstuvwxyz

ABCDEFGHIJKLM NOPQRSTUVWXYZ

1234567890?!$%&*:;"

14/16 CHAPTER V: ADVICE FROM A CATERPILLAR
The Caterpillar and Alice looked at each other for some time in silence: at last the Caterpillar took the hookah out of its mouth, and addressed her in a languid, sleepy voice.
"Who are YOU?" said the Caterpillar.

18/20 CHAPTER V: ADVICE FROM A CATERPILLAR
The Caterpillar and Alice looked at each other for some time in silence: at last the Caterpillar took the hookah out of its mouth, and addressed her in a languid, sleepy voice.
"Who are YOU?" said the Caterpillar.

24/23 CHAPTER V: ADVICE FROM A CATERPILLAR
The Caterpillar and Alice looked at each other for some time in silence: at last the Caterpillar took the hookah out of its mouth, and addressed her in a languid, sleepy voice.

Perpetua

This font was designed by Eric Gill in 1928, based on drawings from old engravings. Its first appearance was in a limited edition of the book *The Passion of Perpetua and Felicity*, for which the typeface was named; the italic form was originally called Felicity. The finely drawn forms and serifs have made this Eric Gill's most popular Roman serif font.

6/9 CHAPTER V: ADVICE FROM A CATERPILLAR
The Caterpillar and Alice looked at each other for some time in silence: at last the Caterpillar took the hookah out of its mouth, and addressed her in a languid, sleepy voice. "Who are YOU?" said the Caterpillar.

8/12 CHAPTER V: ADVICE FROM A CATERPILLAR
The Caterpillar and Alice looked at each other for some time in silence: at last the Caterpillar took the hookah out of its mouth, and addressed her in a languid, sleepy

Quixley

abcdefghijklmnopqrstuvwxyz
ABCDEFGHIJKLMNOPQRSTUVWXYZ
1234567890?!$%&*:;"

Quixley

Quixley was designed by Vince Whitlock in 1991. The capitals can be used alone or combined with the lowercase and should be set with close letter and word spacing. Quixley is an eye-catching condensed display typeface whose unusual angles and marked stroke contrast lend it marvelous visual appeal. It should be set closely for best results.

9/12   "I can't explain MYSELF, I'm afraid, sir," said Alice, "because I'm not myself, you see."
"I don't see," said the Caterpillar.
"I'm afraid I can't put it more clearly," Alice replied very politely, "for I can't understand it myself to begin with; and being so many different sizes in a day is very confusing."

24/24   "I can't explain MYSELF, I'm afraid, sir," said Alice, "because I'm not myself, you see."
"I don't see," said the Caterpillar.
"I'm afraid I can't put it more clearly," Alice replied very politely, "for I can't understand it myself to begin with; and being so many different sizes in a day is very confusing."

30/26   "I can't explain MYSELF, I'm afraid, sir," said Alice, "because I'm not myself, you see."
"I don't see," said the Caterpillar.
"I'm afraid I can't put it more clearly," Alice replied very politely, "for I can't understand it myself to begin with; and being so many different sizes in a day is very confus-

Sabon

abcdefghijklmnopqrstuvwxyz
ABCDEFGHIJKLM
NOPQRSTUVWXYZ
1234567890?!$%&*:;"

6/9

"It isn't," said the Caterpillar.

"Well, perhaps you haven't found it so yet," said Alice; "but when you have to turn into a chrysalis—you will some day, you know—and then after that into a butterfly, I should think you'll feel it a little queer, won't you?"

"Not a bit," said the Caterpillar.

"Well, perhaps your feelings may be different," said Alice; "all I know is, it would feel very queer to ME."

8/12

"It isn't," said the Caterpillar.

"Well, perhaps you haven't found it so yet," said Alice; "but when you have to turn into a chrysalis—you will some day, you know—and then after that into a butterfly, I should think you'll feel it a little queer, won't you?"

"Not a bit," said the Caterpillar.

"Well, perhaps your feelings may be different," said Alice; "all I know is, it would feel very queer to ME."

11/14

"It isn't," said the Caterpillar.

"Well, perhaps you haven't found it so yet," said Alice; "but when you have to turn into a chrysalis—you will some day, you know—and then after that into a butterfly, I should think you'll feel it a little queer, won't you?"

"Not a bit," said the Caterpillar.

"Well, perhaps your feelings

14/16

"It isn't," said the Caterpillar.

"Well, perhaps you haven't found it so yet," said Alice; "but when you have to turn into a chrysalis—you will some day, you know—and then after that into a butterfly, I should think you'll feel it a little queer, won't you?"

"Not a bit," said the Caterpillar.

"Well, perhaps your feelings may be different," said Alice; "all I know is, it would feel very queer to ME."

Sabon

This Jan Tschichold 1964–67 design was in response to a request from German master printers to make a font family that was the same design for the three metal type technologies of the time: foundry type for hand composition, linecasting, and single-type machine composition.

Tschichold turned to the sixteenth-century Garamond font styles for inspiration, especially the 1592 specimen sheet issued by the Egenolff-Berner foundry (previously owned by Sabon before his death in 1580), which included a 14-point roman attributed to Claude Garamond and an italic attributed to Robert Granjon. Sabon was a name that separated the new design from the names of Garamond and Granjon.

Souvenir Light

abcdefghijklmnopqrstuvwxyz

ABCDEFGHIJKLM
NOPQRSTUVWXYZ
1234567890?!$%&*:;"

8/12 "You!" said the Caterpillar contemptuously. "Who are YOU?"

Which brought them back again to the beginning of the conversation. Alice felt a little irritated at the Caterpillar's making such VERY short remarks, and she drew herself up and said, very gravely, "I think you ought to tell me who YOU are, first."

Souvenir

Souvenir was originally designed by Morris Fuller Benton in 1914 as a single weight for ATF. It was revived in 1967 by Photo-Lettering and optimized for phototypesetting equipment. When ITC was formed in 1971, ITC Souvenir, designed by Ed Benguiat, was one of its first font families.

11/14 "You!" said the Caterpillar contemptuously. "Who are YOU?"

Which brought them back again to the beginning of the conversation. Alice felt a little irritated at the Caterpillar's making such VERY short remarks, and she drew herself up and said, very gravely, "I think you ought to tell me who YOU are, first."

14/16 "You!" said the Caterpillar contemptuously. "Who are YOU?"

Which brought them back again to the beginning of the conversation. Alice felt a little irritated at the Caterpillar's making such VERY short remarks, and she drew herself up and said, very gravely, "I think you ought to tell me who YOU are, first."

18/20 "You!" said the Caterpillar contemptuously. "Who are YOU?"

Which brought them back again to the beginning of the conversation. Alice felt a little irritated at the Caterpillar's making such VERY short remarks, and she drew herself

ITC Stone Sans

abcdefghijklmnopqrstuvwxyz
ABCDEFGHIJKLM
NOPQRSTUVWXYZ
1234567890?!$%&*:;"

6/9   "Why?" said the Caterpillar.
Here was another puzzling question; and
as Alice could not think of any good reason, and as
the Caterpillar seemed to be in a VERY unpleasant
state of mind, she turned away.
"Come back!" the Caterpillar called after
her. "I've something important to say!"
This sounded promising, certainly: Alice
turned and came back again.
"Keep your temper," said the Caterpillar.

8/12   "Why?" said the Caterpillar.
Here was another puzzling
question; and as Alice could not
think of any good reason, and as the
Caterpillar seemed to be in a VERY
unpleasant state of mind, she turned
away.
"Come back!" the Caterpillar
called after her. "I've something
important to say!"
This sounded promising,
certainly: Alice turned and came back
again.
"Keep your temper," said the
Caterpillar.

11/14   "Why?" said the Caterpillar.
Here was another puzzling question; and as Alice could not think of any
good reason, and as the Caterpillar seemed to be in a VERY unpleasant state of
mind, she turned away.
"Come back!" the Caterpillar called after her. "I've something important
to say!"
This sounded promising, certainly: Alice turned and came back again.
"Keep your temper," said the Caterpillar.

18/20   "Why?" said the Caterpillar.
Here was another puzzling question; and as
Alice could not think of any good reason, and as
the Caterpillar seemed to be in a VERY unpleasant
state of mind, she turned away.
"Come back!" the Caterpillar called after
her. "I've something important to say!"
This sounded promising, certainly: Alice
turned and came back again.
"Keep your temper," said the Caterpillar.

ITC Stone Serif

abcdefghijklmnopqrstuvwxyz
ABCDEFGHIJKLM
NOPQRSTUVWXYZ
1234567890?!$%&*:;"

6/9   "Is that all?" said Alice, swallowing down her anger as well as she could.

"No," said the Caterpillar.

Alice thought she might as well wait, as she had nothing else to do, and perhaps after all it might tell her something worth hearing. For some minutes it puffed away without speaking, but at last it unfolded its arms, took the hookah out of its mouth again, and said, "So you think you"re changed, do you?"

8/12   "Is that all?" said Alice, swallowing down her anger as well as she could.

"No," said the Caterpillar.

Alice thought she might as well wait, as she had nothing else to do, and perhaps after all it might tell her something worth hearing. For some minutes it puffed away without speaking, but at last it unfolded its arms, took the hookah out of its mouth again, and said, "So you think you"re changed, do you?"

11/14   "Is that all?" said Alice, swallowing down her anger as well as she could.

"No," said the Caterpillar.

14/16   "Is that all?" said Alice, swallowing down her anger as well as she could.

"No," said the Caterpillar.

Alice thought she might as well wait, as she had nothing else to do, and perhaps after all it might tell her something worth hearing. For some minutes it puffed away without speaking, but at last it unfolded its arms, took the hookah out of its mouth again, and said, "So you think you"re changed, do you?"

18/19   "Is that all?" said Alice, swallowing down her anger as well as she could.

"No," said the Caterpillar.

Alice thought she might as well wait, as she had nothing else to do, and perhaps after all it might tell her something worth hearing. For some minutes it puffed away

ITC Stone
Sumner Stone worked together with Bob Ishi to create the Stone family of fonts, which appeared 1987–88. The family consists of three types of very legible fonts: a serif, a sans serif, and an informal style.

As it turns out, *ishi* is the Japanese word for "stone," which precluded any need to find another name for the font families.

Times New Roman

abcdefghijklmnopqrstuvwxyz
ABCDEFGHIJKLM
NOPQRSTUVWXYZ
1234567890?!$%&*:;"

6/9 "I'm afraid I am, sir," said Alice; "I can't remember things as I used—and I don't keep the same size for ten minutes together!"
"Can't remember WHAT things?" said the Caterpillar.
"Well, I've tried to say 'HOW DOTH THE LITTLE BUSY BEE,' but it all came different!" Alice replied in a very melancholy voice.
"Repeat, 'YOU ARE OLD, FATHER WILLIAM,'" said the Caterpillar.

8/12 "I'm afraid I am, sir," said Alice; "I can't remember things as I used—and I don't keep the same size for ten minutes together!"
"Can't remember WHAT things?" said the Caterpillar.
"Well, I've tried to say 'HOW DOTH THE LITTLE BUSY BEE,' but it all came different!" Alice replied in a very melancholy voice.
"Repeat, 'YOU ARE OLD, FATHER WILLIAM,'" said the Caterpillar.

11/14 "I'm afraid I am, sir," said Alice; "I can't remember things as I used—and I don't keep the same size for ten minutes together!"

14/16 "I'm afraid I am, sir," said Alice; "I can't remember things as I used—and I don't keep the same size for ten minutes together!"
"Can't remember WHAT things?" said the Caterpillar.
"Well, I've tried to say 'HOW DOTH THE LITTLE BUSY BEE,' but it all came different!" Alice replied in a very melancholy voice.
"Repeat, 'YOU ARE OLD, FATHER WILLIAM,'" said the Caterpillar.

18/20 "I'm afraid I am, sir," said Alice; "I can't remember things as I used—and I don't keep the same size for ten minutes together!"
"Can't remember WHAT things?" said the Caterpillar.
"Well, I've tried to say 'HOW DOTH THE LITTLE BUSY BEE,' but it all came different!" Alice replied in a very melancholy voice.
"Repeat, 'YOU ARE OLD, FATHER WILLIAM,'" said the Caterpillar.

Washout

abcdefghijklmnopqrstuvwxyz

abcdefghijklmnopqrstuvwxyz

ABCDEFGHIJKLM

NOPQRSTUVWXYZ

1234567890?!$%&*•:;"

Washout

Washout, designed by Barry Deck, self-proclaimed type cynic, produces an image that gives the impression that the printer has failed to ink the presses properly, or someone has made cheap photocopies of the letters to save money. "It's a recipe font. Anyone can do it at home and come up with some result," says Deck.

The creation of Washout involves tools available to almost everyone involved in the contemporary design industry. Type is drawn, auto-traced in Freehand, and then scanned into Photoshop, where it is blurred and the contrast levels exaggerated.

Washout is featured in a poster advertising a one-day conference sponsored by the American Center for Design in Chicago, 1992, titled "Flirting with the Edge." The poster's message is an indication of Deck's perception of the creative process and of his Symbolist approach to visual solutions.

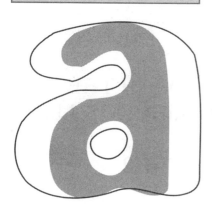

9/12 **Alice said nothing: she had never been so much contradicted in her life before, and she felt that she was losing her temper.**

"Are you content now?" said the Caterpillar.

"Well, I should like to be a LITTLE larger, sir, if you wouldn't mind," said Alice: "three inches is such a wretched height to be."

"It is a very good height indeed!" said the Caterpillar angrily, rearing itself upright as it spoke (it was exactly three inches high).

"But I'm not used to it!" pleaded poor Alice in a piteous tone. And she thought of herself, "I wish the creatures wouldn't be so easily offended!"

"You'll get used to it in time," said the Caterpillar; and it put the hookah into its mouth and began smoking again.

11/16 **Alice said nothing: she had never been so much contradicted in her life before, and she felt that she was losing her temper.**

"Are you content now?" said the Caterpillar.

"Well, I should like to be a LITTLE larger, sir, if you wouldn't mind," said Alice: "three inches is such a wretched height to be."

"It is a very good height indeed!" said the Caterpillar angrily, rearing itself upright as it spoke (it was exactly three inches high).

"But I'm not used to it!" pleaded poor Alice in a piteous tone. And she thought of herself, "I wish the creatures wouldn't be so easily offended!"

"You'll get used to it in time," said the Caterpillar; and it put the hookah into its mouth and began smoking again.

Wide Latin

Wide Latin

Typefaces designated as Latins were popular during the last half of the nineteenth century. Attributed to Stephenson Blake in 1884, Latin fonts are readily identifiable by triangular serifs and sharp terminals on the strokes of some of the lowercase letters.

abcdefghijklm
nopqrstuvwxyz
ABCDEGHI
JKLMNOPQ
RSTUVWXYZ123

This time Alice waited patiently until it chose to speak again. In a minute or two the Caterpillar took the hookah out of its mouth and yawned once or twice, and shook itself. Then it got down off the mushroom, and crawled away in the grass, merely remarking as it went, "One side will make you grow taller, and the other side will make you grow shorter."

Zapf Chancery

abcdefghijklmnopqrstuvwxyz
ABCDEFGHIJKLM
NOPQRSTUVWXYZ
1234567890?!$%&*:;"

6/9   "One side of WHAT? The other side of WHAT?" thought Alice to herself.

"Of the mushroom," said the Caterpillar, just as if she had asked it aloud; and in another moment it was out of sight.

Alice remained looking thoughtfully at the mushroom for a minute, trying to make out which were the two sides of it; and as it was perfectly round, she found this a very difficult question. However, at last she stretched her arms round it as far as they would go, and broke off a bit of the edge with each hand.

8/9   "One side of WHAT? The other side of WHAT?" thought Alice to herself.

"Of the mushroom," said the Caterpillar, just as if she had asked it aloud; and in another moment it was out of sight.

11/14   "One side of WHAT? The other side of WHAT?" thought Alice to herself.

"Of the mushroom," said the Caterpillar, just as if she had asked it aloud; and in another moment it was out of sight.

Alice remained looking thoughtfully at the mushroom for a minute, trying to make out which were the two sides of it; and as it was perfectly round, she found this a very difficult question. However, at last she stretched her arms round it as far as they would go, and broke off a bit of the edge with each hand.

14/15   "One side of WHAT? The other side of WHAT?" thought Alice to herself.

"Of the mushroom," said the Caterpillar, just as if she had asked it aloud; and in another moment it was out of sight.

Alice remained looking thoughtfully at the mushroom for a minute, trying to make out which were the two sides of it; and as it was

18/20   "One side of WHAT? The other side of WHAT?" thought Alice to herself.

"Of the mushroom," said the Caterpillar, just as if she had asked it aloud; and in another moment it was out of sight.

Alice remained looking thoughtfully at the mushroom for a minute, trying to make out which were the two sides of it; and as it was perfectly round, she found this a very difficult question. However, at last she stretched her arms round it as far as they would go,

Key Concepts

AA
an acronym for author's alteration: it is used in proofreading as an indication that changes are requested and will be paid for by the client since the changes are not due to a printer's, or to a typesetter's error.

abjads
consonant alphabets represent consonants only, or consonants plus some vowels. Full vowel indication (vocalization) can be added, usually by means of diacritics, but this is not common. Most of abjads, with the exception of Divehi Hakura and Ugaritic, are written from right to left. Examples of abjads are Hebrew, Dhives Akuru, Arabic (sometimes used as both an abjad and an alphabet), Parthian, Nabataean, Middle Persian, Proto-Hebrew, Psalter, Phoenician, South Arabian, Samaritan, Sabaean, Ugaritic, Tifinagh, and Syriac.

accordion fold
a type of paper folding in which each fold runs in the opposite direction to the previous fold, creating a pleated or accordion affect.

Aldine-French Old Style
a variation of the humanistic hand that began to appear around 1500 CE.

alleys
refers to the space between two columns of set type. It is sometimes called a column gutter or column margin.

alphabet
a set of visual characters or letters arranged in an order fixed by custom. The individual characters represent the sounds of a spoken language. There are three types of alphabets: consonant alphabets (called *abjads*), alphabets (called alphabets) which consist of separate vowels and consonants, and those in which the vowels are indicated by systematic modification of the form of the consonants (called *abugidas*). In addition to English, there are Armenian, Avestan, Bassa (Vah), Beitha Kukju, Coptic, Cyrillic, Elbasan Etruscan, Fraser, Asomtavruli (Georgian), Nuskha-Khucuri (Georgian), Mkhedruli (Georgian), Glagolitic, Gothic, Greek, Hungarian Runes, International Phonetic Alphabet (IPA), Korean, Manchu, Mongolian, N'Ko, Old Church Slavonic, Ogham, Old Italic, Old Permic (Abur), Orkhon (Turkish Runes) Pollard Miao, Runic, Santali (Ol Cemet'), Somali (Osmanya), Sutton Sign Writing, Tai Lue, and Thaana.

alternate character
a secondary version of a letterform that is designed as part of the font, but is not the standard or primary form. The alternate character set commonly includes swashes.

American Type Founders
ATF; a company founded in 1892 that consisted of twenty-six branch plants and who held a monopoly on the typesetting industry in the United States until movable type was replaced by phototypesetting.

ampersand
monogrammatic symbol & that replaces the word "and."

ancient
of or relating to a time early in history, or to those living in such a period or time; especially of or relating to the historical period beginning with the earliest known civilizations and extending to the fall of the western Roman Empire in 476 CE.

angle brackets
these two characters < and > appear on your keyboard as [shift key] + comma and [shift key] + period. They are commonly used to set HTML tags off from the rest of the text on the page when composing a Web page for publication on the Internet.

ante meridiem
normally abbreviated as a.m., this refers to the hours of the day between midnight and noon.

apex
the upper point of letters with an ascending pointed form. The point of the apex usually extends beyond the cap line. There are different types of apices including rounded, pointed, hollowed, flat, and extended.

apostrophe
a mark (') used to indicate the omission of letters or figures, the possessive case, or the plural of letters or figures.

Apple Macintosh
also known as the "Mac," this family of personal computers revolutionized the desktop publishing and digital type design industries throughout the 1980s and 1990s.

arabic number
refers to a numeral between 0 and 9 that can be set as Old Style (lowercase) or Lining (uppercase) figures.

arc of the stem
a curved stroke that is continuous with a straight stem, not to be confused with a bowl; examples include *j, t, f, a, n, m,* and *u.* This is also referred to as a shoulder.

arm
the horizontal or upward diagonal stroke of a letterform that attaches to the stem and is free on one end; examples are included in the letters *E, T,* and *K.*

Art Deco	a style of design and decoration with designs that are geometric and with or of highly intense colors intended to reflect the rise of commerce, industry, and mass production, popular in the United States and Europe in the 1920s and 1930s.
Art Nouveau	a painting, decorative design, and architectural style developed in England in the 1880s that spread to the United States and remained popular through 1910. This ornamental style was not only a protest against the sterile Realism, but against the whole drift toward industrialization and mechanization and the unnatural artifacts they produced. It is characterized by the usage of sinuous, graceful, cursive lines, interlaced patterns, flowers, plants, insects, and other motifs inspired by nature.
Arts and Crafts Movement	both an aesthetic and social movement expressing the widespread dissatisfaction with the quality of mass-produced items brought on by the Industrial Revolution, characterized by an admiration for folk art and for the old guilds of medieval craftsmen. The concept was started by John Ruskin and perpetuated by William Morris.
Art Workers Guild	a group founded in 1884 that is considered the precursor to the formal Arts and Crafts Movement approximately four years later.
ascender	the part of a lowercase letterform that extends above the x-height or waist line; examples may include *b*, *d*, *h*, and *k*.
ascender line	the invisible or imaginary horizontal rule that aligns with the top of lowercase letterforms that extend above the x-height or waist line.
asterisk	the * symbol or glyph denotes a footnote.
A-style envelope	often characterized by a square flap, the A-style envelope is used with announcements, small booklets, brochures or promotional pieces, and more recently for distinctive business stationery; A2 measures 4⅜ × 5 ¾ inches, A6 measures 4¾ × 6½ inches, A7 measures 5¼ × 7¼ inches, A8 measures 5½ × 8⅛ inches, A10 measures 6 × 9½ inches, and the slimline measures 3⅞ × 8⅞ inches.
ATF	American Type Founders.
ATypI-Vox system	Association Typographique Internationale was founded in 1957 at the urging of Charles Peignot, of the type foundry Deberny & Peignot. Its primary goal was to minimize type piracy, however, it is now known for its efforts to analyze and promote quality typography. The ATypI-Vox classification organizes typefaces by their design characteristics into ten distinct groups (Humanistic, Garaldic, Transitional, Didonic, Mechanistic, Lineal, Incised, Script, Manual, Black Letter, and Non-Latins) for the benefit of easy typeface recognition and specification.
BCE	refers to the time before the birth of Jesus of Nazareth, also referred to as Christ; the acronym stands for "Before Christian Era" but is now referring to "Before Common Era."
back matter	the information placed after the text in a book, which commonly includes an index, glossary, bibliography, and appendix.
bad break	is a term that refers to widows or orphans in text copy, or a break that does not make sense in the phrasing of a line of copy, causing awkward reading or unclear meaning.
banner	the type design of a periodical, such as a newspaper, newsletter, or magazine, sometimes referred to as the masthead.
bar	the horizontal or oblique stroke, connected at both ends as in an *A* or *H*, sometimes referred to as a crossbar.
barb	a type of half serif found on the horizontal arms of *E*, *F*, *L*, and *T*.
baronial envelope	a more formal, open-sided (OS) envelope with a deep, pointed flap, often used for invitations, greeting cards, and announcements. A no. 4 measures 3⅝ × 5⅛ inches, a no. 5 measures 4⅛ × 5½ inches, a no. 5½ measures 4⅜ × 5¾ inches, a no. 6 measures 4¾ × 6½ inches, and a Lee measures 5¼ × 7¼ inches.

Baroque	refers to a period of Western art and music that took place generally during the seventeenth century, with the high baroque taking place between 1625 and 1675. Primarily, it designates the dominant style of European art between Mannerism and Rococo. Qualities most commonly associated with the Baroque are grandeur, sensuous richness, drama, vitality, movement, tension, and emotional exuberance.
barrel fold	also called a rolled fold, this refers to a piece of paper folded in spiral folds, that has two or more parallel folds that fold in on each other.
Bartarde	a derivative of the Gothic Littera Bastarda, sometimes referred to as Batarde Minuscule, or French Bartarde, the script existed between the fourteenth and sixteenth centuries. Quickly developed as a fast way to write functional script, it soon acquired its own artistic embellishments. It was eventually replaced by the humanist and italic scripts of the Renaissance.
base	also called the platform, this refers to the large background area of a piece of lead type, upon which the letterform is cast.
basis weight	weight in pounds of 500 sheets (one ream) of a standard basic size. For example, the standard basic size for text paper measures 25 × 38 inches. A ream of basis 70 text sheets in that size weighs 70 lbs. The basic size for cover papers measures 20 × 26 inches. Weighing 500 sheets of any grade of paper in its proper basic size will determine its basis weight. In other words, 500 sheets of 17 × 22 inch, 24 pound bond will weigh 24 pounds.
Baskerville	the name of a transitional-style typeface designed in the eighteenth century by John Baskerville.
baseline	the invisible or imaginary horizontal rule on which all the bottom serifs and terminals align or sit.
basis weight	of a paper stock is the designated fixed weight of 500 sheets, measured in pounds, in that paper's basic sheet size; note that the "basic sheet size" is not the same for all types of paper.
Bauhaus	an art school founded in Weimar, Germany, in 1919 by architect Walter Gropius. The anti-academic character of the school was fostered by Johannes Itten, Josef Albers, Laszlo Moholy-Nagy, Wassily Kandinsky, Paul Klee, and Oskar Schlemmer. In 1926 the school moves to Dessau, Germany, and is finally closed by the Nazis in 1933. The New Bauhaus was founded in Chicago in 1937 under the direction of Laszlo Moholy-Nagy, until his death in 1946.
beak	a type of half serif found on the horizontal arms of *E*, *F*, *L*, and *T*.
bitmap	a binary representation in which a bit or set of bits corresponds to some part of an object such as an image or font. For example, in monochrome systems, one bit represents one pixel onscreen. For gray scale or color, several bits in the bitmap represent one pixel or group of pixels. The term may also refer to the memory area that holds the bitmap.
Black Death	believed to have been a combination of bubonic and pneumonic plagues that entered Europe along Eastern trade routes, and swept across Europe between 1347–1350. It was spread by rats carrying infected fleas, the Plague eliminated between one-fourth and one-third of the population in its first wave. Subsequent outbreaks, which continued into the seventeenth century, were far less severe. The Black Death had profound effects on all aspects of medieval life and deeply affected the psychological outlook of Europeans.
black letter	a family of type characterized by closely spaced and heavy minuscule stems developed during the fourteenth and fifteenth centuries in Europe; this style of type is sometimes named Old English or Textura. A heavy angular condensed typeface used especially by the earliest European printers and based on handwriting, used chiefly in the thirteenth to the fifteenth centuries.
bleed	in printing, an image that extends off the edge of the page or envelope. Envelopes with bleed generally must be printed before they are folded, since the fold line runs through the printed image.
Bodoni	a modern-style typeface designed by Giambattisti Bodoni, known for the contrast between the strokes and the clean, hairline serifs.
body copy	also referred to as *body text*; the main content textual matter commonly set in one font with consistent leading and column width in an article, story, or book.
body line	another name for the line that indicates the x-height or body height of a particular font, in reference to the anatomical identification of the different parts of a letterform.
body text	also referred to as *body copy*.

bold face	a variation of a font with heavy strokes that appears thicker and more massive in which the counter space is minimized; this is used to contrast with regular text for emphasis.
bond weight	typically an uncoated paper, 20 lb. bond paper is the standard for copy machines today while 24 lb. paper is usually used for letterhead.
Book of Hours	popular prayer book of the Middle Ages commonly owned and used by the laity; canonical hours, called horae, divided the day into eight periods named Matins, Lauds, Prime, Terce, Sext, Nones, Compline, and Vespers. Many printers chose this as a topic to print following the proliferation of printing presses and literacy among common people, so a thriving publishing economy developed around the production of books of hours.
book weight	either coated or uncoated paper with 30–100 lb. weights for 500 standard-sized sheets. Book paper is typically used for lesser grade projects like books, magazines, and posters.
booklet envelope	often characterized by a wallet flap, booklet envelopes are available in a wide variety of text papers to match an enclosure such as an annual report, brochure, or sales literature. They are also used for volume mailings and direct mail. The no. 3 measures 4¾ × 6½ inches, no. 5 measures 5½ × 8⅛ inches, no. 6 measures 5¾ × 8⅞ inches, no. 6½ measures 6 × 9 inches, no. 6⅝ measures 6 × 9½ inches, no. 6¾ measures 6½ × 9½ inches, no. 7¼ measures 7 × 10 inches, no. 7½ measures 7½ × 10½ inches, no. 9 measures 8¾ × 11½ inches, no. 9½ measures 9 × 12 inches, no. 10 measures 9½ × 12⅝ inches, no. 13 measures 10 × 13 inches.
boustrephedon	writing with alternating lines in opposite directions; one line is written from left to right, then the next line is reversed (mirrored) and written from right to left. The Greeks called this Phoenician method of writing in alternating directions *boustrephedon* which means "like the ox plows a field."
bowl	the curved stroke that encloses a space within a character. In an open bowl the stroke does not meet the stem, whereas in a closed bowl the stroke meets the stem.
bracketed serif	a serif in which the transition from the stem stroke to the serif stroke is one continuous curve; there are varying degrees of bracketing.
bracketing	the rounded transitional area between the stem stroke and the serif on a letterform.
brackets	the symbols { } used in algebraic formulas.
break	the place where type is divided into a new line or new paragraph.
British Standards	a system of typeface classification developed in 1967 which generally follows the Style Era classification system. There is less distinction between Old Style categories (with the Dutch-English Old Style not defined) and more subcategories in the sans serif category. Additional categories of Glyphic and Graphic are included. In addition, significance is applied to the general shape characteristics of serifs and some general design differences in certain letterforms. The category designations in this system includes: I. Humanist; II. Garalde, III. Transitional, IV. Didone, V. Slab serif, VI. Lineale, VII. Glyphic, VIII. Script, and IX. Graphic.
broken	one of the construction attributes of stroke and stroke relationships identified in Catherine Dixon's descriptive framework.
bubble jet printer	a type of inkjet printing which uses tiny resistors to create heat which vaporizes ink to create a bubble. The expansion that creates the bubble causes a droplet to form and eject from the print head.
bullet	a small, solid circle that is used to introduce listed items or categories
byline	the name of the writer, appearing at the top of an article. Artists and photographers typically get credits. When the reporter's name appears at the end, it often is preceded by a dash and is called a signer.
CE	refers to the time following the death of Jesus Christ, formerly known as AD or anno domini; the acronym stands for "Common Era."

calendering or **calendered**	named for a stack of smooth metal calendar rollers used to smooth the surface of paper during the finishing process. Often the paper is flooded with a liquid claylike coating before it is run through the calendaring stacks to produce a hard, shiny paper surface.
California job case	the large, shallow drawers used to sort hand-set lead type into small compartments; the character compartments were arranged according to their frequency of use.
callout	a selection of a word or phrase from an article or story that is set in larger, often bolder type from the body copy text for emphasis.
cap height	the typesetting term referring to the size of a typeface measured from the baseline to the top of the capital letters
cap line	In studying type anatomy, this is the line that indicates where the top of the capital or majuscule letters align. It is imaginary, or invisible in typeset text.
capital	the uppercase or majuscule letters of an alphabet, the original form of ancient Roman characters, sometimes referred to as caps.
Capitalis Quadrata	was a type style developed by the Romans from the original Greek alphabet, and was ready in its final timeless shape at around 200 BCE. The dominant characteristic part of the style is that all of its letters are designed within a specific relationship to a square that has the height of the type as the length of its sides. Since this alphabet contained only capital letters, and diacritical marks were not yet invented, the side length of that square was always as long as the height of these capitals.
caption	small descriptive copy placed near an illustration or photograph indicating the content of the image.
Carolingian hand	also known as littera gallica, is a script developed during the reign of Charlemagne (768–814 CE), especially in monastaries of Saint Martin of Tours, Corbie, Aachen, Lucca, to propagate reforms in liturgy, scholasticism, and empire, was rediscovered in the 15th century as littera antiqua when it was renovated and later copied by the first printers.
cartouche	the oval band symbolizing continuity encloses hieroglyphs of a god's or pharaoh's name (nomen and prenomen) into one visual entity. Its use was similar to the modern logo.
cast coated	a coated paper with a high-gloss finish. While the coating is still wet the paper is pressed or cast against a polished, hot, metal drum.
catalog envelope	also called presentation envelopes, these usually feature a main center seam running the length of the envelope for greater structural strength. No. 1 measures 6 × 9 inches, no. 1¾ measures 6½ × 9½ inches, no. 3 measures 7 × 10 inches, no. 6 measures 7½ × 10½ inches, no. 8 measures 8½ × 11¼ inches, no. 9¾ measures 8¾ × 11¼ inches, no. 10½ measures 9 × 12 inches, no. 12½ measures 9½ × 12½ inches, no. 13½ measures 10 × 13 inches, no. 14½ measures 11½ × 14½ inches, no. 15 measures 10 × 15 inches, and no. 15½ measures 12 × 15½ inches.
cedilla	the diacritical mark ¸ placed under a letter (as ç in French) to indicate an alteration or modification of its usual phonetic value (as in the French word façade).
Celtic	refers to the old subfamily of the Indo-European language family comprised of the peoples of England, Ireland, Scotland, Wales, Brittany, and a number of Teutonic lands; pertaining or referring to the Welsh, Cornish, or Scots Gaelic peoples.
centered	also referred to as CLL or centered line for line; a typesetting term referring to lines of text whose center points are vertically aligned.
character	a letter, punctuation mark, symbol, or numeral.
character count	an estimation of the number of characters in a particular article, story, or book manuscript.
character per pica	also referred to as CPP; this is a close approximation of the average number of characters of a font that will fit into one pica of space.

chase	probably from French châsse frame, reliquary, from Middle French chasse, from Latin capsa; a rectangular steel or iron frame in which letterpress matter is locked (as for printing).
Civilité	a typeface designed by Robert Granjon, who created a fourth major typeface to be different from and stand alongside roman, italic, and Gothic; reminiscent of a cursive Gothic, it ultimately found its only acceptance as a display face and was not utilized in the printing of books.
Cloister Old Style	a font that was originally designed by Morris Fuller Benton that was widely popular and belonged to ATF; It was based on Nicolas Jenson's roman cut.
coated	a term that refers to paper manufactured with a thin surface coating of clay. This surface coating produces a sharp, finely detailed image because it prevents ink from absorbing into the fibers.
codex	a book of paper or parchment pages bound with board covers; distinct from an ancient volume in scroll form.
coin envelope	similar in appearance to an OE policy envelope, it is much smaller and commonly constructed from kraft paper. A standard coin envelope measures 3⅜ × 6 inches, no. 1 measures 2½ × 4¼ inches, no. 3 measures 3 × 4½ inches, no. 4 measures 3 × 4⅞ inches, no. 6 measures 3½ × 6½ inches, no. 7 measures 4⅛ × 9½ inches.
cold type	the term for photocomposed type, in which no heat is required for typesetting.
colon	a punctuation mark (:) that separates the main portion of a sentence from what follows, usually some form of list.
colophon	an inscription at the end of a printed manuscript or book that contains facts regarding production; usually the artists, designer, printers, typefaces, and paper are identified.
color bar	refers to a series of small blocks and patterns of colors at the edge of a printed piece used to measure and control the quality of the color printing of the piece. These color squares are used to verify the accuracy of the film used to make printing plates, and are used by a press operator to help calibrate the printing press.
column rule	a line used between two columns of type
comma	a punctuation mark (,) used to indicate the separation of elements within the grammatical structure of a sentence.
commercial envelope	is widely used for business and personal correspondence and may be filled using machine insertion. The No. 6¼ measures 3½" × 6 inches, no. 6¾ measures 3⅝" × 6½ inches, no. 8⅝ measures 3⅝ × 8⅝ inches, no. 7 measures 3¾" × 6¾ inches, monarch also known as no. 7¾ measures 3⅞ × 7½ inches, policy, also known as no. 9 measures 4" × 9 inches, no. 10 measures 4⅛ × 9½ inches, no. 11 measures 4½" × 10⅜ inches, no. 12 measures 4¾ × 11 inches, no. 14 measures 5 × 11½ inches, and no. 16 measures 6 × 12 inches.
comp	a slang or shortened term referring to a comprehensive layout that is a close approximation of the final composition; used for communicating to the client for approval and the printer for production cost estimates.
concave	curving inward.
condensed type	type that has been compressed along the horizontal axis, resulting in a tall, thin appearance; sometimes called compressed, a condensed face is taller than it is wide.
connotative evaluation	refers to the subjective associations assigned to the visual characteristics of a font. This includes thoughts and feelings and visual reminders that the viewer associates with the particular aesthetic.
construction	refers to a category of formal attributes in Catherine Dixon's descriptive framework that describes the assembly of the typeface components, such as strokes.
Constructivism	refers to an abstract art movement that appeared in Russia around 1915. Attributed to Vladimir Tatlin, the movement is characterized as the use of art for utilitarian purposes. During this period, art is seen as scientific activity, involving the exploration of line, color, surface, and construction, and the Constructivists sought to apply their ideas to political and social issues.
contrast	refers to opposition or dissimilarity. In visual perception, contrast is the difference in visual properties that makes an object, shape, or form distinguishable from other objects, shapes, forms, and the background.

continuous	an attribute of stroke and stroke relationships in the construction category of Catherine Dixon's descriptive framework.
convex	curving or bulging outward.
copperplate engraving	is a term that may refer to an intaglio printing process in which the image is engraved into copper, inked, and printed; this term is also used to refer to a style of type design that was derived from styles used in copperplate engraving prints.
Coptic	the name given to the latest stage of the Egyptian language, as well as to the script used in writing it. Egyptian is within the category of the Hamito-Semitic family of languages, dating back to the fourth millennium BCE. Egyptian was first written in hieroglyphic script which was later simplified into Hieratic, then Demotic script.
copy	the text for a particular project supplied by the client or by a copywriter on behalf of the client; it comes in typewritten form ready to be typeset.
copy fit	the process of specifying type in a particular font intended to fit into a designated area in the final composition.
counter	a negative space within a character that may be fully or partially enclosed.
cover weight	the heaviest paper that is typically used for postcards, business cards, paperback book covers, and so on. Typical cover stock paper weights are 60–100 lbs.
CPP	acronym that refers to the term "characters per pica."
credit	the small text next to a photograph or illustration that indicates the artist or photographer's name.
crop marks	small lines placed at the edge of the corners of mechanical art to indicate where the poster, brochure, or page should be trimmed after printing.
cross bar	the horizontal or oblique stroke connected at both ends as in an A or H, sometimes referred to as a bar.
cross stroke	the horizontal stroke cutting across the stem of a letter, as in t and f where both ends of the stroke are free.
Crotch	the pointed space where an arm or arc meets a stem; an acute crotch is less than 90° and an obtuse crotch is greater than 90˚.
Crusades	historically, the Crusades were a series of several military campaigns, usually sanctioned by the papacy, that took place during the eleventh through the thirteenth centuries. Originally, they were Roman Catholic endeavors to capture the Holy Land from the Muslims, however, some were directed against other Christians, such as the Fourth Crusade against Constantinople and the Albigensian Crusade against the Cathars of southern France.
Cubism	refers to an early twentieth-century art movement attributed to Pablo Picasso and Georges Bracque, which is based on the simultaneous presentation of multiple views, disintegration, and the geometric reconstruction of objects in flattened, ambiguous pictorial space, so figure and ground merge into one interwoven surface of shifting planes. It appeared around 1908 and continues to be one of the most influential schools of visual representation today.
cuneiform	a written language of characters formed by the arrangement of small wedge-shaped elements and used in ancient Sumerian, Akkadian, Assyrian, Babylonian, and Persian writing, believed to have been developed by the Sumerians.
curly braces	brackets or punctuation marks { } that are used in pairs to set apart or interject text within other text.
cursive	handwriting or type style variation of a script in which the letterforms are slanted but not necessarily connected.
cutline	a caption. The term comes from the day when engravings or "cuts" were used to make the impression on the page.
Dada	this influential international intellectual movement was founded in Zurich in 1916 by a group of artists and writers. The Dadaists rejected and ridiculed the values, ideas and culture of the society that they believed were responsible for the destruction and brutality of World War I. The rejection of traditional values and ideas in art led the Dada artists to pioneer many new and original approaches to art and art making including the use of found objects, chance and irrational thought and performance.

dagger	(†) is a typographical symbol or glyph. It is also called an obelus, from a Greek word meaning "roasting spit" or "needle"; or obelisk. It is used to indicate a cross reference or footnote.
daisy wheel printer	this was little more than an electric typewriter that was capable of accepting data from a computer and producing typewriter-quality output. To print a character, the printer rotates the daisy wheel until the desired letter is facing the paper. Then a hammer strikes the disk, forcing the character to hit an ink ribbon, leaving an impression of the character on the paper. The daisy wheel can be changed to print different fonts.
decoration	is one of the formal attributes in Catherine Dixon's descriptive framework. The term refers to attributes that describe some of the common motifs and treatments used when detailing letterforms. Common motifs include abstract scrolls, medallions, and flourishes or the more pictorial forms of flowers and foliage. Decorative treatments include the use of inline and outline, shadowing, cameos (reversing out), shading, and stenciling.
decorative	refers to typefaces, also known as novelty faces, which are designed to be used for a word or words in display or headings since they are not legible at small text sizes. While one kind of decorative type face seeks to create a mood and is therefore highly emotive, another kind may be designed to represent something else: computer printouts, baseball bats, balloons, etc. The majority of these types are designed as a single font only with perhaps only a handful containing a small family such as normal, bold and outline.
demography	the statistical study of human populations, especially with reference to size and density, distribution, and vital statistics.
demotic script	an Egyptian script that lasted for about 1000 years following hieratic script, and belongs to the last period of ancient Egyptian history. Demotic script was used for business and literary purposes, while hieratic was used for religious texts. Derived from hieratic script, it has a more cursive form, signs are more flowing and joined, and the signs themselves are more similar to one another, and therefore slightly more difficult to read.
denotation	of a specific font is an analytical description of its serifs and bracketing, terminal formation, stroke direction, and stroke weight.
descender	the section of a lowercase character that extends below the baseline, as seen in examples such as *g, j, p, q,* and *y.*
descender line	the invisible or imaginary horizontal rule that aligns along the bottom edge of the lowercase letters that extend below the baseline.
De Stijl	means "the style" and refers to a somewhat purist movement in art, architecture and design that evolved out of the Netherlands, and a magazine published in 1915 of the same name, and is primarily attributed to Piet Mondrian. Also known as "neoplasticism"—the new plastic art sought to express a Utopian ideal of spiritual harmony and order by advocating pure abstraction and universality through a reduction to the essentials of form and color—the vertical and the horizontal directions and the primary colors of red, blue, and yellow along with black and white.
Didot	is the family name of several generations of Dutch printers and typographers. The Didot system of measurement was set forth by François Ambroise Didot. The typeface named Didot is a modern style face originally named for Firmin Didot, a contemporary of Giambattisti Bodoni and the son of François Ambroise Didot.
Die neue typography	refers to a manifesto on modern design by Jan Tschichold, a German designer and typographer, which condemns all fonts but the sans serif as well as centered design (e.g., on title pages). In this publication, Tschichold advocates the use of standardized paper sizes for all printed matter and clearly explains the effective use of different sizes and weights of type to quickly and easily convey information. Although the book remains a classic, Tschichold later abandoned his rigid beliefs and condemned the book as too extreme.
DIN	founded in 1917, the Deutches Institut für Noruing or the German Institute for Standardization sets forth the standard systems of product testing and quality assurance, commerce, measurement standards, environmental protection, and any other area of standardization in the public domain. Specifically as it relates to the printing and type industries, DIN refers to the measurement system used to define paper sizes and envelope dimensions in mm.
dingbat	decorative printer's marks or symbols sized as a font and used for typesetting accentuation.
display	refers to type sizes above 14 points in size, and decorative styles of type usually used to set headline copy.

dot matrix printer a type of printer that produces characters and illustrations by striking pins against an ink ribbon to print closely spaced dots in the appropriate shape. Dot matrix printers are relatively expensive and do not produce high-quality output, and are relatively noisy.

double dagger (‡) a typographic glyph, considered a variant of the dagger with two "handles," and is also called a diesis. It is used to indicate a second cross reference or footnote.

drop cap an initial capital letter that is set larger than the body text by 2 to 4 lines in height for emphasis at the beginning of an article, story, or chapter; it is set so its baseline aligns with a subsequent line of text below

dull-coated refers to a coated paper stock that is low gloss, usually made to standard book sizes and weight, and is suitable for printing fine halftones since the paper does not absorb the ink.

Dutch-English Old Style in the seventeenth and eighteenth centuries vertical stressing appeared on lowercase letterforms as part of the last development stage of the Old Style classification. Typeface examples include: ITC Boutros Setting Medium, Caslon 540, Fairfield, Granjon, Janson, Ryumin L-KL, Times Roman, and Weiss.

ear the small, sometimes rounded stroke projecting from the top of the lowercase g, r, f, and a.

Egyptian refers to roman-style type with heavy slab serifs that appeared during the late nineteenth century. Some believed that they were named as such because of the social preoccupation with Egypt and archeological research being conducted simultaneously; other historians speculate that this style became known as Egyptian because their slablike serifs reflected the rigidity of ancient hieroglyphics.

elite refers to monospaced typewriter text that measures twelve characters to the inch.

ellipsis a combination of three periods (...) set in text type to indicate omitted material or a pause, sometimes used in place of a semicolon.

em refers to a typographic dimension that is equal to the square of the font size; that is, if the type is set in 14-point size, then an em would measure 14 points. An em is the correct measure to indent paragraphs in traditionally typeset text.

em dash sometimes called a mutt dash; a dash that is the length equal to the square of the point size of type, commonly specified to join two phrases together into one sentence instead of using a conjunction, to insert information that could have been included in parentheses, or to add a final thought or emphasis at the end of a sentence, or as a leader before the author's name at the end of a poem, article, or story.

em space sometimes called a mutt space; a space that is the length equal to the square of the point size of type, commonly specified for typeset paragraph indentation.

Émigré magazine an experiemental graphic design journal founded by Rudy VanderLans and Zuzanna Licko; it showcases contemporary typography and entertains contemporary social issues and technological issues with regard to the graphic design community.

en a typographic dimension that is half of an em. If the type is set in 14 points, the em dimension would be 14 points and the en dimension would equal seven points.

en dash sometimes called a nut dash; refers to a dash that is equal to the length of an en, or one half of the square of the point size of type; it replaces "to" in typeset text, as in "6–9 P. M."

en space sometimes called a nut space; refers to a space that is equal to the length of an en, or one half of the square of the point size of type.

envelope converter the name of a manufacturing establishment that specializes in the production of envelopes.

exclamation mark a punctuation mark (!), which is also known informally as a bang or a shriek, is used at the end of a sentence or a short phrase which expresses very strong feeling.

extended also called expanded; this term refers to a variation of a type style that appears to have been stretched along the horizontal axis, and is wider in appearance than the corresponding regular version of the font.

extenders	a term used to refer to both the ascenders and descenders, named such because they extend beyond the body of the font.
eye	the counter or enclosed area at the top of a lowercase e.
family	variations of one primary font that have similar characteristics of serifs, strokes, proportion, and optical balance; variations may include weight or width.
feudalism	the system of political organization prevailing in Europe from the ninth to about the fifteenth centuries, having as its basis the relation of lord to vassal with all land held in fee and as chief characteristics homage, the service of tenants under arms and in court, wardship, and forfeiture.
fillet	also called bracketing, this refers to the curved or straight connection between the stroke of a letterform and the serif.
finial	the non-serif ending added to a stroke, which is classified as ball, swash, spur, or hook; the shape of the finial may taper.
flag	decorative, curved strokes connected to the stem of an uppercase gothic or black letter face.
fleuron	a decorative typesetting unit that may be assembled into borders and fanciful dividers; often floral in appearance.
flush left	a typesetting term for specification of line or paragraph alignment along a left-hand margin; the rag or ragged right edge is inferred if it is not specified.
flush right	a typesetting term for specification of line or paragraph alignment along a right-hand margin; the rag or ragged left edge is inferred if it is not specified.
folio	the page number; may include a type, date, or flourish that is placed with the page number on the page.
font	the set of characters including numbers, letters, punctuation, and symbols included in a particular type design of a specific point size.
force-justified	a type of text alignment in a column where the text is set to align with both the left and right margins simultaneously. From a distance it appears to provide a clean layout solution, but from a reader's perspective, white spaces between the words can become distracting, making it difficult to read and decipher the content. Force-justified refers to the fact that even in the short, ending lines of a paragraph which may contain only a couple of words, they are word-spaced to align with the margins.
formal attributes	describe specifc and detailed characteristics of type design and construction in Catherine Dixon's descriptive framework. There are eight categories: construction, modeling, proportion, key characters, shape, terminals, weight, and decoration.
forms	a typographic format used to collect data. These may be typeset with or without lines or delineated spaces for writing, however the clearer the organization and meaning of each blank, the greater the possibility of collecting legible, usable information.
foundry set	also called machine set; a typesetting term that refers to type composed mechanically on a machine without specific spacing adjustments or kerning.
Fraktur	a sixteenth-century German style of letterforms that incorporate curved strokes to soften the angularity of earlier Gothic styles of calligraphy.
French fold	a sheet of paper printed on one side and folded twice into quarters. First it is folded over from left and right, and second it is folded again from top to bottom. This is not an economic use of paper in most applications, but adds strength when a thin, inexpensive paper stock is specified.
furniture	in typesetting, this term refers to the wood or metal spacing material that is used to fill extra spaces in the chase around handset type to assist in locking it into place.

Futurism	a flamboyant literary and artistic movement that developed in France, Italy, and Russia from 1908 through the 1920s that has visual similarities to Cubism. Futurists added implied motion to the shifting planes and multiple observation points of the Cubists; they celebrated natural as well as mechanical motion and speed. Their glorification of danger, war, and the machine age was in keeping with the martial spirit developing in Italy at the time.
galley	originally this term referred to the frame on a platen press that locks up the handset lead type in letterpress printing; today this term refers to a typeset proof from the service bureau that is printed photographically on a continuous long sheet.
gate fold	a three- or four-panel fold where the two outside panels fold inward to meet in the center. In an open gate fold, there are three panels, the bottom of which is twice the size of the folded panels. In a closed gate fold, there are four panels of roughly equal size where the outer panels are folded inward together.
gloss-coated	a term that refers to paper manufactured with a thin surface coating of clay. This surface coating is polished slightly, and produces a sharp, finely detailed image because it prevents ink from absorbing into the fibers.
Gothic	of or relating to a visual style reflecting the influence of the medieval period including a heavy angular condensed typeface used especially by the earliest European printers and based on handwriting used chiefly in the thirteenth to fifteenth centuries; Also the name of the first sans serif font.
grain	the direction of the fibers in a sheet of paper; it is important to determine the grain length for successful scoring and folding without cracking.
gravure	also called intaglio, the printing process in which the plate is etched and the ink lies in the resulting grooves.
greeking	nonsense type set in a particular font and column width to indicate body copy on a comp.
grid	the underlying structure of a composition determined by the designer that is used to indicate column width and height, margins, gutters, type alignment, and image size and placement.
gripper	the area of a printing press that has a series of metal fingers that hold each sheet of paper as it passes through a printing press; this area of a sheet of paper cannot be printed.
grotesk	or grotesque; the European designation for sans serif type or letters when they first appeared.
gutter	the inside margin of a layout where two pages or panels meet, or the inside of book page that is attached to the binding.
H&J	refers to the hyphenation and justification options in a computer software application; most modern programs allow users to refine the standard settings, changing them to meet their own aesthetic preferences.
hairline stroke	the secondary stroke of a letterform, that is commonly thinner than the stem stroke; this term also refers to the weight of the finest rule a typesetter can set, commonly equal to ¼ point in width.
half-uncial	a lettering style dating from the third century; so named because the letterforms are constructed on four horizontal guidelines one-half uncial (a Roman inch) apart. Half-uncials include ascenders and descenders while uncials do not.
hanging cap	also referred to as a hanging initial. A hanging cap is set larger than the body text and extends beyond the left margin of the rest of a paragraph.
hanging indent	a typesetting instruction used to indicate that the first line of a paragraph is set flush left while following lines are indented. This format is typical for bibliographic information following an article or story.
hanging initial	also called a hanging cap; the initial letter of body text set in a larger display size, extending out into the left margin area next to the rest of the paragraph.
hanging punctuation	punctuation set outside the margin so that the type aligns visually along the right or left side of the paragraph either flush left or flush right; an example are hanging quotation marks that are set in the left margin next to the text so that the letterforms align vertically in subsequent phrases.
head margin	the space above the type, appearing on every page.

header	the top portion of information that may be included in the head margin of a publication. It may indicate the title, the chapter name, and/or the page number or folio.
headline	the introductory title usually set in display type of a different font than the text, used to call attention to the article, story, or chapter.
hierarchy	is a system of ranking and organizing things either from most important to least important, least important to most important, or chronologically.
Hieratic script	ancient Egyptian cursive writing, used from c. 2925 BCE until about 200 BCE which was derived from the earlier, pictorial hieroglyphic writing used in carved or painted inscriptions. Hieratic script was generally written in ink with a reed pen on papyrus; most commonly used by priests.
hieroglyphic	a writing system developed in ancient Egypt that used pictographs to represent words and sounds.
hinting	is the name for the set of techniques for restoring, as far as possible, the aesthetics and legibility of a bit mapped font that is scaled to a particular size and resolution. At low computer device resolutions, undesirable rounding effects mean that parts of some characters can disappear, and other parts can appear too thin or too thick. Hints correct this by equalizing the weights of stems and preventing parts of glyphs from disappearing to maintaining aesthetic appearance and legibility down to as low a resolution as is possible.
humanism or **humanistic**	a doctrine, attitude, or way of life centered on human interests or values; especially a philosophy that usually rejects supernaturalism and stresses an individual's dignity and worth and capacity for self-realization through reason; devotion to the humanities and literary culture with the revival of classical letters, individualistic and critical spirit, and emphasis on secular concerns characteristic of the Renaissance.
Humanistic hand	a sixteenth-century writing style also called "Rotunda" that was a more open, rounded form than the condensed, angular black letter that spread from some of the centers of literary arts of the times in France and Italy. The rounder, more flowing hand was embraced by scribes in the art and educational centers because it was faster to write, and it echoed the Carolingian form from the ancient Roman manuscripts saved from the sacking of Europe at the end of the Charlemagne empire.
hyphen	a punctuation mark (-) commonly used between parts of a compound word or between the syllables of a word when the word is divided at the end of a line of text.
hyphenation	the convention of breaking a word according to syllables so that it will fit on a typeset line of copy; most modern publishing software applications allow user-specified settings for hyphenation establishing how many characters can precede a hyphen, how many character can follow a hyphen, and the number of allowable hyphenated endings in a column of type.
IBC	an abbreviation or acronym for the "Inside Back Cover."
icon	a sign (as a word or graphic symbol) whose form suggests its meaning; a graphic symbol on a computer display screen that suggests the purpose of an available function.
iconography	pictorial material relating to or illustrating a subject or the traditional or conventional images or symbols associated with a subject and especially a religious or legendary subject; the imagery or symbolism of a work of art, an artist, or a body of art.
ideogram	signs that depict the object that is drawn. They are direct examples of an object or an action.
ideograph	a sign or character that represents and idea or concept, often comprised of two or more pictographs.
IFC	an abbreviation or acronym for the "Inside Front Cover."
illumination	or to Illuminate; the art of decorating letters or pages with ink and embossing techniques. The art of illumination is most commonly known from medieval Christian texts, wherein the first letter of a text or section of text was enlarged, embellished, and framed with great artistry. Most illuminations from such texts are unique: the monks and scribes responsible for copying the text did so by hand.

imagesetter	a device that uses laser light to expose film at high dpi resolution, usually 1200 dpi or higher. Most have a maximum dpi of 4000. When generating screens or dots for halftones, each dot is created from the smaller dots that are determined by the dpi resolution. Imagesetters come in many different sizes and formats. They can image one page at a time or they can be manufactured large enough to make imposed film for presses.
Incunabula	a book printed before 1501 CE.
indent	the space placed at the beginning of a line to indicate a paragraph break, or to offset a selection of text or tabular matter.
index	an alphabetized reference list at the end of the text of the names and topics and their corresponding pages on which they are found.
Industrial Age	a period of time (commonly 1860s–1900) following the Civil War when the United States experienced a great period of commercial and technological growth as it moved away from an agricultural society.
inferior character	also called subscript; a small character or set of characters placed below the baseline of text, most commonly used to typeset chemical formulas.
Initial cap	the first letter of body text set in a display size and decorative font intended to introduce a new section of type; intended as a design element to indicate the beginning of text, the initial cap commonly shares a baseline with the first line of body copy.
inkjet printing	output from any printer that fires extremely small droplets of ink onto paper to create an image. The dots are extremely small (between 10 and 30 dots per millimeter); they are positioned very precisely and can have multiple colors to produce relatively inexpensive continuous color images and text.
Inline	a typeface that incorporates a white line inside the letterform to simulate the illusion of a raised surface or chiseled, three-dimensional quality.
intaglio	also known as gravure, the method of printing in which a metal substrate is etched or engraved, and the ink lies in the incisions in the plate surface before being transferred to paper.
International Typeface Corporation	a company (known as ITC) which was founded in 1970 by New York advertising designer Aaron Burns, type designer Herb Lubalin, and Ed Rondthaler of Photo-Lettering, Inc. It was an international leader in the distribution of typefaces for over thirty years, and strived to work against font piracy and to work for fair compensation for type designers of the time.
Intertype	the Intertype Linecaster was a typesetting machine that provided commercial competition for the Linotype originally designed by Alfred and Charles G. Harris. In 1957 Harris-Seybold (originally the Harris Automatic Press Company) merged with Intertype Corporation, and became a world leader in typesetting equipment.
ISO	International Organization for Standardization evolved from the 1906 International Electrotechnical Commission (IEC). In 1946, delegates from 25 countries met in London to create a new international organization, of which the object would be "to facilitate the international coordination and unification of industrial standards." The new organization, ISO, officially began operations in 1947.
italic	denotes a style of type that slants 12 to 15 degrees to the right, and is distinct from roman letterforms in construction and terminal structure; not to be confused with oblique.
ITC	acronym for "International Typeface Corporation."
Jugendstil	the German equivalent of the Art Nouveau movement at the end of the nineteenth century, which is characterised by ornamental and asymmetrical compositions incorporating dreamlike and exotic forms with symbols of nature, sexuality, death, and resurrection.
jump head	a headline positioned at the top of a story that continues from a previous page; a jump head is usually an abbreviated version of the original title.
justified	a typesetting term referring to text type that is aligned vertically along both the left-hand and right-hand margins.

Kelmscott Press   one of the most well-known private presses founded by William Morris in 1891. The quality of the printing and binding was unsurpassed at the time.

kerning   the process of adjusting the space between individual characters.

key characters   identify and describe those characters whose treatment is significant in distinguishing one typeface from another. A basic selection might include a single- or double-story *a* and *g*, an *e* with an oblique or horizontal crossbar, an *f* or *J* sitting on or descending below the baseline, a *Q* with a short or long tail, or a tail bisecting the bowl, and an *R* with a straight or curved leg in Catherine Dixon's descriptive framework.

keyline   the outline on mechanical or camera-ready art indicating the placement of type, illustrations, and photographs.

kraft   a type of brown (unbleached), inexpensive paper commonly used for the construction of paper bags.

laid paper   paper with a surface texture made to simulate that of handmade paper screens.

laser printing   uses an electrically charged, light-sensitive photo receptor drum or belt. When the data is received from the computer the laser exposes the charged drum or belt in the areas which correspond to the image areas. This forms an image out of many tiny dots (dpi). The areas of the photo receptor that are exposed by the laser become oppositely charged from the rest of the photo receptor and will accept the oppositely charged particles of toner (which is a powder). The toner adheres to the drum or belt in those areas exposed by the laser and is transferred to the paper. The paper is then passed through hot rollers or some other heat device to "melt" the toner and bond it to the paper.

leader   a series of characters, commonly dots, that are set to lead the eye across the page from one set of information to a corresponding set of information; a leader is commonly used on a table of contents page to lead the reader's eye from the title to its corresponding page number.

leading   the vertical space between lines of type measured from the baseline to the previous or subsequent baseline for consistency; the term evolved from the thin lead spacers of different dimensions used in letterpress printing to open the space for compositional and legibility reasons.

leaflet   a single printed sheet, folded, but not bound.

leg   a stroke that extends downward at less than 90° is a leg, as seen on the letters *k*, *K*, and *R*.

legibility   the characteristics of letters, numbers, graphics, or symbols that make it possible to differentiate one from the other and therefore easily deciphered and understood.

letterpress   the printing method in which the raised surface of the type or blocks transfers the ink onto the paper with the application of pressure.

letter space   refers to the amount of space that separates letters in a word. Additional space between letters may be added (called letter-spaced) for special effect in limited situations at the designer's discretion.

letter spacing   adding space between the characters beyond what is considered normal for legibility and readability purposes; extending the text or head to a specific pica measure.

ligature   a combination of two or more characters that are joined into one form which are not commonly combined in either Arabic or Persian; originally ligatures were cast as one piece of lead to simulate handwriting and to protect the ascenders and descenders on previous and subsequent lines of text.

light face   a thin-stroked typeface in which the negative space is greater in mass that the weight of the strokes; its appearance is light and airy.

line length   also referred to as line measure, this is the length of a line of type described in picas and points, usually in reference to a column of type.

line spacing   another term for leading; the space between vertical lines of type.

lining figures   numerals that align against the baseline of the font and are the same height as the uppercase letterforms, unlike old style figures which include ascenders and descenders.

link	the stroke connecting the bowl and loop of the lowercase g.
Linotype	hot metal typesetting system invented by Otto Mergenthaler that utilizes a keyboard and sets one line of type as a solid piece of lead (called a slug) when the text is input via a keyboard.
lists	typeset as a category of individual terms, one above the next, often set apart by a bullet or dingbat at the beginning of each line or in front of each list item.
lithographic printing	or offset lithographic printing is a process in which ink is applied to the printing plate to form the "image" (such as text or artwork to be printed) and then transferred or "offset to a rubber "blanket." The image on the blanket is then transferred to the substrate (typically paper or paperboard) to produce the printed product.
lithography	printing method using a flat surface in which the area to be printed is receptive to the ink and the rest of the plate is coated with a chemical that resists ink.
Littera Antiqua	believed to be a rediscovered variation of the Carolingian hand in the 15th century (meaning "ancient letter" or "old letter") when it was renovated and later copied by the first printers. During the 15th century the round, neat, humanistic, or Renaissance hand was introduced in Florence and was employed for literary productions, while the needs of everyday life were met by an equally beautiful, though not as clearly legible, cursive hand.
logogram	a single written symbol that represents an entire word or phrase without indicating its pronunciation; 7 is a logogram that is pronounced "seven" in English and "nanatsu" in Japanese; it is a meaningful unit of language by itself. This contrasts with other orthography, such as syllabaries, abjads, and alphabets, where each symbol represents a sound or a combination of sounds which may or may not have meaning on their own.
logotype	the name, symbol, or trademark that is comprised of typographic characters, used to identify a company or product on all collateral materials.
loop	the lower portion of the lowercase g.
lowercase	also referred to as minuscule or lc, these smaller letterforms include ascenders and descenders and are believed to have originated from the semi-uncial or half-uncial lettering style; the name is derived from the location of the small letters in the lower of the two wooden type drawers used by hand compositors.
lowercase numerals	(sometimes referred to as old-style, hanging, non-lining, minuscule, or medieval figures, digits, or numerals) are a style of Arabic numerals designed for visual harmony with running text. They are known in German as Mediävalziffern ("medieval numerals"), in French as chiffres elz viriens, in Italian as cifre non alineate or numeri minuscoli, in Spanish as n meros elzevirianos or cifras de estilo antiguo, and in Polish as cyfry nautyczne ("nautical numerals").
Ludlow	a hand composing stick usually used for setting headlines and display fonts in lead type.
machine-calendared	a process where paper is run between a stack of polished steel rollers which progressively smooth and compact the paper as it moves through the rollers.
main stem	the thickest stroke of a character.
majuscule	the capital version of a letterform, also called uppercase.
margin	the white space from the edge of the text to the edge of the page, located on all four sides of a printed or lettered work.
markup	the instructions for a typesetter on a typed manuscript to ensure correct typesetting; also called type specification or speccing type.
masthead	This term is used to mean three things and can get confusing. It is used to mean the name on page one of a newspaper or periodical (also known as the nameplate), for the box on the editorial page or a periodical with the names of top editors, and also for the box of names, phone numbers, and addresses that appears in the first few pages of a newspaper.
matte finish	uniformly smooth coated paper stock with a dull finish, without luster or glare.

matrices	plural; more than one matrix.
matrix	the piece of brass into which the punch is driven to create an impression of a character; the matrix is placed at the bottom of the precision mold to cast lead type for printing.
mean line	the imaginary line defining the height of lowercase letters excluding ascenders; also called the x-height, body line, or waist line.
mechanical	also called camera-ready art or CRA; refers to the accurate assemblage of all the components of a composition to be photographically reproduced for printing.
metal clasp	the metal closure on the back of larger envelopes, such as the catalog envelope. Two metal prongs protrude through a hole in the envelope flap, then are separated and folded flat to close the envelope.
Middle Ages	the period of European history from about 500 to about 1500 CE.
minuscule	the set of characters, also called lowercase or lc, believed to have evolved from half-uncial lettering that incorporates ascenders and descenders with a smaller body height than majuscules or uppercase characters.
minus	negative space setting between typeset characters.
minusing	decreasing the space between typeset characters in text settings; sometimes called tracking in modern software applications, this affects the entire selection of text equally.
mnemonic	a device, such as a formula, verse, or rhyme, used as an aid in remembering; a technique of improving the memory.
modeling	refers to the contrast in stroke weight ranging from a consistent weight to a highly exaggerated difference in Catherine Dixon's descriptive framework. In addition to the contrast in stroke weight, the stress and the type of transition between the strokes are included.
Modified-Transitional	refers to one subdivision of the Transitional style classification of typefaces characteristed by less contrast and thicker serifs (also known as "new transitional"). Examples include Caslon Antique, Cheltenham, Maximus, and Melior.
modern style	a mechanical-looking face with no bracketing, thin hairline strokes, thin serifs, and vertical stress; Bodoni is a popular example of this class of type.
monospacing	refers to fonts in which each character occupies the same amount of space; in monospaced type, such as that output from a typewriter, the characters align vertically on the page regardless whether it is an *i* or a *w*.
monotone	also referred to as monoline; a typeface in which all of the strokes appear to be the same thickness.
movable type	an invention attributed to Johann Guttenberg in which each character is cast in lead or carved from wood so that it can be used multiple times for multiple printing jobs on a platen press or letterpress.
Multiple Master	a font format that provides designers with the ability to interpolate smoothly between several design axes, from a single font. The axes can include weight, size, and width. Adobe's first Multiple Master Font was Myriad—a two-axis font with weight (light to black) on one axis, and width (condensed to expanded) along the other axis. In the case of Myriad, there are four "polar" designs at the "corners" of the design space. The four designs are light condensed, black condensed, light expanded, and black expanded.
mutt or **mutton quad**	are alternate terms for an em space, used to differentiate from the term en when spoken.
mutt dash	is an alternate term for an em dash, also known as a long dash that is the width of an em, or the square of the point size of the font.
nameplate	a periodical's name on the first page which is also called the "flag" or "masthead," usually set in a special font or combination of characters visually unique to the publication; sometimes referred to as the banner.

negative leading refers to a typesetting specification that indicates the vertical space as being less than the point size of the type. Depending on the amount of negative leading, the lines of type may begin to overlap making them difficult to discern. For example, type set solid would be written as 9/9, whereas the same type with -3 points of leading would read 6/9. Negative leading is used in display text when the headline or phrase takes more than one line of space.

neon a gas that can be enclosed inside glass tubing and used for decorative, sometimes typographic signage.

newsprint a thin, inexpensive, absorbent paper used in manufacturing newspapers.

non-repro blue a light blue color or ink or lead that is not usually discernible in the photographic process; non-repro or non-photo blue is used for keylining mechanical art so that the layout lines drawn on the camera-ready-art board do not photograph when the final art is converted to film and then to a printing plate.

number sign the character #, also known as pound sign and hash sign.

nut dash an alternate term for an en dash that is the length of an en space.

nut quad also called an en space, the term is used to differentiate from em space when spoken.

OBC the acronym that refers to "Outside Back Cover."

oblong binding a book that is bound along the short dimension or side.

OE an acronym for "Open End" that specifies that the flap of an envelope is located on the short side, or end of the envelope, as opposed to the long side of the envelope.

OFC the acronym that refers to "Outside Front Cover."

official envelope also known as a commercial no. 10 envelope, measuring 4⅛" × 9½ inches.

offset lithography a printing method in which the image is transferred from the plate via a rubber roller to the sheet of paper.

Old English the angular, condensed Gothic style of lettering favored in Germanic areas as early as 1012 CE and continuing through the mid-nineteenth century; also called black letter.

OS an acronym referring to "Open Side" in which the flap of an envelope is oriented along the long side as opposed to it being located on the short end.

Old Style a style of type distinguished by graceful irregularity among individual letters, bracketed serifs, and but slight contrast between light and heavy strokes.

old style figures a set of numerals which do not line up along the base line of type. Also known as non-aligning figures.

open leader also called dot leader, this refers to a line of periods spaced out that lead the reader's eye from one set of information to a corresponding set of information on the opposite side of a page.

OpenType a scalable computer font format initially developed by Microsoft and Adobe that is an extension to the TrueType font format.

optically corrected all characters in a font are sized so that they appear to align along the baseline, x-height line, and cap line regardless of whether they are circular, triangular, or square in overall shape and design.

ornament small typographic decoration such as a floret, a graceful curvilinear swash, or dingbat used to indicate a paragraph break or signifying the end of an article.

orphan the first line of a paragraph left at the bottom of a column of type, separated from the rest of the paragraph, or the last line of a paragraph set at the top of a new column; this is undesirable both aesthetically and pragmatically as it interrupts the reader's flow and thought process.

pagination process of numbering pages in consecutive order.

paleography study of old writing founded by Jean Mabillon, a French Benedictine monk (1632–1707).

Papal Chancery	the chancery hand or script was developed during the Italian Renaissance and originally used for formal and informal work by the scribes in the papal offices; a contemporary font based on this type of handwriting is named Zapf Chancery, and was designed by Herman Zapf for ITC.
papyrus	the pith of the papyrus plant cut in strips and pressed into a paperlike substrate or material to write on.
paragraph mark	a type specification symbol indicating the beginning of a new paragraph; handwritten, the symbol appears as a reversed "P" with a vertical line drawn through it.
paraphrase	the process of reformulating and restating the ideas of another author into your own words, while maintaining the same meaning and context.
parchment	originally a writing surface made from dried, processed calf or sheep skins; today made from cellulose fiber paper by dipping unsized stock in sulfuric acid, to simulate the appearance and feel of genuine parchment; called "vegetable parchment" if made from cellulose fiber paper.
pasteup	the process of assembling mechanical art, often utilizing a heated wax adhesive with which compositional components are positioned and burnished into place, then checked for accurate alignment using a t-square and triangle or drafting arm.
patterns	the third primary description component in Catherine Dixon's descriptive framework, which are defined using the two other basic description components of sources and formal attributes. This refers to the visual repitition of a particular combination of formal attributes in a source (or sources).
PDL	acronym that refers to the terms "Page Description Language."
PE	a copy editing mark indicating a printer's (or typesetter's) error as opposed to a designer's error; this was important at one point in time, so that the appropriate party would pay for the correction to the galley or blueline proof.
petroglyph	an elemental sign or pictograph carved or drawn on a rock.
phonemes	any of the abstract units of the phonetic system of a language that correspond to a set of similar speech sounds.
phonetic	representing speech sounds by means of symbols that have one value only; the sounds of speech represented by a set of distinct symbols, each denoting a single sound; spelling that matches the pronounciation of a particular syllable or word.
phonogram	a character or symbol used to represent a word, syllable, or phoneme.
photocomposition	phototypesetting or cold type; the use of negatives of a font, through which light is passed to expose the type onto photosensitive paper or film.
photographic negative	the image in which light and dark regions are reversed on a photographic film; when light is projected through the photographic negative onto a photosensitive substrate under controlled conditions, then a photographic positive is produced.
Photon	the first photographic type compositor invented by two French engineers, Louis Moyroud and René Higonnet, patented in 1944. The Photon combined the technologies of a typewriter key-based entry system, a telephone relay system, and a photographic unit. Letters were typed in by an operator and simultaneously stored in computer memory. On command, the stored letters would call up the correct position on a glass disc that contained the outlines of 1,400 characters of a typeface in different fonts. Once the revolving disc was positioned to the correct letter, a strobe light would expose the letter outline onto photosensitive film. The exposure lasted for microseconds so the process was relatively fast compared to hand composition, with eight characters per second being written to film.
photosensitive	sensitivity to light or direct sunlight.
phototypesetting	another term for photocomposition that refers to photographically reproduced typesetting or cold type.
phrasing	the way in which words are chosen and grouped in writing so that they are easily translated into logical units of thought and meaning when reading.

pica	a typesetting unit of measure equal to approximately $1/16$ th of an inch, 0.013837 inches or 12 points.
pictograph	a pictograph is a symbol that is used to wholly communicate a simple message without words, such as in traffic signs and restroom door signage. A pictograph may be used as a signature, otherwise known as a distinctive mark indicating identity, such as a corporate logo.
pipe	a typographic glyph or symbol also referred to as the "vertical bar" which is commonly used as a mathematical symbol, or to separate hyperlinks in a navigation bar on a Web page.
platen	a flat plate that exerts or receives pressure (as in a printing press).
platform	another term for the lead base, which measures type high (.918 inch), upon which a letterform is cast for hand composition and letterpress printing.
point	a typesetting unit of measure used to specify the height of a typeface equal to approximately $1/72^{nd}$ of an inch or $1/12^{th}$ of a pica.
point size	a typesetting term that is used to designate the dimensions of a font, as measured from the ascender line to the descender line.
policy envelope	a style of envelope that opens on the end (OE) used to enclose legal papers such as insurance policies and real estate deeds, no. 10 measures 4⅛ × 9½ inches, no. 11 measures 5 × 11½ inches, and no. 14 measures 3⅞ × 7½ inches.
post meridiem	this term is commonly represented by the acronym p.m., and refers to the hours of the day between noon and midnight.
PostScript	an object-oriented, page description language (PDL), meaning that it treats images, including fonts, as collections of geometric objects rather than as bitmaps. PostScript fonts are called outline fonts because the outline of each character is defined. Also called scalable fonts, their size can be changed with PostScript commands. Given a single typeface definition, a PostScript printer can produce a multitude of fonts, whereas, many non-PostScript printers represent fonts with bitmaps. There are three levels of the PostScript language.
PPI	an acronym that stands for "pixels per inch."
precision mold	the mechanical mold developed by Johann Gutenberg used to cast lead type. The brass matrix for individual letters were placed in the mold and held into place by the precision mold. The molten lead was poured into the bottom of the inverted mold to cast lead type.
prehistoric	of, relating to, or existing in times antedating written history, or relating to a language in a period of its development from which contemporary records of its sounds and forms have not been preserved.
press bed	the flat surface of a printing press on which the type form is laid in the last stage of producing a newspaper or magazine or book etc.
press type	also called dry transfer; characters on clear plastic film burnished onto a comp for accurate size and placement of a particular font; popular during the late 1970s and 1980s, this method of comping type has been replaced by the personal computer today.
prime mark	a typographic symbol or glyph most commonly used in mathematical equations. It is also used to represent the word "foot" or "feet" in a measurement. That is, 7' refers to something that measures 7 feet long or tall.
proof	refers to a preliminary copy of the intended final composition or typesetting, ready for trial inspection or "proofing," which means to check for errors and indicate any changes before the actual final printing plate or typesetting galley is produced.
proofreader	the person who checks the final typeset galleys for correct spelling, punctuation, grammar prior to creating camera-ready art and again, prior to burning the plates for printing.

proofreader's marks   a standard series of symbols used by those who read and correct manuscripts and typeset galleys, and indicate any necessary corrections. The series of marks are a system of standardized symbols employed by the typesetting and publishing industries.

proportion   a relationship between the parts of a whole as indicated by a ratio.

proportional spacing   fonts designed with specific amount of space for each character, considered more legible than older monospaced type.

pull quote   a phrase from the body text that is set larger, often in a different typeface, as a quotation that summarizes a main idea of an article.

punch cutting   the cutting of a character at the end of a steel bar so that it can be punched into a brass mold or matrix from which lead type is cast.

quad   a space in lead type that comes from the names of the word spacers in handset type composition.

quotation mark   also called quotes or inverted commas, (" ") are punctuation marks used in pairs to set off speech, a quotation, or a phrase. The pair consists of an opening quotation mark and a closing quotation mark.

ragged center   type specification instruction for type to be set with each line centered above or below the next so that neither side aligns; also called centered, the designer commonly specifies the line breaks at logical intervals of the message.

ragged left   type set aligned along the right margin with an uneven left; also specified as flush right/ragged left, or FR/RL .

ragged right   type set aligned along the left margin with an uneven right; also specified as flush left/ragged right, or FL/RR.

raised cap   another term for an initial cap or raised initial.

raised initial   another term for an initial cap or raised cap that is larger and projects above the first line of body copy and may or may not align with the baseline of the first line of text; also called a stick-up or stand-up initial cap.

ranging figure   another term for old style characters that are not always aligned along a standard baseline.

readability   the quality of written language that makes it easy to read and understand.

rasterize   the conversion of an object-oriented image or vector-based graphic into a bitmapped image. All computer files are rasterized when they're printed.

ream   the standard packaging unit for standard size paper which is usually 500 sheets for bond and 250 sheets for cover or card stock.

rebus   pictures and/or pictographs assembled in an order so as to represent the syllables in a word or words, from which meaning can be deciphered; the origin of the word and custom came from the *basochiens* of Paris, during the carnival, used to satirize the current follies of the day in drawn riddles, called de rebus quae geruntur (on the current events).

recto   the right-hand page in a book or spread, also called the obverse.

reference mark   symbol used to indicate a footnote such as an asterisk, numeral, or dagger; may also serve to inform the reader of side notes to the text.

Reformation   a sixteenth-century religious movement marked ultimately by rejection or modification of some Roman Catholic doctrine and practice and establishment of the Protestant churches.

registration   to make ready in such a way or adjust so the colors on the printing press correspond exactly and align in the printed final.

relief   a projection from a flat surface; embossed. The opposite of incuse, engrave, or deboss.

remittance envelope   comes with a large wallet flap and has side seams, and is used by charities, billing agencies, schools, churches, mail order companies, and by other businesses and organizations for ordering or remittance applications. They provide a large printing surface for order blanks and other information required by the sender. No. 6¼ measures 3½ × 6 inches, no. 6½ measures 3⁹/₁₆ × 6¼ inches, no. 6¾ measures 3⅝ × 6½ inches, and no. 9 measures 3⅞ × 8⅞ inches.

resonance   refers to the visual cues and classification of the visual characteristics according to the connotative associations of a particular font.

reverse or reversal   type or image that is set white against a solid background area, sometimes called negative; reversed type appears slightly smaller and thinner than its corresponding face set in black on a white background.

Renaissance   the transitional movement in Europe between medieval and modern times beginning in the fourteenth century in Italy, lasting into the seventeenth century, and marked by a humanistic revival of classical influence expressed in a flowering of the arts and literature and by the beginnings of modern science.

revised proof   a printing proof pulled after corrections are made.

river   a series of white spaces running through consecutive lines of type, creating a vertical white jagged line through the visually gray area of body copy; these occur most frequently in justified text and should be avoided.

rolled fold   a fold created as the pages of a newsletter or brochure are folded one upon the next, as in rolling up a blanket or sleeping bag for storage.

Romaine du Roi   considered a mathematically perfect font, Romain du Roi (Roman of the King) was developed by the French Academy of Sciences under the rule of King Louis XIV. The face was cut at the beginning of the eighteenth century by the royal punch cutter, Philippe Granjean.

Roman face   denoted the upright vertical orientation of a typeface as opposed to either or the slanted versions of italic or oblique type.

Roman numerals   the base 10 numbering system used by Ancient Romans that uses uppercase letterforms to denote quantities: I=1, V=5, X=10, L=50, C=100, D=500, and M=1000.

romance languages   the group of languages derived from Latin. The most spoken Romance language is Spanish, followed by Portuguese, French, Italian, and Romanian.

romanesque   meaning "in the Roman manner"; it is an early medieval style with crude Roman influences characterized by arches and curves, simple geometric arrangements, coarsely rendered animal and plant forms, and painted in decorative hues. Found throughout Europe, the Romanesque style preceded Gothic styles.

Roman Rustica   or also known as Capitalis Rustica; a handwriting style or face developed by the 1st century and was the standard book hand for Latin scribes from the 1st to the 6th century.

Rosetta Stone   a black basalt stone found in 1799 that bears an inscription in hieroglyphics, demotic characters, and Greek and is celebrated for having given the first clue to the decipherment of Egyptian hieroglyphics.

rotolus   a scroll constructed from sheets of papyrus pasted together, measuring approximately 9 inches × 35 feet, used throughout Ancient Greece and Rome.

Rotunda   a form of Gothic script (black letter) from Italy and southern France, with more rounded letterforms than those of more northerly areas. Originally from Carolingian minuscule, sometimes it is not considered a black letter script, but a script on its own.

rough   a preliminary sketch or mock-up of a composition often drawn at full scale in color representing what the final may look like when the project is complete.

roundhand   a style of penmanship comprised of graceful curves and rounded strokes, written with split-point pens and controlled pressures.

rule   a typeset line that may be used alone or as an outline of a shape available in varying thicknesses specified in points.

run-around	text copy set to wrap around a silhouetted image or other design element which may also be referred to as contour-set or wraparound.
runic	refers to a set of alphabets using letters known as runes used to write Germanic languages in the areas we know today as Scandinavia and the British Isles. Some runic inscriptions have been dated to approximately 150 CE.
run-in	a head incorporated into the first line of body copy or introductory phrase of body text commonly set larger, bolder, in italic, small caps, or a different font intended to attract the reader's attention.
running foot or **footer**	refers to a title, design element, rule, and/or folio repeated on every page within the bottom margin area.
running head or **header**	refers to a title, design element, rule, and/or folio repeated on every page within the top margin area.
runover	refers to text that requires more than one line. In a list with a hanging indent, the runover should be indented to align with the left margin of previous lines, and not extend to the left as in a paragraph.
Rustica	also called Capitalis Rustica, this style of writing was derived from the Roman style of calligraphy thought to have evolved from the Roman square capitals; some historians now believe that based on a recent find, the "Gallos Fragment" dates Rustica to about 22 BCE.
saddle stitch	a type of binding that appears as a staple when complete; wire is inserted and bent back through the middle of the center fold to secure the sheets together, with the bent ends of the wire on the inside of the document.
sans serif	letterforms without serifs.
scaling	determining the desired size for an image that will be reduced or enlarged to fit a particular area in the layout.
scanner	an electronic device that translates an image into digital information that can be saved in a variety of digital file formats (for example, .gif, .tiff, .pict, and .jpg) to be saved on disk or printed.
screen or **halftone screen**	a pattern of shaped lines or dots that appear as different levels of gray when printed, most commonly specified in 10% intervals from 0% (white) to 100% (black); measured in dots per inch (dpi), with a larger dot count resulting in a more refined, even tone of very small dots; a larger screen is required for more absorbent papers (85 line for newspapers) and a smaller screen for higher-quality publications on coated paper stock (300 line and above).
script	typefaces based on handwritten, linked characters usually incorporating a right-hand slant and flourishes on the uppercase letters.
scroll	a roll of papyrus, leather, or parchment for writing a document.
semicolon	a punctuation mark (;) used to connect independent clauses, and indicates a closer relation than does a period or full stop.
Semitic languages	a name used to designate a group of Asiatic and African languages, namely: Hebrew and Phoenician, Aramaic, Assyrian, Arabic, Ethiopic (Geez and Ampharic).
serif	a line crossing the terminal of a character that extends beyond the main stroke; some historians theorize that serifs are residual of chisel-cut letters in Ancient Rome.
set-in initial	also called a cut-in initial or Initial cap; a larger first letter of body text that is inset so that it aligns with the left margin as does the body copy.
set solid	a typesetting term that refers to type with no additional leading between the lines; for example, 12-point type with no additional leading would be specified as "set solid" or 12/12.
set width	refers to the width of a character, including minimal letter space on each side.
shape	in Catherine Dixon's descriptive framework, this attribute describes the basic shapes of the Latin alphabet, which are curves and straight lines which may be angular, broken, or fractured, and then round, oval, square, convex, concave, parallel, irregular, or flared. Reference may also be made to specifically named curves (or parts of curves), such as the bowls, as well as the detailing and position of secondary lines, such as crossbars and the overall treatment of counters.

shoulder a curved portion of the stroke of a letterform that connects to a straight stroke, as in the lowercase letters *m*, *n*, and *h*.

sidebar text that is set in a column off to the side of the main text of an article or story, used to describe or present supporting material that clarifies an important point or provides an example to support the main story; often set in a slightly different, but complementary font.

side head a heading set to the side of the page or column of text; a heading set partially into the outer margin of the text and partially into the column of text is called a cut-in side heading.

signer the reporter's or author's name appearing at the end of an article, often preceded by an em dash.

silhouette an image whose background area has been removed.

Sinaitic Script a writing system found in Sinaitic mines that may link Egyptian hieroglyphs to the Phoenician alphabet.

sink a term for distance to the first line of type on a page usually larger on chapter-opening pages to fit in the chapter head.

short fold when the front page of a newsletter or brochure is a shorter dimension than the rest of the publication so that a portion of a second page shows along the right side.

signature a section of a book or magazine, tabloid or newspaper, ordinarily obtained by the folding of a single large printed sheet into 4, 8, 16, or more pages. The term can also be applied to a printed flat sheet that is to be later folded into a multipage document.

simple fold refers to a single crease along the length or width of a sheet that results in a four-page brochure or newsletter.

slab serif refers to a serif font, also sometimes referred to as "Egyptian" that has large, squared-off serifs, usually of the same weight as the main stem stroke. The Industrial Revolution encouraged the development of very bold printing types that could be used for advertising, posters, flyers, and broadsides, which all completed for attention. Examples of slab serifs include Clarendon, Lubalin Graph, New Century Schoolbook, and Memphis.

slash a diagonal line (/) used to represent "per" as in miles/hour or to represent alternatives as in and/or; also named a virgule.

slug two common references for this term as related to typesetting are: a line of type cast as a single piece of metal from a Linotype machine, or secondly, the strips of metal used for spacers to create vertical space on a page in letterpress printing.

small caps smaller capital letters designed to approximately 75 percent the height of the regular version of the typeface, and most commonly set to the x-height of the corresponding font.

sources describe generic formal influences and usefully draw together broad groupings of typefaces, that share underlying similarities in approach or like visual references. Sources identify influences such as decoration or pictorial references, handwriting, ideas of what a roman type is, and so on, according to chronological developments in type from a historical perspective.

spine the main curved stroke of the letter s.

splayed describes the stem of a character that is wider at the top and bottom than it is toward the center.

spread term that refers to the combination of the left- and right-hand pages in a book or periodical.

spur the nodule descending from the vertical stroke of an uppercase G connecting the straight stroke to the curved stroke.

square serif also known as a hairline serif; the stem stroke and serif are attached without bracketing, resulting in a formal or mechanical-looking font; this type of serif is characteristic of the Modern category or classification of type.

squeeze refers to text that is set with tighter than normal spacing between characters, also called tracking or minusing.

stand-up initial   another name for an initial cap that projects above the first line of text and is commonly aligned with the baseline of the first line of text as well; also named stick-up initial or raised initial.

stem stroke   the main stroke of a character.

stet   term used when editing or proofing copy that means to leave a selection as originally typed, disregarding the typesetting specification or correction; "Let the original stand" is the translation.

stress   the thickening in a curved stroke caused by a flat pen tip changing direction during the making of a mark; the thickest point is called the "maximum stress"; a second definition refers to the angle of the thickest strokes in curvilinear letterforms, either oblique (at an angle other than 90 degrees to the baseline) or vertical (at a 90-degree angle to the baseline).

strike-on composition   type that is made by direct impression, such as in the use of a typewriter.

stroke   any line required as part of the basic construction of a letterform, not including serifs or swashes.

style sheets   refers to a function in a desktop publishing software application that allows the user to specify standard and consistent specifications for typesetting different levels such as headlines, subheads, body text and so on. Characteristics such as font, size, color, hyphenation and justification, kerning, and tracking can be set for the complete document, making them easily altered as needed.

subhead   a subordinate heading usually requiring a different typographic treatment than the primary headline or the body text.

subscript   small characters placed below the baseline of the regular font, commonly used to denote chemical formulas; also known as inferior characters.

sunken initial   another name for a drop cap; a large, decorative initial cap often two to four lines tall, whose baseline aligns with the baseline of the corresponding line of body copy so that it sinks down into the set type; also named a drop cap.

supercalendered   coated paper made using alternating chrome and fiber rollers that make a very smooth, thin sheet of paper typically used for magazines, catalogs, and directories.

superior character   small characters placed above the x-height of the regular font used to denote footnotes in body text, or exponents in mathematical formulas; also known as superscript.

superscript   small characters placed above the x-height of the regular font used to denote footnotes in body text, or exponents in mathematical formulas; also known as superior characters.

Suprematism   a Russian abstract art movement that came about around 1913, attributed to Kasimir Malevich (1878-1935). The term, in Kasimir Malevich's own words means "supremacy of forms." It was characterized by flat geometric shapes on plain backgrounds and emphasized the spiritual qualities of pure form.

Surrealism   movement following Dada, formed in the 1920s around the French writer Andre Breton (1896-1966) and his followers, whose main interest was automatism, or the suspension of conscious control in creating art. They preferred things that happened by accident, and dreams, and anything relating to our subconscious. In art this is usually expressed in terms of unusual situations or combinations of things or events which can help to trigger our imagination.

swash   a fancy flourish that replaces the terminal or serif on scripts and alternate characters.

syllable   the smallest conceivable expression or unit of speech; a unit of spoken language that is next bigger than a speech sound and consists of one or more vowel sounds alone or of a syllabic consonant alone or of either with one or more consonant sounds preceding or following.

syntax   the part of grammar that deals with the way in which linguistic elements (as words) are put together to form constituents (as phrases or clauses or sentences).

tables   a type of visual organization in which the columns of information align with the rows of information in such a way as to communicate an informational relationship. Tables are often organized in a chartlike fashion by dividing the rows and columns by rule lines, creating individual cells.

tabloid   term refers to either a small newspaper measuring approximately half the size of a full-size newspaper, or one of the standard sizes of a sheet of paper measuring 11 × 17 inches.

tail   a stroke or arc of a character starting from the main stroke or structure of a letterform and extending downward, with one end free, as seen in the letters *R*, *K*, and *Q*.

target audience   refers to the group of the most desired consumers for a product or service, listed by characteristics such as demography, lifestyle, brand or media consumption, and purchase behavior.

terminal   the free end of a stroke, available in different variations such as sheared, ball, straight, acute, horizontal, convex, concave, flared, hooked, tapered, and pointed.

terminal attributes   describe the variety of terminals and finishing strokes found within letterforms, as well as where and how they have been applied. Description of baseline terminals include those derived from handwriting, more familiar tapered serifs that evolved from Roman inscriptional lettering models, and other variations such as slab serifs, Tuscan (sometimes referred to as forked, spur, or fishtail) serifs, or the sans serif option.

text   the body copy set in a consistent font with uniform leading, commonly resulting in a block of characters with the appearance of a medium-gray texture on a page; the content includes the main article or story and excludes heads, subheads, callouts or pull quotes, sidebars, headers and footers.

Textura   the first gothic written font was called Textura because of it's dark, tall and compressed letterforms. It originated in France in the 13th century, then spread rapidly to Germany, France, England, the Netherlands, Spain, and Bohemia, where all Latin books were written in this typeface.

text weight   a higher-quality paper than book paper that can be found in better-quality books, magazines and annual reports. A common weight for this kind of paper is 70–80 lb.

thin space   a space used between a bullet and text that is ¼ or 1/5 em space or less than a 3 to the em space.

thumbnail   small rough sketches prepared quickly with little detail, intended to document numerous compositional ideas generated in a relatively short period of time; a type of visual shorthand.

ticket envelope   a small envelope, typically measuring 2 × 5 inches that is used to enclose theater and show tickets for distribution to the purchaser.

tied letters   also known as tied characters or ligatures, this refers to two or three type characters tied, or joined together, to make a single type character.

tilde   a grapheme, that when used as a diacritic mark (~) is placed above an *n* in some orthographies to indicate a palatalized sound, as in Spanish cañon. The same mark placed above a vowel in phonetic transcription to indicate that the vowel is nasalized.

tip-in   an illustration or image that is printed separately and trimmed out, then pasted by hand into the space left for it in a book.

title page   the page in the front of a book indicating the title, subtitle, author, publisher, and date of publication.

tittle   the name of the dot above the lowercase *i*.

TOC   acronym for "Table of Contents."

TR   copy proofing or editorial mark that means to transpose or switch the order of the letters.

tracking   the function in a software application that determines the character-to-character spacing as well as word spacing proportionally; the tracking may be set to a negative number for a tighter fit called minusing or squeezing, or may be set to a positive number for letter spacing purposes.

Transitional Style   formed in the late seventeenth century as an "improved style" and later it was named "transitional" (as a bridge between Old Style and Modern). Transitional style shares some characteristics of Venetian Old Style, yet it features stronger stroke contrast, curves and round letters with vertical stress, and slightly rounded serifs.

TrueType	a vector-based, object-oriented font format developed by Apple (and adapted by Microsoft) intended to compete with the PostScript fonts by Adobe. TrueType fonts can be easily scaled to many different sizes and still maintain quality. One advantage of TrueType over PostScript is the fact that TrueType fonts can be drawn in low resolution on a monitor while still printing smooth characters on a printer. (PostScript requires an additional graphics file format called Encapsulated PostScript in order to represent the characters on a monitor.)
type classification	various systems designed to help group typefaces according to similar visual characteristics and/or time periods.
typeface	the specific design of an alphabet's characters including upper- and lowercase letters, numerals, symbols, alternate characters, and punctuation in all available sizes.
type family	all of the styles of a particular typeface including roman and italic, variations in weight such as extra light, light, book, regular, bold, heavy, extra bold, and ultra, and variations in width such as condensed, extended, and expanded.
type high	a dimension equal to .918" which is the precise height of all characters and imagery to be printed on a letterpress.
type size	the dimensions of a font measured in points from the top of the ascenders (ascender line) to the bottom of the descenders (descender line); during the period of letterpress printing and lead type, the term referred to the dimension or size of the metal platform for a particular font; also known as the point size.
typewriter	a mechanical or electromechanical device with a set of "keys" representing the characters and punctuation marks that, when pressed, cause characters to be printed on a sheet of paper.
typo	a shortened, slang form of the phrase "typographical error."
typography	the style, arrangement, and appearance of typeset matter; typography is sometimes seen as encompassing many separate fields from the type designer who creates letterforms to the graphic designer who selects typefaces and arranges them on the page.
U&lc	an abbreviation for the term "upper- and lowercase" which means to typeset the manuscript text as written; this is also the title of a typographic quarterly periodical published by the International Typeface Corporation (ITC).
uncia	from Latin, meaning a twelfth part, referring to the measurement of an inch.
uncial	a rounded calligraphic style of capital letters, appearing as early as the third century in Ancient Greece, named such as it was drawn using guidelines placed one inch apart divided into twelve divisions; uncials were especially popular for use in Greek and Latin manuscripts of the fourth to eighth centuries.
uncoated	refers to a type of paper that has not been finished with a coating of clay. Soft and absorbent in appearance, there is a wide variety of grades and levels of quality among uncoated papers.
underscore	a character on a typewriter used to underline text for emphasis, or used in a digital format as a place holder in a directory, subdirectory, and when a blank space is an unacceptable format in a particular programming language.
uppercase	the capital letters, located in the upper drawer of a font of lead type used for hand composition and letterpress printing.
uppercase numerals	are also called "lining figures" because they align with the baseline and cap line of a particular font when typeset. Most uppercase numerals are also tabular figures, meaning that each number has the same set width, and will align with numbers above it or below it for easy mathematical calculations such as addition or subtraction. They are sometimes referred to as "modern" figures because they began to appear at around the beginning of the nineteenth century at the time of modern-style typefaces.
vector graphics	sometimes called "object-oriented" graphics, though it's nothing to do with object-oriented programming. The representation of separate shapes such as lines, polygons, and text, and groups of such objects, as opposed to bitmaps. The advantage of vector graphics ("drawing") programs over bitmap ("paint") editors is that multiple overlapping elements can be manipulated independently without using different layers for each one. It is also easier to render an object at different sizes and to transform it in other ways without worrying about image resolution and pixels.

vellum	parchment that is made of calfskin. The word is derived from the Latin vitulus, a calf, whence our word veal. Drum leather is a specialized form variety of vellum, made nowadays in diminished quantities for the purpose indicated by its name. Modern vellum is somewhat translucent paper made from wood and cotton pulps. Like most contemporary papers, the surfaces of these materials are treated and chemically processed to create the translucency.
Venetian Old Style	or Renaissance Old Style faces replaced the black letter style of type. This Old Style is based on ancient Roman inscriptions and these fonts are characterized by low contrast between thick and thin strokes, bracketed serifs, and a left-leaning axis or stress.
verso	the left-hand page in a two-page spread.
vertex	the outer, downward juncture of two angled stems where the resulting point touches just below the baseline; different types of vertices include rounded, pointed, hollow, flat, and extended.
vertical bar	a typographic glyph or symbol also referred to as the "pipe" which is commonly used as a mathematical symbol, or to separate hyperlinks in a navigation bar on a Web page.
Victorian era	a period commonly indicated between 1837 and the early 1900s characterized by high ornamentation and decoration in fashion and architecture during the reign of Queen Victoria in England. It is marked as a sixty-four-year period of change from Romanticism through the Industrial Revolution.
virgule	the name of a forward slash mark (/) representing the "per" in a term such as miles/hour, or to indicate alternatives in a shortened version in a term such as and/or.
Vox system	a 1954 system of typographic classification developed by Maximilien Vox (1894–1974), also called "Classification de Lure." His classification system is an extension of classification first developed by Thibaudeau, based on the formal characteristics, the history and includes the categories Manuaires, Humanes, Geraldes, Réales, Didones, Mécanes, and Lineal.
WYSIWYG	acronym in the digital typesetting and graphics industries referring to the term "What You See Is What You Get," meaning that the image on the screen is a very close representation of what will print.
waist line	the invisible or imaginary horizontal rule that indicates the top of the body height of the lowercase letters, also called the x-height line.
wallet flap	refers to a style of envelope with diagonal seams and a square flap that extends halfway down the back. It is used for mailing legal documents, bank deposits, and statements because of its extra sealing strength and its acceptance of bulky mail. It is available in standard booklet envelope sizes.
watermark	a design or word placed in the screen when making paper, that is visible when the finished sheet of paper is held up against a light from behind, used to identify the paper mill and paper stock.
weight	in the graphic arts professions, this term refers to two different things: first, the boldness of a character stroke in both serif and sans serif typefaces including variations such as extra light, light, book, regular, bold, heavy, extra bold, and ultra; second, the thickness of a particular paper or card stock which is determined by how much 500 sheets weigh.
WF	a copy editing or proofreading mark that refers to the term "wrong font."
widow	the line at the end of a typeset paragraph that is less than half the column width, usually only one or two words; these are undesirable in typeset copy.
width	refers to the horizontal dimension of a typeset character or font. Terms such as compressed, condensed, extended, and expanded indicate how wide a font is.
window envelope	is a style of commercial envelope that has one or more widows cut into the front to allow the address on the contents to show through. These envelopes may or may not have a plastic or glassine protective window in the cutout area.

wood type letterpress or handset letterforms cut from wood, on a type high platform or base, used for large headlines and posters because it is less expensive and lighter than lead.

word space the standard white space between each word in typeset copy, usually $1/3$ em for lowercase body text and one en for caps.

wove paper manufactured with a uniform smooth surface.

wrap-around typeset copy that fits around a silhouetted image or irregular shape projecting into the column of text in a layout.

x-height the height of the body lowercase letters, excluding ascenders and descenders as measured from the baseline to the waist line.

x-height line also called the body height line, it is an imaginary line drawn at the top edge of the lowercase x, or at the body height of typeset text used in the study of type anatomy.

Key Players

Albers, Josef	1888–1976	German-born American artist, author, and teacher who was influential in his teachings at the Bauhaus in Weimar, Black Mountain College, and Yale University. Albers is known for his color theory studies with geometric shapes created in the 1950s.
Alcuin , Flaccus Albinus	c 735–804 CE	Alcuin of York. A monk and famous scholar from York, England. Alcuin was adviser on ecclesiastical affairs in Charlemagne's court and one of the important leaders at the palace school. Alcuin taught classical Latin and liberal arts, and helped to maintain scholarship in the Catholic Church.
Augereau, Antoine	1485–1534	He was and engraver, punch cutter and printer known as Claude Garamond's teacher and mentor and a contemporary to Simon de Colines.
Baker, Robert		Served as the court printer to King James I, head of the Anglican Church who set up a "Translation" Committee of forty-seven men who met respectively in Westminster, Cambridge, and Oxford. These separate committees were responsible for the translation of the Old Testament, the New Testament, and the "Apocrypha" books. Although the King nominated the translators in 1604, they did not begin their work till 1607. When a written copy of the Bible was completely translated, it was delivered to Robert Baker, the king's printer (who up until 1629 had exclusive printing rights to this Bible). There were three separate printings of the King James Bible in the first year (1611) and a total of fifteen editions (reportedly between five hundred and a thousand copies each printing) from 1611–1614.
Baskerville, John	1706–1775	He was an eighteenth-century, English type designer, printer, calligrapher, stone carver, and book designer. Baskerville is ranked among the foremost of those who have advanced the art of printing through the development of a typeface bearing his name, exploration with ink formulas, paper, and page composition.
Bayer, Herbert	1900–1985	He was an influential Austrian artist who went to study at the Bauhaus in 1921 and later became a teacher. He is well known for his geometric, asymmetrical style and the creation of the universal alphbet. He fled Nazi Germany in 1938 when it was no longer possible to work there, and lived in New York until his death in 1985.
Behrens, Peter	1869 1940	He was an architect and painter and a well-known figure in the exploration and development of the field of industrial design and in the Jugendstil movement. He was involved in the beginnings of the Bauhaus and is known for his work as an artistic adviser to AEG (Allemeine Electricitäts-Gesellschaft) from 1907 to 1914.
Benguiat, Ephram Edward	1927–	Prolific New York graphic designer, type designer, and lettering artist known for the design of typefaces Souvenir, Korinna, Era, Fenice, Avant Garde Gothic, ITC American Typewriter, and Edwardian Script.. He has worked on high-profile designs such as the masthead for the *New York Times*, Estée Lauder, and AT&T. He was instrumental in assisting Herb Lubalin establish the International Typeface Corporation (ITC).
Benton, Morris Fuller	1842–1948	He was trained as an engineer, then joined the ATF and is known for designing two hundred forty-six faces for ATF, including Century Schoolbook, Franklin and News Gothics, Hobo, Broadway, Alternate Gothic, Stymie, and Cloister Black. He was the chief type designer at ATF from 1900 to 1937.
Bigelow, Charles	1945–	A type designer, type historian, and professor who is known for his design of the bitmap Apple computer system font Chicago, as well as Lucida Console, Lucida Math, Lucida Sans, Lucida Typewriter, Lucida, and New York.
Bodoni, Giambattista	1714–1813	He was an engraver, typographer, and printer most well known for the design of a typeface bearing his name. With contrast between the thick and thin strokes, and the thin hairline serifs, Bodoni is considered one of the first modern-style faces.
Bringhurst, Robert	1946–	He is an American-born poet, author, book designer, typographer, historian, and linguist most well known for his book, *Elements of Typographic Style*. He now resides in Vancouver, British Columbia.
Brody, Neville	1957–	British graphic designer, type designer and art director who is known for a London-based style magazine, *The Face*, a men's magazine, *Arena*, and his digital medium magazine *Fuse*, as well as the design of a number of typefaces including Arcadia, FF Autotrace, FF Blur, FF Dirty 1, FF Dirty 3, FF Dirty 4, FF Dirty 6, FF Dirty 7, FF Dome, FF Gothic, FF Harlem, Industria, Insignia, FF Meta Subnormal, FF Pop, FF Tokyo, FF Typeface 4, FF Typeface 6 & 7, FF Tyson, and FF World.
Bullen, Henry Lewis	–1938	He was an established printer with scholarly interests who held a high-level management position within the ATF, who later became the head librarian. He worked toward the goal of having it known as "the professional printers' library."

Burgundians		People who were East German tribesmen who emigrated from Scandinavia and became allies of Rome during the fifth century, and have since become part of the area of France known as Burgundy.
Burns, Aaron	1922–1991	American graphic designer, typographer, and teacher who is known as one of the founders of the International Typeface Corporation (ITC) with Herb Lubalin and Ed Rondthaler in 1970.
Burt, William Austin	1792–1858	A justice of the peace, school inspector, postmaster, and inventor who settled in Detroit, Michigan, and who holds the first American patent for the typewriter, from 1829. He is also known for his work in improving the solar compass and his patent on the equatorial sextant.
Butti, Alessandro	1893–1959	Type designer and teacher known for the font designs he developed with Aldo Novarese, including Athenaeum, Normandia, Augustea, and Microgramma.
Carter, Matthew	1937–	He is a contemporary type designer whose career spans four decades and multiple technologies. Carter cofounded Bitstream (known as America's first digital type foundry) with Mike Parker in 1981. In 1991 he left Bitstream to form Carter & Cone with Cherie Cone. His type designs include ITC Galliard, Snell Roundhand and Shelley scripts, Helvetica Compressed, Olympian (for newspaper text), Bell Centennial (for the U.S. telephone directories), ITC Charter, and faces for Greek, Hebrew, Cyrillic, and Devanagari, an alphabet used in India. For Carter & Cone he has designed Mantinia, Sophia, Elephant, Big Caslon, Alisal, and Miller.
Cassandre, Adolphe Mouron	1901–1968	He (born Adolphe Jean Edouard Mouron) studied at the Écoles des Beaux Arts in Paris. Cassandre's work was seen as a bridge between the modern fine arts and the commercial arts. The French artist and designer is known for his work as a poster artist in Paris with Deberny & Peignot (a nineteenth-century type foundry) during the 1930s.
Caslon, William	1692–1766	An English engraver, type designer, and typefounder who is known for the face that bears his name. His typefaces were used for a number of important printed works from 1740 to 1800, including the first printed version of the United States Declaration of Independence.
Caslon IV, William	(1780–1869)	Typefounder who was the great-grandson of William Caslon I; he ran the type foundry from 1807 until 1819 when it was sold to Blake, Garnett & Co.
Caxton, William	1422–1491	He is known as the first printer in England. Caxton is thought to have printed approximately 100 books, many dealing with themes of chivalry. He translated about one-third of the books that he printed from French, Latin, and Dutch, and is known to have written some of the original prologues, epilogues, and additions in these texts.
Charlemagne	742–814 CE	Charles the Great, King of the Franks and eventually the King of the Holy Roman Empire from approximately 800 until his death. Toward the end of the first millenneum CE, Charlemagne's court standardized a written form which included most of the features of our modern lowercase alphabet. Alcuin of York, adviser to Charlemagne, introduced the "Carolingian" minuscule, which spread rapidly through Europe between the eighth and twelfth centuries.
Chwast, Seymour	1931–	Illustrator, designer, and type designer who is founder of Pushpin Studio who is known for his work for clients such as *Time* magazine, Mobil Oil, JCPenny, IBM, General Foods, Chrysler Corporation, Peugeot, MGM, Doubleday, CBS, and AT&T.
Claude, Georges	1870–1960	French chemist and physicist known for the invention of neon to light red signs that were first displayed at the Paris motor show in 1910. He was the founder of the Air Liquide Company, and as a staunch nationalist during the 1930s, a member of the Action Française, and as a candidate for legislative elections, he notoriously endorsed Hitler's Germany and was condemned to life imprisonment in 1945.
Constantine	c 285–337 CE	(Flavius Valerius Constantinus) This Roman emperor is best known for the city named for him, Constantinople (formerly Byzantium) and for the legalization of the Christian religion at the Conference of Nicacea in 325 CE.
Coster, Laurens Janszoon	c 1370–c1440	Many believe that this Dutch sexton was Johann Gutenberg's rival, and was the true inventor of movable type for printing around 1440, though there are no books existing today that bear Coster's name as publisher (but neither are there any of Johann Gutenburg). An account by Hadranius Junius recalls the legend of Laurens Coster's discovery and development of movable type in his *Batavia*, published posthumously in 1568. This account connects Laurens Coster with an employee, Johannes Faust who steals from the printery and escapes to Amsterdam, Cologne, and finally Mainz, Germany.
Craw, Freeman	1917–	New York designer associated with ATF.

da Vinci, Leonardo	1452–1519	He was a renaissance painter, architect, engineer, inventor, musician, mathematician, and philosopher. At the time Leonardo was born Gutenburg had just invented movable type and Leonardo's press was not a new design; his contribution consisted of suggesting improvements on an existing system. Leonardo proposed a modification that added a double thread, which served to increase the travel of the press for each turn made of the lever. Many historians believe Leonardo intended to publish his information on work done in this area, but it did not happen until 132 years after his death.
de Colines, Simon	1480–1546	A Parisian typographer, printer, and publisher who worked with the elder Henri Estiennes, as his editor for a time. A contemporary to Antoine Augereau during the golden age of French typography, de Colines is believed to have been one of the first to mix roman and italic faces in one publication. His Book of Hours (1525) was well received, and helped established book design and fine typography as an art form.
deVinne, Theodore Low	1828 1914	He was considered New York's best and most noble printer of the late 19th century; his writings and by his quality workmanship advanced the cause of good printing. He printed the *Century Magazine* and the *Century Dictionary*, both of them considered fine specimens of the art in that period. He also printed many of the Grolier Club books.
Deck, Barry	1962–	A contemporary graphic designer and type designer, known for his proliferation of interesting fonts since the early 1990s, typical of the "new wave" movement in typography. Deck has become associated with distorted typefaces, which began to appear in publications such as Ray Gun, Emigré, Wired Eye, and I.D. In 1995 he started his own company, Dysmedia, and has worked with clients such as Pepsi, Reebok, Nickelodeon, and VH1.
Didot, Françoise Ambrose	1689–1757	A French printer and Firmin Didot's father, who is known for creating the point system of measurement. Known for his creative technical innovations and sound business practices, he earned several high appointments, including being printer to Comte d'Artois and later Charles IX.
Didot, Firmin	1764–1836	In 1783, at age 19, Firmin Didot created what is now considered the first "modern" typeface, rivaling the work of Giambattisti Bodoni. In the late 1700s he is attributed with the invention of stereotyping (the creation of printing plates cast from a paper mâché mold of handset type). Firmin Didot's typographic expertise was showcased in 1798 when he cut a new font which was used for the *Virgil* of 1798. This new modern look established him as the typographical authority in France, resulting, in a 1814 appointment as the director of the imperial foundry by Napoleon Bonaparte, where worked until his death.
Dixon, Catherine	1970–	Designer, writer, and teacher. Graduated from Central Saint Martins, London in 1992. PhD completed in 2001 as, *A description framework for typeforms: an applied study*. Writing projects further develop interests in letterforms, see http://www.publiclettering.org and the book *Signs: lettering in the environment* (with Phil Baines 2003). Works as a freelance graphic designer. Nominated in 2005 as part of the Penguin design team for Design Museum, London, Designer of the Year award.
Dürer, Albrecht	1471–1528	He was a leading German painter and printmaker of the Renaissance era known for his elaborate and detailed compositions. Few are aware that he was also instrumental in outlining correct proportions and construction methods for a roman alphabet based on square proportions and applied geometry entitled "Of the Just Shaping of Letters."
Eckmann, Otto	1865–1902	An illustrator known for his work during the Art Nouveau period (known as "Jugendstil" in Germany); the movement split between the decorative tendencies of Otto Eckmann and the *Pan* magazine, and the streamlined design of Peter Behrens.
Estienne, Charles	c 1504–1564	Carolus Stephanus. Another son of Henri Estienne who succeeded Robert in the management of the Paris establishment in 1551. He was known for his editing and publication of medical and agricultural texts.
Estienne, Henri	c 1470–1520	The partriarch of a well-known family of French scholars and publishers; the Estienne printers were known for the quality of their work and the accuracy of the content in their publications. When he died, his widow married Simon de Colines who is believed to have worked with him for a number of years.
Estienne, Robert	c 1498–1559	A son of Henri Estienne who took over the printing business that Simon de Colines had been running since the death of Robert's father, Henri. He was known for printing and editing a number of scholarly works such as dictionaries, lexicons, and critical editions of the Bible. As a humanist who supported the Reformation, he found himself fleeing to Geneva around 1550, where he set up his own press and continued working there until his death.

Feininger, Lyonel Charles	1871–1956	An American painter who was instrumental in establishing and teaching at the Bauhaus in Weimar and in Dessau. When the Nazis rose to power, Feininger returned to the United States and helped found the New Bauhaus in Chicago.
Fourdrinier, Henry	1766–1854	Most paper today is made on Fourdrinier machines, which are patterned after the first successful papermaking machine, developed and patented in 1803 by the British brothers Henry Fourdrinier and Sealy Fourdrinier, sons of Henry Fourdriner who was a wealthy paper maker and wholesale stationer.
Fournier Le Jeune, Pierre	1712–1768	Also Simon-Pierre. Engraver, typographer, punch cutter, and printer known for the development of the point system that was later improved upon by François-Ambroise Didot.
Franks		One of several western Germanic tribes of people who entered the late Roman Empire from Frisia; modern descendents of these people are settled in areas of France and the Franconia, Germany.
Friedman, Dan	1945–	Author, graphic designer, and teacher who received his education at the Carnegie Institute of Technology in Pittsburgh, the Hochschule für Gestaltung in Ulm, and the Allgemeine Gewerbeschule in Basel (under Wolfgang Weingart). In the early 1970s he was instrumental in the proliferation of new wave typography. He has worked for companies such as Anspach Grossman Portugal, Pentagram New York, and most recently, himself, developing posters, publications, packaging and visual identities for many corporations and organizations.
Frutiger, Adrian	1928–	Author, type designer and teacher whose education and experience spans both the phototypesetting and digital eras. His work has been concentrated in the areas of typography and signage. Some of his most popular type designs include the Avenir, Linotype Didot, Frutiger, OCR, Univers, and Vectora type families.
Fust, Johann	–c 1466	The financier, goldsmith, and lawyer who made several loans to Gutenberg during the period the great inventor was perfecting the art of printing from movable type. In 1455, Fust demanded repayment of his loans and, when rebutted, brought a lawsuit against Gutenberg. Unable to repay his debt, Gutenberg was forced to yield much of his printing equipment and type to Fust, who then set up a printing shop of his own in partnership with Peter Schöffer. In partnership with his brother-in-law, Peter Schöffer, Fust carried on the work begun by Gutenberg. Fust and Schöffer were the first to print in colors (1457), using red and blue inks as well as black. They printed the first dated book, a great Psalter (1457). Their Greek type was first used in 1465.
Garamond, Claude	1480–1561	Punch cutter, type designer, publisher. Garamond studied the art of punch cutting with Simon de Colines and Geofroy Tory before moving on to design and cut his own fonts between 1530 and 1545, which became popular then and are widely used for inspiration in contemporary variations available today.
Geschke, Chuck	1939–	Charles M. Geschke is the cofounder (with John Warnock) of Adobe Systems Inc. in 1982. Unable to convince Xerox management of the commercial value of Warnock's Interpress graphics language for controlling printing technologies, he and John Warnock left Xerox to start Adobe. At their new company, they developed the PostScript printing language from scratch, and brought it to market. It is now a worldwide industry standard for digital printers.
Gill, Eric	1882–1940	A student of Edward Johnston's, this sculptor, painter, and type designer was influenced by Johnston's dedicated approach to work and decided to join the world of the Arts and Crafts. He designed numerous typefaces, among them Perpetua (for Stanley Morison) and his most famous Gill Sans. He is known for the design of Aries, Gill Display Compressed, Gill Hebrew, Gill Floriated Capitals, Gill Sans, Gill Sans Light Shadowed, Gill Sans Shadowed, ITC Golden Cockerel, ITC Golden Cockerel Initials & Ornaments, Joanna, Jubilee, and Perpetua
Goodhue, Bertram	1869–1924	Also Bertram Grosvenor. Type designer, book designer, and architect known for his design of the Merrymount and Cheltenham Old Style typefaces. His illustrative printing work resembles that of William Morris, Kelmscott Press.
Goudy, Frederic William	1865–1920	A prolific American author, book designer, teacher and type designer known for his design of Bulmer, ITC Berkeley Oldstyle, FB Californian, Copperplate Gothic, Deepdene, Goudy, Goudy 38 RR, Goudy Catalogue, Goudy Handtooled, Goudy Heavyface, Kennerly, Monotype Goudy Modern, Goudy Old Style, ITC Goudy Sans, Goudy Sorts, Goudy Stout CT, Goudy Text, Goudy Trajan, Goudy WTC, Hadriano, Italian Old Style, Remington Typewriter, and Village typefaces.
Grandjean, Philippe	1666–1714	French punch cutter and type designer renown for his famous series of roman and italic types known as Romain du Roi. The design was commissioned in 1692 for the Imprimerie Royale (royal printing house) of King Louis XIV and was carried out by a group of mathematicians, philosophers, and others, who produced carefully worked-out drawings.

Granjon, Robert	1513–1589	French punch cutter, type designer, and printer known for his Meno, St Augustin, and Civilité typefaces. It is believed that he cut approximately fifty fonts during his lifetime, which equates to approximately six thousand punches.
Greiman, April		A graphic designer trained in the United States and in Switzerland (with Wolfgang Weingart), contemporary to Wolfgang Weingart. Her work in the 1980s and 1990s embraced all phases of digital technology. She became a partner at Pentagram in 2000 and frequently lectures at the Art Center College in Los Angeles, California. Famous for her integration of graphic design practices, digital technology, and creative approaches to composition, she is considered one of the founders of American New Wave design.
Griffo, Francesco da Bologna	1450–1518	A talented Venetian type founder, punch cutter, and type designer, best known for his design of Bembo which was used by Aldus Mantius to print a sixty page essay "De Aetna," by Cardinal Pietro Bembo. After the death of Mantius in 1515, Griffo returned to Bologna where he printed some of his own editions until his own death, when it is thought he was hanged for killing his brother-in-law.
Gropius, Walter Adolph	1883–1969	The architect and teacher is known for his work in founding the Bauhaus in Dessau, Germany, and later for his position of chair of the graduate school at Harvard Univerisity School of Design, beginning in 1937.
Gutenberg, Johann	c1398–c1468	Born as Johann Gensfleisch. A German metalworker and inventor who is attributed with the invention of movable type and the printing press, as well as the printing of the first Latin Bible in the 1450s. Gutenberg entered into a partnership with Johann Fust (wealthy lawyer and goldsmith from Mainz) who financed his printing experiments. Eventually Fust foreclosed on Gutenberg and took over the printery near the end of the printing of the first edition of the Latin 42-line Bible, and Gutenberg lost everything, dying in relative poverty a number of years later.
Handy, John	–c 1792	Punch cutter to John Baskerville for approximately 28 years.
Higonnet, René Alphonse		A French inventor, in combination with Louis Marius Moyroud, using an electric typewriter connected with a computer and a photographing unit, developed a successful phototypesetter that used a strobe light and a series of optics to project characters from a spinning disk onto photographic paper. It was eventually known as the Lumitype-Photon machine.
Hoffman, Armin	1920–	Graphic designer, author, and teacher credited for the development of "Swiss Design" while teaching at the Basel School of Design where he taught for 40 years, until 1986.
Jenson, Nicolas	1420–1480	He became a printer, punch cutter, type designer, and publisher who studied printing under Gutenberg in Mainz for three years upon leaving his profession as a coin engraver at the request of King Charles VII of France. His type styles have remained popular throughout time, and has experienced a revival in the digital age.
Johnston, Edward	1972–1944	Author, calligrapher, type designer, and teacher most well known for his work in developing a font for the London Underground, and managing the ensuing identity and signage system design. His publications include: *Writing and Illuminating and Lettering* and *Manuscript and Inscription Letters for Schools and Classes and for Use of Craftsmen*.
Kandinsky, Wassily	1866–1944	Russian artist, musician, lawyer, and teacher was involved with Der Blaue Reiter (The Blue Rider) group and taught at the Bauhaus with Klee, Geiniger, Schonberg, and Kandinsky.
Keedy, Jeffery		Graphic designer, author, teacher, and type designer has been teaching at the California Institute of the Arts since 1985. His designs and essays have been published in the periodicals *Eye, I.D., Émigré, HOW, Design Quarterly, Design, Fuse,* and *Print,* and in the books *The 20th Century Poster: Design of the Avant Garde, Twentieth-Century Type, Typography Now: the Next Wave,* and *The New Discourse: Cranbrook Design*.
Kisman, Max	1953–	Prolific Dutch graphic designer, animator, illustrator, and type designer known for Bebedot Black, Bebedot Blonde, Bfrika, Book And, Cattlebrand, Chip 1, Chip 2, Circuit Closed, Circuit Open, FF Cutout, FF Fudoni, Interlace Double, Interlace Single, FF Jacque, Mata Hari Exotique, Mata Hari Hollandaise, Mata Hari Parisienne, Mundenge Rock, FF Network, Nevermind, Pacific Classic Bold, Pacific Classic Light, Pacific Sans Bold, Pacific Sans Light, Pacific Serif Bold, Pacific Serif Light, Pacific Standard Bold, Pacific Standard Light, Quickstep, Quickstep Sans, FF Rosetta, FF Scratch, FF Scratch Outline, Submarine, Traveller, Traveller Bold, Tribe Mono, FF Vortex, We Love Your, Xbats, and Zwart Vet typefaces. He designs exhibitions, books, magazines, calendars, animations, posters, postage stamps and typefaces.

Klee, Paul	1879–1940	A Swiss Expressionist painter, printmaker, musician, and teacher, was involved with Der Blaue Reiter (The Blue Rider) group, who was instrumental in the development of abstract art. Following World War I he taught at the Bauhaus, then in 1931 he began teaching at Dusseldorf Academy, but he was dismissed by the Nazis, who termed his work "degenerate." His work continued to influence late twentieth-century Surrealist and nonobjective artists and was a prime source for the budding Abstract Expressionist movement.
Koch, Rudolph	1876–1934	Artist, punch cutter, graphic designer, type designer and teacher known for the design of Kabel, ITC Kabel, Koch Antiqua, Koch Original, P22 Koch Signs, Neuland, and Wilhelm Klingspor Gotisch typefaces.
Koenig, Fredrich	1774–1883	German printer who is attributed with the invention of the high-speed printing press. In the early 1800s he attempted to improve the druckpresse to increase the printing time. By 1911, improvements led to the printing of the first book and by 1814 the printing of *The Times* in London.
Lawson, Alexander	–2002	Author and type historian who taught at Rochester Institute of Technology from 1947 until 1977. His most well-known work is *Anatomy of a Typeface*.
Licko, Zuzana	1961–	Cofounder of *Émigré*, together with her husband Rudy VanderLans, she is known for experimenting with the newly invented Macintosh computer and a bitmap font tool, to create fonts for the magazine in the early 1980s. Emperor, Oakland, and Emigré faces were designed to accommodate low-resolution printer output. She is a prolific type designer, known for Base Monospace, Base Nine and Twelve, Citizen, Dogma, Elektrix, Fairplex, Filosofia, Hypnopaedia, Journal, Lo Res, Lunatix, Matrix, Matrix Script, Modula, Modula Round and Ribbed, Mrs Eaves, Narly, Oblong, Quartet, Senator, Soda Script, Solex, Tarzana, Totally Gothic & Totally Glyphic, Triplex, Variex, and Whirligig typefaces.
Lissitzky, El	1890–1941	(Born Lazar Markovich Lisitskii) A painter, architect, photographer, and typographer during the Soviet Contructivist Avant Garde. At Marc Chagall's request, Lissitzky taught at the Vibetsk Art School for a while, beginning in 1919. In the 1920s he joined the German Dadaists Kurt Schwitters and Hans Arp. The following decade he worked as a propagandist for the Stalinist regime.
Lombards		Originally known as the Langobards (referring to their long beards), were a Germanic tribe that slowly worked their way from Sweden into Italy by the sixth century. They settled in the Northern area of Italy, now called Lombardia. Around 751 CE the Franks conquered the Lombards, removing them from power in that area.
Lubalin, Herb	1918–1981	American graphic designer, photographer, and type designer who was known for his role in cofounding the International Typeface Corporation (with Aaron Burns and Ed Rondthaler) where he was the editorial design director for ITC's promotional journal U&lc (Upper and lowercase). The periodical was influential on type design and the type industry in the 1970s and 1980s. He is known for the design of ITC Avant Garde Gothic, ITC Lubalin Graph, ITC Ronda and ITC Serif Gothic typefaces.
Lun, Ts'ai		According to tradition, paper was first made in 105 CE by Ts'ai Lun, a eunuch of the Eastern Han court of the Chinese emperor Ho Ti.
Mantius, Aldus Pius	1449–1515	Also known as Aldo Manuzio. Renaissance scholar, tutor, and publisher of fine books who founded the Aldine Press. He was known for his improvements in typography as he commissioned work from punch cutters and type designer such as Francesco Griffo. He printed small versions of classical scholarly works, making them affordable for larger portions of the population at that time.
Marinetti, Filippo Tomaso	1876–1944	Writer and poet who published "Manifesto del Futurismo," an article outlining the major principles of Futurism (as a modernist movement celebrating the technological advancements yet to come) on the front page of *Le Figaro* in 1909. Inspired by Cubism, the Futurists mixed activism with their art and aligned themselves politically with the Facists who were gaining power, and encouraged youth of Italy to break with tradition in art and poetry to face the challenges of a new machine age.
Meidinger, Max	1910–1980	Type designer most widely known for his design of the Helvetica family (originally named Neue Haas Grotesk) of type, as well as Pro Arte, Haas-Grotesk, Helvetica , and Horizontal.

Mergenthaler, Otto	1854–1899	German emigrant who is credited with the invention of the Linotype machine, patented in 1884 and first used in 1886 by the *New York Tribune* and was one of the major advancements in printing technology since Gutenberg. The Linotype machine automatically assembled a line of 'matrices' forming letters that were then immediately cast inside the machine, giving a solid "line of type"—hence the name.
Moholy-Nagy, Laszlo	1895–1946	Hungarian Painter, photographer, and teacher who joined the Bauhaus from 1923–1928, taking over a portion of the foundation program for Itten. Starting in 1937 he led the New Bauhaus in Chicago, and in 1944, the Institute of Design.
Mondrian, Piet	1872–1944	Dutch painter and primary contributor to the de Stijl movement founded by Theo van Doesberg. He is best known for his nonrepresentational paintings, consisting of rectangular forms of red, yellow, blue, or black, separated by thick, black, rectilinear lines.
Morris, William	1834–1896	Artist, designer, type designer, and publisher best known for founding the Arts and Crafts Movement (loosely linked group of craftsmen, artists, designers, and architects who aimed to raise the status of the applied arts to that of the fine arts) and the Kelmscott Press.
Morrison, Stanley	1889–1967	Author, type designer, and typographical adviser for Monotype, he is best known for his design of the font Times New Roman, used for London's daily *The Times* newspaper. He is known for his designe of the Times, Times Ten, Times Eighteen, Times Central European, and Times New Roman (with Victor Lardent) typefaces and the publications *Four Centuries of Fine Print*, *The Alphabet of Damianus Moyllus*, *The Calligraphy of Ludovico degli Arrighi*, *The English Newspaper, 1622–1932*, *First Principles of Typography*, *A Tally of Types*, and *Typographic Design in Relation to Photographic Composition*.
Moyroud, Louis Marius	1914–1983	A French inventor, who in collaboration with René Higonnet, using an electric typewriter connected with a computer and a photographing unit, developed a successful phototypesetter that used a strobe light and a series of optics to project characters from a spinning disk onto photographic paper (originally named the Lithomat in 1949).
Mueller-Brockman, Josef		Graphic designer and teacher known for his rational approach to the organization of visual information using a formal grid system, carefully presented his book *Grid Systems in Graphic Design*.
Novarese, Aldo	1920–1995	Teacher and type designer known for his Landi Linear, Athenaeum (with A. Butti), Normandia (with A. Butti), Microgramma (with A. Butti), Eigno, Fontanesi, Egizio, Juliet, Ritmo, Garaldus, Slogan, Recto, Estro, Eurostile, Forma, Magister, Metropol, Stop, Lapidar, Fenice, Novarese, Expert, Colossal, ITC Symbol, ITC Mixage, and Arbiter typefaces.
Ostrogoths		The eastern division of the Germanic tribe of Goths who settled in the area North of the Black Sea. When the Goths separated into two groups the Ostrogoths settled in Ukraine. They were subject to the Huns until the death of Attila, when they settled into Pannonia (roughly modern Hungary).
Renner, Paul	1878–1956	German painter, architect, type designer, and teacher known for the design of Futura, Plak, Futura, Futura licht, Futura Schlagzeile, Ballade, Renner Antiqua, and Steile Futura typefaces.
Rondthaler, Ed	1905–	Known as one of the founders of modern photolettering with his company Photo-Lettering, Inc., and of the International Typeface Corporation (ITC) (with Aaron Burns and Herb Lubalin).
Rubel, Ira Washington		American lawyer, engineer, and printer who is attributed with the invention of offset lithography (from the phrase "to set off"). After he accidentally printed on both the front and the reverse side of the sheet, the printed image of the waste sheet was passed from the plate to the blanket of the impression cylinder before it is transferred onto another sheet of paper. Unexpectedly, the indirect copy is higher quality. The elastic rubber surface transfers the ink more evenly onto the sheet's surface than the metal printing plate. Rubel also discovers that this enables printing on paper of inferior quality.
Ruder, Emil	1914–1970	Swiss graphic designer, author, typographer, and teacher of typography, known for his work at the Basel School of Design. Ruder was a frequent contributor to the respected trade journal, *Typografische Monatsblätter*, and cofounder of the International Center for the Typographic Arts in New York in 1962.

Schöffer, Peter	c1425–1502	Printer and publisher who worked in Paris as a manuscript copier early in his career. In 1455 he appeared for Johann Fust against Johann Gutenberg. Upon collection of Gutenberg's debt to Fust (which meant that Fust took over Gutenberg's printery), Schöffer became Fust's partner and eventually married his daughter, Christine. He is not known for any significant technological or aesthetic advances in the printing industry of the time, as he was a conservative business manager and maintained status quo.
Schwitters, Kurt	1887–1948	Early on, this artist known for his collage imagery experimented with the Cubist and Expressionist styles. In the early 1920s, Schwitter met Theo van Doesberg whose de Stijl style influenced his work as he transitioned into Dadaism with poetry and music. Nazis banned Schwitters's work as "degenerate art" in 1937 and he found refuge in Norway until the Nazis invasion there in 1940. He escaped to Great Britain where he remained until his death.
Senefelder, Aloys	1771–1834	German artist and author who is known for the invention of offset lithography and chemical printing.
Slimbach, Robert	1956–	American type designer who has worked for Adobe Systems, Inc. since 1987 and is known for his work on Caflisch Script, Cronos, Adobe Garamond, ITC Giovanni, Adobe Jenson, Keppler, Minion, Poetica, Sanvito, ITC Slimbach, Utopia, and Warnock typefaces.
Southward, John	1840–1902	Type founder, historian, and author of *Modern Printing: A Handbook of the Principles and Practice of Typography and the Auxiliary Arts*, and *The Principles and Progress of Printing Machinery*.
Thibaudeau, Francis	1860–1925	A French typographer who worked out the typographical catalogues of two famous foundries: Renault and Marcou, then Peignot and Co, where he was a head of the services of composition until his death. He worked out four categories in his classification which included " antiques " (without footings), " didots " (with threadlike footings contrasting with the full ones with the letter), " elzévirs "(with triangular footings), and "Egyptian women" (with footings of rectangular form). This foundation became the basis of the character and historical style classification system proposed by Maximillan Vox (born as Samuel Theodore William Monod) and adopted by Association Typographique Internationale in 1962 (Vox-AtypI).
Tory, Geofroy	c 1480–1533	Parisian author, teacher, printer and typographer who worked as an editor, engraver, and bookbinder for Henri Estienne, and eventually for King Francis I. He is known for his superb quality of typography exhibited in his Book of Hours from 1525 and his writing of *Champfleury* (1529), in which he explains and illustrates the theory governing his designs of roman capitals.
Tschichold, Jan	1902–1974	German author, typographer, type designer, and teacher who studied calligraphy and typography at the Leipzig Academy for Graphic Arts and Book Trades under Walter Tiemann. He was influenced by the work from the Bauhaus, as well as by painters László Moholy-Nagy and El Lissitzky early in his career. He is known for the design of Jenson, Bembo, Granjon, Elzevir, Caslon, Fleischmann, Baskerville, Fournier, Bell, Bulmer, Miller, Centaur, Perpetua, Janson, Transit, Electra, Fairfield, Dante, Aldus, Sabon, and Albertina typefaces as well as writings on typography including *The New Typography* (1928).
Twombly, Carol	1959–	A staff type designer at Adobe Systems, Inc, she originally studied under the direction of Charles Bigelow at Rhode Island School of Design, then worked for Bigelow and Holmes. She is known for the design of FB Californian, Adobe Caslon, Chaparral, Charlemagne, Lithos, Mirarae, Myriad, Myriad Wild, Nueva, Pepperwood, Rosewood, Trajan, Viva, and Zebrawood typefaces.
van Blokland, Erik		A graduate of the Royal Academy for Fine and Applied Arts in The Hague, he works separately and together with Just van Rossum under the name LettError. His work now includes type design, illustration, and programming. He is a key developer of the RoboFab, scripting environment for FontLab with van Rossum and Tal Leming. He is known for the design of FF Beowolf Random 21, FF Beowolf Random 22, FF Beowolf Random 23, FF Erikrighthand, FF Kosmik Flipper Plain, FF Kosmik Glyphs, FF Kosmik Plain One, FF Kosmik Plain Three, FF Kosmik Plain Two, The Printed Word, The Written Word, FF Trixie, and FF Zapata typefaces.

Vandals		An eastern Germanic tribe who settled along the bank of the Danube by during the second and third centuries CE and who invaded Gaul, Spain, and Africa. The fact that they were a warring tribe is reflected in today's usage of the word "vandal," as it reflects the dread and hostility the tribe precipitated in other people, especially the Romans, by their looting and pillaging of the many villages they conquered. They entered the late Roman Empire, and created a state in North Africa, centered on the city of Carthage. The Vandals probably gave their name to the province of Andalusia (originally, Vandalusia), in Spain, where they temporarily settled before pushing on to Africa.
VanderLans, Rudy	1955–	Type designer, graphic designer and cofounder of *Émigré* (a journal of experimental graphic design) with his wife Zuzana Licko in 1984. He is known for his work in designing Oblong, Variex, and Suburban typefaces as well.
van de Velde, Henry Clemens	1863–1957	Belgian architect, designer, and teacher known as one of the most prominent and successful practioners of the Art Nouveau style. His Weimar School of Arts and Crafts (1907) provided the foundation for the Bauhaus in Weimar.
Van Doesburg, Theo	1883–1931	(Born Christian Emil Marie Kupper) Poet, art critic, and artist known for founding the group de Stijl and the periodical of the same name, with Vilmos Huszár, Piet Mondrian, Bart van der Leck, and Georges Vantongerloo in 1917. In the 1920s he wrote using the pen name I. K. Bonset and later Aldo Camini. in 1922 he taught at the Weimar Bauhaus with Raoul Hausmann, Le Corbusier, Ludwig Mies van der Rohe, and Hans Richter, where he became interested in Dada, and began working with Kurt Schwitters and Jean Arp
Van Rossum, Just	1966	Now an independent type, Web, and graphic designer in The Hague, he graduated from the Royal Academy of Fine Arts in The Hague with a specialization in typography and worked for MetaDesign. He is known for the design of FF Advert, FF Advert Rough, FF BeoSans, FF Beowolf, FF Brokenscript, FF Confidential, FF Double Digits, FF Dynamoe, FF Flightcase, FF Justlefthand, FF Karton, Phaistos, FF Schulbuch, FF Schulschrift, and FF Stamp Gothic faces. He started the LettError virtual type foundry, with Erik van Blokland. Initial fame came with the release of Beowolf (co-designed with van Blokland), a font whose ragged edges shift randomly each time you print the font.
Visigoths		Originally part of the Germanic tribe known as the Goths, they settled in the region west of the Black Sea around 3CE. Eventually the Goths split into different groups, the Visigoths and the Ostrogoths. They played a key role in the region during the time of Constantine, then later warring with the Huns and finally the Roman Empire. During a number of revolts against the Roman Empire, they moved into the Balkans, eventually Italy, Southern Gaul, and eventually Spain. By the sixth century CE, the leader's conversion to Catholicism facilitated the fusion of the Visigothic and the Hispano-Roman populations of Spain.
Warnock, John	1940–	Is the cofounder (with Chuck Geschke) of Adobe Systems Inc. in 1982. Unable to convince Xerox management of the commercial value of Warnock's Interpress graphics language for controlling printing technologies, he and John Warnock left Xerox to start Adobe. At their new company, they developed the PostScript printing language from scratch, and brought it to market. It is now a worldwide industry standard for digital printers. Warnock has an Adobe font named after him.
Weingart, Wolfgang	1941–	Author, typographer, graphic designer, typographer and influential teacher who began his career hand composing lead and wood type. He has successfully combined numerous technologies to create a new vision of typography for the industry and students alike. Since 1968 he has taught typography at the Basle School of Design/Switzerland, conducted typography workshops at the Yale University Summer Program in Graphic Design at Brissago, Switzerland, and lectured on his teaching methodologies throughout Europe and the United States.
Wells, Darius	1800–1875	New York printer and inventor, found the means for mass-producing letters in 1827, and published the first known wood type catalog in 1828. The usual procedure was to draw the letter on wood, or paper, which was pasted to the wood, then cut around the letter with a knife or graver, gouging out the parts to be left blank. Wells, however, introduced a basic invention, the lateral router that, in combination with a pantograph introduced by William Leavenworth in 1834 constituted the essential material for mass-producing wood type.
Zapf, Hermann	1918–	This German type designer is known for his fonts Aldus, URW Antiqua, Aurelia, Edison, URW Grotesk, Kompakt, Marconi, Medici Script, Melior, Noris LT, Optima, Optima Nova LT, Orion LT, Palatino, Saphir, Sistina, Vario, Venture LT, ITC Zapf Book, ITC Zapf Chancery, ITC Zapf Dingbats, Zapf Essentials LT, ITC Zapf International, Linotype Zapfino, Zapf Renaissance. Optima and Palatino are two of the most widely admired, used, and pirated faces in the type industry.

Credits

Bibliography

5.49   The Estate of Jan Tischold.

6.6   Adrian Frutiger.

6.32   Seymour Chwast.

6.43   The Estate of Herb Lubalin.

6.44   From Avant Gard Magazine.

6.45   © Bill Graham Presents. 1967. Artist Wes Wilson.

6.46   Dorthea Hoffman.

6.47   Wolfgang Weingart.

7.2   Rudy Vanderlans and Zuzana Licko.

7.3   Rudy Vanderlans and Zuzana Licko.

7.9   Rudy Vanderlans and Zuzana Licko.

7.10   Rudy Vanderlans and Zuzana Licko.

7.11   Rudy Vanderlans and Zuzana Licko.

7.12   Rudy Vanderlans and Zuzana Licko.

7.16   With permission from Max Kisman.

7.17   With permission from Max Kisman.

7.18   With permission from Max Kisman.

7.19   Dutch Doubles, an alphabet with designs by: Jaques Le Baily, Aa | Underware, Bb | Wim Crouwel, Cc | Ad Kin Dd | 178 Aardige Ontwerpers, Ee | Peterpaul Kloosterman, Ff | Martin Wenzel, Gg | Petr van Blokland, Hh | Assi Kootstra, Ii | Jelle Bosma, Jj | Sander Kessels, Kk | Onno Bevoort, Ll / Marc Lubbers, Mm | Niels "Shoe" Meulman, Nn | Harmen Liemburg, Oo | Peter Bilak, Pp | Harmine Louwé, Qq | Paul van der Laan, Rr | Swip Stolk, Ss | Richard Niessen, Tt | Gerard Unger, Uu | Martijn Oostra, Vv | Goodwill, Ww | Donald Beekman, Xx | Mark van Wageningen, Yy | Bas Oudt, Zz | Ben Bos, ij IJ | Melle Hammer, 0–9 | Rutger Middendorp, !? | Pieter van Rosmalen, fi fl | Severin Frank, © ® | Erik van Blokland, @ | Peter van den Hoogen, & | Jan Dietvorst, +†‡ | Martin Majoor, Çç* | Martijn Oostra, ‹› | Fred InKlaar, ¥C$£ | Max Kisman, .,:;–_{} [] () = <>"" ' ' .

7.20   With permission from Max Kisman.

7.22   Neville Brody.

7.32   With permission from Barry Deck.

8.4   Meggs. Typographic Design: Form and Communication, 2e, 1993. John Wiley & Sons.

8.7   Lieberman. Types of Typefaces. 1978. Oak Knoll Publishing. New Castle, DE. 1987.

8.8   Lieberman. Types of Typefaces. 1978. Oak Knoll Publishing. New Castle, DE. 1987.

9.13   Courtesy of Catherine Dixon.

9.15   Courtesy of Catherine Dixon.

World Sign Design, No. 2-1994: Marks & Logos. Roman Nippan Books.

Adler, E. 1993. *Everyone's Guide to Successful Publications*. Peachpit Press.

Aldrich-Ruenzel, N. ed. 1991. *Designer's Guide to Typography*. Watson-Guptill.

Annual of the Type Directors' Club Staff. 1990-present. *Typography 11-18*. Watson-Guptill.

Arnold, E. 1969. *Modern Newspaper Design*. Harper & Row.

Berger, A. A. 1998. *Seeing is Believing*. Mayfield Publishing Company.

Bigelow, C. 1977-1988. *Fine Print on Type*. Pro Arte Libri.

Bradbury, T. 1988. *Bradbury Thompson: The Art of Graphic Design*. Yale University Press.

Brier, D. 1994. *International Typographic Design 2*. Madison Square.

Brier, D., ed. 1992. *Typographic Design*. Madison Square.

Buchannan, C. 1994. *Quick Solutions for Great Type Combinations*. F & W Publications.

Carter, H. 2002. *A View of Early Typography Up to About 1600*. Hyphen Press.

Carter, R. 1993. *American Typography Today*. Van Nostrand Reinhold.

Chwast, S.and S. Heller, ed. 1985. *The Left-Handed Designer*. Abrams Publishing.

Clair, K. 1999. *A Typographic Workbook*. John Wiley & Sons, Inc.

Cliff, S. 1994. *The Best in Cutting Edge Typography*. Quarto Publishing.

Craig, J. 1990. *Production for the Graphic Designer*. Watson-Guptill.

————. 1992. *Designing with Type: A Basic Course in Typography*. Watson-Guptill.

Cropper, M., and L. Haller. 1994. *Fresh Ideas in Corporate Identity*. F & W Publications.

Davis, G. 1993. *Quick Solutions to Great Layouts*. North Light Books.

Denton, G., and G. Allen. 1984. *The Doring Kindersley History of the World*. Doring Kindersley Publishing.

Drogin, M. 1980. *Medieval Calligraphy*. Dover Publications, Inc.

Droste, M. 2002. *Bauhaus*. Taschen.

Dürer, A. 1965. *Of the Just Shaping of Letters*. Dover Publications, Inc.

Elam, K. 1990. *Expressive Typography*. Van Nostrand Reinhold, Inc.

Evans, P. 1996. *The Graphic Designer's Sourcebook*. F & W Publications.

Evans, P. 2004. *Forms Folds Sizes*. Rockport Publishers.

Felici, J. 2003. *The Complete Manual of Typopgraphy*. Peachpit Press.

Freidman, M. et al. 1989. *Graphic Design America*. Harry N. Abrams, Inc.

Gottschall, E. 1989. *Typographic Communications Today*. MIT Press.

Goudy, F. 1922. *Alphabet & Elements of Lettering*. Dover Books.

Goudy, F. 1978. *Goudy's Type Designs, His Story & Specimens*. Oak Knoll.

Grafton, C. 1984. *Treasury of Victorian Printers' Frames, Ornaments & Initials*. Dover Books.

Grafton, C. B. 1986. *Treasury of Book Ornament & Decoration*. Dover Books.

Graphis Publication. 1992-present. Graphis Press.

Haley, A. 1992. *Typographic Milestones*. Van Nostrand Reinhold.

Harrower, T. 1989. *The Newspaper Designer's Handbook*. Wm. C. Brown Communications, Inc.

Hartt, F. 1976. *ART: History of Painting, Sculpture, and Architecture*. Harry N. Abrams, Inc.

Harter, J. 1978. *Harter's Picture Archive for Collage & Illustration*. Dover Books.

Heller, S. 1994. *Graphic Style: From Victorian to Post-Modern*. Abrams Publishing.

Heller S. and G. Anderson. 1994. *American Typeplay*. Hearst Books International.

Heller S. and S. Chwast. 1994. *Graphic Style: From Victorian to Post-Modern*. Abrams Publishing.

Henrikson, A. 1983. *Art Through the Ages*. Crown Publishers, Inc.

Hinrichs, K. and D. Hirasuna. 1990. *Type Wise*. F & W Publications.

Howes, J. 2000. *Johnston's Underground Type*. Capital Transport Publishing.

Hurlburt, A. 1977. Layout: *The Design of the Printed Page*. Watson-Guptill Publications.

Hutt, A. 1967. *Newspaper Design*. Oxford University Press.

International Paper. *Knowledge Center*. http://www.ipaper.com/20 May, 2005.

Kennedy, P. E. 1974. *Modern Display Alphabets*. Dover Books.

King, J. C. 1993. *Designer's Guide to PostScript Text Type*. Van Nostrand Reinhold.

Koren, L., and R. W. Meckler. 1989. *Graphic Design Cookbook*. Chronicle Books.

Labuz, R. 1988. *Typography & Typesetting*. Van Nostrand Reinhold, Inc.

Lambert, F. 1972. *Letterforms: 110 Complete Alphabets*. Dover Books.

Lawson, A. 1971. *Printing Types: An Introduction*. Beacon Press Books.

Lawson, A. 1990. *Anatomy of a Typeface*. David R. Goldine, Publisher.

Leader Paper. *Envelope Size Chart*. http://www.leaderpaper.com/info/size_chart.php. 19 May 2005.

Lieberman, J. B. 1978. *Type & Typefaces*. Oak Knoll.

Livingston, A. and I. Livingston. 1992. *The Thames & Hudson Encyclopaedia of Graphic Design & Designers*. Thames Hudson.

Martin, D. and L. Haller. 1996. *Street Smart Design*. North Light Books.

Meggs, P. 1992. *A History of Graphic Design*. Van Nostrand Reinhold.

Müller-Brockmann, J. 1981. *Grid Systems in Graphic Design*. Verlag Arthur Niggli.

————. 1992. *Type & Image: The Language of Graphic Design*. Van Nostrand Reinhold.

————. 1994. *Typographic Specimens*. Van Nostrand Reinhold.

Parsons, B. 1994. *Electronic Pre-Press: A Hands-on Introduction*. Delmar Publishing.

Phornirunlit, S. & Supon Design Group Staff. 1992. *Great Design Using One, Two & Three Colors*. Madison Square.

Phornirunlit, S. ed. 1996. *Innovative Low-Budget Design*. Madison Square.

Pipes, A.1992. *Production for Graphic Designers*. P-H.

Place, J. 1995. *Creating Logos & Letterheads*. North Light Books.

Rand, P. 1993. *Design, Form & Chaos*. Yale Univesity Press.

Re, M. 2003. *Typographically Speaking: The Art of Matthew Carter*. Princeton Archtectural Press.

Seibert, L. and L. Ballard. 1992. *Making a Good Layout*. North Light Books.

Siebert, L. and M. Cropper. 1993. *Working with Words & Pictures*. North Light Books.

Solo, D. X. 1986. *Condensed Alphabets: One Hundred Complete Fonts*. Dover Books.

————. 1979. *Sans Serif Display Alphabets: 100 Complete Fonts*. Dover Books.

————. 1989. *Circus Alphabets*. Dover Books.

————. 1992. *Extended Alphabets: One Hundred Complete Fonts*. Dover Books.

————. 1995. *One Hundred Ornamental Fonts*. Dover Books.

Soloman, M. 1994. *Art of Typography*. Art Direction Books.

Stokstad, M. 1999. *Art History*. Harry N. Abrams, Inc.

Supon Phornirunlit Staff. 1993. *Iconopolis: A Collection of City Iconographics*. North Light Books.

Swann, A. 1991. *How to Understand & Use Design & Layout*. North Light Books.

————. 1989. *How to Use Grids*. North Light Books.

Tschichold, J. 1992. *Treasury Of Alphabets and Lettering*. Design Press.

————. 1995. *The New Typography*. U CA Press.

Van Nostrand Reinhold Staff. 1974. *The Type Specimen Book*. Van Nostrand Reinhold.

VanderLans, R. and Licko, Z. 1993. *Émigré (The Book) Graphic Design into the Digital Realm*. Van Nostrand Reinhold.

Watson-Guptill Staff. 1997. *Graphic Design USA*. Watson-Guptill.

Weingart, W. 2000. *Weingart: Typography*. Lars Müller Publishers.

White, A. 1987. *How to Spec Type*. Watson-Guptill.

White, J. V. 1988. *Design for the Electronic Age*. Watson-Guptill.

White, J. V. 1990. *Graphic Idea Notebook*. Rockport Publishing.

Whitford, F. 1984. *Bauhaus*.Thames and Hudson.

Williams, R. and Tollet, J. *A Blip in the Continuum*. Peachpit Press.

Index

Colophon

All Chapters
Captions: 7/11 News Gothic Medium
Key Concepts: 8/12 News Gothic Medium
Key Players: 8/12 News Gothic Medium
Sidebars: 9/13 News Gothic Medium
Subheads: 10/14 News Gothic Bold

Chapter 1: 10/14 Bodoni
Chapter 2: 10/14 Adobe Garamond Pro
Chapter 3: 9/14 New Century Schoolbook
Chapter 4: 10/14 ITC New Baskerville
Chapter 5: 10/14 Gill Sans Light
Chapter 6: 9/13 ITC Fenice
Chapter 7: 10/14 Adobe Myriad Pro
Chapter 8: 10/14 ITC Officina Serif Book
Chapter 9: 10/14 Adobe Jenson Pro
Chapter 10: 13/14 Sassoon One
Chapter 11: 9/14 ITC Stone Sans Medium
Chapter 12: 10/14 Adobe Chaparral Pro
Appendix A: Various as shown
Appendix B: 8/11 ITC Franklin Gothic Medium
Appendix C: 8/11 ITC Clearface
Credits: 7/8.4 Lucida Roman
Bibliography: 7/8.4 Lucida Roman
Index: 8/9.6 Univers 57 Condensed
Colophon: 9/10.8 City BQ